Soul and Body

Essays on the Theories of C. G. Jung

Prof. C. A. Meier, M.D.

Introduction by Joseph L. Henderson, M.D.

The Lapis Press

Santa Monica
San Francisco

The Lapis Press
1850 Union Street, Suite 466
San Francisco, CA 94123

ISBN 0-932499-00-7 *cloth*
ISBN 0-932499-01-5 *paper*
Library of Congress Catalog Card No. 85-050669

Acknowledgment
Special thanks are due to Paul Anderson, Cristina
Barroso, and Julia Butterfield of San Francisco,
John Peck of Zurich and Lore Zeller of Los Angeles
for their tireless editorial assistance in the prepar-
ation of this manuscript.

Cover
AION—Deity of the Mithraic cult. Persian-Roman
2nd-3rd Century A.D. Collection: Biblioteca
Vaticana. In passing west into Europe from Persia
the worship of Mithras absorbed many foreign
elements including a strong strain of astrology.
This winged, lion-headed deity covered with the
signs of the zodiac and enclosed in the coils of a
serpent has been identified by some as Aion, or
Time, the god of the Astrologers, believed by many
to be the Creator himself.
—*New Larousse Encyclopedia of Mythology*
   The Hamlyn Publishing Group Limited,
   London, 1959.

Soul & Body *was designed by Jack W. Stauffacher
of the Greenwood Press, San Francisco, California.
Production by Mary Farr, Ink, San Francisco,
California. Text type is Sabon, designed by Jan
Tschichold. Digital composition by Kina Sullivan
Typography, San Francisco, California. Display is
Méridien.*

Contents

Carl Alfred Meier

was born in 1905 in Schaffhausen, Switzerland. He
received his medical training at the University of
Zürich and studied as a graduate at the University
of Vienna Medical School. He received his degree
in psychiatry from Burghölzli Psychiatric Clinic,
Zürich. Through his relationship with C. G. Jung,
he became actively involved in many areas related
to analytical psychology. Meier served as a general
secretary of the International Society for Medical
Psychotherapy from 1933 to 1943 during Jung's
tenure as president, and is founder of the C. G. Jung
Institute in Zürich. Upon Jung's retirement in 1949,
Dr. Meier succeeded him as professor at the Swiss
Federal Institute.

Introduction

It is a special honor to be asked to introduce C. A. Meier's volume of collected papers to an English-speaking public. These papers bring to our attention a side of Jung's psychology which one tends to lose sight of in the focus upon the alchemical studies and the vast landscapes of amplificatory symbolic material that were prominent in the writings of his old age. What we tend to forget, and what Jung himself does not often remind us of, is the origin of the science of analytical psychology and what it still can mean for us. Dr. Meier's work fills in this area because he lived and worked from the same model originally used by Jung – the model of natural science as handed down to us from a late medieval source (with overtones of Graeco-Roman philosophy).

To be more specific, C. A. Meier's life closely parallels Jung's: he came from the same region of Switzerland, became a psychiatrist trained at the Burghölzli Hospital in Zürich, enjoys the benefits of a classical education, and has the temperament to understand its deeper meaning. Like Jung's, Meier's Greek and Latin quotations come from a knowledge of these languages, but also from a feeling for their relevance in a deeply cultural sense, and so they are not pedantic, but instead add to the methods of natural science a refreshing sense of rediscovery. From this point of view Meier, like Jung, speaks the language of his profession in an "accent" today's professors will recognize, while speaking with a new and life-affirming interpretation.

A good example of this sensitivity to language and its memories is found in an essay "Cultural Education as a Symbol." Here Meier takes a mundane German word – *Bildung*, meaning education – and in searching its etymological history rediscovers its connection with magic, healing qualities and that kind of "formation," indirectly exposing the fact that education is basically reformation in a spiritual as well as worldly sense. He says:

I shall confine myself to those amplifications that I feel substantiate the psychologically most interesting result of my investigation, namely, *that the traditional concept of* Bildung *and the modern Jungian concept of individuation clearly converge.*

It is no wonder that the scholarly use of cultural memory, as it is represented here, made possible Meier's descent into history. The product of his endeavor was a work entitled *Ancient Incubation and Modern Psychotherapy*, in which Meier revealed the archetype of healing as a process of incubation, a transformation of psychic contents of the collective unconscious.

This study was executed with the same careful blend of scholarly fact and humanistic philosophy that one finds in this collection of essays.

In a major example, "Wilderness and the Search for Soul in Modern Man" (Chapter 17), he speaks of "the Wilderness within," which can be tamed only by the capacity of humankind to live with dichotomy.

The *pièce de résistance* of this collection is to be found in the eighty pages which comprise Professor Meier's series of lectures entitled "The Cutting Lectures: Jung and Analytical Psychology" (Chapter 5), presented in 1959 to the Department of Psychology at Andover Newton Theological School, Newton Centre, Massachusetts. Starting from a theoretical base, Meier explores such specific aspects as the archetypes and the interpretation of dreams, and ends with a review of Jung's attitude towards religion. The latter subject is frequently misunderstood by those who are aware of Jung's interest in religion and who have identified him primarily with some of his more extreme and resounding statements on the subject.

Professor Meier's viewpoint recapitulates the process by which he had to rediscover the importance of religion for himself, following Jung's example. In order to do this, he had to work against the scientific prejudice which is so rife in psychoanalytic circles that religion is often regarded as little more than an illusion springing from a personal complex. Meier did not at first think of religion as being centered in the reality of the psyche, but through his work with patients he finally came to realize that a religious attitude is not derived from the culture pattern but is an instinct *sui generis*, and as such its awakening is absolutely essential for any cure of the soul.

For the ancients, sickness of the psyche or soul was considered to be divine, and it follows that only some epiphany of the gods could cure it. Professor Meier gives examples of the manner in which he learned to recognize the truth of this attitude for modern people as well, as he presents numerous examples to show how the healing principle appears. In this way, he introduces the whole subject of symbol formation and its therapeutic function.

He quotes an alchemical saying that is a personal favorite of mine, and one which Jung wrote out for me himself: *In habentibus symbolum facilior est transitus.* (This expression can be translated as follows: "For those having a symbol, the transition is more smoothly made.") I am sure Dr. Meier would agree that such a transition implies a transformation, in the religious sense, from any kind of psychic disorder, to regain a condition of psychic health. Jung's concept of the individuation process indicates that it may do even more, for as Meier notes in Chapter 5: "This means a person who goes along with this process in such a way as to stimulate both the process and the development by taking an active part in it, which is to show an interest that is properly called religious." All this is amplified with wonderful references to many religious symbols, such as the fish symbolism in the Eighteenth Sura of the Koran. This and other references are used to explain the nature of the cure for a severe case of endogenous depression.

The importance of the religious instinct as a healing factor is underscored in those chapters where Meier speaks to people whose interests are purely cultural. "Some Consequences of Recent Psychological Thought" (Chapter 6), presented to the Zürich Philosophical Society, is such a paper.

There are two other themes which Dr. Meier develops to good advantage in this collection. The one that is most likely to appeal to medical psychotherapists is his discussion of problems of identity and professional procedure, entitled "Thoughts on Medical and Nonmedical Psychotherapy" (Chapter 3). The other, developed throughout the book, reflects the complementary elements of analytical psychology and physics, and of psychology and the scientific investigation of dreaming. There is also a lively response to parapsychology and what a Jungian analyst may bring to its better understanding.

This collection brings together in a single volume major examples of the diversity of Meier's scholarly interests over the last several decades in the interest of enlivening and reactivating the findings of his lifelong studies.
Joseph L. Henderson

Chapter 1

Spontaneous Manifestations
of the Collective Unconscious

The patient concerned is a woman of thirty-one, a talented musician, well-educated and very intelligent. No more need be said about her as a person because the specific phenomena to be depicted here are manifestations of the collective unconscious. She consulted the doctor because she had become aware of certain disturbances in her hearing while playing the violin. She had only been to the doctor a few times, and when she returned after a long interval she presented the following picture:

She came to the street where her doctor lived and looked for his house, but it had vanished without a trace. The houses to the left and right were still standing. It was all so strange; she had the feeling she was in an ancient deserted town. She really wanted to see the doctor, so she tried to do so by entering the garden of the house on the left.

Suddenly she saw the doctor's house and went into his garden, but try as she might, she could not get in the house. She returned to the garden and there she began to go through an odd rite: moving left, she circled some garden beds, a ring and some small squares several times. Meanwhile, the doctor had noticed her, and when he went to her she had reached a point where she

---

Paper read to the "Ninth Congress of the International General Medical Society for Psychotherapy" in Copenhagen on October 3, 1937. First published in German in: *Zentralblatt für Psychotherapie*, vol. XI (Leipzig, 1939), 284ff. English translation by David N. Roscoe.

could go no further: her path was blocked by a smell of heating from the garage, a sulphur vapor. She was glad to be freed from an unpleasant situation by the doctor, who took her into his consulting room and tried to get her to talk. Now she was completely blocked, i.e., she could not say anything or answer his questions. Her eyes were closed, and the more the doctor questioned her, the stronger became the block and the mutism. She turned her head more and more to the left, and slowly there was a change. The mutism gave way to negativism; she responded to the questions now but only with the laconic phrase, "I don't know." Suddenly she asked if she could leave. The doctor said yes, and she left without another word. Answering to his conscience, the doctor followed and, in view of the uncanny situation, asked her to make an appointment for the following day. Laconically, she said she would come at 5 o'clock, but he indicated that he was engaged at that time. She answered, "Oh, no, but I'm coming at 5 o'clock, or no, 3 o'clock will be better," whereupon he shook her hand and said, "Good, go where you will and come back when you will but remember that you must not lose touch with the world; you must 'keep a grip on things.'" She left hurriedly, without her handbag and gloves; the doctor managed to wrap her coat around her, for it was a bitterly cold December day.

That was at 11 o'clock in the morning. The psychotherapist had mixed feelings. A "good psychiatrist" would have diagnosed a perfect acute schizophrenic attack and would reluctantly have had the patient interned. All the symptoms of such a diagnosis seemed to be there: block, negativism, mutism, stereotypes, catatonic-like behavior and lack of contact with external reality, i.e., autism. The psychologist sensed that it could not be schizophrenia; he had a feeling that nothing bad would happen, for he knew that the patient had close contact with him, that she relied on him, and that he understood her. He simply had to respond in the same manner and have complete confidence in her.

I shall show later how this attitude was justified, but first I will present the more unpleasant side of this matter. The psychotherapist had to go back to work, but at about 1 o'clock he was telephoned by friends of the patient asking him where she could be, for she had been invited to lunch and dinner with them and had arranged to stay overnight, but had not yet turned up. The doctor was not surprised, and he recounted the strange circumstances to them. Despite his strong opposition, an immediate search went on all over the town by the police, on motorcycles, in cars and on foot. He was asked where he thought would be the best place to search, and he said anywhere but in town, even though he felt quite sure that that was where she was. He wanted at all costs to prevent her from being disturbed in the process she was going through.

Meanwhile, the patient's friends and relations were on the brink of despair and had even begun to undermine the psychiatrist's convictions. Nevertheless, he went to bed at 11 o'clock and slept well. At 3 o'clock in the morning there was a timid ringing of the doorbell, which he heard at once though it was unusual for him. He got up and let the patient in. At 3 o'clock on a cold December night she had returned as she had said she would. "I'm sorry, Doctor," she said, "for disturbing you so late, but here I am." Her condition was perfectly normal, better than he had ever seen before, and only now did she begin to shiver.

What had happened in the meantime? For sixteen and a half hours, since 11:00 a.m. the previous day, she had been wandering around the town center and showed not the slightest trace of exhaustion. I will describe what the patient did and then will draw some similar parallels. Certain details will have to be omitted, as well as certain parallels, as they do not fall within the scope of this essay.

With a couple of exceptions, verifiable facts are possible because the patient wrote down her experiences soon afterward. On the basis of what she wrote, I retraced her steps *refracta dosi* [in divided dosage] to confirm all that she had said. What was striking was that the patient had been incredibly observant all the time, and for a long time afterward remembered the most minute details, which is very common in sleepwalking states. In French psychiatric circles this is described as *automatisme ambulatoire*, whereas in German, remarkably enough, we have no word for it. The patient's account covers a manuscript of over two hundred pages, so I shall dwell only on what seem the most important aspects of her travels.

On leaving the doctor, the patient had intended to go to her friends where she was invited for lunch, but there were difficulties involved. She felt compelled to keep to the left-hand side of the road and soon she had to walk through the garden of a house. She now felt she had to walk around the house on the left. At the end of this *circumambulatio* she discovered a huge ammonite on the lawn. It fascinated and attracted her enormously; she was totally absorbed and delighted by it. She had a clear impression that this was what she had been looking for. Then she was disturbed by a man asking her what she wanted, so she moved on.

On the next street, still keeping to the left, she noticed more and more that she had a tendency to rise from the ground, as if lifted by a strong wind. This "levitation phenomenon" gradually became so pronounced that with every step she had to hold onto the garden fence, which meant she was making slow progress. This extreme form of "double consciousness," which was with her all the time, was accompanied by a constant fear that her behavior would make her conspicuous, and that people feeling for her would take it upon themselves to look after her, thus disturbing and endangering the whole process.

At this point she abandoned the attempt to locate her friends, as her progress was blocked at every possible stage. The patient was actually being guided only by smells—she literally "followed her nose." Some smells blocked her way (such as the heating smell from the garage in the doctor's garden), and others seemed to invite her to pursue them. Now as you know, anyone being led by the nose is going to end up all over the place. Her scent-directed route throughout these sixteen and a half hours was a very complex one *(see illustration)*.

In addition to smells, colors also were yardsticks for the patient. She came onto a street where there were a number of postal cars and delivery vans, and where all the company door-plates were yellow. She was very pleased about this, for yellow seemed to her to be the right color for her state. At the end of this street, at the west door of a church, she walked around a pillar of four columns, still keeping to her left. She continued with no plan or design, simply following her nose. She noticed in particular that it was not possible to reach the periphery of town, and that she was moving more and more towards its center. Progress was extremely slow, always on the principle of trial and error. She had the feeling she was surrounded by a holy silence that must not be disturbed.

Next she came to one of the main squares, where there was a

huge Christmas tree. The levitation phenomenon reappeared particularly strongly here. As there was no garden fence, she had to look for some other form of counter-spell, which she succeeded in doing. Staring fixedly at her feet helped her to keep them on the ground. By midday she reached another main square, and from then on it seemed to her that she was more in touch with reality. She managed to walk down the right-hand side of the street for a while, but in a bookshop she caught sight of books which called her back into the other world, such as *Holy Tibet, The Devil's Conqueror*, and the like. She crossed back at once to the left-hand side of the road, but when she came to a well-known sweet shop, she was struck with fear. This was not for her, she was not to look at it. (These details are all very important, and I shall have to come back to some of them later.)

In another part of town, the patient once again kept strictly to the left. At almost every house she went into the courtyards and walked around them on the left. She did the same thing with the gardens. As she did so she was constantly struck by the solemn stillness, the atmosphere of death in the air and the fact that the brown earth was covered with dead leaves. In the botanical gardens she wandered around for a long time until she came to a greenhouse, where she discovered a cactus with a small violet blossom. "That's what I was looking for," she said, "the violet color spoke to me of death."

From then on things went even more slowly. All the shop windows were full of Christmas goods; some of them appealed to her, others repelled. She was particularly fascinated by objects of striking colors or when the same object was displayed in large quantities, i.e., the multiplicity of objects. There now appeared a new form of orientation: when the patient occasionally did not know how to continue she just waited until a car went past. When the driver indicated his turning direction, she followed his lead. It sometimes happened that a car did not pass for a while, or that there was no smell or color to guide her, so she tried to work out for herself which way she should go. This approach did not work, however, and regularly led her in the wrong direction, where passage was blocked.

Now something dangerous happened: the patient felt a growing temptation to make an *experimentum crucis* [critical test], to establish whether the walking and the town were really there or whether they were just dream and illusion. So what did she do?

She beat her fist against the wall of a house and found it did exist, for the pounding hurt. Doing this frightened her, for she believed she had offended God by making a conscious decision. Now most of her wandering would become null and void – and she might even have to go back to the beginning. She turned around and walked around a house that she had just walked around before. Fortunately, this seemed to be enough and she could proceed further – the offense had been atoned for.

After a while she came to a butcher's shop window, which held a great fascination for her. There was a black porcelain bull, and half-cows and pigs were hanging on hooks. That was splendid, it was somehow right! Then came a jeweler's showcase with just one stone in it. This was a beautiful sight. Another interesting symbol was Noah's Ark, which was being exhibited in a toy shop. She was struck by the fact that, whenever she followed her nose, she consistently came across the essential and right things, as if it were a matter of course.

Once she tried to get into a church, but it was closed. Then a phenomenon occurred that was very unpleasant. With irresistible force she slowly began to turn on her own axis, once again to the left and on the spot. For a long time she made no progress. After many attempts to move forward, she finally came to a shop where dogs and dog articles were exhibited, which had a particularly deep and calming effect on her.

Often she saw friends and acquaintances from a distance, but when they approached they turned into different people or disappeared altogether.

When the patient came to a well-known pastry shop, some cakes (as she said in her own words) offered themselves. She ate them, but she soon had to move on. After a while she came to the east end of the Romanesque Minster. In her own words:

Suddenly I had to stoop at a right angle and began to rock to and fro. The speed increased rapidly until, with the upper part of my body bent, I was doing a dance on the stone paving of the alley, moving left in a circle with a diameter of about two meters. Then this was extended by the addition of a second circle, one moving to the right. So I danced a figure eight. People walked past me without seeing me. A child looked on, fascinated by my apparition, a man hesitated for a moment without looking at me as he walked past. There were a lot of people on the street, and cars too, but nobody disturbed my circles and I did not disturb the others, for I was, as I noticed, invisible.

When the impetus and the speed of the figure eight dance increased more and more, the patient felt afraid. She knew this rite was dangerous. Once to the left, once to the right – they cancel each other out – and then? – then there is nothing else. She stopped, thinking of her doctor's warning not to lose contact with the world. In the adjoining street she still walked bent at right angles and she met some school children who made fun of her. Realizing that she was visible again, she stood straight.

About 7 o'clock in the evening the wind that had been trying to pick her up off the ground grew particularly strong again. Once she had to cling with all her might to the tire of a parked car. Later, when the levitation phenomenon was even stronger, she stuck her hand into a holly hedge so as not to lose touch with this world. Opposite the concert hall, even though the urge to run away was particularly strong, she walked for a long while on the wall at the banks of the lake until she was finally released and could cross to the concert hall.

From this point onward she was aware that the journey was particularly dangerous, and so she proceeded extremely cautiously. Being a musician, she knew that the concert hall would be a focal point of her *nekyia* [journey of descent] and so she walked around it very carefully. First of all, she walked round the adjacent buildings, moving to the left, and all gardens and courtyards. Some she could not enter because their gates bore the sign of a watch by a security company, an "eye," and this told her that it might be dangerous there. After she had walked around the concert hall in this way for two hours, she came to the main entrance. There was a concert going on, Beethoven's Ninth Symphony, the last one he composed before his death. Moreover, the poster was on violet paper and, as we have seen, for this patient violet signified death. She wanted to go through the main enrance but here, too, the "eye" of the security sign was looking at her and preventing her entrance. She stood at the door. Then came a great vision, which filled her with great happiness because it began to unravel the plot: outside there were two white globular lamps burning, and through the glass doors she could see two similar ones burning inside. They reflected each other in the glass doors and intersected there. That was the image that released her: a light inside and a light outside – both are the same, equally bright and meeting in the center, one also being the reflection of the other.

The patient knew her journey had reached its climax and she could now embark on her return. Joyfully she left the concert hall, which had been the scene of her struggle for two hours. That was at 9:30 in the evening, and there was still a long way to go until 3 o'clock in the morning. The path forward was not a matter of course, even though she knew that she could now return to the doctor, for she still had to follow her nose. From the beginning she had feared that she might have to stand before a tribunal, and between midnight and 1 o'clock in the morning the fear was particularly strong. The situation was still rather sinister because the urge to fly away from the earth was rather strong at times, with the result that she was afraid that the process would be interrupted ahead of schedule. She found a *yantra*—the sewer lids on the pavement. Realizing that when she stood on one of them nothing could happen, that she was perfectly safe here, she ran from one to the next and rested there. From now on she kept to the right-hand side of the road. Any deviations she took were also to the right.

There was one other remarkable aspect of the situation with the sewer lids. Something happened on a specific street on the way back to the doctor's: in several places there were four small lids distributed over the street and a fifth, larger, one at the edge of the pavement, and the patient was convinced that the large one would slowly suck up the four small ones so that at the end there would be only one large one left.

Close to 3 o'clock in the morning the patient ran into two drunken men near the doctor's house, and one of them started to follow her. As fast as she could she ran through the streets to the house of her "leader" and was thus finally driven back into reality. The ghost had been laid aside once and for all.

I shall now attempt to pick up some of the most important motifs depicted here and, by using parallels, explain the symbolic actions. It is not possible to make an exhaustive parallelization, not even with one single motif, so I shall express myself briefly to bring the most important points together.

The first striking factor is that the patient's odyssey consisted essentially of a labyrinthine journey, which is true of every "quest," such as those of Gilgamesh or Parsifal. The origin of the labyrinth motif can be traced back to prehistoric times. In the course of the last two centuries, in the northern hemisphere, new prehistoric labyrinths have been discovered.[1] Some of these prehistoric stone figurations with a labyrinthine character were discovered by K. E. von Baer in 1838. They have such characteristic names as *Jungfrudans* and *Steindans*, indicating some form of ritual dance, but there is also Troiburg (Troy City, Vier, Wisby). The last name can be explained by the recent investigations carried out by W. F. Jackson Knight, which have revealed that the city walls of Troy were, in fact, labyrinth-like, signifying not only military but also "magic" defense.[2]

A surprising parallel to the labyrinthine city walls of Troy is to be found in the huge early Iron Age "Maiden Castle" in Dorset, which has two extensive maze-like entrances to the east and west.[3] In northern regions there are also games, so-called "Troy Games," consisting of peculiar centric dances. Regarding Troy Games, oddly enough, we find a passage in Virgil's *Aeneid* that I should also like to mention: Aeneas' small son, Julius, takes part in a game, which is called *Ludus Trojae*.[4] Apparently it was a processional or parade-like dance, which Virgil himself compares with the turnings of the labyrinth in Crete. Some of the participants seem to have been on horseback. The game was popular later in Rome, as both Suetonius and Tacitus report.[5] I remind you also of the famous Swiss circumambulation in Beromünster, the Ascension Day procession, which is also performed on horseback. One is immediately reminded also of the stone circles in England, such as Stonehenge and Rollright, as well as such early earth-works as Chun Castle, which also have simple labyrinths as their entrances. The most famous labyrinth is the one in Egypt, and I quote Pliny's report of it:

We shall also describe the labyrinths, at any rate the most adventurous work of human lavishness, but not at all, as one might believe, an invention. Even today there is in Egypt in the *Heracleopolic Nomos*, the one that is said to have been built thirty-six hundred years ago by

---

1. Cf. W. H. Mathews, *Mazes and Labyrinths* (London, 1922).
2. W. F. Jackson Knight, "Maze Symbolism and the Trojan Game," *Antiquity* VI, 24 (1932): 457.
3. R. E. M. Wheeler, *The Antiquaries Journal* XV, 3 (1935) and *The Antiquaries Journal* XVI, 3 (1936).
4. Virgil, *Aeneid*, V, 545-603.
5. Suetonius, *Nero* XI, 15.

Petesuches or Tithoes, although Herodotus says it is the work of twelve kings, the last one being Psammetichus. Several reasons have been put forward for its construction: according to Demoteles it was the kingly seat of the *Moeris*; according to Lyceas it was the grave of the *Moeris*; according to several others a sun temple, this being the most common opinion. That Daedalus took it as the pattern for the labyrinth he built on Crete is just as doubtful as the story that he imitated just one hundredth of it, which contained inextricable deviations, counter-paths and retrogressions and not, as we see in our attics or children's playgrounds, a short stretch of some thousand steps, but something with several doors in the counter-paths, creating an illusion and leading one back on one's tracks. I cannot give details about the construction of this work and the individual parts, for it is divided into areas and governorships, whose 45 names are divided into just as many rooms; moreover, it contains a temple for all of Egypt's gods, apart from 40 small temples to Nemesis and several pyramids, 40 ells high and each covering 6 hides from their feet. Just as one is getting tired, one comes to that inextricable maze of paths. . . .[6]

The motif of the labyrinth was particularly common in ancient Egypt and highly honored. For example, we find a primitive form of the labyrinth in the so-called "palace sign" which also meant the grave. The *Horus name* taken by the king at his coronation was written within a rectangular frame corresponding to the palace sign and often found on the dummy doors of his *mastaba*.[7] A later Egyptian example is found on the grave seal of Memphis. According to Sir Arthur Evans, it is the representation of two people trying to find their way through the labyrinth.[8] The first clearly labyrinthine construction in Egypt is probably the grave of King Perabsen, Second Dynasty.[9] Later the meaning of the labyrinth becomes clearer, as in the great step pyramid of Sakkara, the grave of King Zoser. The north side entrance is a labyrinth that is dangerous to go through.[10] In the middle sec-

---

6. Pliny (the Elder), *Naturalis Historia*, XXXVI, XIX, 1-4.

[7. Ed. Note: Mastabas were Egyptian tombs of the time of the Memphite dynasties, oblong in shape with sloping slides and connected with a mummy chamber cut into the rock beneath.]

8. Sir Arthur Evans, *The Palace of Minos* I (London, 1921), 152.

9. W. M. Flinders Petrie, *The Royal Tombs of the Earliest Dynasties* I (1901), 11.

10. Gaston Maspero, *L'Archéologie Égyptienne* (Paris: Maison Quantin, 1887), 152.

tion comes the famous labyrinth described by Pliny in the quotation above, which was the grave of Amenemhet III. This labyrinth was built adjacent to Amenemhet's pyramid.

It has always been explained that the labyrinthine form of construction of the graves and pyramids was designed to hide kings and protect their graves against thieves. It is to C. N. Deedes that we owe the evidence that this is not the case, as the labyrinth system had been fully developed before the Sixth Dynasty, when Egypt was enjoying peace and prosperity.[11] It is much more the case that the significance of the labyrinth is only to be understood from its religious and ritual function. The myth of King-God Osiris's annual resurrection gave rise to an Osiris mystery drama, which was celebrated in these very labyrinths and where, in place of the king, a royal bull was slaughtered and the king reborn. (It must be remembered in this connection how fascinated the patient was by the dismembered cattle in the butcher's shop window and the black porcelain bull.) It has also been proved that at the coronation of the Pharaoh, a *hieros gamos* [sacred marriage] took place in connection with the Osiris drama.[12] The same event is known from Babylon, where the *hieros gamos* took place on the summit of the ziggurat. I mention this because later the patient built a model of a temple in the form of a step pyramid, inside which the *hieros gamos* takes place accompanied by a highly complicated ritual dance on the steps of this pyramid, which she described down to the last detail. We know of the Osiris drama that the climax of the rite culminated in various forms of dance. In some of these ritual dances the dancers inflicted wounds on themselves, as can be seen from a drawing on a grave in Sakkara. (At a certain stage of

---

11. C. N. Deedes, "The Labyrinth," in *The Labyrinth: Further Studies in the Relation Between Myth and Ritual in the Ancient World*, ed. S. H. Hooke (London, 1935), 1-42.

[12. Ed. Note: In antiquity the *hieros gamos* represented the sacred union of a female divinity and her brother/son/lover and was performed in reality as a cult drama by the city ruler and a priestess. Associated with the rite were harvest festivals, themes of fertility, death, and resurrection; more generally, it symbolized wholeness produced by the union of opposites (male/female, human/divine, death/rebirth). Jung has called the *hieros gamos* an image of "the earthing of the spirit and the spiritualizing of the earth." Cf. Jane Wheelwright, *The Death of a Woman*, New York: St. Martin's Press, 1981, p. 282.]

her journey,the patient plunged her hands into a hedge of holly until they bled.)

Pliny moves from the Egyptian labyrinth to those at Lemnos and Crete. The labyrinth of Knossos is in the well-known form depicted on a number of late Minoan and Cretan coins. Daedalus is supposed to have built the labyrinth of Knossos on the model of the Egyptian one. Minos of Crete had imposed on the Athenians a tri-yearly tribute of twelve virgins and young men who were sacrificed to the Minotaur in the labyrinth. The point of the rite was to renew the life of the king. The labyrinth was the cult center. As we know, thanks to the sword and the thread given to him by Ariadne, Theseus was able to kill the Minotaur and escape from the labyrinth. On the way back to Athens, he danced a circular dance on Delos with his companions, a dance that described his journey in the labyrinth and that was perpetuated by the people of Delos. In his book *De Saltatione* [On Dance],[13] Lucian talks about dances with the names "Daedalus," "Ariadne," "The Labyrinth." Here we find united all the elements of the labyrinth motif: the ritual center of the rite, the annual festival, the rebirth of the king-god and the joining with his goddess, victims for the divine bull, the sacrifice of the bull and at the end of the saga – the dance. Alchemy often refers to the labyrinth. In a tract by Morienus in the *Ars Aurifera*, "De Transmutatione Metallorum," Morienus talks at length with King Calid and compares the alchemistic opus with the labyrinth process.[14] That is why later the alchemists identified the *Mercurius philosophorum* and Theseus. Theseus became the friend of Heracles, the artist and philosopher who accomplished the same feats as Heracles. Probably the classic passage in alchemist literature is in *Philaletha*, where the magisterium is compared to the way through the labyrinth.[15] Deedes, in her essay on the labyrinth, provides further evidence of the fact that originally Greek drama was largely defined by dances executed in the form of a labyrinth around the altar in the oval orchestra, which was covered with sand and hence given the name

---

13. Lucian, *De Saltatione (On Dance)*, LCL, vol. V, 211-289.

14. Morienus, "De Transmutatione Metallorum," in *Artis Auriferae Quam Chemiam* (Basel, 1593), 25ff.

15. Eirenaeus Philalethes (pseud.), *An Exposition on Sir George Ripley's Hermeto-Poetical Works*, (Hamburg, 1741), 157-158.

konistra.[16] It is possible that the figure of the labyrinth was described in the sand beforehand.

Let us now turn briefly to the Italian labyrinth. Pliny offered this description:

Mention must also be made of the Italian [labyrinth], which was built by Lars Porsenna, King of Etruria, as a sepulchre but also out of vanity to excel foreign kings in this respect. As this construction is so legendary, let us fall back on the words of Marcus Varro: according to Varro, Lars Porsenna was buried below the city of Clusium in the place where there remains a polygonal monument of square stones; each side is three hundred feet long and fifty feet high; inside there is an inextricable labyrinth and the exit is impossible to find unless one takes a ball of thread. On top of this square block there are five pyramids, four at the corners and one in the center. At the base they are seventy-five feet wide and 150 feet high and pointed in such a way that at the top of all of them there is a brass circle and a single cap, with little bells attached by chains. When the wind blows these bells can be heard from afar, as was the case with Dodona earlier. Above this circle there are four single pyramids over one hundred feet high and above these on a single base five pyramids, whose height Varro was reluctant to give. The Etruscan sagas claim that the height equalled that of the whole construction.[17]

The Etruscan *oinochoe* or wine jug of Tragliatella described by W. Deecke, shows a picture in which two warriors on horseback are emerging from a classical labyrinth that bears the name "Truia."[18] The one in front is protected by a cynocephalus-like animal, which leads one to assume that he was of a divine or at least royal nature. At the end of her essay, Deedes comes to the following conclusion:[19]

Above all, the labyrinth was the center of activities concerned with those greatest of mysteries, Life and Death. There men tried by every means known to them to overcome death and to renew life.... There the living king-god went to renew and strengthen his own vitality.... The labyrinth was the center of all the strongest emotions of the people —joy, fear and grief were given the most intense forms of expression. These emotions were directed into certain channels, producing ritual and the earliest forms of art....

---

16. Deedes, "The Labyrinth," 30-33.

17. Pliny (the Elder), *Naturalis Historia* XXXVI, xix, 7-9.

18. W. Deecke, *Annali dell' Istituto di Correspondenzi Archeologia* (Rome, 1881).

19. Deedes, "The Labyrinth," 42.

Directly connected with the above are the observations of John Layard.[20, 21] With the natives of the New Hebrides, the journey of the dead leads through a labyrinth drawn in the sand. Half of it is erased and must be completed by the spirit of the dead person if he is to reach the "land of the dead." Should he fail to do this, he is eaten up by the female guardian spirit. With a similar aim, the initiations are accompanied by highly complicated labyrinth dances, which are reminiscent of our Polonaises. W. B. Seabrook reports on a similar idea he observed in the blood initiation rites of the natives of Haiti: "The Paploi sealed the open door by scratching a network of lines in the clay ground of the threshold with a couple of circles in the lines. The evil and unwelcome spirits trying to cross the threshold would get lost in the labyrinth of lines and wander from one circle to the other, just like the lost souls wandering from star to star in the ether."[22]

The dances mentioned also recall something else—if, for example, one looks at Figure 22 in Layard (spiral-shaped dance): namely, the ammonite that the patient came across in the course of her first circumambulation.[23] This in turn is reminiscent of the *mundus subterraneus* [subterranean world] of Athanasius Kircher, a Jesuit historian who lived in Rome from 1601 to 1680. The picture represents an ammonite, in the center of which is a *madonna col bambino* on the cresent moon, and the descriptive text runs as follows:

Est et hoc admiratione dignum; Anno 1659 in Helvetia intra montem vulgo Gottes-Wald dictum, lapidem inventum fuisse in spiras convolutum, in cujus centra figura Deiparae non sine stupore adspectantium apparuerit. [Here is something worthy of admiration. In the year 1659 in Switzerland on a mountain called 'God's Forest,' was found a stone engraved with spirals. In the center of this stone appeared the figure of Deiparae—the madonna giving birth to God—displaying an enraptured look to those who gazed at her.][24]

---

20. John Layard, "Maze Dances and the Ritual of the Labyrinth in Malekula," *Folklore* XLVII (1936): 123-170; LXVIII (1937): 115-182.

21. John Layard, "Der Mythos der Totenfahrt auf Malekula," *Eranos-Jahrbuch* (Zurich: Rhein Verlag, 1937): 241.

22. W. B. Seabrook, *The Magic Island* (New York: Harcourt Brace, 1929) [orig. ed. *Geheimnisvolles Haiti*, Berlin, 1931], 83.

23. Layard, "Maze Dances," fig. 22.

24. Athanasius Kircher, *Mundus Subterraneus* (Amstelodami, 1678), 51-52.

In Aryan India we find a similar idea. In the Trichur Museum there is a Shiva-bull bearing a *prabha-mandalam* (shining mandala in Mandorla form). It contains a *Salagrama*, i.e., an ammonite from the Gandaki river in Nepal. The ammonite is depicted as Vishnu's *chakra*. The spiral symbolizes the *avataras*. It is seen as a *naga* which has curled itself up into a ring.[25]

In the picture of the labyrinth from the *Hypnerotomachia di Poliphilo* by Francesco Colonna,[26] in the next to the last tower of this labyrinth lives a *Matrona* (madonna), and in the center *le loup des dieux, qui est sans pitié*, in other words, inexorable death. Here too, as with the patient, there is the idea of a tribunal. In the list of contents of the French edition of Beroalde de Verville the figure is described as follows: "Labyrinth figuré pour représenter les révolutions et contraintes nécessitées du destin." [A labyrinth represented to symbolize the revolutions and constraints entailed by destiny.][27]

As for the eye "of the watch and security company," all I can say is that according to Layard, the points in the labyrinths of the natives that have to be carefully avoided are also the "eyes" of the guardian spirit and have an apotropaic character. There is also the apotropaic eye of the Ka, which is found in Egyptian graves. The fact that the patient could not enter the houses and gardens that had this sign also has the function of an *automatisme téléologique* because it would have been dangerous there. If she had been discovered by the watchmen in any house or garden at such a late hour, the continuation of her journey would have been over, which would have been disastrous as far as her feelings were concerned.

Many labyrinths are found in churches in the Middle Ages. To quote Max Schlesinger:

[The labyrinth of Knossos] probably represented the seven circles of the underworld. It was often pictured in the mosaic plaster of the forecourts of churches and nunneries (it can still be seen in some old French

---

25. *The Hindu Iconography*, I: 10.

26. Francesco Colonna, *The Dream of Poliphilus* (Venice, 1499).

27. Francesco Colonna, *Le Tableau des Riches Inventions... Representées dans le Songe de Poliphile... exposées par Beroalde [de Verville]* (Paris, 1600). Also cf. *The Dream of Poliphilo* related and interpreted by Linda Fierz-David (Princeton, Bollingen Series XXV, 1950).

floors); this had to be crossed by the penitent, slowly and painfully, often on his knees, as a symbol of Israel's wandering through the desert, or in Christian terms, the pilgrimage on earth. At the west end of the naves in the churches in many countries an underground labyrinth was often built; they became tomb chambers. Myths and mysteries, sagas and fairy tales perpetuated this theme; there was still a trace of this in the mazes of the recently lost art of landscape gardening.[28]

An example of such a church is St. Savino in Piacenza, where there is Carolingian floor labyrinth. Remains are also to be found in St. Vitale in Ravenna and Sta. Maria in Trastevere, as well as Sta. Maria in Aquiro in Rome. There is also a relief on the portico of the cathedral in Lucca.

In addition to the tales in alchemistic literature, there are also pictures of labyrinths, for example in the alchemistic codex *Marcianus graecus*, p. 102v., and a Greek manuscript of *Ambrosiana* ("Labyrinth of Solomon").[29]

Now that the central motif of the patient's journey has been covered, that of the labyrinth path, we note other striking details. If one follows the patient's route on the map of the town, one is reminded of the track of a worm in damp earth. It follows the principle of trial and error and recalls the intestines and the *Plexus solaris*, which is related to the whole *nekyia*. Moreover, we also find close parallels in the northern hemisphere where, according to one version, the sun on its nocturnal sea voyage in winter is found in the so-called worm position. On the other hand, the whole motif of the labyrinth and the labyrinth dance is closely connected with the circumambulation repeated so frequently during the patient's journey. As for the psychological significance of this motif, recall the ritual of the founding of Etruscan cities with the drawing of the *sulcus primigenius* [original boundary furrow]. In our region there is the custom of riding around the territory blessing the land (fertility spells). Finally one may recall the circumambulation of the Boro-Budur (classically described by H. Zimmer), and the *stupas* in Sanchi, which

---

28. Max Schlesinger, *Geschichte des Symbols* (Berlin, 1912), 392 [Concerning landscape, cf. Matthews, *Mazes and Labyrinths* xv and xvi.]

29. G. Carbonelli, *Sulle fonti storiche dell' Chimia e dell' Alchimia in Italia, tratte dallo spoglio dei manuscutti delle Biblioteche con speciale reguardo ai Codici 74 di Pavia e 1166 Laurenziano* (Rome: Istituto Nazionale Medico Farmacologico, 1925).

still takes place today.[30] The point of all these rites is the displacing of the creative energy to the center by contemplation. What is important for us here is that the inward journey was always circumambulated to the left and the outward journey to the right, where the left led to the unconscious and right to the conscious.

Another striking motif is that of being guided by the nose. The nose represents the state of the atmosphere, the intuition, perception by the unconscious. It is for a similar reason that the patient was so interested in the dog exhibition: dogs are "nose animals"; in Persia they are guides into the beyond. They also embody sure instinct.

Even more interesting is the matter of the sewer lids. It is clear that they represent a magic circle with protective powers, but listen to the patient's own explanation. She says: "The sewer lids protected me because they are square outside and round inside and have a center in the middle." This simple description contains all the constituents of the mandala.[31] The figure four is also recalled in the walking bent at right angles on the east side of the Minster and in the figure-eight dance. The two right and left-moving circles of the figure eight cancel each other out and, thus, cancel both the conscious and the unconscious. Nothing is left; it is gone. The right angle is the starting for the squaring of the circle, a problem whose relationship to the symbolism of individuation is clear, hence the helpful effect of this rite. We are familiar with it in alchemy.[32]

Many of the symptoms given – the feeling of being in an ancient city, the holy hush, the multiplicity of the objects, etc. – are typical characteristics of the journey through Hades.

To conclude: In the following section I will state the patient's symptom and then the relevant passage from the *Tibetan Book of the Dead*.[33] I justify the use of this text to explain the patient's

---

30. Heinrich Robert Zimmer, *Kunstform und Yoga* (Berlin, 1926).

31. R. Wilhelm and C. G. Jung, *The Secret of the Golden Flower* (New York: Harcourt, Brace & World, 1962) [original German edition, 1929].

32. Michael Maier, *Secretioris naturae secretorum scrutinium chymicum* (Francofurti, 1687), Emblema XXI.

33. *Bardo Thödol (The Tibetan Book of the Dead or the After-death Experiences on the Bardo Plane)*, according to Lama Kazi Dawa-Samdup's English rendering, by W. Y. Evans-Wentz (London: Oxford University Press, 1927).

state during her journey because in psychiatric terminology we have no expression as apt as that of the *Bardo existence* to describe this exceptional state.

First of all, it should be remembered that the patient felt she must not stop and think, otherwise the journey would go wrong or stop altogether. In the *Thödol* it is written: "Thou are now in the Bardo state, wherein all things are like the empty, cloudless sky, and the bare, spotless intellect like a transparent vacuum without circumference or focal point. Ordinary people call this the state in which the conscious principle has fainted. Oh thou of noble birth, thy present intellect, its true nature being empty, naturally empty, is the true reality...." And later: "...the shapes here block my empty thought forms...." In the *Bardo Thödol* it is pointed out that the process of release is jeopardized once the deceit of thoughts is not acknowledged.

Secondly, recall that the patient was seized by a wind and almost swept off the ground. In the *Thödol* we also find: "Oh thou of noble birth, at about this time the mighty wind of the Karma, terrible and difficult to resist, will drive you from behind with awful gusts."

Thirdly, the patient was afraid of the tribunal. We discovered a similar motif in *Poliphilo*. In the *Sidpa Bardo* the dead one is faced with this tribunal, but his guru gives him encouragement. "Before this tribunal you will be sore afraid, subdued and terrified and will tremble. But be not afraid, be not terrified."

A fourth element to consider is the fact that the patient was hungry and yet could only once eat cake, which, as she says, offered itself to her. In the *Sidpa Bardo* there is the following instruction: "As for food, you can only take what is offered to you and nothing else."

Lastly, the friends and acquaintances she met on the journey were unable to see her and had either changed or disappeared as she approached. For this and other reasons she made the *experimentum crucis* as evidence of her material existence and pounded her fist against a wall, only to withdraw, as it seemed to her a sin. It is a known fact that spirits often refuse to believe that they have no body and have to be exhorted to pass through a wall, which they can do effortlessly. This enables them to be convinced of their pure spirituality. Listing the characteristics of existence in the Bardo state, we find: "As far as friends are concerned in this state, there is nothing sure about them...."

And further: "You see your kith and kin and speak to them but receive no answer" (i.e., because you have no material existence anymore).

Among further instructions for the dead one we find: "Oh thou of noble birth, thy present body is equipped with the power of unimpeded movement, not being made of coarse material, so that you now have the power to walk through cliffs, hills, rocks, earth, houses and even through Mount Meru without hindrance. Nor does your body cast shadows."

The patient is afraid of such temptations, which she revealed in the figure-eight dance in the street near the Minster. It says in the *Bardo Thödol*: "But do not wish for the various forces of deception and transformation of form – do not wish for them."

In conclusion, we must examine the phenomenon of the central light illusion at the concert hall, which brought about the dénouement. There it was immediately made clear to the patient what in the *Bardo Thödol* is constantly referred to as the essential perception for anyone in the Bardo state: "Oh thou of noble birth, these kingdoms do not derive from somewhere outside yourself. They come from the four departments of your heart. They come from within you and shine on you. Nor have these divinities come from elsewhere; they have existed since eternity within the powers of your own intellect. Know that they are of such a nature…. May the time come when we all perceive the rays of our own rays."

By drawing parallels of the patient's initiation process with the initiation process of the dead, as represented in the *Bardo Thödol*, it seems to me to make clear the essential meaning and main function of the peculiar process the patient went through: any initiation is a preparation for death, but not usually physical death as much as the death of the level of consciousness that had hitherto prevailed, in other words, a reversal of the attitudes hitherto adopted.

Chapter 2

Surgery-Psychology

At first glance, the attitude of the surgeon seems to be un- if not to say antipsychological. The doctor active in the field of psychology (the psychotherapist or psychiatrist) is usually "unsurgical" by his very nature. Despite the fact that the contrast in the relationships between exponents of the two disciplines emerges again and again, the extremes seem to be so far apart that at their opposite poles they coincide. It is at this intersection of surgery and psychology that we find the "common unknown factor" of the two fields – the *spontaneous healing tendency of Nature*. Without this, skill is of no avail, either in the somatic or in the psychic sphere. The dexterity of the surgeon creates nothing but destruction, and the skill of the psychologist is reduced to a dangerous experiment of the sorcerer's apprentice. *Naturam si sequemur ducem numquam aberrabimus* [Following Nature as our guide we shall never go astray]. In that the surgeon experiences daily how his *contra-naturam* incisions are healed without rancor by the very same "wounded" Nature, he is bound to be amply convinced of her self-healing tendency. Unless this were the case, he would not even dare reach for his scalpel. It is only this unshakable, though occasionally unconscious, belief of the surgeon in the integrating powers of Nature that has made possible the incredible developments in operative surgery, with its often brutal and seemingly ruthless incisions.

First published in German in: *Schweizerische Medizinische Wochenschrift*, vol. 73 (Basel, 1943), p. 457 ff. English translation by David N. Roscoe.

At the seemingly indestructible roots of Nature, however, there lies the soul working alongside in indivisible unity, although the post-operative process rarely provides the surgeon with an opportunity for psychological observations. It is only publications such as those of Erwin Liek that have once again encouraged doctors to think along such lines.[1] Recently, even August Bier,[2] as witness for the functions of the soul, has stepped into the field of surgery; and nowadays, when there are complications after an operation (discounting organic or psychological causes), the surgeon also bears psychic factors in mind. If, in so doing, he talks of the "lack of will to recover," this is usually a *lucus a non lucendo* [light from the unapparent], for in that will lies the psychic energy available to the conscious mind. In such cases, recovery is rarely a question of will, and any attempt of the conscious mind to free itself is doomed to failure. At this "rear front" the surgeon is once again bound to encounter psychology —in fact *with* its "rear front," i.e., *with* the psychology of the unconscious mind, providing energy for the "will to recover," — and thus is coincidental with the spontaneous healing tendency of Nature.

In the medical psychology of our times, a similar development has taken place. Once people freed themselves from the conviction of the sole domination of the conscious mind (e.g., Dubois) and acknowledged the role of unconscious factors (e.g., Janet and Freud), it was thought that a discovery of the method and instrument for treating psychic disturbances (especially neuroses) had been made. For a long time there was a risk that analytical psychotherapy would be reduced to issuing a prescription for a medicine, thereby making it possible for doctors to provide "cures" for the treatment of neuroses. This method of venturing into the psyche of man would be heroism equated to that of the surgeon's anatomical operations. Although the destructive effects were surprising, it was equally surprising to see how, in the right circumstances, Nature herself assisted in the healing process. Later, people became more cautious, which was

---

1. Erwin Liek, *Der Arzt und seine Sendung* 9th ed., (Munich, 1934); *Das Wunder in der Heilkunde* 3rd ed., (Munich, 1936).
2. August Bier, *Die Seele* (Munich, 1939).

to the advantage of the patient, and it was discovered that in the psychological sphere, too, there is a self-healing tendency of Nature. This discovery made a vital contribution to what emerged from the unconscious – dreams, for example. Almost as a side effect, the fact that considerable progress had been made in the understanding of the neurosis and in the acknowledgment of its meaning helped make up for the more painful experiences of this epoch of heroic therapy.[3]

For this reason, the dream, as a product of Nature, has an outstanding practical significance in modern psychotherapy. An impartial observation of the products of the unconscious (dreams, fantasies, visions, occult phenomena, hallucinations, voices, and delusions),[4] often enables one to realize that such products, even without the patient's knowledge, present thorough and precise functional or organic diagnoses and even make suggestions as to therapy. What has to be done is to raise the patient to the level of this acknowledgment, and thus imbue him with respect for the self-healing tendency of Nature thereby indicated – in other words, encourage him to follow the "doctor" within himself. (I must point out that I have no wish to generate over-optimism in therapy of this kind, especially with psychotic cases.) The following casuistic report serves to illustrate how far such things can go:

A couple of years ago, a 61-year-old man consulted me because he was having alarming dreams. He was mentally and physically very fit and was still active in sports. For thirty years he had successfully run a large industrial concern, then slowly fell into a depression, experiencing those dreams. In other respects, his psychic functions were perfectly intact. The dreams showed that he had got stuck in the well-known ideal, "you are only as old as you feel." The purpose now was to lead him away from this unhealthy illusion to an acceptance of death as the natural progression of life. When this was achieved, the depression and

---

3. C. G. Jung, "Psychotherapy and a Philosophy of Life," *The Practice of Psychotherapy* (Coll. Wks. 16, 1954), 76-83 [original German version, 1943].

4. C. G. Jung, "On the Psychology and Pathology of So-Called Occult Phenomena," *Psychiatric Studies* (Coll. Wks. 1, 1957), 3-88 [original German version, 1902]; "The Psychology of Dementia Praecox," *Psychogenesis of Mental Disease* (Coll. Wks. 3, 1960), 211-225 [original German version, 1907]; "The Content of the Psychoses," *Psychogenesis of Mental Disease* (Coll. Wks. 3, 1960), 153-178 [original German version, 2nd ed., 1914].

disturbing dreams vanished, and the patient gratefully stopped the treatment. A short while later he died.

The *anamnesis* revealed that he had developed a luetic infection in Paris thirty years earlier. First, he had been treated with an ointment cure; later he had taken many combined courses of treatment. Ten years before therapy there appeared a *tabes dorsalis* [dorsal putrefaction], with disturbances of the arterial system playing a dominant role. Consultation with a psychiatrist followed, then lumbar puncture. Malaria therapy was suggested.

During this period, without having moved in spiritualist circles, the patient had received occult "messages." If he had to face any difficult problem at work or in his private life, he would always find a note on his bedroom floor in the morning, and this note, in unfamiliar handwriting, would give the solution to his problem. He always followed this advice faithfully, with excellent results.

On the morning after the psychiatrist had recommended malaria therapy, the patient was amazed to wake up and find, written in huge letters on his bedroom wall, the words: "Take burnt sponge powder." He read this literally, rejected the malaria therapy, went to a chemist and asked whether such a powder existed. On being told that this was so, he took the powder for a long time and had good results. At least all the troublesome symptoms disappeared. (The writing on the wall faded away in the course of the day.)

I must ask indulgence with regard to the extraordinary aspects of this case. I am no adherent of the occult and have no intention of introducing it into medicine, nor is this the place for a discussion on the existence or nonexistence of occult phenomena. The psychology of such manifestations cannot be discussed at this point either, especially as there is still little useful literature on the subject. However, critical investigations on "automatic writing" could be relevant here to an understanding of the case.[5] To attribute it to cryptomnesia[6] would not detract from the significance of the case as it regards the question of self-helping

---

5. T. Flournoy, *Des Indes à la planète Mars* (Paris, 1900); *Journal of the American Society for Psychical Research* (1907) and *Proceedings of the American Society for Psychical Research* (1907), New York; *Journal of the Society for Psychical Research* (1907) and *Proceedings of the Society for Psychical Research* (1907), London; *Journal of Parapsychology* (North Carolina: Durham, 1937).

6. C. G. Jung, *Psychiatric Studies (Coll. Wks.* 1, 1957), 138ff. [original German version, 1902, 110].

Nature, just as the question of *post hoc ergo propter hoc*[7] can have little effect on the fact of the improvement. Important about this case from our point of view are the following:

1. Although the malaria therapy did an excellent job with the progressive paralysis, it was almost a total failure with the Tabes.

2. Nature justifiably warned the patient about this very different treatment and, on the genuinely natural principle of *primum nil nocere* [primarily to do no harm], put forward a more natural proposal, i.e., corrected the psychiatrist. The only thing that was "unnatural" or illegitimate, as it were, was the manner chosen by Nature to achieve this. Apparently she had difficulty in asserting herself over the authority of the psychiatrist, so had to resort to an unusual method of achieving her aim even if it went "against her nature."

3. The irrational aspect is compensated at once by the fact that what happened bears the test of scientific criteria. It may be assumed that the remedy suggested to the patient by his unconscious mind was an iodine medication, which leads to the conclusion that the "burnt sponge powder" was *Spongia usta*. This is what we know about it:[8]

Spongia usta, carbo spongiae, spongia tosta, burnt fungi, sponge carbon, *éponge torréfiée.*
Sponge, burnt till partially carbonized, brown-black to black, fine powder, heavier than carbo ligni powder, odorless or faint burnt smell and salty taste. In water soluble components; larger quantities are dissolved in hydrochloric acid with effervescence.

components:

Carbon	30-40%
Calcium carbonicum	25-30%
Silicic acid	8-12%
Iron oxide	5-10%
Ca, Mg, sulphate & phosphate	8-12%
Iodide sodium	2-3%
Cl, Br and cyan-salts	traces

It is evidently *Euspongia officinalis L.,* the official use of which, as the name shows, has a venerable age. Tappeiner[9] has this to say on the subject:

[7. Ed. Note: *Post hoc, ergo propter hoc* literally means "After this, therefore because of this," and refers to the fallacy of arguing from temporal sequence to a causal relation.]

8. Hager, *Hdb. d. pharmazeut. Praxis* (1878).

9. H. v. Tappeiner, *Lehrb. d. Arzneimittellehre,* 10th ed. (Leipzig, 1913), 334 ff.

Iodine combinations are constant components of sea water and therefore are passed into sea fauna and flora and their remains. Even before the existence of iodine was known, carbonized seaweed and sponges were used for goiter ailments (*Ethiop's vegetabilis* and *Spongia usta*). After iodine had been discovered in 1812 in the remains of sea flora, the obvious step to take was to search for the effects of the commonly used preparation in this element, and to use it instead....

Application: the indications for the use of iodine have a purely empirical basis. They are directed mainly at the elimination of pathological excrescences and hypertrophies and the after effects of chronic inflammations.... The best results, often quite surprising ones, are achieved with the various affections of tertiary syphilis (introduced by Wallace, 1836).

With regard to the psychology of the unconscious processes, it is of theoretical interest that our patient was given an "old-fashioned" Galenic preparation. As C. G. Jung has shown, the unconscious has at its disposal a treasure trove of "knowledge" which consists of the countless experiences man has undergone in his history.[10] Hence both its "primitive" archaic form of expression, as often imparted to us so strikingly in dreams, and also its *virtus* of manifesting itself as a spontaneous healing tendency of Nature. If such a "message" used the chemical preparation or a specialty of the modern pharmaceutical industry, instead of the German term for a Galenic remedy, we could hardly avoid explaining it except by the hypothesis of a cryptomnesia.

The above remarks also imply that if we are to understand such phenomena, we would benefit by drawing historical parallels. In ancient times sick people went for treatment to the temples of Asklepios where, in particularly favorable surroundings, in the incubation rooms on the *klinē* (the name our clinic still proudly bears), they lay down and waited for the dream. This dream, once it had been interpreted by the priest-doctors, gave the diagnosis and the therapy.[11] In those days there seems to

---

10. Jung, *Archetypes of the Collective Unconscious* (*Coll. Wks.* 9, Part I, 1959), 3-41 [original German version, 1934]; "Individual Dream Symbolism in Relation to Alchemy," *Psychology and Alchemy* (*Coll. Wks.* 12, 1953), 39-213 [original German version, 1935]; "Concerning the Archetypes," *The Archetypes and the Collective Unconscious* (*Coll. Wks.* 9, Part I, 1959), 54-72 [original German version, 1936]; *Psychology and Religion* (*Coll. Wks.* 11, 1958), 3-105 [original German version, 1940].

11. L. Deubner, *De Incubatione* (Leipzig, 1900); R. Caton, *The Temple and Ritual of Asclepius* (London, 1900); M. Hamilton, *Incubation* (London, 1906); R. Herzog, *Die Wunderheilungen von Epidaurus* (Leipzig, 1931).

have been confidence in the healing powers of human nature to a quite different "superstitious" degree. This confidence prevailed throughout the Middle Ages and was glimpsed for the last time with the Romantics.[12] Just how far modern clinical psychiatry is divorced from this can be seen in a work by Kehrer[13] about the extraordinary achievements of dreams, where the vitality of the soul is literally killed off by a ruthless process of systematization.

Here once again it is the surgeon Bier who helps the extraordinary quality of the powers of the soul to come into their own. For example, he indicates the discovery of the ring structure of the benzole molecule by Kekulé[14] in the daydream or the conception of the "artificial bloodlessness" by Esmarch in the dream. In this context I also recall the deciphering of the Egyptian hieroglyphics by Champollion while in the dream state.[15]

It would be easy to quote further such examples from day-to-day practice, as was the case with the aforementioned casuistic report, but examples usually are much less conspicuous than in the situation just noted.

12. G. H. v. Schubert, *Die Geschichte der Seele,* 5th ed. (Stuttgart, 1878).

13. F. Kehrer, "Wach-und Wahrträume bei Gesunden und Kranken," *Sammlg. psychiatr. u. neurol. Einzeldarst. Bd.* IX (Leipzig, 1935).

14. F. Kehrer, *Ber. dtsch. chem. Ges.* (1890), 1306 ff.

15. Hartleben, *Champollion, sein Leben und sein Werk* (1906).

Chapter 3

Thoughts on Medical and Nonmedical Psychotherapy

Noli esse stultus ne moriaris in tempore non tuo. Fingunt se cuncti medicos: idiota, sacerdos, judaeus, monachus, histrio, rasor, anus.
Do not be stupid that you may not die before your time. They all pretend to be doctors: the private man, the priest, the Jew, the monk, the actor, the barber, the hag.
(Inscription on the local doctor's house in Cavigliano, Tessin)

The thoughts I put before you here apply exclusively to what is known as analytical psychology. This form of treatment is practiced successfully by many nonmedical analysts; in fact probably more nonmedical than medical analysts practice it. This fact is much more a problem for the doctors than for their patients, for the former find themselves confronted by two insoluble problems:

1. The doctor is inclined to regard his patients as ill people, and considers quite rightly that their treatment should be in his hands. But in the realm of psychology it is never clear, even in the case of the doctor himself, where the normal ends and the pathological begins.

2. There are not enough doctors who have mastered analytical psychology, and there never will be enough. The few doctors who are interested in mental phenomena remain mostly in psychiatry, partly for apotropaic reasons and partly on account of a lack of philosophical training.

The arguments that the doctors bring against lay analysis are justifiable from their point of view, but on many other grounds

Paper read to the "Sixth Convention of the Swiss Society of Psychology" in Fribourg, Switzerland on May 18, 1946. First published in German in: *Schweizerische Zeitschrift für Psychologie*, vol. v (Bern, 1946), 300ff. English translation by Frances E. Smart, M.D.

they are feeble. Long before it was recognized as such, psychotherapy was, in all ages, a form of divine healing, and its practice
lay exclusively in the hands of priests. I have already tried to
show in a special study how exceedingly modern the psychotherapeutic equipment of the priest-doctors was, even in ancient
Greece.[1] One cannot but marvel at the medical acumen they
possessed. Actually, it was a doctor, Hippocrates, who, through
the founding of his essentially materialistic medical school, was
responsible for the later limited use of dreams in psychotherapeutic treatment, although he was the first who believed it was
possible to dispense with the help of Asklepios. Since his time,
medicine has become progressively more materialistic in its
development. Clearly, it is now, therefore, the duty and obliga-
tion of the medical profession to place the psychological factor
once again at the center of treatment (where, indeed, it has
belonged for more than twenty centuries).

Seen historically, ancient medical science was handed down
through Cassiodorus, who transferred the care of it to the Christian monasteries. Just as the monks were forbidden to carry out
surgical interference or perform autopsies, so, in later times,
religious scruples forbade the priestly ministry from occupying
itself with certain diseases of the soul, which were not considered
respectable according to clerical concept. For this reason, then,
psychotherapy once again passed into the hands of doctors, who
have become the founders of modern psychotherapeutic treatment. It is a strange paradox of history that his training in natural science – and not in philosophy, which is quite lacking in his
training – enabled the modern doctor to undertake this task
successfully. The enlightened phase of modern medicine promul-
gated by the doctors has, on the one hand, drained the ecclesiasti-
cal ministry of its powerful water and, on the other hand, filled a
grievous lack caused by the failure of just this religious
institution.

The fundamental features of medical training have remained
the same for centuries, and not without very good reasons. The
doctor-to-be receives in his premedical course a basic and many-
sided introduction into the methods of natural science. It seems

---

1. C. A. Meier, *Ancient Incubation and Modern Psychotherapy* (Evanston,
Illinois: Northwestern University Press, 1968) [original German edition, 1949].

odd, therefore, that Freud, in his article on lay analysis, should describe this part of medical training as superfluous for the training of the future analyst; apparently he was unconscious that *his own merit* lay exclusively in the undeviating application of just these methods. Freud's philosophic training, however, was insufficient to enable him to see this inconsistency clearly, and this factor of his personal equation remained unconscious to him all his life. Freud worshipped the *déesse raison*, who was never a goddess, however, but merely a quality of the divine figure. The psyche, however, is "like a butterfly, gaily glittering and difficult to catch," as Hippolytus says. At any rate, the methods of natural science never have sufficed to catch it, especially in the case of the modern neurotic.

Freud unquestionably deserves the credit for having performed the sheer pioneer work in this area. Even in 1926, in the article entitled "Die Frage der Laienanalyse" [The Problem of Lay Analysis], he was the first to intercede, with the whole force of his personality, on behalf of lay analysis.[2] Paradoxically, this very article, which otherwise contains some very good arguments, gives us the starting point for enumerating many invaluable advantages to the analyst that a medical training provides.

Freud places the emphasis generally on the training of the analyst. Doubtless the degree of professional training stands in reciprocal relation to the square of the vanity of the individual, and the well-trained analyst will make significantly fewer mistakes in his work than the one who is only adequately trained. Knowledge makes one humble, but what is it that Freud calls training and knowledge? Aptly, the master puts the emphasis primarily on the value of the training analysis and the control analysis. We all know how little these have to do with real knowledge, so this requirement is equally important for the layman and the doctor. The actual specialized knowledge Freud demands includes purely material and technical requisites that, according to him, should be possible to learn in two years:

1. The theory of psychoanalysis
2. The most thorough understanding of the psychology of the unconscious that is possible today

---

2. S. Freud, *The Problem of Lay Analysis* (New York: Brentano, 1927) [original German version, 1926].

3. Instruction in sexual matters
4. Learning the delicate technique to which belong
   a) the art of interpretation,
   b) the overcoming of resistances, and
   c) the handling of the transference [3]

I must confess that it has taken me eight times as long to "learn" these things, and I still have not completely mastered them.

In a 1927 publication, "Nachwort zur Frage der Laienanalyse" [The Postscript to the Question of Lay Analysis], Freud puts the following paragraph at the head: "The decisive thing in the training is to become an analyst and not to become a doctor."[4] This maxim which neither we nor many of Freud's own pupils accept unreservedly, is inadvertently explained by Freud in an autobiographical note.[5] He tells us that he has never been a *pur sang* doctor, and has never perceived the need to help suffering humanity. He was, indeed, a research worker, and a student of natural science. Out of pure scientific curiosity and with the equipment of natural science, he has successfully entered the tabooed realm of the neuroses. Thus, he became responsible for a very large number of cures, in spite of the fact that he was no *pur sang* doctor. It would be better to say he was a doctor *malgré lui* [in spite of himself]. At any rate, we can hardly believe that these therapeutic successes just happened to him *contre coeur*. Finally, besides the theory of the neuroses, he has also given an account of a *therapeutic* method that certainly betrays a medical attitude. It is just this attitude in himself to which he never wants to draw attention and, therefore, finds unimportant for the analyst as well.

For this paradox in Freud's conception, I think I can give an explanation. In "Die Frage der Laienanalyse," Freud speaks, as I have already said, almost exclusively of the training, and unless one counts the third item, knowledge of sexual matters, it contains no medical material. Only incidentally is the need for "medical" discretion mentioned.[6] Similarly, only once is moral

---

3. Freud, *Lay Analysis* [German version, 83-84].

4. Freud, "Nachwort zur Frage der Laienanalyse," *Gesammelte Schriften* XI (Vienna, 1928), 385.

5. Freud, "Nach wort," *Ges. Schr.* XI (Vienna, 1928), 388-389.

6. Freud, *Lay Analysis* [German version, 45].

responsibility addressed.[7] Otherwise, he says, a certain tact is necessary for handling the resistance and the transference neurosis,[8] and for the rest, some skill, patience, calmness, and self-denial are needed.[9] Toward the end of the article it is once more stated[10] that the analyst must have personal qualities that make him trustworthy—all that is demanded of the lay analyst in the way of character *desiderata*. Then, suddenly, at the end of the "Nachwort zur Frage der Laienanalyse,"[11] it is said that doctors and lay analysts should work together so that the latter may be stimulated to raise their moral and intellectual level. Only the lay analysts have this need, and the doctors are the "society for raising the fallen." Doctors are morally and intellectually in a higher position, then, and *eo ipso* [for that very reason] superior. The involuntariness of this confession by Freud makes it, a posteriori, something very suspicious. One should never write an appendix without need. I suppose even the brave champion of lay analysis was in need of *a rider over Bodensee*, and, in spite of his convincing championship for the layman, he has still been obliged to add: "We doctors are indeed better men!"

Now, I think we must entirely excuse this drawback to Doctor Sigmund Freud. He and many of his medical followers have proved through their work that the study of medicine is not an unqualified handicap for the practice of analysis. As I said at the beginning, I am of exactly the opposite opinion. Certainly it is difficult for the doctor to fulfill the demands of the alchemist Gerardus Dorneus: "mentis a corpore distractio necessaria est [a separation of the mind from the body is necessary]."[12] But it helps him little in psychology if he masters the philosophical material and understands nothing of the methods of natural science. There is even a very great danger that he may lose himself in the undergrowth. In all events, the danger of losing himself in the natural-scientific method is much less. At worst, the

---

7. Freud, *Lay Analysis* [German version, 46].
8. Freud, *Lay Analysis* [German version, 70].
9. Freud, *Lay Analysis* [German version, 83].
10. Freud, *Lay Analysis* [German version, 113].
11. Freud, *Gesammelte Schriften* XI, 394.
12. G. Dorneus, "Philosophia Meditativa" in *Theatrum Chemicum* I, (Ursellis, 1602), 453.

spiritual phenomena are reduced to nothing, as in psychiatry with its taxonomy, materialism, and electric shock treatments. The doctor who is only interested in observing the spiritual phenomena from a safe distance remains firmly planted in psychiatry and is, therefore, unlikely to become dangerous as "an untrained analyst" as Freud feared.[13] Therefore, it is only to be welcomed if in such candidates the materialistic spirit of medicine, as Freud says, does not awaken an interest in the spiritual aspect of the phenomena of life.[14] But whoever goes through the holometamorphic development from the premedical natural sciences to become a clinical doctor and a psychiatrist, and eventually an analyst, also goes the way of the natural development of analysis. Was this not the way taken by its founders, Freud and Jung? Is not modern psychotherapy an offshoot of modern medicine? Regarded as a form of spiritual healing, psychotherapy is certainly a heresy, and doctors must be willing to have the reputation of being heretics. On the other hand, one cannot make them responsible for the fact that analysis did not arise from philosophy or theology, or even from academic psychology; at all events, they are no more responsible for this than for the godlessness of modern times in general. At any rate, the young doctor who becomes an analyst by this route follows the basic law of biogenesis, for ontogenesis is really a shortened recapitulation of phylogenesis. If Nature could make it easier, she certainly would. In all events, Freud's argument that medical training for the analyst is uneconomical seems to me largely materialistic.[15] In analysis itself, the analyst experiences soon enough that he must be ready at any time, in any given case, to courageously throw overboard his whole natural-scientific and medical equipment, and change it for philosophical equipment, which he must acquire. He can, however, draw on it again at any time, in a given case. At any rate, I personally have never yet suffered from a too heavy ballast of natural science; on the contrary, my *consiliarii* of specialized knowledge in many spheres have been indispensable. Thanks to my medical career, I have

---

13. Freud, *Gesammelte Schriften* XI, 392.
14. Freud, *Lay Analysis* [German version, 88-90].
15. Freud, *Lay Analysis* [German version, 115].

sufficient knowledge in mathematics or physics, for example, to recognize the hidden problems in the corresponding material of my patients.

I do not want to speak of these arguments, *pro domo medica*. Ultimately, the lay analyst could also acquire a suitable preclinical training and, moreover, this is of predominant importance for dealing scientifically with analytical material. Nowadays, however, medical training consists for the most part of clinical work, and here, in my opinion, lie some very decisive advantages, only two of which I would particularly like to emphasize.

First, the young doctor receives basic practical instruction on the importance of discretion. This training is lacking even for the potential lawyer and, what is still more dangerous, for the student theological minister. The latter, of course, certainly receives instruction on the meaning of the *sigillum confessionis* [secrecy of the confessional], but not, as in the case of the doctor, before he takes up his duties after having several years of practice already to his credit. Certainly the Catholic priest, it seems to me, is eminently protected against the *fractio sigilli* [betrayal of the secret] by reason of church law and dogma, but the Protestant minister is at a disadvantage because of this lack of protection. In my experience, it is one of the most common mistakes of lay analysts that they do not take the duty of discretion seriously enough.

Second, and this is the most essential, it is only medical training that provides opportunity for the student to obtain direct experience of suffering humanity. This opportunity is not even given to the theologian, for whom it is especially regrettable that he must go straight out into practice without it. It is, unfortunately, only the doctor who can have experience, during his training, of the dignity of illness and suffering, the human being afflicted by it, and the powers brought in to play through it. This advantage is obtained in no other training. An old alchemist says, "The soul, by which Man is distinguished from other forms of life, certainly has that particular function in the body [namely, the above-mentioned directing of the mind, i.e., understanding, and its effect on the activity of free will], but it has its more important effect outside the body, because there it rules independently. In this lies the difference from the animals, which only possess *mens* [intelligence], but not the *anima deitatis* [divine soul]."[16] Whoever does not become aware of this at the bedside, during his training, remains a somatic doctor or psychiatrist, but does not become a good doctor, and certainly not a safe analyst; but neither is he any danger to us if he should throw psychotherapy into the same pot with magic and quackery. Whoever is aware of this becomes a good somatic doctor, and will always be a good psychotherapist, and is our most valuable colleague, not to say rival. He may instead become an analyst and, without knowing it, again close the circle begun by Hippocrates more than two thousand years ago when he laid the foundations of scientific medicine. So the medical analyst goes a longer way around. Is it really as uneconomical as Freud supposed?[17] "Qui patientiam non habet, manum ab opere suspendat" [He who lacks patience should keep his hand away from it], says the *Aurora consurgens*.[18]

I have nothing to say about the training of lay analysts. For the doctor, the postgraduate training leading to analysis is via a long series of philosophic disciplines. I do not believe in institutions, still less in Institutes. I believe more in the close human contact with a great psychotherapeutic personality, in the sense of master and disciple, in which the development of one's own personality is stimulated. In addition, I do not believe in a method that can be learned, for in our work, as nowhere else, the man is the method, as has been said so often. I also do not believe it is so urgently necessary to manufacture psychotherapists by mass production. Those who do not go to psychotherapists still would not go even if these name-plates decorated more buildings in their town. I have never yet had to turn away anyone seeking help, and, moreover, if I could not take time myself, I have always been able to find a most suitable colleague, whether lay or medical in training.

For the rest, I believe every patient deserves the psychotherapist to whom he eventually goes. It is fitting here to quote the

---

16. "Anima autem, qua homo a caeteris animalibus differt, illa operatur in corpore, sed majorem operationem habet extra corpus; quoniam absolute extra corpus dominatur, et his differt ab animalibus quae tantum mentem non animan deitatis habent." *Musaeum Hermeticum* (Francofurti, 1677), 617.

17. Freud, *Lay Analysis* [German version, 115].

18. Morienus, *Harmonia Imperscrutabilis* (Francofurti: ed., Joh. Rhenanus, 1625), 191.

Musaeum Hermeticum, which says:

Indeed, doctors [medical doctors] and scholars and others are not able to find this thing, because they have never paid attention to it, and they do not trust it, although it has in itself such power. And none can teach them so long as they follow their nature and their intellect; thus by sheer knowledge they cannot find it, because it exceeds the possibility of their comprehension, for it is the work of God and Nature, and is obtained through Nature. Therefore they remain inexperienced in these things.[19]

---

19. "Quodque idem viri Doctissimi, utpote Doctores, & alij, reperire nequeant, in caussa est, quod numquam ad rem istam intenti sient quamvis eamdem cottidie prae oculis suis habeant, nihilominus tamen illi fidem nullam tribuunt, quod videlicet tantam in se virtutem habeat: Ipsis quoque nemo, illud persuadere potest, dum naturam, intellectumque suum sequuntur: idcirco etiam illud, nimia prae sapientia, reperire non possunt, quum captum ipsorum transcendat, Dei opus siet, & natura siet, & per naturam operatur. Quocirca rerum imperiti permanent." *Musaeum Hermeticum,* 212-13.

Chapter 4

Projection, Transference, and The Subject-Object Relation in Psychology

It is too often forgotten that Jung's beginnings lay in clinical psychiatry. As the young assistant physician at Burghölzli, he quickly made a name for himself through his work on Galton's association experiments. It was thought at the time that these experiments would lead to a better knowledge of the elementary phenomena of psychology and psychopathology. With unerring scientific instinct, Jung directed his attention to the very phenomena his predecessors had neglected, the statistically rare *reaction disturbances*, and in so doing discovered an even more fundamental phenomenon to which he gave the name *complex*. It was soon proven from the experimental side that this discovery opened the way to a realm that had been discovered shortly before from the clinical side, by Freud. After that, almost the whole of Jung's work was devoted to exploring this *terra incognita* of the unconscious.

Advancing boldly along paths that sometimes ran parallel and sometimes diverged, Freud and Jung travelled deeply into this vast continent. Pioneers encounter new natural phenomena for which new concepts have to be formulated. Both explorers have done this, and the new expressions they introduced were often intuitive strokes of genius. Armed with these, for fifty years countless psychotherapists and psychologists of all denomina-

---

Paper read to the "Internationaler Kongress für Philosophie der Wissenschaften" in Zürich. First published in German in: *Dialectica*, vol. 8 (Neuveville, 1954), 302ff. English translation by R. F. C. Hull. Also published in *The Journal of Analytical Psychology* 4, 1 (1959).

tions have pooled their experience and amply confirmed the existence of those phenomena and processes for which the new technical terms were coined. Indeed, one sometimes gets the impression that nothing really new has been discovered since those early years, at any rate in psychoanalysis. Jung, it is true, continued to enrich the world of psychological theory, and he always remained true to his pioneering spirit. On the other hand, one can also see how he endeavored constantly to adapt the old concepts of the *libido, unconscious, archetype,* and the like to his growing experience and to formulate them anew. He left everything open and in flux, so that readers who cannot see his development in perspective easily get confused or think they can spot contradictions, and they are doomed to disappointment if they expect a nicely rounded theory.

It seems to me that any intellectual advance in psychology today depends very much on whether it is possible to revise these old, established concepts in the light of the experience that has accrued through their practical application. Jung himself endeavored to do this in one of the most important of his later works. He recounts how, the first time he met Freud, the great psychologist asked him at the end of their conversation, "And what do you think about the transference?" Jung replied that it was the "alpha and omega of the analytical method," whereupon Freud, visibly gratified, dismissed him with the remark, "Then you have understood the main thing." [1] Forty years later Jung came back to this central problem in the light of the experience he had gathered in the meantime.

The *transference* is the *pièce de résistance* of psychotherapy and consequently one of the phenomena in most urgent need of revision. As Jung showed, however, it is an extremely complicated affair, so it may be advisable to begin our investigation with a simpler psychological phenomenon.

The fundamental phenomenon on which the transference rests is projection. If we disregard, for the time being, what Jung called *active projection,* [2] then projection is a process that has

---

1. C. G. Jung, "The Psychology of the Transference," in *The Practice of Psychotherapy. Essays on The Psychology of the Transference and Other Subjects (Coll. Wks.* 16, 1954), 172 [original German version, 1946].

2. C. G. Jung, *Psychological Types (Coll. Wks.* 6, 1971) [original German edition, 1921].

been found to occur between a *projecting* subject and a *receiving* object. I use the perfect tense here because we are able to establish only the effects of the process; the process itself operates unconsciously. Projection is not *made*, it just *happens*, so that all one sees is its effects. Since the actual process works unconsciously, it is reasonable to suppose that the content of a projection is unconscious, too, and should therefore be ascribed to the unconscious of the sender. If the sender has an opportunity to discuss this state of affairs with the carrier of the projection, it will be possible for him to become conscious of the content projected, though this is certainly not easy, as it presupposes a fair amount of objectivity on both sides. Sometimes the brute facts are enough to make the necessary corrective, but the result is not an ideal one from the analytical point of view, for in that way the projected content simply disappears again into the unconscious of the sender. In a proper discussion the sender stands to gain something: he becomes conscious of the content he originally projected and thus increases his range of consciousness. The original content has probably had to adapt itself a bit, but it now really belongs to the subject and, because it is conscious, will not be projected again. That is the basic advantage of analysis: the scope of the personality is gradually increased.

Apparently this scheme underlies the development of consciousness in general and, moreover, in a double sense. First, the qualities projected, provided that they can be withdrawn or led back to the subject, are only now recognized as belonging to him. And since this process repeats itself spontaneously from earliest childhood right up to old age, it must be one of the most important sources for increasing and strengthening the scope of individual consciousness, and certainly the most vital factor for self-knowledge. This view obviously implies that the unconscious is a theoretically inexhaustible matrix consisting not only of contents that are capable of becoming conscious, but also of contents that for some reason or other have sunk below the threshold.

There is, however, a second sense in which the process just described plays an important part in the development of consciousness. Projections fall on all manner of objects, animate and inanimate; in the latter case, for instance, on matter. We shall come back to this later on. Here I would only mention how important projections on matter were for the alchemists, as Jung was the first to demonstrate.[3] The growth of the natural sciences seems on the one hand to be connected very largely with projections falling on a certain realm of matter, so that the scientist was fascinated by it, and on the other hand to depend on how far it was possible, in the course of centuries, to objectify the contents hiding behind the projections. Not only does the choice of material realm, and of a profession, for instance, seem to be determined in this way, but it also seems that some of these projections, when suitably corrected, finally prove to be objective facts. The realm in question is gradually emptied of its magic and mythology, and, as if in compensation, their place is then taken by scientific knowledge, which increases the sum of collective consciousness,[4] as W. Pauli has shown in the case of Kepler.

At any rate, we know from psychological experience that a certain correspondence exists between the contents of a projection and its carrier. That is to say, it is not *any* content of the unconscious that is projected on *any* carrier. On impartial investigation it generally will be found that the carrier provokes certain projections. Objective discussion on this point is, of course, only possible if the analyst (the carrier) is in a large measure conscious of himself. This self-knowledge underlies the absolute requirement for a training analysis. If it is not met, the so-called analyst will only be drawn into disagreeable arguments with the analysand and will miss the whole point. Not taking the projection seriously, he will cheat both the analysand and himself of an important truth.

In everyday analytical parlance we call this correspondence the *hook* in the carrier that *catches* the projection. This theory is often easy to demonstrate, but it introduces a new principle into our original scheme of projection – the principle of symmetry or reciprocity. It may be assumed that the catching of projections by a hook cannot be without effects on the carrier, and that a countereffect will not be lacking. This symmetrical situation can exist even in the case of an inanimate carrier: the retroactive effects which the alchemist's projections upon inert matter had

---

3. C. G. Jung, *Psychology and Alchemy* (*Coll. Wks.* 12, 1953) [original German edition, 1944].

4. W. Pauli, "The Influence of Archetypal Ideas on the Formation of Scientific Theories in Kepler," in *The Interpretation of Nature and the Psyche*, Bollingen 48 (London: Routledge Kegan Paul; New York: Pantheon, 1955).

on himself have been convincingly proved by Jung.[5] One is tempted to make the same process responsible for the origin of astrology, though it would certainly be difficult to say whether *Heimarmene* [the absolute influence of the stars] is the retroactive effect of psychic contents projected onto the stars, or whether the objective, extra-human existence of something like Fate is simply projected onto the stars for lack of better understanding.

Let us return to the question of projection on a human partner, and try to understand what happens when the projection is *withdrawn* in the technically correct manner. The analysand has not only had a good chance to become considerably more conscious of himself and his partner, he has also experienced something of his own unconscious and made an important discovery concerning the nature of the projection-making factor. Withdrawing the projection does not mean merely recognizing the hook or the grain of truth which was magnified into the whole; the essential thing is to recognize how much the projected quality belongs to the subject. Once this is recognized, we are faced with the further question of what it was that caused the subject to "make" precisely that projection. As anyone with analytical experience will agree, there seems to be a certain method in this choice; in other words, there must be some factor at work still further back in the unconscious which seems to have the "total plan" of the personality in view. This factor generally appears personified, as a numinous figure of the opposite sex. Jung, as we know, has called these dream and fantasy figures the *anima* and *animus*. It is, therefore, one of these figures which we have to consider as the projection-making factor (in the case of the anima an illustrative example would be the Vedantic *Māyā*[6]). The above-mentioned method can, accordingly, be represented in the following triadic system, where *a* is the projecting subject, *b* the object that carries the projection, and *c* the projection-making factor:

5. Jung, *Psychology and Alchemy* (*Coll. Wks.* 12, 1953). [original German edition, 1944].

[6. Ed. Note: Māyā is a key philosphical, mystical and practical concept which dominates much of Indian thought. It is creative, cosmic illusion in magic, art and phenomenal existence. The belief is that all experiences in the manifested universe are illusory – that true and essential reality is obscured.]

Figure 1

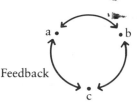

Feedback

a in his discussions with *b* on whom his projection falls, will recognize (1) that the projected content belongs to himself, and (2) that its origin lies in *c*. The analysand has thus recognized the projection-making subject in himself as a result of discussions with the outside object, the analyst, which means nothing less than the subjective discovery of what Jung sometimes calls the *objective psyche*.

In this process the arc *c*——*a* amounts to a feedback system, since *c*, after assimilation of *a* of the projected content, will not cease to constellate further components in *a*, whereupon the process can begin all over again in changed form. Herein lies the *totalistic* function of *c*, which justifies Jung and others in speaking of an objective psyche. We shall come back later to the significance of factors not dependent on consciousness as objects of the ego.

This formulation of the projection problem gives rise to a new question, namely the attribution of *c*. It is not at all clear to whom the projection-making factor belongs. Normally, at the beginning of analysis, contents are projected which can, without further ado, be attributed to the subject. However, as soon as *archetypal* contents appear in projection, the situation is no longer so clear. This problem becomes particularly acute in the case of a full-fledged transference. The contents can then easily assume forms which are both more and less than human, sometimes reaching an intensity for which we can offer no explanation. Such situations, as we know, harbor many dangers:

1. The affective reactions are overwhelming, which means that the subject is unable to cope with these contents;

2. The carrier too is affected by them, so that his behavior will not be adequate to the situation;

3. A well-known analyst's disease, resulting therefrom, is positive or negative inflation, positive or negative according to the

nature of the content or the predominance of one of its aspects;

4. Inflation, meaning at least partial identification with the projected contents.

What frequently happens in these circumstances is that the analysand projects onto the analyst, the "knower." He is the professional who is supposed to know everything about the almost impenetrable darknesses of the human soul. This may be partially true in rare cases, and it is then only partly a projection. Usually the claim goes much too far, however, and must be taken as projection and nothing else. If the analyst identifies with this projection, he will give the patient advice like a wise old man or interpret dreams like a Chaldean. The result is in any case highly questionable, if not dangerous. Not only does he make the patient fatally dependent on the analyst, he also cheats him of the realization of those qualities which the patient has projected upon him. If we now assume that the authority delegated to the analyst is a projection of the analysand, we are saying in effect that the projection is a content of the analysand's unconscious. We are therefore logically compelled not only to acknowledge this unconscious authority's right to exist in the analysand, but also to awaken it in him and make it conscious. We must do this if only to stop the patient from getting an inflation instead of the analyst, for only consciousness can prevent this danger. If there are analysts who have learned how to cope more or less adequately with the demands of the human soul, then surely other people, including our patients, can learn to do so, too, and thus learn to withdraw this particular projection.

The situation becomes more difficult in the instances I have already mentioned, where the projection assumes dimensions which simply refuse to submit to this technique, and cannot be reduced either to the carrier or to the sender alone. One can try in one way or another to reduce the excess of emotion in these situations, and occasionally one succeeds in robbing the projected image of its power. Yet the result is not particularly gratifying, since it becomes quite obvious that the analysand is impoverished and bored by the whole procedure, which is not surprising when one considers, as I have said, that he has been cheated out of something important.

Besides, there are always cases where this method fails completely and the projection resists all our therapeutic efforts. However that may be, I suggest we examine this special situation once more, on the principle that in these cases, too, we are still dealing with the scheme of projection we have described.

The hook in the analyst that catches the projection can naturally be either conscious or unconscious. If he is conscious of it, then the chances for unravelling the tangle are more favorable. We all know that either real knowledge will help the patient, or a reputation based on real powers of healing increases the chances of a cure. For the analyst as well, it is true that consciousness is a safeguard against identification with the archetype of the wise old man or with that of the savior, to take the two possibilities already mentioned. As we have said, it is only at times that this consciousness on the part of the analyst still does not stop the patient from making more than human projections. The question then arises as to where the patient gets these emotional affluxes from, and what ought to be done to alter the process. If they assume superhuman dimensions, it can readily be understood that they will resist being reduced to the all-too-human figure of the analysand. Nor would it be good medical treatment to inflate the unfortunate patient with these contents – he would get a psychic emphysema and burst!

Faced with these overpowering experiences, we may remind ourselves how mankind has always reacted to them in the past. To take the most frequent content of projection, the erotic aspect: all psychotherapists should be convinced Platonists at least in this one point, that Eros is a "mighty daimon."[7] Antiquity regarded erotic projection as a state in which the lover is the helpless and innocent victim of a supernatural power that has wounded him with its *telum passionis* [dart of passion], and this seems to me to be well worth considering in the light of our projection theory. That is to say, people in antiquity experienced an effect whose cause was missing because it was unconscious, and they proceeded to posit this cause in the concrete form of Eros. Now, were they justified in exteriorizing Eros like this, or must we be psychologically consistent and say that it was a projection for which they themselves were responsible? In other words, has modern psychology "cleared up" the old mythologem? Which is right: to ascribe all these contents to oneself, or, cost what it

---

7. Plato, *Symposium*, 203 A1.

may, to insist on a corresponding hook in the object, whether it is demonstrable or not? In neither case is the "superhuman" quality of the projection explained.

Here we may be helped by an observation which we do not at first like to admit: (1) projections often have very marked effects not only on the sender but also on the receiver, even when the latter can, in no conceivable way, have known about the existence of the projection, that is, when we cannot imagine any mechanism of transference. Here our classical causality breaks down. (2) We must also admit that the asymmetry of the old quasi-causal scheme of projection, which simply assumes that the unconscious of *a* projected something onto *b* (see Fig. 2), is unsatisfying.

In view of these absurdities, we put forward an idea that may be more satisfactory. If we treat the symmetry of the projection process seriously, we surely know of the transference being followed by a countertransference. I suggest we assume that in every case of transference something similar is happening to the projection carrier, and that the same kind of arrangement or pattern is taking shape in relation to *a* and *b* (Fig. 2). That which falls into the same pattern would be what we ordinarily describe as the transference between *a* and *b*. If we think of examples where a mechanism of transference—i.e., a transmission of energy—is inconceivable, then our reason posits an arranging or constellating factor A, which is entirely abstract and invisible, while the similarity of pattern between transference and counter-tranference is a visible phenomenon. The positing of a constellating factor naturally arises from a causal need, which exists even when—or rather, just at the point where—the missing link remains in the unconscious. It would then be nothing but another projection, as it were into empty space. In view of the difficulties of such an hypothesis on the one hand, and of the inconceivability of causal transference mechanisms on the other, it might be advisable to understand the model as an acausal relationship, in accordance with Jung's principle of synchronicity. Let us not forget that the expression *transference* derives from folklore,[8] where, for instance, the transferring of an illness to a tree for purposes of healing is thought of purely in magical terms, that

---

8. P. Kemp, *Healing Ritual* (London: Faber, 1935).

is, acausally.[9] Terms such as *arrangement, pattern*, and *constellation* are, of course, based on a formal principle. In this sense the identity of the formal principle with the archetype, as defined by Jung, is obvious.[10] The invisible or "irrepresentable" nature of the constellating factor also enters into this definition.

The object we have postulated, the constellating factor, must be conceived as transcending the subject. This likewise suggests that we are here concerned with an archetype. If we speak of projection of transference in such circumstances, that is only a special way of observing the similarity of patterns from a point outside it, C, on the assumption that *a* is the active partner and has illusions about *b*.

Figure 2

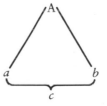

Eros with his arrow would be an example of a causal representation of the irrepresentable constellating factor A, and more satisfying than the old projection theory. It also avoids the danger of inflation with contents whose attribution to the subject would be injurious to psychic health.

This symmetrical view of the transference phenomenon gives rise to yet another problem. For *a* and *b* would then be either (1) partly identical (so far as similarity of pattern is concerned) and thus indistinguishable from one another, or (2) unconsciously identical, which means that they would be undifferentiated.

In the second case, the contents of projection would be reducible to qualities that belonged to the subject, and the process would satisfy causality: *b* would have entered the system only as a kind of catalyst and would be extruded at the other end unchanged. The symmetry of these situations seems to manifest

9. C. G. Jung, "Synchronicity: An Acausal Connecting Principle," *The Interpretation of Nature and the Psyche* (New York: Pantheon, 1955) [original German version, 1952]; also in *The Structure and Dynamics of the Psyche* (*Coll. Wks.* 1960), 417-519.

10. Jung, "Synchronicity."

itself chiefly in the form of synchronistic phenomena. In the first case, however, though the situation would be just as symmetrical, the similarity of pattern cannot be reduced to *a* and does not satisfy causality. We have, rather, one of those meaningful coincidences which Jung calls *synchronistic*. Moreover, since it is impossible and therefore meaningless to discriminate from *b* as regards pattern, the situation has a totalistic character and the subject is transcended by A. In the language of analytical psychology a true symbol has come into being, and the subjective situation is characterized by the appearance of a creative element.[11] Where the situation is symmetrical, *b* is included in it just as much as *a*, and both are changed by the experience and by the knowledge they have gained.

Figure 3

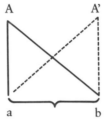

In the classic transference situation as described by Jung,[12] our constellating factor A would be replaced by anima and animus (Fig. 3, A + A'), thus producing a quaternary constellation.

It is known that in such situations synchronistic events are experienced with some frequency, and this alone suggests that we should revise our ideas of projection and transference in the light of this new principle.

It may be that the quaternary model underlies every mental creation or conception and explains much of the fascination of sex. Again, one thinks of the *Symposium*, which says of this mysterious genesis: "For the coming together of man and woman is a bringing forth," meaning that together they will have beautiful and immortal children.[13]

---

11. C. G. Jung, *Mysterium Coniunctionis. An Inquiry into the Separation and Synthesis of Psychic Opposites in Alchemy* (Coll. Wks. 14,1963) [original German edition, 1955].

12. Jung, "Transference," 221ff.

13. Plato, *Symposium*, 206c.

We can see the problem of projection and transference more clearly when we observe it from the standpoint of the subject-object relation. If we take the psychologist as subject, and particularly his conscious ego, then his object can either be *outside*, animate or inanimate, a thing or an idea, or *inside*, an idea, image, fantasy or some emotional state in himself. *Relation* may be specified here as the way in which the subject affects the object and vice versa. It is only these effects that we can establish directly. There are then, in principle, two possibilities: either the effects are asymmetrical, or the effects are symmetrical or reciprocal.

In order to have the simplest possible conditions, one will try first of all to establish the first case. The phenomena under discussion are especially clear in analytical work. Here, as elsewhere, so-called projections occur, a specific instance of which is the erotic projection, or transference. Freud, following Occam[14] (*Entia praeter necessitatem non sunt multiplicanda*) [Entities must not be multiplied unnecessarily], assumed that the effects are asymmetrical, but was soon forced to admit that in actual fact there is always a tendency towards symmetry or reciprocity, in other words, that there is a countertransference at work.

Let us try to observe this complication in the light of the subject-object relation. The analyst pushes deeper and deeper into the object, so that the "cut" between subject and object is moved further and further into the latter. Meanwhile the analyst's insight into the object is becoming so intimate that he cannot tell whether he is still dealing with the object or partly with himself. In addition, the situation in psychology is, as we have said, reciprocal, and thus more or less symmetrical:

Figure 4

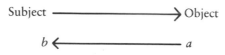

[14. Ed. Note: William of Occam, an English scholastic philosopher (1290-1349).]

To the extent that the analyst (*b*) affects the analysand (*a*), we must assume that the analysand is also having an effect on the analyst. The action from right to left (Fig. 4) may in ideal cases be less, insofar as the analyst's range of consciousness is assumed to be greater; that is to say, the cut moves more into the object, since the analyst knows more about the analysand than vice versa. The only question is, what has been gained?

Naturally the analyst can communicate his greater knowledge of the analysand to him, and thus increase his range of consciousness, though this is no simple matter on account of the resistances. There is, however, another difficulty of fundamental importance: the moving of the cut into the analysand and the uncertainty as to its localization, bring with them an uncertainty as to the attribution of the facts observed. In analytical psychology the principle holds that the analyst must not only be analyzed himself, but must also keep his own reactions in mind all the time. He has to relate his own dreams to the system, on the assumption that they have a corrective or compensatory value with respect to his consciously acquired knowledge of the object.

It is probable that this extra knowledge which the analyst has (or which the analysand thinks he has) is a source of projections for the analysand. Practically every analyst becomes a savior-god to his patient, and this constellates an archetype which brings the analysand powerful affluxes of emotion. Once again we are faced by the question of an attribution. To whom does this image with its emotional charge belong? In analytical psychology we apply the hypothesis of the *collective unconscious* and arrive at the following triadic system:

Figure 5

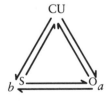

The system is triadic because we cannot attribute the collective unconscious to either partner personally. It stands rather for the objective psyche and is thus a second object for both *a* and *b*.

Once it is constellated, however, this image will not leave the analyst untouched. Emotions are infectious. The channel for infection in the analyst may be the archetype itself, since, as a content of the collective unconscious, it is the common denominator of *a* and *b* (arrows CU ⟶ S and O, Fig. 5). The analyst's greater consciousness and more stable personality will damp down his emotional reaction so that he will be in a better position to put the whole phenomenon in the right perspective and answer out of his own totality. Characteristically, however, we are operating all the time in a system which constellates a third quantity for *a* and *b*, an object which acts on both of them. Thorough analytical investigation of this object has two main effects: first of all, it increases *a*'s consciousness in particular and rouses the powers of the healing in him; secondly, it has a reactive effect on the collective unconscious, so that the original image changes or so that other images appear (arrows S and O⟶CU, Fig. 5). This sets up a movement (note the analogy with Fig. 1) which, because it seems to follow an inherent pattern, Jung has called the *individuation process*. For, as far as we can see today, the collective unconscious proves to be identical everywhere.

From what we have said, five points of considerable importance emerge for our theme:

1. The psychologist works with his patient, but from time to time a third element, the objective psyche, appears. As it belongs to both partners, the analyst must also work on himself, whether he likes it or not. The process thus gets a kind of oscillatory character. When things are going well, and *a* and *b* are in phase, there is a building up of oscillation; when things are going badly, a destructive interference. The last-named effect narrows down the personality and is found, unfortunately, among not a few analysts, a fact which says much for the totalistic character of the situation. At any rate, we have here a symmetrical system (see the second case above).

2. The *vis motrix* [moving force] of the process seems to be the emotional charge of the archetypal images. *E-motio* means literally "being moved out of something." The partners in such a process are, in fact, moved out of an initial situation: the analyst out of a supposedly stable situation, the analysand out of a labile or a stagnant one—hence the oscillation or seesaw motion. We shall not dwell here on a factor of some importance for the course of the analysis, namely the specific form in which the constellated archetype appears as a *causa formalis*, and shall

merely remark that we cannot do without emotions in effecting transformations of personality.

3. The process begins, as we have said, with projections and their emotional charge. They act on the analyst or on the third quantity, sometimes without there being any demonstrable, or even conceivable, mechanism of action. I suggest that the mode of action becomes more understandable if we accept the hypothesis of the "cut" moving into the object. What is present in the object then, to some extent, passes over to the subject, even though neither of them may be aware of this fact.

It is difficult to find a clear example where projections are effective despite unconsciousness of their existence on both sides. But in 1927 the American child psychologist, Frances Wickes, described cases of children who showed symptoms which disappeared after the problems of the parents had been successfully treated. The marriage problems of the parents were completely unknown to the children on whom they were projected. Many of the girls were not told for years that their parents had wanted boys instead, and yet it had severe effects on their feminine development. Similar experiences in men may lead even to homosexuality. One can always object that the emotions of parents are simply there and cannot be hidden, and that children have a very fine nose for these things. Unless the parents are completely lacking in self-control, however, that is not a sufficient explanation.

On the strength of our discussions, in 1955 Mrs. Wickes published three case histories from her own experience, the last of which should satisfy the most exacting criteria regarding the inconceivability of a mechanism of transmission.[15] Her exposition is very detailed and ought, for that reason, to be read in the original. One case concerns a mother-son projection of which both were unconscious, and the main point is that the cessation of the sender's projection under analysis had well-attested synchronous and synchronistic effects on the carrier, although he did not know about the treatment and was three thousand miles away at the time. So the whole system collapses as soon as *a* changes. The reliability of this observation is beyond question

---

15. Wickes, *Three Illustrations of the Power of the Projected Image*, Studien Zur Analytischen Psychologie C. G. Jung's, (Zurich: Rascher Verlag, 1955).

and its theoretical importance still holds, even if this was only a rare example.

4. Finally, I would like to mention a further category of cases where special importance attaches to the arrow S ⟶ CU (Fig. 5). In many therapeutic situations the analyst (S) has to occupy himself intensively with the phenomena of the collective unconscious. This active application of attention amounts to what Jung calls *active projection*.[16] Active projections seem to underlie certain ritual actions whose purpose is to influence and animate a particular cult object. They also have a special therapeutic effect. An impressive case of this kind has just been published by R. Lindner.[17] The patient, "Kirk Allen," a state-employed atomic physicist, suffered from a complicated system of delusions, which got so bad that they affected his ability to work. His superior, therefore, sent him to the psychoanalyst Lindner for treatment. The contact was unsatisfactory and the psychoanalytical procedures all remained without result. This intrigued the analyst very much. In his bewilderment he resolved to enter actively into the delusional system of the patient, and, by intense concentration, succeeded so well that he himself began to develop alarming symptoms. The immediate effect, however, was that the patient was able to stand off from his system, so that the system collapsed and he was cured.

Bearing in mind Fig. 5, we would say that Dr. Lindner (S) had caught archetypal contents of the collective unconscious by diverting them from the patient to himself through his emotional interest (arrow CU ⟶ S). The total effect of the constellated contents on doctor and patient (CU ⟶ S and O) may be assumed constant, but if the doctor, as the more stable personality, is able to hold out, then the patient obviously has a better chance of cure.

5. In cases of active projection we are obliged to go a step further. We have already mentioned that the object can be a *thing*. Here again we can describe intense preoccupation with a lifeless object as an attempt to carry the cut between subject and object as far as possible into the latter. Owing to the uncertainty of its position, it is conceivable that the lifeless object will take

---

16. Jung, *Psychological Types*, 582ff.

17. R. Lindner, *The Fifty-Minute Hour*, (New York: Rhinehart, 1955).

over qualities that we usually ascribe to living beings or people. Such effects are generally described as *magical*, and modern experimental parapsychology has successfully interested itself in some of them. Results such as those obtained by Rhine with Zener cards or with dice,[18] which now seem to have been corroborated by Soal and Bateman, can be regarded from this point of view.[19] Jung thought emotions played an important part in these experiments.[20] Bearing in mind what we said under (2) and (3), it would be interesting to see how far affects are *de rigueur* in "magical" procedures. Schopenhauer assumes this on the authority of Bacon, Paracelsus, and van Helmont. The theory, as Jung showed, goes back to Albertus Magnus.[21] According to the view we have put forward, the door through which these affects enter would seem to be the archetype or common denominator, and the vehicle for the displacement of the cut would be projection, though of the active type in this case. Evidently magical practices are resorted to when there is a very delicate line of division between subject and object, that is, when the subject must have the object and wants to devour it, or integrate it, or understand it, and cannot do so in any other way. This is just the situation that produces emotion, on the evidence of biology.[22] If, at this juncture, we remember the case of Kirk Allen, this is not to accuse Dr. Lindner of practicing magic, but to draw attention to the painfully obscure nature of all therapeutic action.

18. J. B. Rhine, *The Reach of the Mind* (Harmondsworth: Penguin Books, 1954).

19. S. G. Soal and F. Bateman, *Modern Experiments in Telepathy* (London: Faber, 1954).

20. Jung, "Synchronicity."

21. Jung, "Synchronicity."

22. Hans Jonas, "Motility and Emotion," *Actes du XIe Congrès International de Philosophie* (1953) 7 (Amsterdam-Louvain, 1954): 117ff.

Chapter 5

The Cutting Lectures

I. JUNG AND ANALYTICAL PSYCHOLOGY

During months of preparation for these four lectures, I became aware that my layman's view on the possible theological implications of analytical psychology and its practice, analysis, was limited, and that I had to give more thought to the matter. I became tremendously interested, more so than I had anticipated, and as a result of my thinking, I came to the conclusion that whatever we do in analytical psychology, and particularly in personal analysis, is far from being explained only by psychological means. I came to the conclusion, which I had tentatively formulated some ten years ago, that the effects analysis may have, particularly in cases with disturbed patients or in cases where there are definite neurotic symptoms, cannot be understood by psychological knowledge alone. This, I am sure, many analysts and psychologists would not accept; not too long ago I myself might have taken exception to any such statement.

The question of healing as such is complicated, complex, and many known and unknown factors are involved in it. Therefore, it may not be too astonishing if a psychologist, in summing up his experiences, or in trying to give an explanation for whatever he may have experienced in the more or less convincing successes of his practical work, is really confused by the multiplicity of

The Cutting Lectures given to Andover Newton Theological School at Newton College. First published at Newton Centre, Mass. in 1959. Reprinted by Southern Illinois University Press, Carbondale, Illinois, 1977.

unknowns in his equation. After nearly thirty years of experience in this field, the cure or the healing of a mental disease or neurosis is still a riddle or a miracle to me, even more so now than when I was a beginner.

You may be astonished that it took me such a long time to realize the vital importance of what I may call the religious factor in the treatment and healing of neurotic people, but as we describe the complicated problems in psychotherapy the reason for this may become clear. The religious phenomena occurring during psychotherapy are concealed in a subtle way, so that if one does not see things from the point of view of a participant in religion, he may miss this altogether; in other words, he may try to understand those facts, those effects, those phenomena in terms that are nonreligious. We know very well that the Freudian school still maintains that phenomena of such a nature should really be reduced to their biological origins, believing it is a misinterpretation to call such phenomena *religious*. This sort of prejudice can be attributed to the medical training of most psychotherapists and psychiatrists. Too often such training is devoid not only of the knowledge that is needed in order to understand religious phenomenology, but also devoid of a proper kind of logical thinking that will allow a doctor to draw necessary inferences and conclusions from material of this sort. A doctor is biased in a particular way, so that he tends to explain all the phenomena he may observe in his own terms. As a result, he eliminates religious phenomena, and is inclined not to admit that there may have been certain factors in the decisive part of the treatment that cannot be, and must not be, explained on the level of science, particularly natural science.

Since I am a physician, I had to go a long way to come to the point where I realized that the religious factor is of vital importance in the treatment and healing of people suffering from mental illness and neurotic disturbances. In spite of the fact that I have had the privilege of being a personal pupil of Jung, who has always recognized the religious factor, my medical training long prevented me from realizing the vital importance of the religious factor in the treatment and healing. As far as I can see, Jung himself did not support his belief in the importance of the religious factor with the necessary proof until 1932, when he read a paper at a conference of Alsatian parsons. I hope, therefore, that I may be forgiven for not having reached this conclusion earlier myself. As a matter of fact, I may say that this is rather an advantage, for in this way it cannot very well be said that I took this conviction over from my teacher. I had to learn the lesson myself, and I believe that this is in harmony with one of the basic tenets of analysis, namely, that a given realization can be considered as being a definite one and a real achievement only when we discover its truth ourselves. We simply cannot take it on, either from books or from what our teacher tells us, however wise he may be. I shall go into these deeper problems in a later lecture.

I should now like to outline the basic concepts of Jungian psychology. In itself this is a difficult task, because there is no definite Jungian system which will let us proceed methodically to outline Jung's ideas. I have, therefore, chosen another method, which is biographical or chronological. Something of Jung's background and his personal and professional development and career should be known since all his findings stem from his own life or experiences with his patients. The remarkable quality of Jungian psychology is that its founder, C. G. Jung, has always applied his own findings first on himself. This fact justifies a rather chronological-biographical way of outlining Jungian thought, as his whole approach even in its most advanced development grew slowly, almost, shall we say, in a biological way. Not only has Jung's thought had a close connection with his own personal life, but every new discovery has always been intimately connected with the preceding one, and has always been very carefully checked against all the preceding ones. This means that the whole of analytical psychology is empirical, or in other words, that all of Jung's ideas are based on empirical data, empirical facts. These empirical facts are themselves connected closely with Jung's life. This does not, however, make his findings systematic. Instead, its system can be discovered only in Jung's life, and any system that lies at the bottom of human life is usually only discovered *après coup*, which means that a person's life is given a certain meaning only retrospectively.

Jung was born on the 26th of July, 1875, near Lake Constance in Switzerland in a little village by the name of Kesswil, where his father was a parson. Jung came from a line of clergymen and physicians. One of his relatives and his namesake, Carl Gustav Jung, is still held in great esteem for having reformed Basel University Medical School. The Swiss are proud of the fact that Basel University, founded in the year 1460, is one of the oldest existing universities. Jung attended school in Basel and then graduated from Basel University Medical School. Then he went to the Psychiatric Clinic of Zürich University, the "Burghölzli," where he became assistant and later on an *Oberarzt*, which is the chief assistant, to the director of the clinic, Dr. Eugen Bleuler. Bleuler was one of the most famous psychiatrists of his time. He made a special study of schizophrenia, which then was called *dementia praecox*. In fact, the whole concept of schizophrenia goes back to Eugen Bleuler. With Eugen Bleuler, Jung started to introduce experimental methods into psychiatry, with the purpose of explaining more accurately the strange mental phenomena appearing in schizophrenia. Schizophrenics have ways of expressing themselves that are tremendously puzzling, and in the light of the then rather fashionable point of view of association psychology, they were explained as disturbances in the association of ideas.

In order to investigate these particular phenomena more in detail, Jung used an experimental method which had been developed by the famous German psychologist Wilhelm Wundt, according to certain ideas of Galton's. The word association method as used then by Jung, which developed into what is called the Word Association Test, still forms the backbone of Jungian psychology. The method is very simple, which is its greatest advantage. Jung's modification of it goes as follows: the doctor has a list of a hundred single words. He pronounces word after word to the test person, who is instructed to answer each word as soon as possible with the first word that comes into his or her mind, as the result of this stimulus word. When the doctor writes down the answer word, he observes the time elapsing between the moment he pronounced the stimulus word and the moment the test person reacted to it. This is all very simple. I cannot go into all the intricacies of this experimental situation, but I shall now summarize the conclusions arrived at from thousands of tests given in those days. First of all, it has to be said that the experiment did not work out in the way it was designed by Jung, for it was intended originally to help with the diagnosis of mental diseases, particularly schizophrenia. The findings were of no importance for this purpose. The test had also been thought of as a means to probe into the schizophrenic's tortuous ways of thinking and speaking. This it did to a very interesting degree, but I can only go into this point after having dealt with those findings which had not been planned and which proved to be more important and interesting than anything which was expected.

Jung discovered that in the course of such an experiment, no matter whether the test person was healthy, mentally disturbed, or truly psychotic, there appeared a disturbed reaction to one or more of the stimulus words. This disturbance showed itself in a number of different ways: the time lag between stimulus word and reaction was longer than the average; the test person was unable to answer in one word but reacted with a whole phrase or with several words; the test person repeated certain reactions, certain words or answers too often, even when the particular reaction did not fit; the test person reacted with a translation of the stimulus word into another language, or used foreign expressions instead of the obvious ones. All those indications of an interfering disturbance were carefully investigated statistically, and Jung came to a conclusion as to their origin. His findings were new, although later he discovered that in the area of the psychology of neuroses, his conclusions were similar to those of Freud.

It must be very strongly emphasized that these important new findings and their interpretation revealed a special trait in Jung's scientific approach which applies to virtually every single step in the development of Jungian psychology.

When Jung graduated from medical school he wrote for his M.D. thesis a small book entitled *On the Psychology and Pathology of So-Called Occult Phenomena,* a psychiatric study that was published in 1902. This was highly unorthodox, for occultism was always, and particularly in those days, looked down upon as not being worthy of scientific research. However, Jung found interesting phenomena in the study he made and arrived at helpful explanations for those phenomena. In this Jung showed an unerring scientific instinct which ever since has led him to approach a subject matter or topic seriously, even though it had previously been neglected or not seen. In other words, his intuition led him to make discoveries and in that sense seems to be a true scientific instinct. This characteristic appears in Jung's dealing with the Word Association Test, for before him those who had been working with this method in the clinical or purely psychological field had disregarded the disturbed reactions on the ground that they did not serve the purpose of the experiment. Jung, however, became intrigued with the difficulties people had in following instructions for the test. By concentrating upon those difficulties instead of the natural reactions, Jung discovered the complex, which has today become a commonplace term. This term was created by Jung at the time and was later adopted by all schools, including the Freudian and Adlerian. The disturbance of a normal sequence of thought or verbal expression proved to be a *via regia* that opened up a new vista with regard to the effects the realm of the unconscious has on our conscious reactions and intentions. The particular way in which unconscious elements interfere with our intentions was made accessible to experimental research.

In summary, the results of the use of the word association method, as it had been specially devised by Jung for diagnostic purposes in psychiatry, was the discovery of the complex; in other words, the result was the experimental proof of the fact that something of which we are not conscious has the power to interfere with our conscious intentions. This proved to be the key to many of the strange phenomena observed in psychiatric and neurotic cases. For example, Jung found that there was a peculiar relation between the disturbing factors discovered in the association experiment and the patients' neurotic or bodily symptoms (which Freud called *conversion symptoms*), and also the patients' dreams at that particular period of time. The experiences Jung had, proved to be an experimental confirmation of certain ideas Freud had published a few years earlier, when he approached the problem of neurosis with his newly devised psychoanalytic method. Jung, of course, was delighted with these parallels, and it was with extreme interest that he met Freud personally in 1907. At that time they discussed at great length these very striking parallels between their findings, which had been reached independently. This meeting of two scientists was the beginning of an extremely fruitful relationship; later Freud said that Jung was his most important disciple, as well as his successor or heir apparent. Unfortunately the two scientists separated in 1912 when Jung published his paper on symbols and transformations of the libido. But that is another matter, which does not concern us here.

I should now like to deal with the results of Jung's early experimental work and its later developments. For this I shall go into what might be called "a general theory of complexes." Not only has Jung's experimental method provided the possibility of understanding psychopathological phenomena such as certain neurotic symptoms, but it also has given a new understanding of normal phenomena, or more or less normal phenomena. These are such things as slips of the tongue, forgetting, or the famous phenomenon of the *déjà vu*, in short, phenomena occurring during our daily occupation and interfering with it mostly in an unpleasant way. Freud dealt with these later on in a special study called *The Psychopathology of Everyday Life*. In the light of Jung's findings, practically all of them can be explained as the effects of complexes that, on each particular occasion, are stirred up by something which would equal the stimulus word in the Word Association Test. From these experiences, the conclusion is that certain stimuli constellate a certain complex. Others, of course, do not. The stimuli have been shown to be related to the complex by that which can be best called an emotional tone. A complex is an entity consisting of a number, sometimes a great number, of elements among which there is a nucleus, the original crystallization point. Around this nucleus new elements seem to gather in the course of time. In this way a complex has a tendency to grow in content, to assimilate all kinds of other elements. And this assimilation makes the complex something like a hungry animal which tries to swallow whatever is near it. This assimilating tendency of the complex shows that the complex has a certain autonomy which gives it the power to interfere with man's conscious intentions. This means that the effects of the complex are beyond man's conscious control. The complex, thus, is something like a second will, which at times can be stronger than man's primary will or man's conscious will. In the course of the experimental investigation of the complexes, it was found that many of them had the qualities of a personality, so that a fully developed complex had the qualities of an *alter ego*. Now this is a strange condition for man to be in. It means that within man there is another ego apart from his conscious ego, living its own life so to speak, which can interfere with his conscious life at the slightest provocation. How can we look at free will in light of such entities in our system? Now, the autonomy of the complexes seems to be very neatly illustrated by myths or fairy tales or folklore all over the world. They may, in fact, be the origin of the widespread idea of animism which by no means is found only among so-called primitives.

A general theory of complexes will have to make clear that complexes must be regarded as perfectly normal contents of man's psyche, even though the theory will also have to show that when they become too powerful, too autonomous, too all embracing, they are more or less pathological phenomena. In the normal process of man's conscious activities, he depends to a great extent on the existence of some autonomous processes, which at certain junctures of his activities, as in his thinking, are capable of exerting influence. If this did not happen—if, in other words, the spontaneous activity of the complexes had no chance to find its way into man's consciousness—he would very soon run out of thoughts or intuitions. I point to what we call a hunch or a brand-new idea. This comes suddenly in the twinkle of an eye; at first it looks completely fantastic and out of harmony with the trend of our thoughts, but it may be a truly creative part of our thinking. Such experiences are often described by creative people such as musicians, writers, and artists. They are exactly of the same dignity as those phenomena we have described as interferences or disturbing factors which can be traced to the existence of a complex in man's unconscious.

Now we return to the more unpleasant effects that complexes can have. We have to admit that those unpleasant effects make it necessary for the human being to do something to cut down the autonomy of these daemons, shall we say. The more autonomous the complex, the more urgent the need to reduce its hold. A typically full-blown complex can show all the qualities, or most of the qualities, of a personality. This fact is most probably responsible for the appearance of complexes in dreams where the dream figures represented as human beings must be regarded as personifications of those complexes. Such dream figures behave entirely, or to some extent, in an autonomous way and do things that do not coincide with man's conscious intentions. The general theory of complexes, then, should include suggestions of methods of approaching the complexes in a way that will render them more harmless. This can be done by making them more conscious, in other words dissolving them as complexes (i.e.,

entities separated from the rest of the psychic system) and introducing them into the conscious system, thus giving them a
chance to cooperate with the conscious mind rather than manifesting their existence in unpleasant ways.

The existence of fully developed complexes in normal as well
as pathological personalities has another interesting aspect,
which explains phenomena most frequently observed in pathological cases, in particular, cases of hysteria and severe cases of
neuroses. One of the most obvious traits in such cases is what
the French psychologist Pierre Janet has described as the dissociation of the personality. In cases of dissociation there seem to
exist more than one personality within one and the same person.
Morton Prince has done a great deal of research with such cases
of dissociation, and in these cases it is clear that the partial personalities that appear are in fact fully developed complexes. So
all the research done by applying the Word Association Test has
had far-reaching consequences in respect to psychopathological
phenomena, to phenomena of dreams, and to the creative
activities of the human mind.

I should like to dwell a little longer on other consequences of
the results of the Word Association Test. It appeared very early
that the common denominator of the various elements that built
up a complex was a particular emotional tone, an emotional
tone that seemed to link the various elements together and to
attach them to the complex itself. All the elements seemed to
possess the same affective tone. Now from this, the reason why
complexes can affect the body and why they affect it in a particular way became clear. The early investigators, all pupils of Jung
then at Burghölzli Clinic, started to investigate the effects that
complexes have on the body. Today we know from the findings
of what is called psychosomatic medicine that there is practically
no organ in the human body that cannot be affected by emotional processes. In the days of Jung's early research, however,
little was known about such connections, except that breathing
was affected by emotional processes. Under elation or depression, the habitual type of breathing is greatly changed, so investigators tried to combine the word association experiment with
a careful record of the breathing movements of the patient's
chest. Such studies were made particularly by Peterson, who was
highly interested to discover that whenever in the word associa-

tion experiment there appeared a disturbance, the test person's breathing activity was affected. The breathing became shallower or deeper, according to the nature of the reaction. Furthermore, one other physiological reaction was combined with the Word Association Test with equally interesting results. It was known that the resistance of the human skin to an electric current changed under certain affective reactions. It looked as if the skin, which protects man from the influences which the outer world has on his body, became more transparent, or opened up somewhat, during an affective and emotional reaction. This Psychogalvanic Skin Response was combined with the Word Association Test to give another complex indicator, and the combination was used subsequently to investigate the effect of complexes and/or emotions on the body.

I now go back to the early years of Jung's career when he was in close touch with Freud, and speak of the first original book of Jung's, called *Symbols of Transformation*. In that book Jung dealt with a clinical case he had never seen himself, but which had been described by a psychologist at Geneva University. The case contained what is now called unconscious material, consisting of a fantasy of the patient. That gave Jung a chance to study the parallels in mythology and religion that seemed to correlate with certain elements of the patient's fantasy. In the course of his research Jung had to develop some ideas about psychic energy, which we now call the dynamism of the unconscious. This dynamism had previously been called libido by Freud, but whereas Freud had given this libido an exclusively sexual connotation or origin, Jung concluded that this dynamism of the unconscious was not restricted to sexuality, but that there were in it all kinds of other sources of primary energy. Adler had already said something to this effect when he made power the primary interest of man in contradistinction to Freud's singular emphasis upon sex. When Jung studied the clinical case in question, he began to doubt the truth of Freud's dependence upon sex alone to explain the dynamism of the unconscious, and he also began to doubt the Adlerian point of view, for he saw that while both men were partially correct they were not wholly so. Thus it became important for Jung to find out how the difference between the two men could be explained and, if possible, reconciled. In the effort to deal with this matter, Jung undertook to clarify the difference theoretically. The result of this work is found in the book called *Psychological Types*.

In this book Jung pointed out two different types of attitude or two different ways in which man directs his interest to objects about him. These two types he called the extravert and the introvert, or the extraverted and the introverted attitude. In the case of the extravert, the attitude is directed to the outer object, and when this is habitually so, it obviously has existed almost from the earliest moments of the individual's life. In the introvert's case, attention is mainly directed toward the inner object—that is, toward the subject. Strictly speaking, what the introvert primarily is concerned with is what Jung called the *subjective factor*. This means that the introvert's interest is habitually caught by the way in which he or she reacts to all incoming information. How this information strikes him is more important to him than the information itself; it is this reaction that Jung calls the subjective factor. Jung then went on to try to clarify the varieties of human reactions and human behavior in still another way by speaking of four different elementary psychological functions. According to him these elementary psychological functions, or functions of orientation of the conscious mind, are *sensation, thinking, feeling* and *intuition*. In order to show what this is about, I shall construct an example: I have a certain visual impression of something standing before me here, glittering, round, of such and such shape, etc. These are the sensory data, shape, color, position, and these sensory data are perceived by the use of sensation, in Jung's terminology. Sensation, therefore, tells me that there is a certain thing before me and that this thing has such and such qualities, but this is in no way sufficient. We have to try to understand what this thing is, and this understanding is given by what Jung calls *thinking*. Thinking now allows me to say that the thing I just perceived is a glass, and that the content of this glass is apparently water. Or in case the content is red, I should say it is probably wine. What I have done, in addition to noting the perception given by sensation, is to diagnose the object in terms of my preexisting system of knowledge, a process which is usually called apperception. I now know what I see. By the sensation function I know that there is something and how it looks, and by the thinking function I know what there is. Now this may still not be satisfactory, for most probably there is something else to be said about the object. For example, I will know that either this glass of wine is indifferent to me or not. Suppose I am a teetotaler; in that case I will say it is a terrible poison, and will reject the object. In other words, I will come to a negative conclusion with regard to its value. If I am a connoisseur, I will say, "How wonderful, I hope it's good." This process of evaluation of an object Jung calls *feeling*, inasmuch as it tells a man that a perceived object is something he likes or something he dislikes, or something that means nothing to him. Feeling defined as a function of values is what Jung means when he uses the term *feeling*.

Jung goes on to say that even this is not all man knows about an object, or all he can know, or all he wants to know. He may still want some other information, yet there seems to be no other channel through which he can get it, at least no conscious channel. But there may be information furnished in a different way, that is via the unconscious; and the information one gets in this way Jung calls *intuition*. As I look at the glass of wine my intuition suggests that it looks as if it were the famous Pommard I gave my friend three years ago on his fiftieth birthday. I may be right, but I cannot possibly know. Jung says that such information and such a way of getting information is questionable, for it may just as well be right as it may be wrong, but when it is right it is astonishing. Jung holds that intuition plays an important part in life, for people often find themselves confronted with situations where they need certain information that is not given. In such cases intuition may be of vital importance.

By isolating the four fundamental psychological functions of the conscious mind, Jung realized gradually that they constituted pairs of opposites in such a way that two of the four always formed a pair. Thinking and feeling, for example, are mutually exclusive. They both are rational functions, capable of forming a judgment, but while man is thinking and to the degree he is thinking, he must exclude feeling, and vice versa. Sensation and intuition, on the other hand, are functions that are irrational, for there is no rational way by which a man can explain why he has such and such a sensation or such and such an intuition. Both functions are perceptive, but they are also mutually exclusive, for in case man depends upon sensation and scrutinizes the particular qualities of the object before him, he must exclude intuition which would give him information about the object that the senses cannot perceive. And exactly the reverse is true.

Now when he grouped the four psychological functions in two pairs of mutually exclusive opposites, Jung came across a fundamental problem in psychology, which is the problem of opposites in general. After encountering this problem, he gave a great deal of attention to the work of collecting illustrations of the way it shows itself in the history of all kinds of human activities, such as literature, religion, psychiatry, psychology, and so forth. The bulk of his book *Psychological Types* deals with such examples from the history of culture. He was also able to show that the differences between the main trends of the new psychology of his time, namely the Freudian and the Adlerian schools, rest on this principle of opposites – that Freud's school is really based on an extraverted attitude, whereas Adler's is based on an introverted one. Jung believed, and I think he was correct, that the Freudian and the Adlerian points of view actually can be explained on this principle of extraversion and introversion. Now the question remains whether such opposites can be reconciled, and how. In order to deal with this question, Jung spent a good deal of his time on the phenomenon of the symbol.

But at this time I need say only that in dealing with the principle of the opposites, it is necessary to remember that the unconscious must be included in the system for the simple reason that almost always in any individual case one or two of the psychological functions will be differentiated or, in other words, will belong to the conscious system or be available to the conscious intention and function properly within the realm of consciousness. The rest of the functions, either three or two, because of the exclusion principle are bound to remain relatively unconscious; in other words they are undifferentiated and are caught up in the unconscious. Consequently, they do not work in the way that can be properly called conscious. Yet they have their autonomy, and for this reason appear mostly as interfering or disturbing factors in man's conscious intentions.

Jung made another interesting discovery at this juncture, which is the fact that a differentiated function always unites with the habitual type of attitude. For example, when a man is a thinking type, his thinking will be extraverted if he is an extravert, or it will be introverted if he is an introvert. The differentiated function thus unites with the habitual type of attitude, the attitudinal type. Contrariwise, the inferior undifferentiated psychological function, the opposite of the superior differentiated function, remains in the opposite attitude. Thus the feeling of an extraverted thinking type will remain in the unconscious and unite with the introverted attitude. This seems to be fairly abstract, but these findings are corroborated by the many examples from history and from all sorts of mental activities Jung relates in his book on types.

There is one more thing to be said in connection with the subject of types. This may be the most important conclusion drawn from the study of the type problem: it has become clear in the course of the development of Jungian thought that during a person's life history the type adopted to begin with slowly and gradually undergoes, or rather must undergo, a change. In other words, in the course of a person's life the functions and the attitude that have been in the unconscious, which have not been differentiated, become more and more important. This development goes on in such a way that it looks as if life tries to create an all-around personality by the gradual development of the opposite attitude and the opposite functions, the inferior functions. This struggle for the development of the opposite attitude and functions, according to Jung's idea, becomes urgent and imperative only during the second half of life. This is, of course, a relative concept. The second half can never be defined in terms of numbers of years, but there obviously is a turning point in the life of most people, which frequently shows itself phenomenologically or even clinically in a certain crisis that demands a completely new orientation or reorientation. This serves to draw out and emphasize the opposite attitude and the inferior function, thus making the person better rounded and more complete.

II. ARCHETYPES AND THE COLLECTIVE UNCONSCIOUS

Archetypes and the collective unconscious are two concepts that have given rise to much controversy and, among the principles of Jungian psychology, have been the most misunderstood and misinterpreted. I believe, however, that an objective reader of Jung's books can see that both concepts are well-founded and that evidence for them can easily be checked, provided a person has no prejudice—particularly prejudice which comes from resistance of a personal nature.

I shall introduce the concepts of the archetypes and of the collective unconscious in an historical way, that is, by tracing the way the two concepts were created by Jung during his empirical experience with certain phenomena in the human psyche. It is important to note that both concepts have to be regarded as exclusively empirical concepts. Jung always insisted that others should go the same way he went and experience the same phenomena themselves. The best way to experience the existence and reality of the archetypes and the collective unconscious is to observe carefully our own dreams. It is easy to deal with other people's material, and by discovering parallels between that material and pathological material, to say that obviously there is something pathological about them. In this way we remove ourselves from such a charge since we are sure we are normal, healthy individuals. But psychopathology must be looked at in an unprejudiced way, and we must understand that psychopathological phenomena are in fact only normal psychological phenomena grossly exaggerated to a bizarre degree. We can, therefore, learn a great deal from them about the normal functioning of the human mind. I remember very well when years ago at the Burghölzli Clinic I had to guide a visitor from the government through the clinic, and I showed him a few typical cases. When he left he thanked me and said, "This has been a most illuminating experience for me as a layman, because I begin to see that this clinic is really a cross-section of the town of Zürich. The population of Zürich is full of characters who are better understood in the light of the patients you have shown me today."

I know that such a point of view, in which one uses pathology to explain the normal, can be very dangerous. Yet I must say that the riddles of normal psychology, if we are humble enough to admit that there are many, can best be solved from this perspective, and that by such a comparative method we have a much better chance of understanding the somewhat startling reactions and actions of ourselves and our neighbors.

We start with the first experience that Jung had, which can be explained only by the use of the concept of archetypes and the concept of the collective unconscious. We find the report of this experience in the book, *Symbols of Transformation*. Jung used as a parallel for a certain motive in a patient's fantasy his own experience with another patient at the Burghölzli Clinic. This man, whom I happened to know when he was an inmate at Burghölzli, had a most vivid hallucinatory fantasy and used to hallucinate night and day. One day during his ward rounds, the doctor came across this "Dr. Schwyzer," as he was called. The patient took him to the window and said, "Stand here and look at the sun. What do you see?" The doctor said, "Well, I see the sun." Whereupon the patient said, "But don't you see the tail on the sun?" The doctor answered, "I am not so sure." "Well," said the patient, "look carefully and move your head as you look; you will see the tail move. That moving tail is the source of the wind." That certainly was not a very common image, and the doctor, although puzzled by it, dismissed it as pure nonsense.

The incident was then reported to Jung. It happened that Jung had been reading a book published at the time by the German philologist Albrecht Dieterich, entitled *Eine Mithrasliturgie* (A Mithraic Liturgy). In that book Dieterich dealt with what I think nowadays would be called a magic papyrus, and in the book was the *editio princeps* [first printed edition] of the text of that papyrus, which was written in Greek. The book was available only to a few scholars of Greek and classical antiquity. Jung had noticed in the book that at a certain junction in the liturgy the initiate was asked to look at the sun, where he would see a tube hanging down, swinging first to the right producing the East wind, and then swinging to the left, producing the West wind. The patient in the Burghölzli Clinic had been there for a number of years; he was completely uneducated and knew no Greek. There was not the slightest possibility that he had seen the Greek papyrus—and he could not have read it had he seen it—yet the similarity between his hallucination and the Mithraic liturgy was clear. This could, of course, be dismissed as sheer coincidence, but as I have told you, Jung always stopped and asked questions about any strange phenomenon which came to his attention. As with the Word Association Test, where he concentrated upon the unusual, so on this occasion he concentrated on this unusual coincidence with the same challenging scientific spirit and gained the same success.

The coincidence in that particular case proved to be something that was by no means rare, for when Jung went on to compare fantasies of mentally deranged people with other mythological texts or with folk literature, he saw that such coincidences were found rather frequently. Later on he discovered that in dreams of children, between the ages of four and (shall we say) eleven, there are often elements that are obviously mythological, yet that could not have been consciously acquired. The dreams contained parts of myths, or whole mythic events, that the children could not possibly have known. In general, however, it is difficult to find cases where serious knowledge of the relevant mythological material can be excluded completely. In the case of "Dr. Schwyzer" I believe that it was firmly established. Today it can be proved in some cases that there have been no known conscious normal channels through which the mythological elements entered the particular person's unconscious material. So the only possible answer to the occurrence of such elements in unconscious material is that the unconscious mind as such apparently consists, to a large extent, of mythological material.

Mythological research made shortly before Jung did this work had brought to light the fact that myths of different peoples showed striking similarities. Sometimes those similarities were general and sometimes they were special or specific. Sometimes the similarity was in a strange minor detail, something that we would dismiss as being wholly incomprehensible. Yet the existence of such a detail in the myths of two separate peoples was hard to understand unless there had been migration between one tribe and another. Yet in certain cases it was shown that such correspondences could not possibly be attributed to migration. Statistically, I would say, such similarities are so widespread and so frequent that we would have to attribute them to a complete *consensus gentium* over the entire surface of our planet. From studies in comparative religions or mythology, and the occurrence of striking similarities in fantasies of insane as well as normal people, Jung reached the conclusion that there is something like an ubiquity of the unconscious or its main contents.

In his studies of this subject, Jung was led to a second conclusion, which was that in individual cases there are often differences in the conventional imagery. He found, for example, that in a dream where the main imagery was obviously religious, where Christian symbolism appeared, that the conventional Christian imagery did not cover the image of the particular dream completely. In other words, he often found minor, subtle, or even strikingly blatant differences between a dream and the orthodox symbol, myth, dogma, or creed.

The question, of course, is how to account for these differences in conventional imagery. Before I go into this question I need to point out that we now know it to be highly unusual for dreams or fantasies showing religious imagery to be conventional. We might correctly say that the unconscious is highly heretical. We therefore need an explanation for the fact that the unconscious of a Christian appears to be much less Christian than his conscious system is. As an example I shall relate a dream of a relatively young girl who is a devout Catholic. This girl decided as a result of a dream that she needed to study psychology, and that perhaps she had the ability to train in analytical psychology with the purpose of using it practically later on. Here is the dream:

I saw my sister who, radiant, mighty, and superior, looked like a mother of God or a fairy queen. She wore a blue cloak and on her head a golden crown, the points of which were set with rubies and emeralds. Astonished and enraptured I exclaimed, "Paula, how beautiful!" Smiling she answered, "Yes, a snake, or the snake, has produced this," and she added, "Nobody can henceforth doubt this or claim that the snake found this crown ready-made and induced it into me from outside, for this would be technically impossible." Then she said, "Sometimes the snake produces something that looks like the scepter of the Antichrist," and at that very same moment she held it in her hand. It looked like a bishop's cross of gold filigree, with a subtle touch on a mechanism in the horizontal bar; the cross opened in a vertical cut similar to a reliquary and exposed two rows of rather small, round-cut, clear blue turquoises, arranged close to each other in the manner of a cobblestone pavement. My sister asked, in a preoccupied voice filled with doubt, what would happen if the scepter or the cross were not given to the priest and if it began to urge her to use power? With that painful question, I woke up out of depths such as I have never experienced before in my life.

That dream was in many ways highly unorthodox. It shocked the patient so badly that she had a therapeutic need to go into analysis. All I need say here is that after she had given thought to the subject, the dream became a great comfort to the patient, for it really gave her all the support she needed in dealing with the difficulties she had experienced in her faith and particularly with regard to her confessor and spiritual guide. Her analysis consisted, to a great extent, of a careful investigation of the comparative and historical background of her imagery. The fact that we find very few dreams containing orthodox or conventional religious matters and many dreams containing heretical material is an interesting fact in itself

After all, as a psychologist I am in the company of St. Augustine who says, "The thing itself [*res ipsa*], which is now called the Christian Religion, was with the ancients [*erat opud antiquos*], and it was with the human race from the beginning to the time when Christ appeared in the flesh: from then on the true religion, which already existed, began to be called the Christian."[1]

If you think I need a further justification, I quote from the Bible, where St. Paul says to the pagans, "For in Him we live, and move, and have our being; as certain also of your own poets have said."[2]

In order to explain such unorthodoxies, and in order to be able to help a person to an understanding of them, one needs a good deal of knowledge of the comparative history of religion, the history of the Church, and the mythologies of the ages. If one does not know this material, he will not recognize the religiousness of a dream or fantasy, nor see or understand the individual differences; he would therefore miss the point, and cheat his patient. It is not strange that most people who criticize Jung's concept of the collective unconscious say that the dreams that Jung relates in his books are either made up, or specially dreamt for him, or altogether faked. Such criticism cannot be met unless the critic takes the trouble to become acquainted with the related material. As long as people remain ignorant of mythological material, they are bound to overlook such allusions in dreams and come to the same conclusion as the opponents of Jung's psychology.

It is necessary to bear in mind that the religious imagery which exists today is the product of a long historical development. The more that is known about the literature of the early centuries, the clearer it is that even the Scripture is a composite of material,

---

1. St. Augustine, *Retractationes*, I. XIII.
2. Acts: XVII, 28.

which goes back to various sources, and that Christ himself had obviously been in touch with a number of religious systems existing in his time. Further than this, throughout the centuries new ideas or new versions of other ideas have appeared, and have either remained one person's particular fantasy or have become the accepted doctrine of a particular group or sect. Some of those ideas have been condemned by the Church as being heterodoxical, while others have been accepted and incorporated into the teaching and later into the dogma. Occassionally ideas that once were refuted have been taken up later on and accepted. The history of mythology, religion and the Churches shows that these elements have always fluctuated, which may be regarded as proof of the life that has been in the Church or the religion of the people. Even the dogma of the Catholic Church has undergone remarkable changes, as additions to it have been made throughout the centuries, and this process has not come to an end even in our day.

Now, in an individual case where religion can be observed in the making, and where the products of the unconscious mind can be carefully observed, it is not strange that in certain instances the images bring up ideas, thoughts, and symbols that can be traced back to earlier stages of development. These stages may be related directly to a particular school or sect in the early centuries or in the Middle Ages, or to further variations of those sects. In order to interpret such products, it is necessary to keep in mind that not only today, but all through history, they cannot be understood only in the light of the collective conscious thoughts and ideas and convictions of particular faiths or particular religions, but also must be considered in light of the actual situation of the person involved, for that situation is found to be something unique. The situation of any particular person has the characteristics of certain general problems, but those problems are encountered in an individual way. Thus, I think, whenever a new religious orientation takes place or is reached, it is bound in part to be conventional or orthodox, and in part *unconventional* or *unorthodox*.

I should like to call your attention to the fact that, if there were no such personal systems popping out of the unconscious — if, in a dream or fantasy which obviously has religious meaning and traits, there were no personal variations, or if in a myth there was no evidence that the dreamer had deviated from the conventional myths or religious imagery – then Freud would be correct in saying that religion is only an illusion and consequently *delenda* [must be destroyed]. If we could find collective traits in such material produced by a single person, that is, elements or whole parts of religious systems that had not been specifically altered or adapted to the person's actual inner or outer situation, then the ideas could be regarded as being taken over *consciously* from the parents without having any life of their own.

In order for us to see how Jung arrived at the conclusion that there are archetypes of the collective unconscious, and that there is a collective unconscious as such, I shall choose one example of the many archetypes that can be observed. This one is particulary characteristic of Jungian psychology and has been described by Jung himself. It is the Jungian concept of the *anima*, which he dealt with theoretically in a paper entitled "Concerning the Archetypes, with Special Reference to the Anima Concept."[3] In this paper he tried to give proof for the existence of the anima, the image of the anima, by referring to a motif widely known in the history of religion, namely the motif of the *syzygy* (in Greek συζυγία, literally "yoking together" – the exact Latin equivalent would be *conjugatio* or conjunction) – the male/female divine couple. We know from ethnologists that many primitive tribes hold the conviction that at one time there was a being who was, and sometimes is still, the supreme being, and of double sex, and that the double condition of this highest being was once the condition of all men. According to the ethnologist Winthuis, the highest being, this being of double sex, was not only the origin of mortals but also their goal.[4] Man expects and hopes to unite again with the opposite sex, and in such a way as to gain original totality. All that man strives for in his cult practice, according to Winthuis (we don't necessarily have to go as far as he does), is to

---

3. C. G. Jung, "Concerning the Archetypes, with Special Reference to the Anima Concept," in *The Archetypes and the Collective Unconscious* (Coll. Wks. 9, part 1, 1959), 54-72 [original German version, 1936].

4. Winthuis, "Das Zweigenschlechterwesen bei den Zentralaustraliern und anderen Völkern" [The Double-gendered Being Among the Peoples of Central Australia and Elsewhere], *Forschungen zur Volkerpsychologie und Soziologie 5* (Leipzig, 1928).

make an attempt to regain this original and perfect condition. However true or wrong this explanation may be, we are reminded of something we find in Greek philosophy, in particular in Plato.

In the *Symposium*, Plato tells us the following story about the genesis of man:[5]

And first let me treat of the nature and state of man, for the original human nature was not like the present, but different. In the first place, the sexes were originally three in number, not two as they are now; there was man, woman, and the union of the two, having a name corresponding to this double nature [which was once called Androgynous]; this once had a real existence, but is now lost, and the name only is preserved as a term of reproach. In the second place, the primeval man was round and had four hands and four feet, back and sides forming a circle, one head with two faces, looking opposite ways, set on a round neck and precisely alike; also four ears, two privy members, and the remainder to correspond. When he had a mind he could walk as men now do, and he could also roll over and over at a great rate, leaning on his four hands and four feet, eight in all, like tumblers going over and over with their legs in the air; this was when he wanted to run fast. Now there were these three sexes, because the sun, moon, and earth are three; and the man was originally the child of the sun, the woman of the earth, and the man-woman of the moon, which is made up of sun and earth, and they were all round and moved round and round like their parents. Terrible was their might and strength, and the thoughts of their hearts were great, and they made an attack upon the gods; and of them is told the tale of Otus and Ephialtes who, as Homer says, dared to scale heaven, and would have laid hands upon the gods. Doubt reigned in the councils of Zeus and of the gods. Should they kill them and annihilate the race with thunderbolts, as they had done the giants, then there would be an end of the sacrifice and worship which men offered to them; but, on the other hand, the gods could not suffer their insolence to be unrestrained. At last, after a good deal of reflection, Zeus discovered a way. He said: "I have a notion which will humble their pride and mend their manners; they shall continue to exist, but I will cut them in two and then they will be diminished in strength and increased in numbers; this will have the advantage of making them more profitable to us. They shall walk upright on two legs, and if they continue insolent and won't be quiet, I will split them again and they shall hop about on a single leg." He spoke and cut them in two, like a sorb-apple that is halved for pickling, or as you might divide an egg

---

5. Plato, *Symposium* (189 d. 1 and 192e).

with a hair; and as he cut them one after another, he bade Apollo give
the face and the half of the neck a turn in order that the man might
contemplate the section of himself: this would teach him a lesson of
humility. He was also to heal their wounds and compose their forms.
Apollo twisted the face and pulled the skin all around over that which
in our language is called the belly, like the purses which draw in, and he
made one mouth at the centre, which he fastened in a knot (this is
called the navel); he also moulded the breast and took out most of the
wrinkles, much as a shoemaker might smooth out leather upon a last;
he left a few, however, in the region of the belly and navel, as a memo-
rial of the primeval change. After the division the two parts of man,
each desiring his other half, came together, and threw their arms about
one another eager to grow into one....

Suppose Hephaestus, with his instruments, were to come to the pair
who are lying side by side and say to them, "What do you people want
of one another?" They would be unable to explain. Suppose further,
that when he saw their perplexity he said: "Do you desire to be wholly
one; always day and night to be in one another's company? For if this
is what you desire, I am ready to melt you into one and let you grow
together, so that being two you shall become one, and while you live,
live a common life as if you were a single man, and after your death in
the world below still be one departed soul instead of two—I ask
whether this is what you lovingly desire, and whether you are satisfied
to attain this?" There is not a man among them when he heard this
who would deny or who would not acknowledge that this meeting and
melting in one another's arms, this becoming one instead of two, was
the very expression of his ancient need. And the reason is that human
nature was originally one and we were a whole, and the desire and
pursuit of the whole is called love. There was a time, I say, when the
two were one, but now because of this wickedness of men, God has
dispersed us, as the Arcadians were dispersed into villages by the
Lacedaemonians.

As you can see, the idea of this complete original being is, of
course, taken from Empedocles, where it is called σφαῖρος,
sphairos, the sphere,[6] the all-round being.

Two things I proclaim: once out of several parts one whole grows, once
the One disaggregates into many. Mortal things create themselves out
of the immortal elements partly when the things procreate out of the

---

[6. Ed. Note: Empedocles' idea of the *sphairos* was the condition of the
universe (*kosmos*) when brought together by love (*eros*).]

sphairos, partly when they return again into it. In both cases, however, they perish again, once by continuous separation, once by continuous union. Uninterruptedly these processes change and never come to an end. Now united in love everything comes together in One, now disunited in hatred everything tends to separate again.

It is rather striking that a primitive tribe in Central Australia has an idea about this original being almost identical to the one developed by pre-Socratic philosophers and by Plato; no migration hypothesis can explain that similarity. From the fact that there are these striking similarities between two peoples so far apart, mentally and geographically, it is possible to conclude that the human mind, in certain respects, works almost exactly alike, no matter in what level of culture it is found. The hypothesis of the collective unconscious strongly recommends itself in light of the above and other similar facts. At all events Jung says that the motive of the *syzygy* is as universal as the fact that there are man and woman, and consequently he maintains that wherever there is a male psyche or psychology, there is always a feminine psychology, or the image of a correlated feminine being. This image corresponds exactly to what Jung calls an archetypal image, and in this particular case the archetypal image is the image of the anima, the image of what Jung also called the soul. Historically it must be said that Jung took the word *archetype* from St. Augustine, who in his theory of ideas used the Greek synonym τὸ αρχέτυπον εἶδος translated *to archetypon eidos* [archetypal form]. But the term *archetypon* is older than St. Augustine, for it is found in the neo-Platonic *Corpus Hermeticum*, dating from the third century, where there is the term *to archetypon eidos*, which corresponds exactly to the archetypal image.

Philologists may be interested to learn that Cicero knew this word, that it is found in Philo in the *De opificio mundi* 71, and that since then its use became widespread. St. Augustine's definition of the *archetypon* is an idea or ideas "quae ipsae formatae non sunt, quae in divina intelligentsia continentur" [which are not themselves represented forms, but are contained within the mind of God]. This most obviously is a Platonic idea; in Plato we have this concept of an image being located ἐν ὑπερουρανίου τόπωι (*en hyperouranio topo*), in a place above the heavens or beyond the stars. This idea is in the *Phaedrus*. Jakob Burckhardt used the expression of *urtümliche Bilder* when he spoke of such ideas, an expression that can hardly be translated into English; yet the term can be translated easily enough into the Greek *archetypon eidos*. These archetypal images coincide with what the German ethnologist Bastian long ago called *Völkerideen* – peoples' ideas – or what the French ethnologist Lévy-Brühl called *représentations collectives*. In both cases it is obviously a matter not so much of definite images, but rather motifs, as we would say in mythology. We would call them mythological motifs – motifs that can be found practically everywhere and on every level. The motif of the *syzygy* is widespread in innumerable variations. There are the famous constituents of Chinese, and in particular Taoistic philosophy, the Yang and the Yin, the bright and the dark, the masculine and the feminine. In the Tantric system in India there is the eternal couple of Shiva and Shakti living in eternal embrace, and there is the gnostic idea of Νοῦς (*Nous*) [mind] and Σοφία (*Sophia*) [wisdom]. In the Christian religion, there is Christ and the bridal church. In the medieval period, the motive of the *syzygy* was taken up particularly by alchemistic mythology, where *sol* and *luna*, or *rex* and *regina*, play exactly the same roles.

Why this is so is a very difficult question to answer, but it is highly probable that with the fact that there are the two sexes in reality, in observable reality, the idea simply pointed to the fact; but it is also highly probable that the idea would have originated in an individual who had never seen a specimen of the other sex. In other words, it is highly probable that not only the existence of people of the other sex and the experiences we have with members of the opposite sex account for that formulation of the image of the opposite sex, but also the qualities that each of us has as an individual. In each person there are genes which are not particularly differentiated as to a particular sex but that belong to the opposite sex – for there are always feminine genes in a man and masculine genes in a woman. Only the relative preponderance of one set of genes accounts for a person's belonging to either one or the other sex. The fact that the motive of the *syzygy* is so universally given in itself makes it clear that the origin of this image of the other sex does not completely go back to the existence of living beings of this other sex, since the peculiarity of the *syzygy* is that the couple is always a divine one, which means that it is more than merely the human couple. The *syzygy* is a theistic idea, and as such shows us that behind it there is more than simply the image of the parental couple. It is much more a projection of unknown contents that necessarily must come out of man's depths—for only contents of his unconscious can be projected. One cannot very well say that the parental couple is unknown, in other words that man is unconscious of them; consequently, they cannot be projected as long as they are conscious contents of our conscious mind.

I will give three more examples in order to show that the existence of an image of the opposite sex is particularly strongly constellated, and that it offers itself readily in our dreams or fantasies when the divine background of our experience is involved. One example is almost universally known, found in the ritual of the baptism of children. In most of such rituals the parents are kept in a relatively humble and unimportant position even though the event is of importance for them, and other people step in who are called godfather and godmother.

The second example is in the third vision of the only Swiss saint, Niklaus von Flüe, who in that vision perceived God once as the Royal Father, and once as the Royal Mother.

The third example is in the vision of Anna Kingsford as related by Edward Maitland.[7] The relevant part of the text of the vision is: "It was God as the Lord who by his duality proves that God is substance as well as power, love as well as will, feminine as well as masculine, mother as well as father." From all the parallels I have used to illustrate the origin of the archetypal image of the anima, it should be rather clear that whenever there is a masculine being, there is simultaneously something correspondingly feminine given. The masculine compensates itself by a feminine element.

This view comes close to the idea Jung developed later on that the feminine is to the masculine the most unknown, and that in such a way the anima in fact represents the unconscious of the man. Yet this being of the opposite sex, since it is the unknown, unconscious counterpart, always appears in the projected form,

---

7. Edward Maitland, *Anna Kingsford: Her Life, Letters, Diaries and Work* (London: 1896).

and as Jung pointed out, the anima proper is the projection-producing factor par excellence in a man. Since there is this projection-producing tendency in the anima, it can be compared to the *Māyā* of the Hindus, the illusion-producing dancer who is always projected onto every woman; this makes it difficult for a man to establish the true identity of the woman. Consequently, whatever remains of the image a man has of a certain woman after he subtracts the real woman from the image is the anima, her divine background; and it is not strange to find that such a dream figure has all kinds of mysterious qualities.

The clinical importance of the anima image becomes important mainly in the second half of life, for the simple reason that in the first half of life a man has to grapple mostly with a mother complex, and only in the second half of life can he approach the matter in a somewhat different way, i.e., when all the values begin to change in their meaning, so that then he has to turn away from mother in order to return eventually to her for good. Clinically, the anima has to be defined as a function. As she represents the unconscious, a man's unconscious, it is extremely important, in particular during the second half of life, that this figure is changed into a *function of relation to the inner world of man*. She must become the initiate into the unknown counterpart of man. Once man succeeds in transforming this personification into a function, he will have achieved a relationship to the inner world that will give him a new dimension, which is what I would call a maternal eros. Man will then be related, not only to the inner world, but also to the external one, in a different way than he used to be before the anima had been turned or developed into a function. He would show a real relatedness which I would call *Eros* in its most general meaning. Similarly, in the course of human life all the various images, archetypal images, should be turned into functions. Before Jung spoke of archetypes, he used to call these phenomena *dominants of the collective unconscious*, in order to emphasize their functional quality.

What I have said so far about the image, the *archetypal image* of the anima, has been to give the theoretical justification for the formulation of that concept by Jung. However, this concept is only one out of many Jungian concepts that have been formed over the years as a result of Jung's clinical experience with his patients. This has always been done in the same way as it was done in the concept of the anima: Jung observed his patients' dreams and fantasies, and in the course of time began to notice that certain personifications, dream figures, tended to repeat themselves, particularly when long series of dreams or fantasies were observed, and that at specific junctures the accumulations of certain figures, situations, or motifs became quite apparent. Such a phenomenon justifies the creation of a particular name for the figure, situation, or motif involved. The question, of course, is always the meaning of such repetitious dream figures or images. In the course of his long practical experience, Jung has given names to a small number of such typical dream figures or situations, some of them coinciding literally with the motifs known from comparative studies of fairy tales, mythology, or religions.

Jung not only made the observations just mentioned, he also observed another rather striking phenomenon. This was that such figures and motifs appeared in regular succession. In the course of a longer, more thorough and more complete analysis, it was possible to outline a hierarchy of the figures. It became apparent that when one figure appeared, another figure or motif frequently preceded it. In light of this, it had to be said that accumulations of one or the other of the images usually occurred only in a certain order. This order seemed to be an inherent one which could only be explained as the result of a repercussion that the process of analysis had on the unconscious. Only after your consciousness has increased by having assimilated a particular content from the unconscious can another aspect of the unconscious psyche appear. As a rule, it is necessary first to assimilate contents of such-and-such a nature before the contents of another nature can appear. This appearance then becomes the next step in analytical development. Thus after the motif of figure A has been dealt with sufficiently, the motif of figure B begins to be more frequent in dreams. When those elements have been integrated into the conscious system and dealt with properly, figures or motifs of class C will begin to be more frequent. If an analytical process is observed, without having a particular idea or theory as to its prescribed course, a natural sequence of elements will be seen.

The very first opportunity to increase consciousness will be the encounter of what Jung calls the *shadow*. This figure is well known, as illustrated by the French expression of the *bête noire* or the famous phenomenon of the scapegoat. Sir James George

Frazer's book, *The Scapegoat*, constituting Volume 6 of his *Golden Bough*, gives a great deal of information about the scapegoat and its function.[8] The idea of the scapegoat is best known in the ritual of the Jewish Day of Atonement, described in Leviticus 16:6-22. The personification of this darker side of an individual's system is sometimes very striking. A dream of a young American psychologist will illustrate this concept. In the dream the young man is helping his friend Frank to empty his cupboard because Frank has to return home. Frank is overloaded and weighed down with all kinds of objects, and the young man helps him to carry some of the objects out of the room. But he sees that his friend can never reach home with so many things, more than half of which are balloonlike. The young man recommends to Frank to let the air out of all the objects, roll them up, and thus have more room to pack.

In order to understand what this dream means, we have to know a few things about the role Frank plays in the dreamer's mind. In other words, we have to collect the associations connected with Frank. The dreamer tells us that he dislikes Frank for the simple reason that he thinks he is inflated. Moreover he characterizes Frank as an introvert, while he himself is an extravert. Literally, in that case, we can say that Frank represents the introverted shadow of the extraverted dreamer.

The dream tells us something about the difficulties the extravert has understanding the introvert. It tells us also that the introverted shadow of the extraverted dreamer appears to the latter as something inflated, which must be understood as a projection. The dreamer makes such projections onto someone who possesses a number of creative qualities, which, however, as long as they are in the shadow part of the personality, are devoid of value to the dreamer because they cannot be realized. Jung devoted a whole chapter of his book *Psychological Types* to this subject. In that chapter he deals with Jordan's book, *Character as Seen in Body and Parentage*, and points out that the author is an introvert who gives a wholly unsatisfactory and unjust description

---

8. Sir James George Frazer, *The Golden Bough; A Study in Magic and Religion* (New York: Macmillan, 1960) [original edition, 1890].

of the extravert and a highly incomplete description of the introvert.

In order to say something theoretical about this figure of the shadow, I will call him "the dark brother within" or "the dark mirror reflex." I have already noted some of the personifications of "the dark brother within" found in folklore. In addition, we have to think only of goblins and evil spirits and the fact that among primitives the shadow has great significance, so that they treat it with all the necessary precautions to have added protection. Primitives take the shadow literally, and the way they deal with it goes so far as to make them liable of a serious crime if they step on it. In certain instances they believe they are justified in killing the person who steps on their shadow. We also know of cases where the shadow gets lost. In German literature there is a very famous story by Chamisso, called "Peter Schlemiehl." Then we have stories like Stevenson's "Dr. Jekyll and Mr. Hyde" where a light and a dark side of man somehow are living in a symbiosis. The primitive man's "bush soul" would correspond in many ways to what Jung calls the shadow.

The shadow always represents that aspect of a man's system which is refuted, rejected, repressed, and which he hides from other people. The less respectable qualities of a person are always represented in shadow figures, so that the existence of the shadow really points to a moral problem par excellence. The shadow is always represented in our dreams and fantasies by a person of the same sex, of our own sex, who is in contradistinction to the animus or anima who are of the opposite sex. This is seen particularly in the beginning of analysis, when tramps, murderers, alcoholics, or drug addicts, and all kinds of unpleasant figures of the man's own sex appear in his dreams. It becomes a problem for one to have to admit that such tendencies exist within oneself. It always constitutes a major difficulty in analysis to get analysands to come to terms with the shadow figures, or in other words, to take the shadow figures, as Jung would say, on the *subjective level*. There is no doubt that the shadow has a personal aspect, or belongs more or less to what Jung calls the "personal unconscious," which as such would be equivalent to the Freudian unconscious. However, when one deals with the widely held prejudices that arise out of the darker aspects of the human personality, it is doubtful how much of the shadow belongs to the personal unconscious and how much remains on the subjective level. This raises the question of the extent to which the individual can be held responsible for this in the true sense of the word. To find illustrations, we only have to think of collective prejudices of this kind, for instance anti-Semitism or other such "isms," that have to do with the unreflected condemnation of something human. Such prejudices are immediately projected not only onto certain persons, but also onto some particular group with some particular creed, or onto particular political convictions that cover up the incompatibilities in our own system. These things, which all of us know very well, poison the atmosphere of virtually the entire planet. In other words, when we deal with collective shadow projections where men not only forget about the beam in their own eyes, but criticize their neighbors for the mote in theirs, it is doubtful whether the situation can be dealt with on a personal level. Since this is at the same time a moral problem, we have to admit that the collective aspect, or the collective roots of a shadow projection, most clearly originate from the collective unconscious and no longer from the personal unconscious. For this reason it can be said that the collective shadow is a problem that simply has to do with the objective existence of the moral problem or the question of good and evil.

The relativity of good and evil in Jungian psychology has been given a great deal of thought and has been discussed at great length, particularly by theologians. In order to see the significance of Jung's teachings, we must go back to the first dire necessity that occurred in our life, which made it inevitable for us to deal somehow with the dark aspect of our own nature or, as it were, to take up that life in us which had hitherto not been lived, but with which we have to come to terms. As soon as we meet with this problem, we experience its ambivalence. Not only do the shadow figures represent all kinds of obviously negative qualities, and not only will we have to deal with those qualities in a way that gives them a chance to be lived, or to be considered, reflected upon, and made peace with, but we also will discover rather positive qualities in those figures, which in themselves are perfectly valuable, but which for some external reasons have never been cultivated and lived, and therefore have degenerated. This condition demonstrates what can be called the ambivalence of the shadow figure. In those cases where the shadow contains both sides, it has in its ambivalence all the qualities of what we may call, in Jungian terminology, a symbol, which, according to Jung's definition, always unites two sides. Here we have then this quality of the shadow, which we call the double, our double – the shadow which is at the same time a poison and a medicine. May I remind you of a famous passage of Omar Khayyam's in which he says, "If a sage hands you poison, drink it. If a fool hands you the antidote, pour it out." The problem amounts to the relativity of the value of the shadow, and thereby to the relativity of the value of evil. We may also, at this point, quote from the Koran:[9]

And when they had journeyed farther on, Moses said to his servant: "Bring us some food; we are worn out with travelling."

"Know," replied the other, "that I forgot the fish when we were resting on the rock. Thanks to Satan, I forgot to mention this. The fish made its way into the sea in a miraculous fashion."

"This is what we have been seeking," said Moses. They went back the way they came and found one of Our servants to whom We had vouchsafed Our mercy and whom We had endowed with knowledge of Our own. Moses said to him: "May I follow you so that you may guide me by that which you have been taught?"

"You will not bear with me," replied the other. "For how can you bear with that which is beyond your knowledge?"

Moses said: "If Allah wills, you shall find me patient: I shall not in anything disobey you."

He said: "If you are bent on following me, you must ask no question about anything till I myself speak to you concerning it."

The two set forth, but as soon as they embarked, Moses' companion bored a hole in the bottom of the ship.

"A strange thing you have done!" exclaimed Moses. "Is it to drown her passengers that you have bored a hole in her?"

"Did I not tell you," he replied, "that you would not bear with me?"

"Pardon my forgetfulness," said Moses. "Do not be angry with me on account of this."

They journeyed on until they fell in with a certain youth. Moses' companion slew him, and Moses said: "You have killed an innocent

9. The Koran, Sura XVIII, 64:81, 4TH ed., trans. N. J. Dawood (London: Penguin Books, 1974).

man who has done no harm. Surely you have committed a wicked crime."

"Did I not tell you," he replied, "that you would not bear with me?"

Moses said: "If ever I question you again, abandon me; for then I should deserve it."

They travelled on until they came to a certain city. They asked the people for some food, but they declined to receive them as their guests. There they found a wall on the point of falling down. His companion restored it, and Moses said: "Had you wished, you could have demanded payment for your labours."

"Now has the time arrived when we must part," said the other. "But first I will explain to you those acts of mine which you could not bear to watch with patience.

"Know that the ship belonged to some poor fishermen. I damaged it because in their rear there was a king who was taking every ship by force.

"As for the youth, his parents both are true believers, and we feared lest he should plague them with his wickedness and unbelief. It was our wish that their Lord should grant them another in his place, a son more righteous and more filial.

"As for the wall, it belonged to two orphan boys in the city whose father was an honest man. Beneath it their treasure is buried. Your Lord decreed in His mercy that they should dig out their treasure when they grew to manhood. What I did was not done by my will.

"That is the meaning of what you could not bear to watch with patience."

As we can see, evil here becomes the teaching and this is something not totally unknown in analysis. There are times when the analysand has to deal with the problem of the shadow; then the analyst may appear as a shadowy figure, thus giving to this shadow quality a healing influence. This whole problem of the relativity of evil is dealt with in the Catholic Church according to the sentence, *Omne bonum a deo, omne malum a homine* [All good is derived from God, all wickedness from man]. Here evil appears as no real being, against which the real being (the Greek ὄν (*on*) [literally "that which is"] only belongs to the good – making the evil a nonexistent "reality," which is the absence of good (*privatio boni*). I think we have perfectly good reasons to turn this theory upside down and to say with Wilhelm Busch that "the good ... is always the evil which is left out."

One of the purposes of analysis is to make the person capable of coming to terms with this inferior personality consisting of laziness, evil, negative values, moral and spiritual inferiorities, and backwardness of all sorts, and to come to terms with the effects this inferior part of his person has upon him. These effects are naturally automatic as long as this inferior part remains in the unconscious, and it is a problem of the first order to learn about not only these autonomous unconscious tendencies, but also to control them, for if they gain the ascendency in the life of a person, a neurotic dissociation of the personality results. The task of linking this part of the person to the conscious personality is, of course, a major technical and moral problem. In this task man will have to keep a balance between the various tendencies and will have to accept some of them by using the necessary critique. Such a procedure will inevitably make it necessary to be disobedient, because man will have to develop an independent sort of position. The moral problem actually exists only because man must be able to will differently. It is essential that man must be able to do things that are not generally accepted by the majority of people, because only if he is able to do so, do ethics make sense. If man is just an animal who piously obeys the laws nature imposes on him, no ethical question comes up, and it is consequently of no particular merit if he simply obeys laws. Thus, the possibility of disobedience is necessary in order to make the moral problem a reality. It can, of course, happen that man gets stuck in this conflict or in a dissociation, so that he starts to live a double life. In order to get out of this condition, man needs something like a therapeutic myth, which can appear in a dream. Dreams almost always have something of a mythic quality, and whenever a dream is seen as an attempt to increase consciousness, or an attempt to create consciousness, it always has some similarity to cosmogony. Every dream appears as a small cosmogony, or the creation of a microcosm, simply because there is in it an interrelation between the conscious and the unconscious. It is for this particular reason that care must be taken not to attribute dream figures *in globo* [in mass] to the dreamer's conscious personality, for this in many cases would give rise to the danger of an inflation—positive or negative. In view of this danger it would be much more correct to treat the dream figures as forces in which man participates rather than forces with which he is identified. Examples of therapeutic myths, which are helpful in dealing with this conflict of a shadow or with this moral conflict, are the myth of the Virgin Birth, the myth of the redeeming work of Christ, and to some degree the more modern myth expressed in the new dogma where Mary, with her body, is received into Heaven. In this myth Mary's body, in other words matter, as the substratum of corruption, is sanctified.

In literature there are many other examples. There is Othello with his shadow counterpart Iago, or there is a myth of venerable age that is particularly striking in this respect, the famous Gilgamesh epic in which the hero Gilgamesh meets with two different aspects of the shadow, first a personal one who is represented by Enkidu and then a collective one, represented by Chumbaba. The latter one has to be overcome *tale quale*, whereas the first one has to be befriended. This is the therapeutic aspect of the Gilgamesh epic. When the hero has integrated the personal shadow figure into his ego, he gains a new dimension by which he becomes less of an individual and more something generally human. If man did not have his shadow, he would not be real, for only ghosts do not cast shadows. In spiritualistic experiences, this is always thought of as being a shibboleth for the reality of an unreal apparition.

The next step in the analytical process is what Jung calls the *persona*. The persona, according to Jung, is a certain system of adaptation, which is built up during the first half of life in order to protect man from the influences of the outer world, and in order to allow him to appear more or less decently in the outer world without giving himself away too much. This system can also be called a *role* that man wants to play. Thus Jung took the term of the persona, which is actually the Latin word for the mask used by actors in the ancient theater, where the mask represented a particular role. From this mask, as a *pars pro toto* [the part stands for the whole], we go to our clothes, therefore the costume we wear. In French, for instance, costume or *coutume* is synonymous with *habit* — which also means a relatively solid habitual complex of functions. Considered as a function, the persona is the function of relatedness to the external world, and as such is a correlative concept to the ones I shall presently describe as anima and animus, for *they* represent the function of relation to the inner world. The persona is formed in the course of life partly by the effects the outer world has upon us, and partly by our reactions to those effects. Schopenhauer put it very neatly when he described it as "that which somebody represents in contradistinction to what he actually is." If we identify ourselves with this persona, then we are *personal* in contradistinction to *individual*. And so, for people who are identified with their personae, *personalities* play such an important part. It must be noted, however, that the stronger the persona, the more rigid it becomes and the more the bearer of this persona is jeopardized by influences from within. In such a case, for instance, a strong man or a confirmed rationalist suddenly shows superstitious traits. I should like to report here an experience I had during my last trip to the United States, when I visited a world-famous scientist whom I had known from Europe. He received me on the porch of his house which was adorned with a horseshoe. I tried to make a funny remark by saying, "But Professor, you don't believe in that sort of thing, do you really?" whereupon he answered quite naïvely, "Of course not, but you know I have been told that it works even when you don't believe in it."

We all know examples of people who have identified so completely with their persona that their lives consist only of the role they play, their profession, or their position, or the use of their particular gift. Certain famous singers are examples of this. Perhaps the most obvious example of such an identification in history was Louis XIV, the French king, with his conviction that *l'Etat c'est moi*—I am the state. In dreams the persona is rarely personified since the persona is something we *wear*, like our clothes, rather than something we *are*; thus it becomes a dream motif rather than a dream figure. This becomes particularly clear when something goes wrong with our persona. In such cases we have dreams in which such speech metaphors as "losing one's shirt" or "losing one's face" (i.e., the mask we wear) are illustrated, or in which something is wrong with our clothes or we are exposed by being naked or partly naked, or our persona, our mask, has become defective or transparent. In cases where the persona is actually personified, it is always represented by someone of the same sex. As we have already seen, this is true with the shadow figure in the beginning of analysis, and with the dream figure that looks like our father or mother in earlier years of life. The father and mother images play a considerable part as examples in the building up of our own persona. Here is an example of such a dream: the dreamer is a young American psychologist, who dreams that he sees himself being carried out of the house in a coffin—he is not particularly moved by this, except that he is upset by the fact that he sees himself lying in the coffin in his best dark blue suit, which he realizes will now be destroyed. This young man was greatly interested in his outer appearance and had always paid particular attention to his clothes. His face scarcely ever showed any mimic reactions for he always put a lot of emphasis on correct behavior. Consequently he was very impersonal.

The persona is usually much more elaborate and much more rigid with men than it is with women. This fact has its mirror-reflex in the well-known fact that women's clothes and hair styles are ever so much more adaptable, changing much more frequently with fashion than they do with men.

The next step in a typical analytical development is the appearance of and the dealing with the anima—in the case of a man—and the animus—in the case of a woman. Previously I offered some justification for the creation of the term anima; here I shall point to the kind of experience that made Jung think of such a term and the objective material that can be used in order to justify these concepts of archetypes of the collective unconscious. In order to do this I need to give you an idea of the development in the realm of anima or animus that takes place in a typical case of analytical psychology.

We deal with the anima first, in other words, with a hypothetical case of a man in order to illustrate the effects of the anima on the man's system. The anima is the projection-producing factor par excellence and, consequently, the anima always is seen by the person in a projected form, i.e., as all women, or most women, or certain women. The man will be affected very strongly by this projection. Such projections have a high degree of autonomy so that they produce strong emotional reactions, which are one of the main features of any anima projection. The existence of such a projection exaggerates or vitiates all the human relations so that relationships to people, particularly women, are weakened and to a strange degree mythologized.

If such a condition were to be analyzed, a good deal of fantasy would be found in it; in other words, there are unconscious fantasies that automatically stain the object of fantasy and make the sender of the projections very irritable, very touchy and moody. Man apparently becomes possessed by his anima image and that makes him something less than a man, producing an effeminate set of reactions. Thus he is not only moody but also very jealous; he reacts like a dandy; he is unadaptable and effeminate. He becomes a strong man with a tender sort of kernel. Now, if this anima is made the subject of analysis it undergoes a certain development, which can be outlined in various stages, of which there seem to be five. To begin with, the anima image will be projected onto the mother. As long as this is the case, the whole problem can just as well be called a mother complex in the ordinary Freudian sense of the word. The image of the mother will quite automatically be contaminated with the pre-existing image of the anima. While the mother carries this projection, there is a condition that is highly undesirable and the mother complex can properly be called a *complexus delendus*; it simply has to be somehow dissolved. If it is not, it will have all kinds of unpleasant effects, ranging from promiscuity to homosexuality, from Don Juanism to criminality. In the second stage, which occurs somewhat later in life, in adolescence or perhaps earlier, the image of the anima is projected on a mother substitute, the older girlfriend of a young man, or in days when there were still maids or cooks in homes, the maid or the cook. The third stage I should like to call the stage of the prostitute type. At this stage, the anima image takes on a somewhat androgynous nature. A prostitute may be considered androgynous because she *is* and *is not* a woman. Obviously she is not a mother type, which accounts for the fact that with the prostitute type the mother complex gets dissolved. A prototype for this third stage is "Baubo," the inspirer of the unchaste and obscene jokes of the women during the Demeter festivals in Eleusis. The fourth stage I should like to call the priestess type. This image is usually projected onto nurses or beautiful nuns, or onto women with some sort of a holiness, or onto women whose backgrounds are unknown or most varied. The fifth stage can be represented by what we used to call the *femme inspiratrice*, that is a lady with a salon, in the French sense of the word, who has a brilliant, witty, clever, and rather mysterious quality, or a lady with a quality that cannot be penetrated, or one who is rather taciturn and mystic. This aspect of the anima image is illustrated by Ninon de Lenclos, Diane de Poitiers, and other *grandes dames* of the

French past. All these figures, all these stages of anima figures, when projected, produce or exert a very peculiar influence on the man, the upshot of which is completely demonic.

This list of five stages is admittedly a clumsy sort of simplification of the problem, but there are a number of clinical examples of this phenomenology in published dreams of the Jungian literature. Instead of giving more such examples, I would note some of the ways in which the problem of the anima appears in non-psychological literature. It is interesting to study the Gnostic myth where there are several stages of feminine figures portrayed. The first stage is the mother type represented by Eve. The third type, the whore or prostitute, appears strikingly in Helena and particularly in the famous story of Simon Magus, which is found in Acts 8:5-24. Simon Magus, who declared himself to be "the great power of God" and was by his followers likened to the Holy Ghost, was a rival to Peter and John. He had found the girl Helena in a brothel in Tyrus and he called her his "first thought." She is the ἔννοια (*ennoia*) [notion, conception], the power contained in the αἰων (*aion*) [age] who is also a χάρις (*charis*) [grace] and who makes *aion* long for the women, so that the situation becomes creative and the ἄνθρωπος (*anthropos*) [man] is begotten. This story is also known from Irenaus and Hippolytus. The next stage, that of the priestess type, appears in the Gnostic system in Maria, and the fifth stage, the *femme inspiratrice* type, most clearly in Sophia. In English literature an excellent example, always quoted by Jung, appears in Rider Haggard's novel *She*. The "she" has the attribute of "she who must be obeyed" — in other words, she is a woman of strict or almost absolute authority. Many aspects of the anima image can be found described in Rider Haggard as well as in a parallel book in French by Pierre Benoit, *L'Atlantide*. There is also an interesting description of the experience of the anima in a famous book of the Renaissance period, written by a Venetian monk, by the name of Francesco Colonna, with the strange title *Hypnerotomachia di Poliphilo*. It was published in 1494 and is one of the most expensive incunabula because of the beautiful woodcuts with which it is adorned. The book has been made the subject of a special study by Mrs. Linda Fierz, published by Bollingen in 1950.

The various stages of the anima are naturally projected onto actual women, and as long as they remain unconscious, a period of time identical with the period of their projection, they must do so, for as soon as a contact is made with the conscious they are no longer projected. The ways in which these images usually appear are various and may be of the following types: the dream figure is an unknown woman, sometimes of dubious character; or a diseased woman, a despicable sort of character, a *femme qui se fait suivre*; or very often a primitive, or particularly in America a black girl; or a stranger; or perhaps to a non-Jewish dreamer, a Jewish girl. The image may also have historical traits, or may be untimely or even outside of time, so that she is not subjected to our terrestrial time. She may have qualities of a virgin, mother, queen, or goddess. She may have the qualities of a sister, mother, wife, and daughter, all telescoped into one. This is what I mean when I say she may be outside terrestrial time. She also can be represented in theriomorphic form, e.g., as a snake, or an animal of prey, a cat, a tiger, and the like. The carriers of these projections usually are somewhat outstanding women, preferably actresses, dancers, heavily made-up persons, at all events women with rather striking and extraordinary features, very dark or very blond, etc. When in the course of analysis these qualities are discussed, and when some kind of an understanding of their existence within the dreamer's own system is reached—in short, when this content of the collective unconscious is more or less integrated—it has one outstanding effect on the consciousness of a man. It will produce what I would like to call an eros of consciousness. Such a man will possess, because of this eros of consciousness in addition to his masculine consciousness, the quality of relatedness not only to women but also to everything that comes his way. For being aware or conscious rather of the effects of the anima and her content, he will have an entirely different attitude to many phenomena of life. While the integration of the shadow enables a person to have a much better relationship to the members of his own sex, the integration of the anima has still more of an effect on a man's relations to the other sex. A man will find that in the course of such a process a triad is produced. This triad consists of the male subject, the female subject (namely his *vis-à-vis*, his partner), plus the third element which is transcendent and which will have to be called the anima.

The correlative concept to the anima in a man's case is the concept of the animus in a woman's case. I think this can be summed up by saying that it represents the masculine element in a woman's system. This element usually comes to the fore in the second half of life where it manifests itself more or less biologically. Women begin to grow mustaches, their voices get lower, they become more energetic and so on. The psychological phenomenology of the identity with the animus would be that such a woman becomes a nagging individual, who likes to fight merely on principles and ideas, and who develops a kind of logic that is doubtful yet persistent. She begins to know everything better, she is possessed with ideas, tends to become sectarian religiously, or to adhere to some fashionable latest philosphy, and so forth. Again, there are certain stages of the development of this phenomenon, which I should like to outline briefly.

The first stage would be represented by the father complex in early life. A girl will feel attracted to older men and will particularly be interested in paternal sort of men friends. The second stage I would call the stage of action. In this stage the woman will admire men who are outstanding in any kind of action, such as a pilot or a strong suntanned sportsman. In the negative case, it can be even a notorious yet physically attractive criminal. The third stage I would call the spiritual stage. In this stage professional men will be singled out: parsons, teachers, doctors, actors, perhaps artists and the like. Negatively, it can be a swindler, or a genius misunderstood, or even a garrulous idiot. In dreams during these stages of development, the animus may be personified as a pilot, or in a racecar driver, or perhaps in a negative form as an eagle or some other kind of a bird, particularly when it is a question of the third stage. The third stage too can be represented by a priest, or by some sort of sorcerer. When the animus is projected onto a real man, this can have very serious effects, for a woman can become an absolute slave to such a man, and it can lead to a helpless sexual bondage. Again I should like to refer you to some examples from literature, which seem to describe the phenomena of the animus projection rather clearly. Read Ronald Fraser's book, *The Flying Draper*, or H. G. Wells' *Christina Alberta's Father*, where you can see another peculiarity of the animus I have not mentioned yet, namely the fact that the animus very often is a plurality, consisting of a group of men, in contrast to the anima which is usually only one woman. In this book, *Christina Alberta's Father*, the animus is represented by what the heroine calls "the court of conscience." A good example also is Mary Hay's book, *The Evil Vineyard*. It is, in fact, much more difficult to describe the animus than it is to describe the anima, and I therefore must refer you to these examples in literature rather than to any particular psychological papers.

Now as for the integration of the animus we again have to say that the animus as such, that is, the archetype of the animus, cannot be integrated, any more than can the anima. What you can integrate are its effects, by a discrimination in the personification of this archetype. You will thereby create a relatedness to what at a later stage, when it has been made conscious to a great extent, will be a *logos*. This logos will give the feminine consciousness something like a reflectiveness or meditativeness, and will give the mind a perceptive quality. This achievement will show mainly in the relationships with other people, and in particular with the partner. It will bear fruit as it goes along with the development of the anima in man and his ability to build up a relationship. Similar to the triad I described as being the result of this integration of the anima, there is also a triad when the animus is integrated, namely, (1) the feminine subject, (2) the masculine subject in the partner, in the real man, and (3) the animus transcending both.

Let us think briefly about the effects that animus and anima have in everyday life. Animus and anima are responsible, in a large degree, for sympathy and antipathy. As ideal images they attract each other fatally, eventually causing the utter disappointment of the individuals in question. The projection is always made at first sight. It produces a strange feeling of old acquaintanceship, that once upon a time one has already known the other. What is worse, the ability to see reality is lost. Almost everybody is possessed by these figures. It has to be remembered, however, that at this juncture our consciousness is still in full development, and that there always have been and always will be more conscious and less conscious individuals. When we stop understanding ourselves or others, emotions are always produced. In other words, there are gaps in our system of adaptation, where emotions immediately push through; when emotions rule, discussion becomes impossible. Whenever this is the case, our arguments are hopelessly involved, and we are victims of our prejudices. Then, of course, one single experience is sufficient to conjure up the whole weight of all the *a priori* judgments, or in the opposite case, one single good experience can make us see everything in an unrealistically positive light.

In an article of this length it is impossible to give a full picture of the Jungian theory of analysis. I should like, however, to add two more things that are of great importance, particularly for the later stages of Jungian analysis. I have been talking about the triad in connection with the animus and anima. I should like to say that in a man's case we will see, in the course of time, that this triad is no longer sufficient, and that at a certain juncture another figure appears in dreams or fantasies, which will likewise have to be integrated, at least to some degree. This fourth figure would be the figure of what Jung termed "the wise old man." In the woman's case something equivalent will take place, and the fourth figure with her would be what Jung calls the "great mother." Both figures have something to do with what we may boldly call wisdom.

Very often in Jungian literature you will find that the author talks about the "individuation process." What I have been doing thus far is, in fact, an attempt to describe this "individuation process," inasmuch as these dream figures, images, motifs, and fantasies showing such elements are in the course of analysis made conscious, or inasmuch as they are in a continuous process assimilated to the conscious system and integrated into it. This kind of development, in whose successive stages these images turn up one after the other, makes a triadic system that winds up with the realization of a fourth element, which must be added to the system. From his experience that under given conditions such a development seems to take place more or less spontaneously, Jung felt justified in talking about it in terms of a process. I shall say more about this later, but I should like to note here that the existence of such a process as this makes it likely that individuation, which is nothing less than becoming conscious of the totality of the human personality, is something which is basically present in life, so that it is only necessary to follow this course of development consecutively in order eventually to attain this totality. Individuation means nothing less than consciously becoming what one actually is. With such a definition the assumption is that this final being exists *in nuce* before man starts on this enterprise. This is something we shall have to investigate later when we discuss the relation between psychology and religion.

III. INTERPRETATION OF DREAMS

I need not tell you that dreams have been held in high esteem from Biblical times until recent years. Not until the coming of the natural sciences in the seventeenth and eighteenth or, more precisely, eighteenth and nineteenth centuries, was this belief affected, and then only among people who could be considered educated. Popular belief never abandoned the conviction of the importance of dream revelations.

In dealing with the place the interpretation of dreams plays in Jungian psychology, I shall proceed chronologically.

In a volume entitled *Studies in Word Association*, which was published during the early years of Jung's psychiatric clinical work, there is one contribution called "Association, Dream, and Hysterical Symptom." In this work, Jung described the treatment of a girl who showed obviously hysterical symptoms. In that treatment he used both the Freudian method of interpreting the patient's dreams and his own word association experiment. In the course of the investigation it became clear that in the association experiment, and in the dreams, and in the symptoms of the patient, the same complex showed itself in various disguises. The complex that seemed to be at the root of the patient's trouble was an erotic one, connected with what was then called *the mother complex*.

A few years later, stimulated by this and other findings of Jung's, Herbert Silberer in Vienna inaugurated an interesting experimental approach to the unconscious, which he combined with the word association method, a technique he called *lecanomantic gázing*. This is a technique taken from ancient methods of divination, from which came the more modern practice of crystal gazing. Instead of a crystal he used a bowl filled with water, with a few lighted candles set around it. The bowl and candles were placed in a dark room and the patient was asked to gaze into the surface of the water. Various kinds of visionary impressions or fantasies developed. The word association experiment that was done at the same time with the test person showed clearly that the associations produced were not based on the visions produced during the lecanomantic gazing, but that both the associations and the lecanomantic visions were based on the same complexes. Silberer concluded that the visions and the associations mutually support their interpretation by pointing concentrically to the same groups of complexes. Silberer also was able to demonstrate that the figures of the images tended to develop in the course of time, becoming more elaborate and clear. He noted that they began to be psychological potencies, turning into types or typical images. All this is interesting, but it must be admitted, that none of those experimental methods produced pure causal relations—rather there seemed to have been some kind of a "translating" element at work. Furthermore, this "translating" element seemed to be rather autonomous, independent of the originally intended effects. The conclusion to be drawn is that a definite causal explanation cannot be given to any of the dreams, symptoms, or effects observed in the association experiment, but a statement can be made about the conditions out of which the phenomena come. This conclusion is important because it bears upon the whole question of how to approach dreams in order to find out about their deeper meanings: it indicates the difficulty of knowing that a particular dream element goes back causally to a specific fact or a certain preexisting condition. In light of this difficulty it may help to recall some points made in section 1 of this chapter, concerning the results of the Jungian word association method. We noted then that through his experience, Jung discovered the existence and effects of what he called complexes. In the course of time he developed a general theory of complexes, in which it was shown that these complexes are like partial personalities and that as such they behave autonomously. They are charged with a considerable emotional tone, and very often are incompatible with the attitude of the conscious mind. These qualities of the complexes are close to the results found in Silberer's experiments, so that it can be said dream figures are personifications of these complexes. In the dreams, complexes are able to act, to perform, to play their parts uninhibitedly, because conscious control during sleep is weak.

Another interesting result of Jung's research in the field of complexes coincides with the theory of the *niveau mental,* the level of consciousness, developed by the French psychologist Pierre Janet. Janet worked out a theory to explain all kinds of phenomena in hysteria, and Jung used this theory to explain some of the effects of complexes. Janet talked about *l'abaissement de la tension psychologique* or *l'abaissement du niveau mental,* which is a phenomenon taking place whenever an emotional condition exists. Various kinds of unusual, strange or even pathological mental disturbances can be explained adequately by this concept of the mental level or level of consciousness. In a later paper of 1937, "*Les Oscillations du Niveau Mental,*" Janet says that the notion of the *abasement of the psychological tension* makes it possible to deal readily with the psychological peculiarities of sleep and dreams.

Jung observed that whenever a complex is stirred up by a critical stimulus word in his word association experiment, something happens that corresponds to the *abaissement du niveau mental* of Janet; the level of consciousness remains lowered for a period of time, varying from a fifth of a second to minutes, which is a fairly abnormal state. It is clear that when a complex is constellated, that is, stimulated or stirred up, the tension or attention of consciousness is lowered. It is also clear that in sleep the level of consciousness is physiologically lowered until consciousness is almost completely wiped out. Thus, it is understandable that in sleep the complexes which are normally down in the unconscious realm will be closer to the frontier of consciousness and in that way exert an influence or make an impression on the conscious mind. It is possible that these impressions account for dreams, since in such a state the complexes will be active.

This point of view can be expanded further by another suggestion Jung made about the psychology of dreams. I refer to the suggestion that dreams have dramatic structures, that they can be looked at as being real *drames intérieurs* [inner dramas], and that they can be analyzed just as a stage drama can be analyzed to uncover its hidden structure. Schopenhauer once said that the ego was the secret stage director of a person's dreams, or, as he put it on another occasion, "In a dream everyone is his own Shakespeare." Jung, in his early seminars on children's dreams conducted at the Swiss Federal Institute of Technology, made the members of the class analyze certain dreams according to the classical pattern of the drama. This pattern has a number of parts in it. First there is the list of characters, or the *dramatis personae*, and the statement concerning the time and place of the action. Second, soon after the action begins, there is a portrayal or exposition of the problem with which the drama will deal. The plot begins to develop and leads to a certain set of complications. Third, the lines in the plot are drawn together into a conflict or crisis; this is the high point of the play in which something decisive, either for good or ill, must occur. Fourth, there comes the solution which must be a reasonable and meaningful ending for the crisis.

To amplify this I shall use a particular dream, which will enter into the discussion later on as well. The patient said, "I was fishing for trout, not in an ordinary stream or lake, but in a reservoir divided into compartments. For a time I fished with the usual equipment of flies, etc., but I caught nothing. Becoming exasperated, I took up a three-pronged spear, which was lying nearby, and immediately I succeeded in spearing a fine fish."

Now I shall apply the pattern of the dramatic structure to this dream. The first sentence, "I was fishing for trout, not in an ordinary stream or lake, but in a reservoir divided into compartments," is the same as the first part of the drama; it gives the *dramatis personae*, which are, in this particular case, the dreamer, the time, and the place. The second part of the drama, the exposition, is given by the next phrase, "For a time I fished with the usual equipment of flies, etc., but I caught nothing." The plot leads to the problem. The third part of the drama is in the first half of the next phrase, "Becoming exasperated, I took up a three-pronged spear, which was lying nearby." This is a critical high point, which must be followed by some kind of resolution, as in the rest of the sentence – "and immediately I succeeded in spearing a fine fish" – which corresponds to the fourth part of the drama.

Keep this dream in mind, and I shall go into its deeper meaning later on. At this point I only want to use it as an example of the Jungian concept of the dramatic structure of dreams. I would note, however, that the suggestion that dreams have a dramatic structure has certain consequences. It means that: (1) The dream is a whole, with a beginning and an end, with a conflict and its resolution. The Greek word *drama* means action, so the action of the dream would lead to the *lysis*, the Greek word for liberation or salvation. (2) It is very likely that the stage drama had its origin in dreams. Note how the solution in the dream under consideration was brought about by the appearance of an entirely new element, the three-pronged spear. This was often the case in the ancient drama, where the solution came about through a *deus ex machina*. In antiquity, when Artemidorus, Macrobius, and Synesius wrote about dreams, they cited examples in which divine intercession brought about the solution, and in all those cases the authors were convinced they were dealing with *somnia a deo missa* [dreams sent by God]. (3) The dramatically acting personifications in the dreams are moved by fate in the same way as fate was the dynamic of the ancient drama. Illustrations of this are the famous oracle in the Oedipus dramas, or the curse of the Atridae. (4) There is a close connection between dreams and the old kind of dramas, which were, as had been pointed out by Nietzsche, *mystery plays*. A dream is a therapeutic myth, which is exactly what the mystery dramas or mystery plays were. (5) Nietzsche said that in the dream, man repeats the experience of earlier humanity, which seems to be an anticipation of the Jungian idea of the collective unconscious.

Dreams have several discernible effects. The first is that the dream wakes the dreamer. This happens relatively frequently, in many cases because the fourth part of the drama is lacking so that the resolution to the drama is left to the conscious mind, which throws the dreamer back into consciousness. Second, a dream has a salutary effect—an immediately salutary effect. A great deal has been said about the cathartic effect of a drama upon an audience. People who attend the performance of a drama are affected by what is going on on the stage because they identify with the hero or heroes, the protagonist or the antagonist. The cathartic effect comes through the strongly emotional reactions produced in people by this identification, and they emerge from the experience liberated by the resolution of the drama. In antiquity, Plutarch provided an excellent example of this when he reported that during a performance of Euripides' *Medea* pregnant women began to give birth and men started having crying fits.

Jung introduced another important matter into dream

analysis. Schopenhauer's statement that a person is his own stage director in his dreams suggests that there may well be some kind of responsibility on man's part for what goes on in his dreams. In the identification of the spectator with the hero or heroine of the drama, somewhat the same thing is true. The matter Jung introduced has much to do with this characteristic of the drama or the dream. Jung pointed out that dreams can be interpreted on two different levels. On the one hand, dreams can be interpreted on the objective level. This means that all dreams may be regarded as reporting something about those persons, figures, and situations appearing in them as they exist objectively. This principle of interpretation is valueless when the dream figures and dream motives can no longer be traced to actual objective figures or situations in outer reality. At this point, the second level of interpretation is needed, which is to take everything happening in the dream on a subjective level, i.e., to attribute all personifications to the dreamer's own system. Interpretation on the objective level is justified as long as dream persons are well known to the dreamer and conditions which exist in the dream are a known part of the dreamer's external world. This principle becomes questionable when the dreamer's boss, or his wife, or his father – all persons who in one way or another are fairly well known – enter his dream. When clearly mythological figures enter the dream, an interpretation on the objective level becomes absolutely impossible. The same thing would apply if situations which the dreamer has never come across in reality enter his dream. The necessity of interpretation on the subjective level raises the problem alluded to earlier when I spoke of the problem involved in the shadow. It is difficult to explain how some of the qualities found in certain dream figures belong to a person's own system. If the *bon mot* of Schopenhauer quoted is correct – if man is his own Shakespeare in his dreams – then he will have to accept the fact that there is something not only like Othello in him, but also something of Iago, of Shylock, and, as it were, of the whole cast of characters: Portia, Antonio, Bassanio, and all the rest.

A few other qualities of dreams, which seem to be fairly typical and which are observed much more frequently in dreams than in other realms of experience, must now be noted. In a collection of several thousand dreams there are several characteristics that appear in a varying degree of frequency; these are peculiarities of dreams in contrast to waking experience. By the way, I believe that such a comparative study of dream material and conscious material is the only method by which knowledge can be gained about the nature of the unconscious, the function of dreams, the conditions under which dreams appear, and the conditions under which certain particular dreams appear. Such comparative study is the only approach I can think of whereby a theory of dreams can be built.

The first quality of dreams to which I point was strongly emphasized by Jung. He called it the compensating or complementing function of dreams. By this Jung meant that dreams have to be looked at in the light of the conscious attitude, condition, and situation of the particular dreamer's life. He thought that dreams in many cases completed the picture of a person's life given in a study of the conscious. The Latin word *compleo* means to fill up completely, and in that sense the complementary function of the dream would be the function that adds to man's conscious picture of his own situation, that which was left out for one reason or another, e.g., repression, resistance, or wrong moral judgment. This element could come into the dream because the unconscious does not suffer from any such prejudices or repressions, because what is in it is not judged, as there is no ego that can pass a verdict.

Something similar has to be said about the compensatory function of dreams. The Latin word *compenso* means to weigh one thing against the other and to smooth out. A dream can have an aspect which can only be seen and understood in contradistinction to the conscious condition of the dreamer. The idea of compensation presupposes the existence of some more complete standpoint for the individual, one that is superior to or different from the one he takes in consciousness. To illustrate, there is the case of a distinguished lady who has a series of dreams in which she meets a harlot lying in the gutter completely intoxicated; or there is a young engineer, a very rationalistic man, who has repeated dreams that he constructs a *perpetuum mobile* [perpetual motion machine] of the first order, which he knows is an impossibility. In these cases the dreams must be regarded as having a compensatory meaning, bringing something highly irrational into the very rational and very sound or very safe system of the dreamers.

Another peculiarity of dreams is that they often produce images, elements having a typically symbolic quality. Here I want to go into the Jungian concept of the symbol at some length. The Jungian concept of the symbol was the reason for his break with Freud. It is given as the cause for all kinds of misunderstandings and misinterpretations, and still is not understood completely by most people who disagree with Jung's thoughts. It is therefore necessary, in spite of the fact that Jung has published a good deal of material on the subject that gives any unprejudiced reader a clear picture of his meaning, to speak of the definition of the symbol in the Jungian sense.

The term *symbol* was used by a great many predecessors of analytical psychology and of Freudian psychology. For instance, Scherner did a great deal of investigation of the relation of dreams to bodily disturbances; he coined the term *body symbolism*. Scherner showed that the dream imagery expressed certain conditions in certain organs of the body. An illustration was the imagery of a furnace filled with flames blown upon by a powerful wind in a case of pneumonia or an inflammation of the lungs. The fire represented the inflammatory process and the wind the breath. Such imagery was called body symbolism; it is nothing more than the translation of something physiological or pathological taking place in the body into an image. There is no doubt that such translations take place in dreams; the ancient Greek authors and doctors, such as Hippocrates and Galen, diagnosed bodily diseases from dreams of this kind. Tantric yoga also has an elaborate system of correspondences between certain bodily locations and corresponding psychological experiences in the system of the chakras. Herbert Silberer gave a well-authenticated description of certain phenomena in dreams having to do with physiological transitions that occur, such as falling asleep or waking up. He calls the imagery related to such physiological effects the *symbolism of the threshold*. He pointed out, by way of illustration, that the dream motif of leaving for a voyage or a trip very often is related to the transition from one psychological condition to another, e.g. falling asleep. This recalls what Janet had to say about the *niveau mental*, and what the English neurologist Hughlings Jackson (who first described Jacksonian epilepsy) had to say about levels of cerebration. According to Jung, all this so-called symbolism is not really symbolic but semiotic, from the Greek word σημα (*sema*), which means sign, thus a sign for something perfectly well known. For instance, we use analogies, yet an analogy is actually an abbreviated expression for something well known and concrete, as the emblems used by employees of an airline. Usually these consist of small wings with the initials of the firm on them, indicating that the person wearing such a sign in his buttonhole is an employee of the airline. If we meet a Frenchman with a red rosette in his buttonhole, we know that he is a *Chevalier* of the *Légion d'Honneur*; or think of Justice represented in a statue, usually a woman carrying a balance, a sword, and with her eyes blindfolded. In all such cases, the observer can find out what is meant simply by using his common sense. Now, with regard to these semiotic expressions, Jung would say that an actual symbol is something different because it is the best possible description of a relatively unknown but posited thing. Inasmuch as it is the expression of something relatively unknown, it always has further possibilities of meaning in addition to the obvious one. Jung would say that as soon as all those further possibilities of meaning become known, the symbol becomes useless. It will be easy to make this clear to theologians. The Christian cross, as long as it was used to signify Christian love, was an allegory according to the given definition and consequently not a true symbol; but as soon as the cross was taken as the expression for something hitherto unknown, something transcending the ego, something beyond any rational explanation, and made the best expression for all this, then it became a real symbol. I think that Jung in his definition came close to what the ancient Greeks understood when they used the word σύμβολον (*symbolon*) [a striking together]. Plutarch spoke of *symbola mystica* in *Consolatio ad Uxorem* 10. There the knowledge of these *symbola* by the initiate of the Dionysian cult meant that he or she knew something which went beyond what could be experienced and was directly knowable. In this sense of the word, symbolism becomes a very important idea in dream interpretation. Through an investigation of tens of thousands of dreams, it becomes perfectly clear that the unconscious has the *virtus* [power], shall we call it, of forming true symbols.

Now I want to report a dream in which this is clear. The dreamer was a man of nearly fifty years; he was a psychologist working as an assistant professor at the psychological institute of a European university. The dream occurred in the course of analysis at a point where he began to realize what Jung calls the existence of the objective psyche. Here is the image which gave him this impression of having to do with something he had almost no conscious part in: he saw a red sphere revolving around a frontal axis in such a way that it moved away from the onlooker. The red sphere was within a blue one, a blue outer sphere, which was revolving sideways and backward around the inner sphere. The movement of the outer sphere was faster than that of the inner sphere. In the inner sphere he perceived what he called a "cross of light." This was a rectangular cross lying in a horizontal plane, as it were in the equatorial plane of the inner sphere. The beams of light from this cross were white and along those four beams the white light was, as he said, pumped rhythmically from the center toward the periphery of the sphere. The rhythm was of about the frequency of his own heartbeat. The white light, which was pumped rhythmically from the center to the periphery, dissolved at the periphery of the sphere into what he called clouds of a red gleam. Outside this whole structure he saw a feminine figure holding her arm out toward the microcosm, with an impressive gesture as if she wanted to say, "You had better contemplate this phenomenon."

Now, this image—it is not really a dream since there is not much of an action in the sense of a drama in it—appears to me to be a symbol of the psycho-physical totality of the dreamer's being, which would be indicated by the fact that it is a highly abstract, geometrical structure, and yet has a peculiar connection with his heartbeat, the pulsation of the light being directly related to his pulse. More specifically, we might call this central pulsation system or central circulation system a heart symbolism, *sensu strictiori* [in a stricter sense]. You will, perhaps, at this juncture remember the famous circulation-of-light symbolism in Taoistic Chinese philosophy. There is also color symbolism in the image—the blue and the red spheres, and the white and the red of the light. The blue and the red are opposites, the red having more to do with the blood, shall we say, and the blue having more to do with the spirit, or the red with feeling and the blue with thinking. Then there is the symbolism of shape or form which was strictly geometrical: the two spheres, the rectangular

Greek cross, the center, and the periphery. In all this taken together there is a symbolism of totality. Last but not least, some kind of a dynamic symbolism is given with this circulation or pulsation on the one hand and with the two movements of rotation on the other hand. In addition, there was a function of time, in the frequency of rotation of the spheres; and there was the more obviously anthropomorphic symbolism of the woman, who belongs to the phenomenology of the anima, although in this case she would play the part of a mystagogue.

The image contained a number of elements that the dreamer himself was able to trace back to conscious contents, and a few elements that the doctor was able to trace back to elements of the unconscious he had come across earlier during the course of analysis. To conclude: the image contained conscious as well as unconscious material, rational as well as irrational elements, and a number of pairs of opposites. To Jungians, it must be clear that the whole structure must be attributed to those symbols that with Jung are called *mandalas*. It also should be clear that inasmuch as the image contained such a large number of opposite qualities and united them in one image, it can be called a true symbol. According to Jung, the symbol has a transcendent function, which means that it is capable of uniting opposites. For this reason a true symbol very often is called by Jung a *uniting symbol*.

To continue with the list of peculiarities of dreams, I speak now of what is best called the occurrence of *typical motifs*. Here are some examples: the motif of a departure; the motif of a passage or crossing like the crossing of a river, either by a ford or by a bridge; the motif of falling or of flying; the more complicated motif of the cave and its dangers; the motif of the treasure guarded by some monster, dragon, etc. and thus hard to be attained; the motif of animals, such as the snake, or more generally the motif of the helpful animals; the motif of the *circumambulation*, when man walks around something repeatedly three times or more; and the "motif of the night sea journey." Recall the story of Jonah. A remarkable amount of parallel material has been collected in Frobenius' book on the night sea journey called *In the Age of the Sun God*, published in 1904. All in all, these typical dream motifs have a very close relationship or similarity with the motifs that ethnologists and mythologists and people who have made studies of fairy tales have pointed out. This phenomenon of typical motifs always bears a relationship to the level of culture of the people involved, so that the interpretations of such motifs must be within the same level of cultural history as that in which the motif is best represented. The cultural connections must always be taken into account.

Another feature of dreams, especially of certain elements of dreams, is what is called the *contamination*, which simply means that dreams are soiled with material that has little or nothing to do with the original element. Such contamination always happens as an effect of stirring up complexes, and in the realm of such contaminations the method of free association, inaugurated by Freud, has its use. For example, a handkerchief appears in a dream and the dreamer jumps from the handkerchief to Desdemona in *Othello* and the connection between the handkerchief and the jealousy of Othello. This is free association, justified inasmuch as in the unconscious realm there is little, if any, discrimination. Everything is connected with everything. Cases of contamination have consequently been analyzed successfully by use of the word association method. Jung, in a little book *On the Psychology of the Dementia Praecox*, which is schizophrenia, has given a few very amusing examples of such contaminated expressions of schizophrenic patients, analyzed as to their meaning. One was an old patient, an inmate of Burghölzli, who used to say: "I am the Lorelei." Jung found out that she had taken this title because of the fact that whenever the doctor came to the ward and said a few words to the patient, and the patient replied to the doctor, the doctor used to leave her shaking his head and saying, "I don't know what this means," referring to her statements, which were full of neologisms. Now, "I don't know what this means" ("Ich weiss nicht, was soll es bedeuten") is the beginning of the famous "Lied of the Lorelei," by Heine. The same patient used to say, "I am the Socrates substitute" – by which she wanted to indicate that she had been locked up in the clinic as unjustly as Socrates had been put in jail.

Another feature of dream elements is what is called the *condensation*. A dream figure may have qualities of the patient's husband, of her lover, of her analyst, or even of some other man, but at the same time the dream figure will be a dentist or a certain animal who is neither fish nor fowl, so that the figure at one and the same time will be something like a winged serpent, like Quetzalcoatl, a chimera. These are examples of condensation. Contrary to this there is the phenomenon of *multiplication* — which is that one particular dream element appears in great numbers, from two to several specimens, all identical. This phenomenon is obviously connected with the fact that when a person is intoxicated he begins to see double. There is a fine example of this in the Chinese meditation text, called *The Secret of the Golden Flower*: "the Book of successful contemplation said, the sun sinks in the great water and magic pictures of trees in rows arise."[10] These multiplication phenomena are closely related with what the French psychiatrists have described as *troubles cénesthesiques*.

Another feature of dreams is that they make concrete more or less abstract psychological inner facts. The words *bête noire* mean, in psychological terms, the carrier of a shadow projection. In a dream a *bête noire* may actually appear as a black ram or something of that sort. Complexes, as I said, tend to be personified, and not only personified but also acted out, which has the effect of giving a dramatizing quality to dreams. Instead of a certain thought, the dreamer hears the whole story, or instead of a certain fact, a whole drama is produced to illustrate the fact. Dreams tend to express themselves in an archaic way so that an animal which appears in a dream may talk, just as a certain animal talks with primitives because it is the carrier of or is identical with his bush soul. This seems to be so because of the fact that the unconscious has actually historical qualities inasmuch as it contains both the history and the prehistory of mankind, so it is able to express itself in a primitive or archaic way.

I shall now draw the theoretical conclusions that can be reached from all I have said about the peculiarities of dreams, and then I shall apply these conclusions to the dreams I have been quoting. It has to be said, first of all, that according to Jung's conviction, the dream is a natural phenomenon, occurring spontaneously in man's psyche. It is not produced by an act of

---

10. Richard Wilhelm, trans., *The Secret of the Golden Flower*, with a commentary by C. G. Jung (New York: Harcourt, Brace & World, 1962) [German edition: Munich, 1929].

will and is apparently not influenced by man's conscious mind. Consequently, any method of explaining the dream cannot be causalistic but must be a method that shows the conditions leading to the production of the dream. The causalistic explanation is impossible because there are no causes that would of necessity produce such and such a dream. All that *is* possible is to demonstrate the conditions that are connected with the creation of a particular dream. Again, every attempt to define the roots of dreams must of necessity remain very vague; all that can be said is that on the one hand the contents of a dream derive from the conscious mind and come from facts known by the dreamer (such contents Freud calls the *remnants of the day*), and, on the other hand, contents come into the dream that stem from the unconscious. These are usually called the constellated contents of the unconscious, and can be of two different natures: (1) they can in turn be constellated or stimulated by a content of the conscious mind and (2) they may have no such connection with the conscious mind and consequently have to be regarded as spontaneous, coming from creative processes in the unconscious mind. The latter possibility we have come across when we talked about complexes of the unconscious and their autonomy – this autonomy more or less equals the spontaneous creative quality.

Now we are ready to deal with the meaning of dreams. This must be formulated in such a way that what the dream has to say is seen in light of the attitude of the conscious mind of the dreamer. There are at least four possibilities in the relation between the conscious and the unconscious in dreams. First, the dream is simply the unconscious reaction to a conscious situation. This possibility is described by the Jungian concepts of complementarity and compensation, completing or compensating. Here, all the impressions of the conscious life provide the conditions needed for the production of such a dream. Second, the dream shows a situation that results from a conflict between the conscious and the unconscious. In this case the independence of the unconscious mind is a prerequisite for the creation of such a dream. Third, there is the dream in which the unconscious plays a still stronger part, so that the dream represents a tendency of the unconscious that seeks to change the attitude of the conscious mind. Such a dream would be possible only when the unconscious influence is stronger than the conscious one, and naturally such a dream would make a particularly strong impression on the dreamer. Fourth, the dream describes the unconscious processes, which have no relation to the conscious mind. Such dreams give the impression of utter strangeness and impress the dreamer deeply. Dreams of this category have the nature of a sudden inspiration, and appear oracular—what the primitive calls a "big dream," or what the ancients call a *somnium a deo missum* [dream sent by God].

When we differentiate the various stimuli that can influence the contents of dreams, we find a number of them. Somatic sources can affect a dream content in such a way that certain disturbances in the body, or certain physiological conditions of the body, can appear in dreams as, for example, hunger or thirst or sexual urges. As a second category, there are the facts in the external environment that come into the dream, physical facts such as sounds, e.g., church bells or a pistol shot. Such physical factors have been investigated carefully by the Norwegian, Mourly Vold, and also by the Frenchman, Maury. A third category is the psychological facts that can come into dreams. Psychological facts of the environment may be illustrated by the psychological problems of the parents, which appear in the dreams of the children. These most probably come into the system of the child by subliminal perceptions. Jung gave an example of a small child who dreamed that her mother was going to commit suicide—the dreamer woke up and rushed into her mother's bedroom only to discover that the mother was, in fact, attempting suicide. When we think of the time factor connected with dream elements, two more categories of sources of dream elements can be discriminated, namely, the experiences of the past and the experiences that may occur in the future. Jung has shown, particularly with children's dreams, that they often foretell the future development of the child. But future developments can also be anticipated in dreams later in life. I should like to quote one particularly impressive dream Jung observed in a middle-aged American patient. This dream came with surprising suddenness; its meaning only became clear later. The dreamer was alone in a house, it was evening and she began to close all the windows. When she went to lock the back porch door, there was no lock on the door, so she tried to push pieces of furniture against the door in order to block it against intruders. The night grew darker and darker and more and more uncanny. Suddenly the back porch door was flung open and a black sphere came in and moved forward until it had penetrated her body. The house was the patient's aunt's house in America. She had visited her aunt in that house more than twenty years before. The family was completely disrupted because of a conflict between its various members, especially with the aunt. The patient had not heard anything about the aunt for twenty years. The striking fact was that about ten days after the dream the patient received a letter from America informing her that the aunt had died at exactly the time of this dream.

In arriving at a possible meaning for a dream, several more facts must be considered. Dreams are never simple photographic reproductions of events that happened previously; there are always minor alterations made in the dream in contrast to the actual facts of the happening. In a dream where a patient perceives the doctor, the image seems to be really of the doctor as he actually looks. Upon closer inspection, however, both the dreamer and the doctor discover that a little difference can be seen so that it becomes doubtful whether the image actually means the doctor as he is, or whether the dream has not shifted the emphasis from the facts known about the doctor to some observation the dreamer made about him that had little to do with him. In other words, the image is a projection the patient has about the doctor. As far as we know, there is only one exception to the rule that dreams are never simple repetitions of previous happenings; the exception is the "shell-shock dreams," which were frequent neurotic phenomena occurring during and after World War I. In these dreams people who had been under gunfire, and had either been wounded or covered with dirt by an exploding shell, kept repeating their experience in their dreams.

It has to be borne in mind that the dream illustrates unconscious contents that may either have lost their original connection with the consciousness or may never have had any such connections. The dream may show contents of the personality that have not been uncovered in the life of the dreamer up to that time; the dream thus may portray particular qualities in the dreamer's personality which may develop in the course of time. All of these statements actually boil down to the fact that there is an autonomous factor at work in dreams, which has great freedom in portraying facts of the past, present and future, and is capable of showing things the conscious mind cannot possibly know or may have forgotten completely. I only have to remind you of certain cryptomnesias to link this statement with observations made in psychology and psychopathology.

When it comes to the matter of the technique for analyzing dreams, I need first of all to emphasize that it is almost impossible to analyze a single dream properly, and that it is much better to attempt dream analysis when a series of dreams of the same dreamer is available. There are important reasons for this. A series of dreams is usually not a sequence where one dream is the result or product of a preceding one, in such a way that A of necessity produces B and B of necessity produces C, and so on. The arrangement in a series — if there is one — is concentric; the various single dreams of a series deal with one and the same central problem, and thus group themselves around this problem. Moreover, a series of dreams gives a number of different aspects of one and the same situation in such a way that one dream gives one aspect and another dream another, so that through the series the situation becomes clear. Under analytical conditions, the interpretation of dream A may have been quite good but still not absolutely satisfying or convincing. Dream B may well add whatever has been overlooked in the interpretation of dream A, and thus make up for the lack of completeness. This characteristic of dreams to circumambulate a problem is illustrated by the behavior of an individual who is confronted with a situation about which he knows next to nothing. Think of a man lost somewhere in an unknown country or in the jungle. If he is wise, he will try to find out more about his situation by investigating the area in sections or by going around his camp in ever-widening circles. This is somewhat like the method Nature has used in describing the unknown aspect of a certain situation by giving a person news about it, through dreams, from various points of view.

Having dealt with these preliminary matters, we now can say something about the technique of the interpretation of dreams. First, it is essential to get a complete description of the actual situation of the dreamer. Then, an investigation into the preceding experiences of the dreamer in the conscious realm must be carried on. Next, it is necessary to collect what is technically called the *context*, which consists of all the associations and the material of subjective nature the dreamer is capable of contributing to the text of the dream. It may well be that if there is an archaic motif in the dream, the possible mythological or folkloristic parallels will have to be studied. (Presently we shall go into the importance of this feature.) Whenever dreams occur in the course of analysis, it may become essential not only that the analysand produce the contents of his or her conscious and, if possible, unconscious mind, but that the analyst may have to do the same thing. This is most certainly of vital importance whenever the analyst plays a part in the analysand's dream. If the situation is complicated, the analyst would need to get information of an objective nature about the dreamer's situation from other sources, such as the dreamer's wife or husband, family, and so forth.

Let us return for a moment to the necessity of producing parallels of mythological nature to the archaic motifs in the dream. This practice is typically Jungian, and its theoretical justification lies in the fact that whenever the dream is not clear, it becomes wise to use the method of amplification in order to interpret the particular motif to the point where its meaning becomes clear. The method of amplification actually rests on the fact that the meaning of a dream is not and cannot be known in advance. This is the opposite of the Freudian idea that actually we know very well what is hidden in a dream and that a dream, the meaning of which is hidden, is no more than shadow boxing. Freud thought that a dream is the guardian of sleep because the infantile tendencies of our unconscious, which are incompatible with our conscious attitude, become alive during sleep, and they have to be blurred by a dream in order not to stir us up too much and interfere with sleep. If this were so, the method used in the Freudian school would be perfectly correct, for the free association method actually is, logically speaking, a *reductio in primam figuram* [reduction to the first figure, as in Aristotelian syllogism]. The Jungian method of amplification is the exact opposite of this. It consists in practice of a technique as follows: the analyst asks the dreamer, "What comes to your mind in connection with this dream element?" Then the analyst asks again, "And what else comes to your mind with regard to this dream element?" The analyst continues to ask questions until he collects many thoughts of the dreamer, concentrating upon the one element. In other words, the element is amplified by bringing in correlated material, whereas in the free association method of Freud the first question is repeated for each answer. The answer to question A is B. So the same question is asked of B, which results in the answer C, and so on for C, D, etc. By this method the analyst leads the patient away from the original element until in the long run the final answer leads back to that original element. This is, in a way, the famous Aristotelian *anagoge* or logical reduction. In contrast, the method of amplification is closely connected with the Jungian concept of the symbol, where – as I noted earlier – the assumption is that a symbol always contains qualities unknown as well as known, qualities that transcend the ego, qualities that at the time could not possibly be known, yet must be accepted, nevertheless, as existent.

With these premises in mind, I shall return to the American patient who dreamed that he had no luck fishing for trout with the conventional equipment and, getting exasperated, picked up a three-pronged spear lying nearby and immediately speared a fish. Here are a few particulars about this patient which describe his actual conscious situation and some of his previous experiences. The patient had been a very successful American businessman – a banker – fifty-six years old. When he came to the analyst, he had been in a very serious melancholic depression for over three years and had been in various excellent American mental institutions where all possible efforts had been made to cure him. He was without any hope; he was completely paralyzed and could not really speak or listen. He was literally dragged into the analyst's consulting room by his wife, and he was quite unable to answer any of the analyst's questions. The analyst saw him once a day for twenty minutes or so, and engaged in a kind of monologue in which the analyst tried to make him see that such depressions may have some deeper meaning and that it would be particularly helpful if he would tell of his dreams. But as he never answered any of the analyst's questions and appeared completely unimpressed by the analyst's words, he was always dismissed after a relatively short period of time. After about one week of this rather one-sided conversation, his wife told the analyst that he had had a dream and that she had written it down for him; it was the dream quoted earlier. From then on, the patient had one dream each night for more than a week, at the end of which time he was cured and remained cured for the rest of his life. The outcome of this entitles us to attribute a major importance to the dream. We have to think of the connection between the *lysis* [dissolution] of the dream and the cure, for it appears that the dream made a forecast of the cure. In order to understand how such a thing is conceivable, it will be helpful to use the amplification method, particularly with regard to one item in the dream. First, however, I want to say a few things about other elements in the dream. Fishing had been the patient's hobby, but the hobby no longer seemed satisfactory as he did not succeed in catching any fish; the reservoir divided into compartments was a peculiar place, not only because it was not a usual arrangement but also because the water was stagnant. The stagnation was a very apt description of his paralysis. The various compartments meant that everything in life was neatly divided up and concealed; that is an illustration of what we call *compartment psychology*. But then something unusual happened, unusual for his present state or frame of mind. He became exasperated. This was an emotional reaction that took place spontaneously; it was connected with a faint realization of his inadequacy in respect to his situation. The literal meaning of the word *emotion* means *to be moved out of* something, in that case, I would say, out of his paralysis. When he got emotional—exasperated, as he put it—there was a connection with his perception of the three-pronged spear. This was the culmination of the dream, which brought in an entirely new element. The inference was that the spear had always been there but he had not seen it. Immediately after he became excited he did see it, and the *lysis* followed as a matter of course in the spearing of the fine specimen of trout. I consider the three-pronged spear to be the famous trident of Poseidon, or Neptune. I will show the importance of this by using the amplification method; the importance comes because the image provides an explanation for the fact that this was a healing dream. The *triaina*, Poseidon's spear, is the main attribute of this Greek god. In other words, it *is* this god himself. Who is this god, then? He has a great many qualities, which have to be found in amplificatory material. It is interesting to read what Homer has to say in the *Iliad*:[11]

Windswift Iris of the fleet foot obeyed these orders promptly and set out from Mount Ida for sacred Ilium, dropping in her eager haste like the snow or chilling hail that falls from the clouds when a squall comes down from the bitter North. She went straight up to the great Earth-shaker and said: "Girdler of the World, god of the Sable Locks, I have come here with a message for you from aegis-bearing Zeus. He commands you to stop fighting, to retire from the field, and to rejoin the other gods or withdraw into your own sacred sea. If you disregard his explicit commands, he threatens that he too will come here in person to take the field against you. And he warns you not to come to grips with him, maintaining that he is by far the strongest god as well as your senior by birth. Not that that appears to deter you, he says, from claiming equality with him, of whom the other gods all stand in dread."

The great Earthshaker was infuriated. "This is outrageous!" he cried. "Zeus may be powerful, but it is sheer bluster on his part to talk of forcing me, who enjoys the same prestige as he does, to bend my will to his. There are three of us Brothers, all Sons of Cronos and Rhea: Zeus, myself, and Hades the King of the Dead. Each of us was given his own domain when the world was divided into three parts. We cast lots and I received the grey sea as my inalienable realm. Hades drew the nether dark, while Zeus was allotted the broad sky and a home among the clouds in the upper air. But the earth was left common to all of us, and high Olympus too. So I am not going to let Zeus have his way with me. Powerful as he is, let him stay quietly in his own third of the world. And do not let him try to scare me with threats of violence, as though I were an arrant coward. He would do better to give his own Sons and Daughters a piece of his mind. He is their Father, and they will have to listen when he orders them about."

"Girdler of the World, god of the Sable Locks," said wind-swift Iris of the fleet foot, "do you really wish me to convey Zeus this contumacious and peremptory reply? Will you not change your mind? It is a mark of excellence to relent. And you know how the Avenging Furies always support an elder brother."

"Lady Iris," said Poseidon the Earthshaker, "you are right in what you say. How excellent it also is for an ambassador to show discretion! But it galls me, it cuts me to the quick to be bullied and scolded by a

---

11. Homer, *Iliad*, 15, 189ff.

god with whom Fate has decreed that I should share the world on equal terms. However, I will give in now, though not without resentment. But let me add a word of warning about my own feelings. If Zeus, against my wishes and those of the Warrior Athene, of Hera, of Hermes and of my Lord Hephaestus, spares the citadel of Ilium and will not have it sacked, giving the Argives a resounding victory, let him know that there will be an irreparable breach between us two."

With that the Earthshaker left the Achaean army, much to the regret of those gallant men, and withdrew into the sea.

Poseidon is the brother of Zeus, Hades and Hera. When they divided the world among themselves, Poseidon got the sea, Zeus heaven, and Hades the underworld. They are equals inasmuch as all three of them have the whole cosmos and rule it. Poseidon, more particularly, is the god of earthquakes; he produces earthquakes by driving his trident into the earth. With such an act, the whole globe shakes. Poseidon is not only destructive, however; he is creative inasmuch as each time he uses his trident something creative happens, such as the welling up of a spring (e.g., Hippokrene) or the opening up of a valley (e.g., the Hellespont and the Bosphorus or the Peneus in Thessaly). Besides this, Poseidon is the god of storms. He also is a stormy lover, and has affairs with all sorts of creatures producing many offspring, so that he is creative also in this sense. He is the god of the earth and as such is responsible for fertility, in particular plant fertility; he is in that respect called *georgos*, worker of the earth. He is a horseman par excellence and created the first horse by using his trident. Then he is called γενέθλιος (*Genethlios*), the father of men, particularly the Ionians, and as such the father of the tribe and its protector. He has a number of other qualities, of minor importance: he is an oracle god in Delphi, and he is a doctor, the father of the two famous doctors in the *Iliad*, Machaon and Podaleirios. From all these attributes we can see that he is a creative god, and the trident is his main creative instrument. As such, it has a typically phallic connotation. I want to point out in this connection that the *phallos* in the Greek sense is never conceived of as being a symbol in the Freudian sense of meaning only a *sema* [sign] for the male organ, but that it means a real *symbol* in the Jungian sense, pointing to the power of creation in nature, which far from being understood, appears to possess a mystical quality. This amplification of the trident as *deus ex machina* gives us a much better chance to understand why the appearance of this divine element in the dream was found to have such an obviously healing effect.

Now, because it is difficult to analyze one single dream correctly, and to say something conclusive about dreams, unless we have a whole series of dreams which can be cross-examined and checked against each other, I will present one or two more dreams of this same dreamer. Here is the text of the second dream, which took place the second night:

The dream began as I dropped my eyeglasses and broke them. I immediately got into a Ford and drove off towards the optician's office (I never drive automobiles myself in conscious life). On the way I saw an old man, a respected friend and advisor of mine. I asked him to come with me, which he did. On the journey to see the optician, I told the old man of my worries and difficulties and received from him much good advice.

Now I should like to compare the two dreams in respect to motifs. The dropping and breaking of his eyeglasses represents a conflict; it can be likened to his unsuccessful fishing in the first dream. The glasses, in this case, were broken, and that created a tension or an impasse comparable to the emotion appearing in the first dream. At the impasse in this dream he got into a car that was close at hand. The car had a similar function to the trident in the first dream: it came to his help, to his rescue. He began to be astonishingly active compared to the absolute passivity he displayed in his depression (shown by the remark he made that in conscious life he never drove automobiles himself — he always had a chauffeur). Thus we can say that he got into motion — he became emotional, as it were. While the automobile was driven by him, it is something that moves autonomously, not by conscious forces but by forces of a different sort. I noted that Poseidon was a great horseman and charioteer; the automobile can be compared to Neptune's chariot, driven by his horses. The man the dreamer wants to see, the optician, who is to mend his broken glasses, is in some way an allegory of the analyst, whereas the old friend he met and whom he called a respected friend and advisor would be like the "wise old man." The friend and advisor, however, corresponds to the fish he caught in the first dream, inasmuch as the fish was the solution, the *lysis* of the dream. In the second dream the *lysis* was the good advice he received from his friend. With regard to this advisor I should like to come back to Poseidon who is the ἅλιος γέρων (*halios geron*), the old man of the sea, and who has many of the qualities of the advisor in the old myths. As I said, Poseidon was an oracle god and a doctor, and he was also related to the fish. From these two qualities, I arrived at the conclusion that the old man advisor whom the patient met was closely connected with the Poseidon figure, thus closely connected with the fish in the first dream. Again I should say that the fish, as well as the old friend, both came to him spontaneously. In the first dream he seized upon the possibility given to him by Poseidon in such a way that something was achieved or came to him, or came back to him, which had hitherto been lost. In this sense, we have to interpret the fish in the first dream as a typical libido symbol, and from the epicrisis of the case we know that this libido actually did come back to him shortly after he had the first dream. When I said that the wise old man of the second dream was parallel to the fish of the first dream, I was reminded of another parallel which I find very interesting, and which precedes the passage from the 18th Sura of the Koran which I quoted earlier. This time it is verses 60-64, the scene where Moses and Joshua meet Khidder or Alkadhir:

Moses said to his servant: "I will journey on until I reach the land where the two seas meet, though I may march for ages."

But when at last they came to the land where the two seas met, they forgot their fish, which made its way into the water, swimming at will.

And when they had journeyed farther on, Moses said to his servant: "Bring us some food; we are worn out with travelling."

"Know," replied the other, "that I forgot the fish when we were resting on the rock. Thanks to Satan, I forgot to mention this. The fish made its way into the sea in a miraculous fashion."

"This is what we have been seeking," said Moses. They went back the way they came and found one of Our servants to whom We had vouchsafed our mercy and whom We had endowed with knowledge of Our own. Moses said to him: "May I follow you so that you may guide me by that which you have been taught?"

When the text says "this is what we have been seeking," it means that the loss of the fish is a sign that they have found the man they were seeking, Alkadhir, the reputed vizier of Dhulkarnein, also known as the two-horned (which is another name for Alexander the Great). He is said to have drunk of the fountain of life by virtue of which he still lives and will continue to live till the Day of Judgment. He is said to appear clad in green robes (hence his name, Khidder, "the green one") to Moslems in distress, and he promises longevity. One of his outstanding qualities is that he is a very good friend of Dhulkarnein and, therefore, a friend and advisor of Moslems in general. As advisor he reveals divine secrets to his friends, and he is to be met on the road as they hike along. This is exactly what happened to our dreamer; he met his friend and advisor on the road. Alkadhir is likened also to Elijah who was immortal and who went to heaven on a fiery wagon. Khidder, by the way, still has a maritime character with the Mohammedans; in the folklore he is called the Khawwad-al-buhur – "the one who traverses the seas" – and as such is the patron of the sailors who still sacrifice to him when a new boat is launched. The loss of the fish in the Sura quoted would correspond to the loss of the instinctual soul or of the psychic energy in the dreamer of our case, which accounts for his being so tired and so depressed. The fish he catches in the first dream would then be the opposite, namely the new life gained, or rebirth.

In the myth of the Australian aborigenes, the *aljiranga-mijina*, the fish in its archetypal aspect, is thought to be the animal ancestor of the tribe or, in other words, the totem animal of the tribe, just as Poseidon is the ancestor of the Ionians.

The return of energy in the psychological sense was indicated over and over again in the series of dreams the patient had. I shall give only three more examples. The fifth dream said: "In this dream I went to the railway station, apparently the Hauptbahnhof in Zürich, to receive a large amount of money, which had to be taken from the station to one of the banks. I made several trips but before doing so I arranged for a guard to follow me on the street, keeping a little way behind me. After one or two trips I glanced around and I could not see the guard, so I quickly turned around and went back to the station. Then I found the guard sitting down on a comfortable bench in a small park. I accused him of neglecting his duty; I was quite bitter in my remarks to him. His only reply was that the arrangement was foolish since there was no danger of anyone in Zürich attacking me." In the seventh dream he said: "I was standing on Fifth Avenue in New York City watching the return of the Rainbow Division from the Great War. I saw many old friends in the marching troops. After the parade had ended several of us met for dinner. Among the party was a very humorous officer who made prophecies about our future. Some of his remarks were very funny – but he did not get to prophesy my future before the dream ended."

At the end of this whole series, he had the following dream: "I went to the home of the great male eels somewhere in the South Atlantic. I watched billions of eels starting home and could see them in the water as far as the horizon." The homing of the eels is one of the most astonishing phenomena in nature. Some of the many eels stop feeding in the autumn and become silvery; then these silver eels descend to the sea and travel across the Atlantic to breed in an area southeast of Bermuda; they die after breeding. Larvae called *Leptocephali*, which are transparent, travel back to Europe in the course of two and a half years' time. It has been proven that these larvae find their way back to the same waters from which their long-dead parents came when they started on their honeymoon trip to the Bermudas. In view of this fact we may safely draw the conclusion from these dreams that the instinct is infallible and energy will find its way back to the dreamer in due course.

IV. PSYCHOLOGY AND RELIGION

It may be out of place for me to apologize for dealing with this subject, but there are one or two reasons for doing so. William James dealt with the variety of religious experience as a psychologist and was a pioneer in the subject. C. G. Jung dealt with the same topic some thirty-five years later in his Terry lectures at Yale. Thus two of the most competent people have dealt with this theme, and I expect that their work is well known. I am not able to speak as competently as they did. Another reason for making my apologies is that I am a dilettante in one of the two parts of the theme, the theological. On the other hand, there are grounds that give me some assurance as I proceed. In analysis, and particularly in Jungian analysis, religious problems appear very clearly. And then for nearly twenty years I had been dealing with the institution of incubation as it was practiced in Greek and Roman times, so I have been highly occupied with the irrational or the religious aspect of healing. When I studied the records of this incubation rite, I came across the fact that in the Hellenistic period and later on in Christian times, people who devoted themselves to the cult of a certain deity were called θεραπευτής (*therapeutēs*) [servant, worshipper], which is our modern word *therapist*. Today analysts are called *psychotherapists*, which means people devoted to the cult of the psyche. Although the psyche is no longer a goddess in our day, the Latin equivalent of the Greek word *anima*, meaning soul, is considered to be of semi-divine nature. When Tertullian spoke of the *anima naturaliter christiana* [naturally Christian soul], it is doubtful that he was convinced that the human soul is naturally Christian. If human nature were said to be Christian, the statement would logically lead to pantheism, which is not Christian.

Jung in his work discovered what he calls a religious factor in nature. He found it in dreams, and dreams are products of nature. On this basis it appears that there is such a thing as a religious instinct. Theologians may be deeply disappointed or scandalized by such a statement since it appears to be a new version of the old medical materialism of William James. In 1901 and 1902 William James showed that the idea that various religious phenomena are "nothing but" the effects of certain chemical changes in a person was in no way satisfactory. Such is certainly not Jung's idea. When he said that there is a religious instinct innate in man, he was not speaking in terms of medical materialism. Since 1912 when he published *Symbols of Transformation*, and more particularly since 1937 when he gave the Terry lectures, he has provided evidence for the fact that the religious factor is something *sui generis* – that it exists in the same way as other instincts exist, which means that they cannot be reduced to anything more elementary.

In Greek antiquity there was the belief that dreams are *somnia a deo missa*, that is, dreams sent by God. The idea that man's soul or unconscious serves, under certain conditions, as the door through which the divine or religious element is capable of reaching his conscious mind has always been believed. If man's soul has a divine spark in it, or in other words if it participates in any way in the realm that transcends the conscious self, it is a ready-made instrument for that purpose. There are certainly other channels to the transcendent realm; records from the past are full of instances and ways in which man has participated in this realm. Aldous Huxley's *The Perennial Philosophy* and William James's *Varieties of Religious Experience* give many examples of the different ways such phenomena take place. To deny the possibility of a variety of ways by which man is related to the transcendent is either to place a limitation on the religious factor or a limitation on the functions of the human soul or psyche, in particular the unconscious psyche. This suggests why in the Freudian system there is no room for an autonomous religious function. In Freud's system the unconscious and its products are looked upon as being only a façade, so that they always have to be reduced to more basic roots or elements. Consequently, the Freudian system has to be understood as an impressive yet effective method for doing away with the unconscious. Unconscious products have to be unmasked because they never mean what they appear to mean, and a person who has undergone such a treatment will feel liberated from many useless, silly, and superstitious preoccupations.

Jung said that he never really cured a patient in the second half of life unless, in the course of the treatment, that person found access to the religious function. As this statement was made as a result of Jung's vast experience, we simply are compelled to believe it. The difficulty is that the two concepts – the healing of the patient and the religious factor *sui generis* – are not clearly defined. For this reason, if we are to advance our understanding of the subject, we must investigate further.

The concept of the healing or the cure is complicated. In order to illustrate how complicated it may be, I use the case of a neurosis with a simple, clear-cut symptom, with which I was involved during the early years of my private practice. During the second year of my practice as a psychotherapist, I was consulted by a man who suffered from impotence. The man bored me intensely. When he told his story, I discovered that he was absolutely uneducated and completely stupid. I realized that it would be impossible for me to have a decent discussion with him; I let him talk on, and at the end of an hour's interview I dismissed him with a few palliative words. I never saw him again. But from that time on, at regular intervals of one year, five other men came to consult me for the same complaint. When the last one came, I decided that I was going to find out what the strange coincidence was all about, so I asked this man how he happened to have come to me. He replied that when he told a friend of his physical disability, the friend suggested that he see Dr. Meier in Züric¹ since he cured him of the same thing in one session and subsequently did the same for four other men whom he knew. Such an experience presents quite a problem. It might be said that the cures which took place in five of those men were due to suggestion, so that my fame as a miracle-working doctor was really the cause. That would not account, however, for the cure of the first man.

As another illustration of the complexity of a cure, we may be reminded that many patients who consult a doctor for this or that neurotic symptom and are cured, sooner or later begin to develop what is called a transference; that is, for those patients, the analyst begins to represent the "Healer" with a capital H. The doctor may be tempted to make it clear to his patient that he is not the healer and that the idea that he is is an illusion, but such a means of dealing with the matter will not work. It is absolutely essential for the doctor to take the projection very seriously and actually make it a major issue in his subsequent work. The point here is that in mental illness it is practically impossible to combat the sickness. Instead, the analyst, by going along with the sickness, engages in the process at work in the patient. The doctor learns that the sickness is something of what the ancients called a "divine sickness." Yet this appears to suggest the age-old belief that sickness not only is a punishment but also, if it is approached in the right way, can lead to a change of the old being or to an entirely different existence. However, a neurosis can no longer be explained causally, as resulting from a lack of the religious factor. If that were the case, pious people would never be neurotic, which is not true. This theoretical conclusion, confirmed by practical experience, shows that the religious factor cannot be introduced by medical means in such a way as to do away with the neurosis.

Freud is right in many cases in assuming that a neurosis can be causally traced to conflicts of early childhood, and that shows there is no religious problem involved. If it were possible to proceed by introducing the religious factor as a substitution for the illness, the implication would be that a whole neurotic or psychotic condition had actually developed from the beginning in order to compel the patient to accept the religious demand. This would be to declare that the sickness as such was unreal and only a neurotic arrangement in Adler's sense. Not only would the sickness in this way be degraded to something completely wrong, thus devoid of any deeper meaning, but it would also suggest that all sickness is only a neurotic arrangement imposed on a person, and that is a contradiction in fact. From this contradiction alone the conclusion must follow that what actually is hidden behind the sickness is the neurosis as an *unknown* complex. This is further shown by Jung's assertion that a real cure is reached only after the religious factor has been assimilated, for this takes place only after a long period of work. Because so much time and effort are involved in order to bring about the realization of the existence of the religious factor, the factor itself must then be unconscious.

This reminds me of a remark Jung once made: "The astonishing fact about the unconscious is that it is really unconscious," which means that it cannot be reduced to anything well known. Consequently, it would be methodologically wrong if, in view of Jung's finding that the religious factor is indispensable to a cure, a doctor were to try *à tout prix* to extricate it like the Manichean spark of light out of the unconscious matter. This would be a *petitio principii* [begging the question] and would be wrong for many reasons, the most important of these being that an analyst who was prejudiced in such a way would never be capable of dealing adequately with a manifold variety of cases. A person who used his own panacea could never be an analyst, as in his work with other people he would only prove the reality of his own monomania, and thus project his own complex onto everybody and everything. Moreover, since the religious factor is subjective reality, and since a person needs this factor in order to be cured, he must discover it himself as the result of his own personal research and effort. In the effort, the analyst can accompany him carefully and in a subtle way, for only in such a way will his discovery have the necessary convincing quality. The analyst can accompany the patient in this search only if he has made the journey himself. If the search is successful, that would point to the fact that the discovery of the religious element is the product of the sickness and the treatment. Such a result can be expected only on condition that the analyst and the patient ask about the purpose of the suffering.

Many religious people used to think of disease or a stroke of bad luck as something sent by God. I should think that such an idea makes more sense than the idea that bad luck or disease is caused by blind fate or by the stars. Even so, to believe that God sends diseases is to believe in a god who plays a rather dubious part in life. This was the idea men had of Jahweh in the old days. He kills and cures; He is the one who says in (Vulgate) Isaiah 45:67: "Ego dominus et non est alter faciens bonum et creans malum" [I am the Lord and there is none other who both does good and creates evil]. But the same was true of Apollo, and even of the Christian God up to the Baroque period; the statues of God portrayed Him sending plagues with bows and arrows. In antiquity there is also the healing god who is himself sick or wounded; this motif is closely connected with that of the poison as medicine, or the weapon which serves as the cure. In Richard Wagner's *Parsifal*, "only the spear that cleft can close the wound."

Such mythologems cannot be explained rationally as threats used by priests: "God made you ill, so restore your faith and he will cure you in gratitude." Patients are usually more sophisticated than that. They would be inclined to accept the explanation that the sickness is something self-inflicted. This would also be a rationalistic or causalistic conception, however. Psychologists have learned that there is no such simple connection between *causa morbi* [cause of disease] and the medicine. To know this is important from the point of view of mental hygiene for the following reason: if it were possible for a person to make himself sick and also to cure himself, he would be like one of the gods who have both powers. This god-likeness would be a very dangerous thing inasmuch as it would show that the person not only had a neurosis but that he also had some kind of a megalomania.

The goal of the integration of the religious factor can be reached when a creative use has been made of the disease, in other words, when the disease has not only been successfully combatted, but when it has been made a meaningful part of the patient's life. This is not a simple thing to achieve, for it is not easy to understand the deeper meaning of a neurosis. To speak of a deeper meaning amounts philosophically to speaking of the *causa finalis*. Psychiatrists are much more in danger of being impressed with the nonsense mental diseases produce, so that it is difficult for them to see sense in such things. This continues to be true even after Jung's discovery, because by applying the Jungian technique the psychiatrist can understand what the patient wants to say, but the strange, bizarre style the patient uses, and the reason why the patient seems compelled to express himself so enigmatically, remain unexplained. It is interesting to note that in the few papers in which Jung wrote about the psychology and psychotherapy of schizophrenia, he said that those diseases have the same function as other mental disturbances, namely that they are a pushing through into consciousness of collective unconscious material, and that as such they are equivalent to a compensatory reaction of the unconscious, compensatory with regard to the conscious attitude or Weltanschauung. If this is so, it is necessary to work with schizophrenic patients constructively, so that the destructive demons may be changed into something really creative and the patients may be helped to build a new personality. In recent days much has been said about the analytic treatment of schizophrenics, but as far as I know, such a view with regard to the cure has never been mentioned. The *telos*, or meaning of the disease, does not seem to worry the psychiatrists who deal with the treatment of schizophrenics; they seem to be satisfied with the causalistic-reductive interpretation of their cures.

Personally, I have had limited experience with the analytic treatment of schizophrenics, and all my cases date from the early thirties when there was little known about the subject. Nonetheless, I would like to quote one of my cases. At the time, I was a young intern at the psychiatric clinic of Zürich University, the Burghölzli, and in my early years of analysis with Jung. I was very enthusiastic and eventually took a few patients who were typical schizophrenics into analysis. The case I report was that of a young man who had been confined for seven years. When I took on his ward, my predecessor warned me never to approach him because he was so aggressive and dangerous. He was a catatonic schizophrenic who stood in the corner of his room, practically immovable, for almost twenty-four hours a day. When I first saw him I could not believe that condition because in the patient's eyes there was a certain warmth and human expression that did not fit with the rest of his appearance. When I visited him the next day, I went up to him and stretched out my hand to shake hands with him; to my astonishment he immediately reacted, took my hand and held it for some time, although he did not say anything. The next day I took him to my room. This created tremendous excitement among the hospital personnel. However, the visit went well; I talked to him and he began to talk, which he had not done for years. He told me his problem, which was that there was a cleft between the two halves of his brain. The right and the left half were separated and the left half consisted of silver ore whereas the right one consisted of coal. This fact, he said, accounted for his condition. In the course of the next few days he continued telling me about his delusional system. I took him out to the park, went for walks with him, and discussed this system and his dreams. After a few days what you would call an analytical situation was created. A day or two later he told me that something had happened in his brain, that in the cleft between the right and the left halves a blue flower had started to grow. Strangely enough, from that moment on, the patient could be regarded as cured. He was soon dismissed from the clinic. Eight years later I met him on the street. He looked extremely well; he told me all that had happened since we had seen each other last. He had worked regularly. He introduced me to a young lady who he said was his fiancée. Upon taking leave of me he said, "Well, Doctor, if I hadn't lived through this, I wouldn't believe what good can come from such a disease." The way in which he said this and the expression on his face made absolutely clear that he had been capable of assimilating the whole psychotic experience in a creative way, that he was deeply grateful for the experience, and that he was looking at it in a religious way. I was convinced that the man was cured, that he was healed, a word synonymous with "whole." I was reminded of Saint Ignatius of Antioch who said in the *Epistle to the Romans* 6:2: "Once arrived there I shall be a man" – ἄνθρωπος ἔσομαι (*anthropos esomai*). Using the mythologem contained in Apollodorus who gave the text of an oracle of Apollo: "ὁ τρώσας ἰάσεται (*ho trosas iasetai*) [he who wounds will also cure], I would say that the catatonic schizophrenia of my patient was at the same time his specific remedy. The disease acquired the dignity of medicine. This is the old homeopathic conviction of *similia similibus curantur* [like cures like], where the poison is the remedy. There is a tremendous psychological problem involved in this, and it is hard for analysts to learn that the principle of this *trosas iasetai* actually has to be carried to its extreme in some cases – the extreme being that the patient becomes the doctor and the doctor the patient. About this paradoxical situation I will have more to say later.

To speak of a patient as becoming whole calls to mind another rather puzzling statement made in the texts of ancient incubation rituals which sounds rather pagan. According to the ancient idea, the two concepts of νόσος (*nosos*) and πενία (*penia*) are practically synonymous – *nosos* meaning disease and *penia*, poverty – likewise ὑγίεια (*hygieia*) and πλοῦτος (*ploutos*) are synonymous – *hygieia* meaning health and *ploutos*, plenty. In Swiss German, when we ask a patient what he is suffering from, we say, literally, "What is it you are lacking of?" which is exactly *penia*. Correspondingly, a man who is healthy has plenty, πλοῦτος (*ploutos*), he is whole. In the ancient temple medicine, *theurgic medicine*, there was only one possibility of cure: that the god who wounded or sent disease or was himself diseased or wounded, personally interfered. A divine intercession always took place when the patient in the temple of Asklepios was cured. Recall the dream of my American patient in which Poseidon made an epiphany in the guise of his trident, and the cure took place almost immediately after that epiphany. For many years writers and others have thought that in the old theurgic clinics in antiquity there was a medical staff. This is definitely wrong. The cures were irrational and exclusively religious. There was no causal therapy whatsoever. Instead of the principle of causality, there was a principle of analogy, the same principle upon which later homeopathy rests, *similia similibus curantur*. When it comes to the question of the integration of the religious factor as being a *conditio sine qua non* of the cure, there is a parallel in antiquity where the patient who has been cured in the temple of Asklepios has to make an offering to the god in such a way that he is related to the god for good. From then on the ex-patient is known as a *"religiosus."* It is significant to see that through the millennia certain correspondences regarding the criteria of healing remain the same.

Now we will look at the Poseidon dream in light of the compensatory function of dreams and note how that applies. The dreamer was in an apathetic condition and was not capable of any strong psychological reaction. In the dream he got "exasperated" — in other words, emotional (*emotio* means "to be moved out of" something) — and sought release from the paralysis, whereupon he immediately realized that he was given the instrument he needed, the trident. In such a way the compensatory meaning becomes quite clear. The patient only had to let himself be sufficiently annoyed by his state of inefficiency and the help appeared. I would not insist that this dream is in any obvious way bringing in a religious theme or motif, but I would note that the helpful element in the dream was represented in a divine attribute, even though it was a pagan one. It may not be merely coincidental that the help came first by a pagan or ancient motif. We might ask ourselves why the help did not appear in the Christian way of the miraculous Draught of Fishes, which is a motif of venerable age. All we can say is that obviously a still further regression was needed in order to let the patient finally find access to his energy and make it possible for him to catch the content of the stagnating condition of his unconscious, the fish which he will be able to assimilate, to eat, to integrate into his own system. In the end, the patient did catch the fish, as you will remember.

I need also to point out that the use of an obviously pagan symbol instead of a Christian one can be explained by the principle of compensation, because what the patient needed most was a more emotional, more primitive, more instinctual reaction. In any case, I would maintain that the trident must be regarded as a divine intercession, if only for the absolutely decisive part it played in the cure of the disease. Only the later development of the case could show whether the patient was able to relate to this divine element and in such a way develop a religious attitude. This does not mean that he would be a church goer, but simply that he would rightfully claim for himself the ancient term *religiosus*. Such an effect can be observed rather frequently, which is why Jung made the statement that he had never really cured a patient until the patient had found access to the religious function within.

Returning to the concept of compensation in the Jungian

sense, I think that what it really means is that the unconscious products, as soon as they have been assimilated into the conscious system, counterbalance insufficient or wrong conclusions or actions of the conscious mind in such a way that a balance or an equilibrium is produced.

I want to discuss the concept of compensation at some length because it has given rise to many misunderstandings. Compensation can be likened to what is nowadays well known from cybernetics as the *regulating circuit*, which is a device used in automation. This analogy can also be applied to certain biological actions, in particular to what used to be called a self-regulating system, but this serves only for a time in connection with the conscious system, for the border of that is soon reached. Norbert Wiener, the father of cybernetics, makes this clear in his book, *The Human Use of Human Beings*, in which he makes fun of the purely rationalistic attempts to explain the higher functions of consciousness by saying, "To them there is no God and Marx is his prophet."[12] As soon as there is a duality of conscious and unconscious, the analogy will not always work. In all the cases where something is lacking in the patient's system, it could be conceived that the lack would be made up by the self-regulating process in the psyche. But such a process would only be a quantitative one and consequently would have to be called complementary rather than compensatory. A complement may be illustrated by the way an answer to a question is found: by increasing one's knowledge, by more experience, or by having an expert—a doctor or what have you—tell you the answer. This seems to be the case in almost all of the problems with which Freud or Adler dealt. I must point out, however, that the general opinion regarding Adler's point of view is not quite correct. The popular belief seems to be that Adler's point of view is a finalistic one, e.g., what a person gains by his neurosis is supposed to explain its existence. Thus a successful analysis would make it impossible for the patient to stick to his fictitious goal, which would amount to the dissolution of the problem and thus be the cure of the neurosis. In my view this amounts to the correct solu-

---

12. Norbert Wiener, *The Human Use of Human Beings: Cybernetics and Society* (London, 1950).

tion given as the "output" of the computer, called analysis, as against the wrong one which the patient gave himself before he came to analysis and in support of which he needed the neurosis. Inasmuch as the true answer in such an Adlerian case is already contained in the system from the beginning, but is simply not wanted by the ego, this answer is not really finalistic—rather it seems to be identical with the cybernetic model. Philosophy would call this *immanent teleology*, which would correspond to the principle of the regulating circuit. Over against this *immanent teleology*, the concept of compensation in Jung's sense would be one of *transcendent teleology*.

The knowledge gained from observing the contents of the unconscious in Jungian analysis has to be applied to the conscious system, as the patient thinks about the elements and discusses them. Jung has shown that if this method is applied ruthlessly, it is possible to see that not only the conscious mind is changed but the unconscious as well, and this interplay begins to produce a new phenomenon, which Jung called the *individuation process*. This development has a *telos*, a goal. It could not have been guessed either from the neurosis or from the patient, but it could have been prefigured long before its realization in a symbolic way; it could be known that the goal was the totality or rather the completeness of the human personality. Earlier I noted that completeness, wholeness, is synonymous with healing, and this with the "holy." It is to be expected that the moment such a symbol of wholeness appears, something of the religious function is at the same time given in experience, since the religious belongs to wholeness of the human personality. Only retrospectively can it be seen that this goal, this *telos*, was a *causa finalis*; nor could this *causa finalis* be found had not the *theorema* of compensation been applied consecutively. The subjective experience connected with a religious phenomenon and with healing is actually one of transcendence, and this transcendence is a new element not in the system from the beginning. At this point I remind you of the dream of the Dutch psychologist, which is an excellent example of a dream wherein the symbol of totality of the human personality appears. This symbol is usually called a *mandala* in Jungian terminology, from the Sanskrit word for circle. In this case the mandala was certainly a very particular one. The symbolism of that mandala was strikingly similar to a dream Jung described and commented upon in his Terry lectures, *Psychology and Religion*. I quote what he has to say about that dream since his words apply almost literally to our case. My patient's dream came two years before Jung's Terry lectures, and my patient was a different type of a person from Jung's patient. The common denominator of the two is that they both had an extremely well-developed intuition. Here is the text of the vision:

There is a vertical and a horizontal circle with a center common to both. This is the world clock. It is carried by the black bird. (The patient refers here to a preceding vision, where a black eagle had carried away a golden ring.) The vertical circle is a blue disk with a white rim, divided into $4 \times 8 = 32$ partitions. A hand is rotating upon it. The horizontal circle consists of four colors. Four little men are standing upon the circle carrying pendula and the golden ring (of the former vision) is laid around it. The world clock has three rhythms or pulses:

1. The small pulse: the hand of the blue vertical disk moves one thirty-second ($^1/_{32}$) at a time.

2. The middle pulse is one complete rotation of the hand. At the same time the horizontal circle moves on by one thirty-second.

3. The great pulse: thirty-two middle pulses are equal to one complete rotation of the golden ring.

And now let me quote part of Jung's commentary on this dream:

It is, of course, difficult to understand why a feeling of "most sublime harmony" should be produced by this abstract structure. But if we think of the two circles in Plato's *Timaeus*, and of the harmonious all-roundedness of his anima mundi, we might find an avenue leading to an understanding. Again, the term *world clock* suggests the antique conception of the musical harmony of the spheres. It would be a sort of cosmological system. If it were a vision of the firmament and its silent rotation, or of the steady movement of the solar system, we would readily understand and appreciate the perfect harmony of the picture. We might also assume that the platonic vision of the cosmos was finally glimmering through the mist of a semiconscious mental condition. But there is something in the vision that does not quite agree with the harmonious perfection of the platonic picture. The two circles are different in nature. Not only is their movement different, but their color, too. The vertical circle is blue and the horizontal one containing four colors is golden. The blue circle might easily symbolize the blue hemisphere of the sky, while the horizontal circle would represent the horizon with the four cardinal points, personified by the four little men and characterized by the four colors. (In a former dream, the four points were represented once by four children and again by the four seasons.) This picture reminds one immediately of medieval representations of the world in the form of a circle or of the *rex gloriae* with the four evangelists or of the melothesiae, where the horizon is formed by the zodiac. The representation of the triumphant Christ seems to be derived from similar pictures of Horus and his four sons. There are also Eastern analogies: the Buddhistic mandalas or circles, usually of Tibetan origin. They consist as a rule of a circular padma or lotus which contains a square sacred building with four gates, indicating the four cardinal points and the seasons. The center contains a Buddha or more often the conjunction of Shiva and his Shakti or an equivalent dorje (thunderbolt) symbol. They are yantras or instruments of ritual for the purpose of contemplation, concentration and the final transformation of the yogin's consciousness into the divine all consciousness. No matter how striking these analogies are, they are not satisfactory, because they all emphasize the center to such an extent that they seem to have been made in order to express the importance of the central figure. In our case, however, the center is empty. It consists only of a mathematical point. The parallels mentioned depict the world-creating or world-ruling deity, or else man in his dependence upon the celestial constellations. Our symbol is a clock, symbolizing time. The only analogy to such a symbol that I can think of is the design of the horoscope. It also has four cardinal points and an empty center. There is, moreover, another peculiar coincidence: rotation is often mentioned in the previous dreams and this is usually reported as moving to the left. The horoscope has twelve houses that progress to the left, that is, counterclockwise.

From the motif discernible in my patient's dream and from Jung's remarks on the dream of his patient, it is clear that we are dealing with a typical symbol for the totality of the personality. In my patient it was clearly a prefiguration of this totality, for outside of this system there was the figure of the anima who pointed at the system as if she were calling the dreamer's attention to the symbol, pointing in a way that deeply impressed the dreamer. This is the role of the mystagogue—naturally enough, this part fits the nature or the function of the anima very well. Such mandalas play an important part in Christian iconography, but they are not limited to this religion, for they are found in practically every known religious system. Jung found such a structure with the first patient he had, the girl who was the subject matter for his doctoral thesis. At that time Jung ventured the idea that the structure was a prefiguration of the totality of the personality which was not then understood. In most of the known religious mandalas, the center is usually occupied by a symbol or the figure of a god. This is not so in the Taoistic or Lamaistic mandalas, particularly the Tibetan ones, where the center is occupied by the *great void*, an empty space. One might be tempted to conclude that a structure without the representation of a god in it is empty in the religious sense of the word, but this is most certainly not so, at least not subjectively in the individual case. The contrary actually is true, for the dreamers are always very deeply impressed by what Rudolf Otto called the numinosity of this image or vision. The numinous belongs to the few most characteristic qualities of a religious experience, and whenever a patient is as deeply shaken by a vision as was the case with the Dutch psychologist, the assumption can be made that the religious element has expressed itself in such an image.

In thinking of this matter, we must not be prejudiced by any particular religious way or creed because, as I pointed out before, the imagery that may appear may not be orthodox or dogmatic. Quite the contrary, for if it were orthodox it could be traced back to known contents of the consciousness and thus would not be a living symbol. A symbol, according to the Jungian definition, always contains elements that are known, and more importantly, elements that cannot be reduced to known facts. We can go so far as to say that a symbol that contains only conscious elements is no longer alive; it is a dead symbol inasmuch as all its contents have already been integrated into consciousness and, consequently, it will no longer contain any new possibilities and will be worthless for life. For this reason, it may be the shocking discrepancy with regard to well-known symbols in our religion that is responsible for the numinosity of a spontaneous product of the unconscious, which can shake a person to the core.

I related earlier the illustration of the dream of a pious Catholic girl. Her older sister was in analysis, which affected her deeply enough to produce the dream that had a shattering effect on her because it was so heterodoxical. The dream was tremendously ambivalent in the fact that the dreamer's sister was represented as the mother of God in all her canonical garb. The ambivalence showed in the text when the dreamer did not know whether to call the image sister, mother of God, or fairy queen. Then there is the snake, which we know can be a symbol of the healing god Asklepios, or of the evil principle, or a symbol of the Savior, as was the case with the Ophites. This ambivalence is an equivalent of the principle I pointed to earlier of the poison becoming the medicine. Another striking example is that of the "scepter of the Antichrist," which is a bishop's cross. The bishop, or *episcopos*, is the person who sees to it that Satan or the Antichrist has no place in his diocese, yet here it is he who wears the cross. In the dream it was the sister, a woman, who played the part of the bishop. Now the sister, who was the mother of God, was at the same time in danger of using her power instead of, as is believed by the orthodox, being an *ancilla domini* [handmaid of the Lord], which is the exact opposite of power. From this it would seem that the dream described the existence of a tremendous temptation to misuse power – obviously power of a magic quality. This is exactly what it would mean if the power of consciousness was used for egotistic purposes. This is the reason why the cross, the scepter of the Antichrist, has to be given to the priests. Here evil is a relative entity, and a human being has some kind of a choice, which is a blessing as well as a curse and a good reason for praying, "Lead us not into temptation." The subtle point here is that when it comes to making the choice, man has no choice; he simply has to make it, trusting that it will be within the prefigured plan. All we can say with regard to this prefigured plan empirically is that it seems to exist and express itself in images, dreams, and visions where the symbol of totality appears. The existence of this totality has to be thought of as being *ante rem* [prior to the universe's beginning]. This preexisting totality may well be likened to the divine *pronoia* [forethought, providence] since the *pronoia* was in pagan religion, and in Christian, one of the essential attributes of God. The Jungian concept of compensation contains a principle which may be called the principle of omniscience – as there has to be some authority who knows everything – in order to make compensation possible. The subject of this absolute knowledge does not necessarily have to be an anthropomorphism, but it must be agreed that once the existence of such a complete or absolute knowledge is admitted, metaphysics is introduced.

That is why I have said that the *physician* who deals with the unconscious in an analytic way is bound to become a *metaphysician*.

This raises the problem of the immanence or transcendence of such a principle. To deal with this we must assume that there are *somnia a deo missa*, dreams sent by God. In view of the problem I suggest that all man can do is to be religious in the original sense of the word *religio*, which, as Jung has pointed out, is "careful observation." This practically amounts to "going along with the process," going along implying a relatedness to the facts revealed in dreams, and relatedness referring to the position of the ego and the center of the drama. As long as the ego plays the primary part, no real relatedness is possible. Only when the center plays the primary part, and the ego begins to be properly related to it, is the person no longer egotistic; only then can he start from this superordinated center and engage in actions that will no longer be selfish or egotistic; only then will he *really* be related, not only to his true self, but also to his fellow beings, and only then will he be able to give, *really give*.

Up to this point I have tried to make things rather simple by not talking about two points in the practice of Jungian analysis that are of primary importance. These two points, which complicate the matter considerably, are the phenomenon of transference and the function of the symbol and the archetypal image. Transference is a special kind of projection occurring to some degree in every analysis but, as Jung says, fortunately only developing to a full-length classical transference in a few cases. Those are the cases I mentioned earlier as being not satisfied with a symptomatic cure, but still needing more analysis, still feeling a need to go on with the process. Once an analyst responds to such a demand he will have to deal with an utterly complicated situation, in which he will find that the projections the analysand makes on the analyst go far beyond human dimensions. The patient will project the savior or the "wise old man" on the analyst, or if the analyst is a woman and the analysand a man he will project the "great mother" or some similar archetypal image. Such images are more than human; they are superhuman. The problem of how to reduce such projections, in other words, how to lead them back to their source in the dreamer, is a classical one in analysis. In the cases where the contents projected on the object can be relatively easily reduced to the dreamer's own system, the matter is simple enough. When the image is superhuman, however, the dreamer simply refuses to have the contents attributed to himself, either because his resistances are too strong or because the contents are simply beyond him. In such cases it is vitally important that both the patient and the analyst understand that the projection-producing factor is actually trying to drive home to the patient that he has to deal with facts and powers that transcend him. The process thus becomes a matter of understanding and accepting the archetypal origin of such projections. Practically, this means accepting the existence of a third entity, an entity that can neither be attributed to the dreamer nor to the analyst but that has to be regarded as a representative of the collective unconscious or as an archetype of the collective unconscious. Jung calls this the *objective psyche*. Here again we are reminded of the point made earlier about the analyst's ability to handle such a case, which is only possible when he has gone through the condition himself and has acquired a more balanced system of his own, in contrast to the more labile system of the patient. Here once more a deeper psychological justification for the principle of *ho trosas iasetai* [he who wounds will also heal] can be seen. It is very important that both patient and analyst understand that at such a juncture they are actually dealing with something that is beyond them, for if they attributed this content to one or the other of them, either of them would be in danger of becoming inflated and consequently of losing adaptation to reality.

Now I come to the second point: symbols of such power. Symbols representing powerful archetypes usually appear only when the actual situation is full of tension, when there is an impasse of some sort. This is clearly the case in a strong transference situation that goes beyond practical possibilities. Such symbols appear only when man finds himself in dire necessity, and this is so because only when there is an extreme tension between opposites (example: the erotic projection on the part of the patient and the moral responsibility of the analyst) will saving grace come in. The symbol will be the saving grace inasmuch as it will provide man with the tertium that logically is not given. Jung says that symbols of this sort have a transcending function, which simply means that they are able to reconcile the opposites.

They produce a cooperation of the conscious and the unconscious systems or they make it possible to create a symbiosis of the two realms. As Jung says in *Psychological Types*: "The birth of the symbol stops the regression of the libido into the unconscious. The regression becomes progression, the repression flux," and again in the same book he says, "The stagnation of the vital powers is ended, life can go on and develop towards new goals with new forces" — *Habentibus symbolum facilis est transitus* [to those having a symbol, the transition is easy]. You will recall what I said about the trident of Poseidon having exactly such effects in the case of my patient. Many of these reconciling symbols show paradoxical qualities inasmuch as they embrace both thesis and antithesis. I remind you of the symbol of my Dutch psychologist, the world clock, in which as the light pulsated, the light became matter, and the blood became light almost in the sense of a "subtle body" — in such a way that the matter became immaterial and the immaterial became matter.

About the archetype I would say that the *archetype as such* cannot be represented, but will always appear in what Jung specifically calls an *archetypal image*. The archetypal concepts as such are not representable as long as they are not clad in such an image. In other words, the archetypal images are the representations of the archetypes as such; the images translate physical facts into psychological images or into psychological language.

I must emphasize one point: it is probably impossible to find a development such as that described in the many examples given by Jung for what he calls the individuation process, unless it is somebody who lives his personal myth. This means a person who goes along with the process, in such a way as to stimulate this process and this development by taking an active part in it, which is to show an interest that is properly called religious. Lately Jung expressed the view that the symbol of the Self, with a capital S, which more or less coincides with the symbol of the mandala, coincides with the symbol of God. I quote what Jung has to say about this problem, in *Psychological Types*:[13]

---

13. C. G. Jung, *Psychological Types*, trans., H. G. Baynes (London: Kegan Paul; New York: Harcourt Brace, 1923). Also found in *Coll. Wks.* 6, 1971.

Veneration for the great natural mysteries, which religious language endeavors to express in symbols consecrated by their antiquity, significance, and beauty, will suffer no injury from the extension of psychology upon this terrain, to which science has hitherto found no access. We only shift the symbols back a little, thus shedding light upon a portion of their realm, but without embracing the error that by so doing we have created anything more than a new symbol for that same enigma which confronted all the ages before us. Our science is also a language of metaphor, but from the practical standpoint it succeeds better than the old mythological hypothesis, which expresses itself by concrete presentations, instead of, as we do, by conceptions.

May I remind you that whenever Jung talks about the problem of the symbol he talks from experience and, more particularly, from experience with his patients and himself. You must also note that the patients of modern psychotherapists are practically all persons to whom the collective symbols have become inefficient, which is identical with the fact that their particular religion no longer holds the highest value for them. The collective symbols furnished to them by their religions have become dead. Most of such cases have been looking for new systems, preferably Eastern ones, as you know—particularly in the United States. The fact that they eventually take refuge in psychotherapy indicates that they have failed in that way to find their proper symbols. No substitute religion will do in their cases. I hope you understand that the Jungian solution is not a substitute for religion, either—all it can do for such people is to try to make them find access to the symbol-producing quality in their own depth. But the way such lost souls have to travel in order to arrive at a point where new symbols appear out of their unconscious is a *longissima via*, and is far from being a safe one or one that promises any definite solution. In any case, the solution that will be found by the individuals who seek cannot be known in advance; the unknown part or factor of the symbols must remain unknown. It must be said, then, that such a goal of analysis is not meant for everyone, and will become decisive only in comparatively few cases. But once we have witnessed the achievement of such a goal, we will not escape the impression and conviction that to a lost soul in our day there are possibilities and hope, even if they may appear to be parareligious possibilities. As doctors we cannot be grateful enough for the help that comes to the rescue of our patients and ourselves.

To close, I shall cite another example from my own experience: it is of a man who had been in analysis with me some years ago. The practical result of this analysis had been very successful and the man left gratefully at the end of the period of work. Then suddenly, after a year had elapsed, he appeared again in my consulting room because he had had a series of six dreams within a week's time that interested him tremendously. I shall read the last of these six dreams to you, but first I would like to give you the epicrisis of the case. I had to tell the man as the upshot of the series of dreams that he was obviously being reminded of the fact that he was going to die before long – he was at that time sixty-four years of age. He was shocked by this interpretation, but eventually he faced it with equanimity. Exactly nine months later he died quietly of a stroke, having attended to all of his worldly affairs in view of his approaching death. He reported his last dream as follows: "At the base of a high rocky wall a huge fire of wood was burning. The flames rose high up into the air and there was much smoke. The place was lonely and romantic. High in the air a number of big black birds were revolving directly above the fire. Now and then one of the birds dove deliberately into the fire and as it died its color was changed into white." This dream, he added, had a strong and lasting effect. It is an unfortunate truth that Western culture has lost to a large extent the ritual preparations for death. The East certainly still has them. There is a touching example of how death is met with, not too long ago in China, in the book by Nora Waln, *The House of Exile*. In Book 1, chapter 5, she describes how the elder of the house had a dream in which he saw his soul stand beside him, dressed in travelling clothes and carrying a scroll; thus he knew that his earthly scroll was filled. So through the seasons in which he continued in robust health, he made ready to die, and the family went through a long ceremony of preparing his tomb, his coffin, his deathbed and everything, most carefully. As you can see in this case, the unconscious produced most impressive symbolic images, the last of which most clearly gives the dreamer the certainty of rebirth or, as you would call it in Christian terms, the resurrection of the soul.

Chapter 6

Some Consequences
of Recent Psychological Thought

I am not a philosopher but a doctor. More particularly, I am a psychiatrist, and more particularly still, an analyst of the Jungian school. As I am taking it upon myself to present something (which to you as philosophers may be of interest), I beg you to keep this initial negative confession in mind.

Hippocrates said, ἰατρὸς γὰρ φιλόσοφος ἰσόθεος (*iatros gar philosophos isotheos*) [for a doctor who is at the same time a philosopher is godlike]. I make no pretense of being a philosopher and am, therefore, unafraid of such a comparison. For you see, we doctors are empiricists – a matter that C. G. Jung emphatically and repeatedly stressed whenever he was reproached for allowing himself to encroach upon the domains of philosophy and even theology. I would like to place a few questions before you that we doctors are not in a position to answer satisfactorily; and in so doing, I hope you may be able to help us to make further progress.

It would be very welcome indeed if the faculties could see their way to complete the circle hinted at in the quotation from Hippocrates – the circle between doctor, philosopher, and God, i.e., between the medical, philosophical, and theological facul-

Paper read to the "Zürich Society for Philosophy" in Zürich on February 26, 1959. First published in German in *Studia Philosophica*, vol. xix (Basel, 1959), 137ff. English translation by Edward Thorton.

ties. For me as a doctor it would, of course, be all the more gratifying if particularly the medical faculty were able to contribute to the healing of this still gaping wound. The recently deceased Karl Reinhardt contended that in olden times, when theology was still a part of philosophy, it was possible to speak without reserve about these problems. When, however, philosophy became scientific, theology became independent and absolute. Consequently it has become dogmatic, intolerant, and uninteresting. Be that as it may, I personally hold with Cicero's view, which, after philosophizing long and diligently *de natura deorum* (on the nature of the gods) makes a sharp turn-about and exclaims, "Contra deum licet disputare liberius" [When we wish to speak against the Deity we each do so freely]. Such an attitude appears to me to be more worthy and suitable where such an important subject is concerned.

I shall not speak to you now about God, as unfortunately I have no sound experience on that subject. Direct experience of God appears to have become indeed exceedingly rare (or was it not always so?) and is, probably with good reason, at all events officially not specially encouraged. What I would like to lay before you rather are experiences, which, at first, give rise to the impression of remoteness from God, namely phenomena which manifest themselves as symptoms of illnesses. In our dialect one inquires after the nature of an illness by asking the patient, "Was fehlt Ihnen?" [What do you lack?]. In the former temples of Asklepios of the Greeks and Romans, the answer to this question was given unequivocally by an occasional epiphany (manifestation) of the deity, in one or other of his forms, either in the waking state or in a dream; and the epiphany was the cure. That which the patient lacked (*fehlt*) was then again manifestly integrated, and the cure thus completed. For such effects polytheism would appear to present a more favorable prerequisite than our monotheism, but the latter is not yet too deeply rooted in us, so that our patients have still another possibility alongside this in believing in one or other chemical compound, in the sense of the *Arcanum* and, as is well known, thereby obtaining a considerably better chance of therapeutic efficacy.

Certain considerations of such disadvantages of monotheism are taken by the Catholic Church in the institution of the fourteen auxiliaries. Furthermore, almost every saint became established in a particular medical domain as a specialist-physician although, however, rather in the manner of ancient Egypt where doctors specialized in individual illnesses and not, as is the case with us, in diseases of particular organic or functional systems. Certainly this is not the case where the Blessed Virgin is concerned. For this and other good reasons, she is without question our most interesting colleague. At her main place of pilgrimage, Lourdes, she manifests herself particularly by curing illnesses of all kinds. In particular, by virtue of the new dogma she acquires the rank of a goddess, and as comparative religion shows, she is closely related to the Virgin Mother Hygeia of the Greeks on whom Asklepios, it appears, was dependent to a very great extent for his cures.

Many years ago when I engrossed myself with the methods that in ancient times were demanded and available for the cure of the sick, it finally became clear to me how manifestly ubiquitous and identical these methods are in all ages of time. They suffice with the two already mentioned properties to satisfy the definition of an archetypal situation, in C. G. Jung's sense.

It is impossible for me to go into the details of the similarities that are found in the arrangements of the ancient Asklepieia and those of present-day Lourdes. Two of the most important to be mentioned in passing, however, are the spring and the *piscina* (bathing pond) as chthonic elements. The earthly, the chthonic, is strongly stressed in all healing cults, and this appears particularly significant in our age, as all the efforts of the great powers are aimed at freeing oneself from the earth. To a mythological way of thinking, there is offered here the unavoidable picture of Antaeus and his destiny. Let us hope that our modern efforts to get away from Mother Earth may finally serve to lead us to the nobler goal of the attainment of the apples of the Hesperides.

You will ask yourselves, what have ancient healing cults to do with modern psychology? First of all it should be remembered that in ancient times he who dedicated himself to the cult of a particular deity was a θεραπευτής (*therapeutes*) [servant, worshipper] – and such a claim we doctors also make. In Hellenistic and early Christian times certain ascetics and monks called themselves *therapeutēs* without relating to a medical activity. I wish to point out how closely cult and cure have been related since time immemorial.

But you may again ask the question: is modern psychotherapy

a cult? This reproach has indeed been raised all too often against Jungian analytical psychology. It is even said to be a secret esoteric cult. Horrible! We only need to point out, with a glance at Jung's tremendous opus, that scarcely any other giant of our time has incessantly endeavored to describe and study anew the results of his research and practice, in order to see that truly no acts of secrecy are performed and no esotericism is carried on (unless some individuals persist in this subjective superstition, placing Jung's writings on their private index).

It is true, however, that in the course of his work Jung found something in an empirical way that makes a close point of contact with ancient cults of healing. He ascertained two facts that are relevant here, namely:

1. that the human psyche possesses an autochthonous religious function; and

2. that he never cured a patient who found himself in the second half of life without the patient having found access to this genuine religious function.

One would assume that in the face of such statements the theologians would flock to Jung's consulting room, but this is by no means the case (possibly because the theologians have no need for such a cure). Certainly they could at least rejoice about the fact that there now exists something in the nature of an experimentally proven *theologia naturalis*. What is the reason that this reaction, too, is absent? The question is not simple to answer, and the answer is by no means the same in every case. For those of us who are medical psychologists, however, this experience of Jung's is interesting enough for the simple reason that it is highly relevant for our practical motives.

It has been established (as seen from the aforementioned statement of Jung) that in the realm of neuroses the cure depends upon whether the religious function of the soul is discovered and acknowledged, and we might conclude that remoteness from God was the "cause" of the "effect," then called "neurosis." The reintroduction of the religious function, then, would accordingly constitute the causal therapy. In other words, that which Jung's many patients lacked, as indicated above, was just this very religious function or its conscious recognition.

I could be reproached, perhaps, for presenting a logically and philosphically inadmissible simplification or generalization.

Also, the comparison would really only be valid in the relatively rare cases for substitution therapy (as it is called medically, e.g., diabetes-insulin). In reality, the circumstances of the case may be much more complicated. If, for instance, there is only a grain of truth in the Freudian conception that the genesis of neurosis goes back to early infantile conflicts, then there scarcely remains here a place for religious aetiology. In any case, one can easily understand that with this method of approach, Freud would not come to the same conclusions as Jung.

What interests us here, however, is the question of whether the aetiologically causal questioning suffices or, for that matter, is meaningful where neuroses and psychological disturbances are concerned. If then the lack of, or an error in, the religious element can be the cause of illness (as is so in those cases which appear to satisfy the Freudian mechanics), and its correction or substitution according to Jung is nevertheless the *conditio sine qua non* of the cure, then the causal-reductive method of observation will not lead us far.

The success of the cure achieved can only be explained if one assumes that the whole system (patient, illness, and doctor) has undergone a certain meaningful transformation during the course of the treatment, and that only because of this has the solution become possible. By virtue of this solution, something additional would have been achieved which does not represent simply a regression into the past but is, in effect, something completely new. One might be inclined to say that the whole neurotic or psychotic interval had been prearranged so that the person in question might be better able to accept the religious demands. The illness itself would then be declared unreal and be degraded almost to a neurotic arrangement, in the manner noted by Alfred Adler. The question of the motive could not then be entered into with the all-embracing Adlerian explanation of the "will to power," so it must be asked what other unconscious complex might be hidden behind it. If this complex first makes itself apparent in the process of healing (i.e., only at the end of a sustained effort called analysis), it must really have been unconscious.

The most exciting part about the unconscious is that it really is *un*-conscious, not only repressed or forgotten, and cannot, therefore, be related to something known. Consequently, it would be a false method and would falsify Jung's mentioned discoveries if we used the analytical treatment to extract an unconscious religious factor from the darkness of the unconscious material as if it were the Manichaean spark of light. Begging the question in such a manner would be wrong for several reasons, the most important being that an analyst, prejudiced in such a monotonous manner, could never possibly do justice to the majority of cases. Whoever operates with a panacea cannot be an analyst because in so doing he merely proves the reality of his own monomania. He is consequently possessed by a complex, and rides this "hobbyhorse" perforce, in that he introduces it into each case he examines. Nothing is based upon the subjective conviction as much as the religious element. If I need this for my cure, it must be discovered by myself, in myself, and to my own greatest surprise be discovered from the consequences of my personal search and endeavors. My analyst may only protectingly accompany or, at best, guide me.

When I noted earlier that in such a case, during the course of an illness and treatment, the system must have undergone an important transformation, it means that the religious element had not lain hidden in the illness from the beginning, but that it was a *product* of the illness and, perhaps, also of the treatment. It is true that with an attitude, religious from the outset, every illness, just as every blow of fate, would appear as decreed by God and, in consequence, as serving the plan of cure that also existed from the outset. This would also be valid even when the illness appears to be concerned only with punishment.

One observes a finality here that is preferable to a blind trust in the power of the stars (at least where the stars are no longer gods). The corresponding god is given, at least initially, a dubious role, in that it is he who is believed to make people sick with his powers. Jahweh did this, then Apollo and then the Christian God, at least into Baroque times. A psychologically interesting variation of this subject is the healing god, who is himself either sick or wounded, and with him the closely connected motif of poison as a means of healing, or the healing effect of the weapon that inflicted the wound (as in Wagner's *Parsifal*).

Today, the idea of the sick-making god is not relished. I wish to stress that I do not share the lifeless, rationalistic idea according to which these mythologems are a priestly deception on the model of "God made you ill: believe, and as a reward He will make you well again." Today one appears to get closer to the patient when one expresses the suspicion that the illness may somehow have been brought about by his own guilt. However, this expressed suspicion is only allowed in the case of those sick persons who already are "enlightened" — such as, shall we say, intellectuals and rationalists — because fundamentally the concept is a rational-causalistic one. If, however, the cure as according to Jung depends on the successful connection to the religious element, and if we cannot explain this as simple substitution, then the connection of *causa morbi* [cause of the illness] and means of healing falls by the wayside. Looked at from the viewpoint of mental hygiene it would be even better, because if it were possible to make myself ill as well as cure myself, then I would be like the aforementioned gods. This godliness would have its incumbent dangers, not to be underestimated, because with such a conception, I would have added to my neurosis a delusion of grandeur.

It is now time to ask ourselves the question, "Where have these reflections brought us?"

It has been shown that in all times there has been a succession of opinions or theories concerning the whence and whither of illnesses. In the realm of neuroses and psychoses, a purely aetiological-causal analysis appears to produce particularly unsatisfactory results. The therapy, or even the cure, does not derive from it; and if Jung's observations are correct, the latter can only take place when the patient is successful in establishing a relationship with a newly added element, namely the religious element. We must not suppose, therefore, that the genesis of a neurosis or psychosis necessarily represents a remoteness from God, as I call it at the beginning. If this were so, religious people would be unable to develop such disturbances at all. Rather, at some point in the process of such an illness, the remoteness from God must be realized in order that the defect can be felt and a remedy found, in accordance with Jung's prescription for a cure. It will sometimes even happen that a person who finds himself stricken with such an illness experiences separation from God as a result of this blow of fate. One is reminded of Job and the melancholy of King Saul: "And God is departed from me; and would not hear me, neither by the hand of prophets nor by dreams." [1]

---

1. 1 *Kings* 28.15.

How this remedy takes place cannot be described simply for it is, in any case, an extraordinarily complicated subject. But since the Terry Lectures in 1937, Jung has made it his task to portray these occurrences in all his greater works. The answer to the question discussed, on the other hand, is indicated in the first of the two affirmations that were mentioned earlier, namely that a naturally religious function is demonstrable in the human psyche.

One cannot get around the question of how the cure is defined in this connection, according to Jung. Unfortunately, it is not explicitly defined, but one can see clearly enough from the other parts of his writing that a symptomatic cure is not suggested. Symptomatic cures in fact take place daily in the consultation rooms of all doctors of all denominations, and are regarded as successful both by doctor and patient, quite independently of whether they subscribe to the Jungian criterion. Neurotic symptoms also disappear without trace in certain cases under, or in spite of, any kind of therapy. Rather, Jung had a goal of treatment in mind that led the patient to an understanding of the meaning of his life, the meaning of his suffering, and why he is the kind of person he is. With that, a fundamental religious attitude is attained, and at the same time, the result of the treatment would not only be a remission but a real cure, which also, I suppose, would have to be regarded as a transformation.

We can also formulate this goal in another way, a way concerned with the creative employment of the illness, that the illness is not only combatted but that it is meaningfully arranged in the totality of the life in question, and that the patient has learned and understood the lesson of the illness. Only then can one be certain that the danger of a relapse has been overcome. This goal, however, is an achievement not easily attained. For one must succeed in extracting a meaning from the illness. As you see, in this manner we return to that conception to which the devout mind has paid homage since ancient times, that at the root of an illness there must be a hidden meaning which it is necessary to recognize. Philosophically speaking, here lies the fundamental question concerning a *causa finalis* [final cause] as pointed out, but with the demand to recognize the meaning of an illness. Every psychiatrist is first of all reminded of the impressive accumulation of apparent nonsense in the case of illnesses and neuroses. It is one of the first surprising facts in modern psychology that Freud offered us an explanation of the nonsense contained in neurotic symptoms, slips of the tongue, and dreams. With the same success, Jung then undertook to exhibit the hidden meaning in schizophrenic neologisms.[2] Until today, however, even after the key for deciphering this peculiar code has been found, it is still unclear what compels these patients to express themselves in such a bizarre fashion. The question of the meaning of these unusual phenomena still remains in the dark.

With somewhat more success, one can then turn to the more general question, "What could possibly be the meaning of a psychosis?" I am using the term "meaning" in this connection as having the same significance as "function," namely the function of a breakthrough of predominantly collective unconscious material into consciousness. The question of meaning is also concerned with the possibility of a cure and consequently of a possible therapy. The latter would mean the same as the constructive employment of the hitherto destructive demons, and would produce a totally changed situation as compared with the pre-morbid initial situation. "Meaning" has to do here with the *telos* (goal) and, to a great extent, is identical with the question of a *causa finalis*.

Jung has made the proposal that schizophrenic illnesses are to be understood as a "gigantic attempt at compensation" by the unconscious—compensation for a narrowness of consciousness, or as he once said, of the Weltanschauung of the individual concerned. Analogous to his cited conclusions about the cure of neuroses, one would venture to say also that a cure may scarcely be diagnosed without the *telos* including the realized religious element. In spite of the fact that there is much talk today concerning the analytical treatment and cure of schizophrenic patients, I have hitherto heard nothing about this criterion.

As far as I can see, one is still satisfied with the causal-reductive interpretation of the results. Personally, I have at my disposal corresponding experience of the analytical treatment of only

---

2. Cf. "I am the Lorelei" in C. G. Jung, "The Psychology of Dementia Praecox," in *The Psychogenesis of Mental Disease* (*Coll. Wks.* 3), 1960 [original German version, 1907].

two schizophrenic patients, and these go back to the early nineteen thirties when there was no talk of the analytical therapy of schizophrenia. One of these I wish briefly to place before you.

It concerns a youngish man who, because of a serious catatonia, had been interned in the clinic for several years. When I took over the department for violent patients, of which he was one, I was warned by my predecessor of the alleged aggressiveness of this fearsome patient, who stood in the corner of the dayroom in an almost cataleptic state. The next day I examined the patient more closely and observed that, contrary to his general attitude, there was something quite unusually warm and living lighting up his eyes. Soon I went up to him, offering my hand in greeting. To my great amazement he reciprocated the greeting and without a word clasped my hand very firmly.

On the following day I took him along with me to my room, a matter which caused no small excitement to the nursing staff. The patient began to talk hastily and described to me in the course of the next sessions the whole system of his delusions. In the course of two weeks, the patient was psychologically normalized and could be discharged from the clinic after a further two weeks.

Nine years later I met him by chance on a city street, and he introduced me to his fiancée. (A short catamnesis showed that after his discharge from the hospital he had worked successfully without interruption, and he was not in danger of suffering a relapse.) He took leave of me with the words, "Yes, yes, Doctor, if I had not experienced it myself, I would never believe what good such an illness could bring." His expression was unambiguous and left no doubt that the years in the Burghölzli had brought about a deep religious experience that cured him—in fact made him whole.

Now individual cases are lacking in statistical significance, however impressive they may be, and because of their impressiveness they are easily overestimated in their general importance. In order to obtain a broader basis, however, we must search for analogous experience in related spheres and place the single case in a larger connection, but without committing a μετάβασις εἰς ἄλλο γένος (*metabasis eis allo genos*) [shifting into another form].

If we believe ourselves authorized to connect the meaning of an illness so closely to its cure, we are reminded of the concept of the old mythologem, *ho trosas iasetai* [the wounder will heal] – an oracle of Apollo, from Apollodorus. Here the illness shares the dignity of the remedy, just as the poison is the remedy and vice versa. For many reasons, the principle even extends so far that the patient becomes the doctor and the doctor the patient. In accordance with the ancient view, the two concepts νόσος (*nosos*) [disease] and πενία (*penia*) [poverty] do not allow themselves to be separated, nor do ὑγίεια (*hygieia*) [good health] and πλοῦτος (*ploutos*) [wealth]. Therefore, illness means poverty and health means wealth. Whoever is ill lacks something as our idiom expresses itself; whoever is healthy has fullness/wholeness (*ploutos*).

In this mythological realm there is consequently only one possibility of cure, namely when the sick-maker, or he the sick or wounded god, personally intervenes. This is clearly the case in the temples of Asklepios, but it must be stressed that no medical treatment was carried on there. They were, however, often concerned with obvious organic changes, according to the case histories still in existence. The procedure was, therefore, an entirely irrational one: there was no causal therapy, but in the place of the principle of causality appeared a principle of analogy, which in homeopathy later became the well known *similia similibus curantur* [poison-remedy]. This remedy is known only to the healing god, and perhaps a necessary intervention is accomplished by him personally (in the dream), wherewith the cure is completed. The cure is an *intercessio divina* (intercession of the god), in other words the appearance of a personified divine principle. The cured patient shows recognition of this fact through a votive offering to the temple, as in the instance of Asklepios, as he departs from the scene of the cure but remains united with that god as a *religiosus – terminus technicus* [in a technical sense].

I invite you to accept these ancient principles as still valid: on the one hand when restricted to my special branch of medicine that is concerned with psychological illnesses and difficulties, and on the other hand, keeping in mind the two Jungian conclusions and the aforementioned psychiatric-clinical experiences. Over thousands of years the correspondences speak for themselves. Jung's conclusions emanate from the tremendous amount

of material based on his experiences. The material was collected
by taking into consideration the phenomena occurring at the
unconscious level, simultaneously with and parallel to problems
in the conscious realm, such phenomena being dreams, first and
foremost.

When one is successful in coming to a conscious understanding of these phenomena, there are two consequences:

1. A development can be observed that terminates in the particular person finding admittance or accession to the religious
(Jung's point).

2. It can be established that the aforementioned parallelism
between consciousness and the unconscious is rather like something of an antiparallelism. For this Jung has introduced the
term *compensation*, and by that he means that the products of
the unconscious have the significance of counteracting insufficient or false conscious performances, so that an equilibrium
can be produced if these effects can be raised into consciousness.

Both facts are at first found empirically and are in many cases
convincingly demonstrable. They also then verify themselves as
heuristic principles in daily practice. The compensatory function
of the phenomena of the unconscious, opposite those of consciousness, demands a still closer theoretical investigation.

It is conceivable that we were concerned here with closed-loop
systems, as they are known today, from automation. This model
allows itself to be used for certain biological regulations, as they
are described as "self-regulating systems." However, even in the
realm of conscious functions we soon arrive at a frontier where
the feedback is no longer sufficient as an explanation.

In his book *The Human Use of Human Beings*, the founder of
cybernetics, N. Wiener, makes this clear enough: "There is no
God and Marx is his prophet."[3] The cybernetic model suffices
still less for the relationship between consciousness and the
unconscious, not to mention the simple idea of the communicat-
ing vessels. We said that in the case of illness of a psychological
nature, the patient lacked something. It would be easy to imagine
that this lack could be remedied by the self-regulating events of
the psyche, although this process would be a quantitative one,

---

3. Norbert Wiener, *The Human Use of Human Beings*, London, 1950.

and one to be defined therefore as complementary (from *compleo*), not to be confused with the concept of compensation in the Jungian meaning of the term.

A complement would be like an answer to a question, one arrived at in the course of personally acquiring knowledge or having it provided by a professional who already has the answers. This appears to be very much the case in all those psychological problems that are capable of a Freudian or Adlerian solution. Here a generally widespread opinion, existing with respect to Adler's view, must be confronted and contradicted. His theory is usually described as based upon a final point of view. The profit of the illness shall not only explain the neurosis but in its purpose also sanctify it. In successful analysis the patient loses fictitious goals and solutions and, with them, the neurosis. In other words, there comes out of the computer (called analysis) a correct solution as "output," in contrast to the false one that the patient gave before the analysis, and for the support of which he needed the neurosis.

In my opinion, the Adlerian concept is not really a "final" one, as if the correct answer lay hidden in the system from the beginning, but one that the ego is entirely opposed to accepting, preferring a false one. On the other hand, the cybernetic model appears here to cover the circumstances considerably. Philosophically, the nearest term to describe Adler's system would be that of immanent teleology, which satisfies the principle of the closed-loop system. By comparison, the concept of compensation in the Jungian sense doubtlessly belongs to the realm of a transcendental teleology.

The consistent use of the proposition that the manifestation of the unconscious has a compensatory meaning in relation to the conscious attitude and orientation leads also to a feedback which, however, changes consciousness as well as the unconscious. There emerges an issue or process which is described by Jung as the *process of individuation*. This happening has a *telos*, as is shown empirically, that is not previously perceived either in the neurosis or the individual concerned. The *telos*, however, can be symbolically prefigured before its realization and, with the use of comparative viewpoints, allows one to perceive that it describes a "wholeness" — a wholeness of the human personality.

Whole and healed are synonymous. He who has been healed

has become whole. As we learn from Jung, both include the religious function, which in fact is included in the experience of the emergence of this symbol of totality. In retrospect, this *telos* becomes a *causa finalis* that, without consistent use of the theory of compensation, would never have been found.

The religious phenomenon and the cure are practically identical and are experienced subjectively as transcendental, i.e., as a new element, which was, however, deeply hidden in the system from the beginning. In consequence of this, no one was in a position to have known the answer from the outset. As you can see, with such conclusions we find ourselves in agreement with the clinical experiences of ancient times, where the *intercessio divina* [divine mediation] is identical to the cure.

I hope that my inability to offer simple solutions to these immensely difficult questions is understood, and that I merely endeavor to circumambulate them meanderingly, prudently, and, as far as possible, without prejudice. Final causes assume an absolute knowledge or prescience, which is indeed an epistemological aporia of the first order. Furthermore, as I said at the beginning, we doctors are empiricists, and empiricists are generally inimical to metaphysics.

What happens, then, when our empiricism (i.e., casuistry) forces us to accept final causes? Their existence is made probable already through the *consensus gentium* [consensus of mankind] for instance, in the form of the already oft-quoted ancient concepts concerning sickness and cure.

In psychiatry we are much more impressed by the meaninglessness of the phenomena than in somatic medicine. At this point, however, it is all the more intriguing to inquire about the meaning. The question is of substantial practical importance because we have seen that should we find the answer, a plan for the cure has been found for the patient. Of course, "the nonsense had method," but let it be understood that it would have been impossible to have seen through this earlier and to have understood it. I must stress that even after this understanding is found, the great secret remains a mystery. Where, then, do we stand with regard to the question of meaning?

Here we must go well beyond our specialized point of view in order to recognize that it really looks as if "the whole gigantic nonsense" were only there to force us to find the sense or plan of the cure lying therein, and this is not only so in psychopathology. In the search for an answer, we meet various suggestions. To name only one, in the case of Poseidonius the question of the purpose belongs in the realm of theology as it presupposes a particular power – a reasoning power, λογικὴ δύναμις (*logike dynamis*) – and therefore has nothing to do with physics. Poseidonius also speaks of a ζωτικὴ δύναμις (*zotike dynamis*) [life-giving power] which Cicero, as always, so correctly translates as *vis vitalis*. This, as you see, is not identical with vitalism.

We cannot escape the question: if there are these final causes and they even become evident after one has succeeded in understanding the whole *quid pro quo* – if this absolute knowledge exists, who has so artfully confused it and brought it about? I willingly admit that this question contains a concealed anthropomorphism, but is it on that account a mere projection? We cannot forget that religions since the Old Testament and ancient times have spoken of πρόνοια (*pronoia*) [foreknowledge] as one of the most essential divine attributes. Or is it also more anthropomorphism when I conclude that this absolute knowledge must after all have a subject? Here I discover myself in the act of bringing in a proof of God – and that from the experiences of psychopathology! This, however, is not my intention. The problem appears rather to belong to that question of Eckehart's, of whether to us "God has not yet become world."

Again, I revert to the Institute of Lourdes, as mentioned at the beginning, in order to close the circle. There the modern motto runs, *per Mariam ad Jesum*, as I hear from Father James Aylward. The Virginal Immaculate Conception leads accordingly to the Son-God or Son of God, which is the Anthropos, the Whole Man. With this, the pre-existent wholeness is attained when the Mother mediates as Virgin. The analogies to Hygeia and Asklepios are striking. In like manner, those among you who are conversant with Jung's representation of the process of individuation will be struck by the analogy to its phenomenology.

In conclusion, you will ask yourselves now, or at least tomorrow, what the consequences of recent psychological thought really are. If my conjecture proves right, then I shall be quite satisfied with this result of my deliberations, for when in psychology we are concerned with consequences, they must be drawn from within the psyche of each individual. Therefore, I must ask you to grant me extenuating circumstances if I have mainly asked questions and answered only a few. One question I will at least disclose to you: "What are the inferences that a doctor draws from these cited facts?"

I will conclude in the form of a pun only: in English the doctor is called a physician. In actually considering the facts described, every physician should then also become a metaphysician.

Chapter 7

Psychosomatic Medicine from the Jungian Point of View

I understand the invitation to speak on this subject as implying that a survey is not required. A survey must be presupposed if we are to investigate what the specifically Jungian point of view has to contribute or what new questions it may perhaps raise. The latter approach is indeed the more fruitful one when we are engaged in research.

With this end in mind, I wish to pursue two questions: (1) the origin of the psychosomatic idea in Jung, which in a sense is a historical question; and (2) the connection between the cure of somatic illness by means of psychological process, and the phenomenon of synchronicity.

To take the first question: when we think today of Jung's complex psychology, psychosomatic medicine will not, as a rule, be the first association that occurs to us. At any rate, when I told one of my nonpsychiatric colleagues, who is well versed in Jungian literature, that the Jungians seemed to take an interest in psychosomatic medicine and that I therefore had to read this paper, he said, "You are upsetting everything for me!" This was followed by a second, rather malicious remark: "In that case it would really be better to let the laymen speak right away." As

---

Paper read to the "Fourth Scientific Session of the Swiss Society for Analytical Psychology" in Fribourg, Switzerland in 1960. First published in German in: *Psyche*, 15 (Stuttgart, 1962), 625ff. Enlarged in English in: *Journal of Analytical Psychology*, 8 (London, 1963), 103ff.

we are used to taking spontaneous utterances seriously from the psychological point of view, I considered what deeper reasons these statements might have, and came to the following conclusion. The first remark is likely to have four roots: (a) the priority of the psyche in Jung; (b) in so far as the psyche is the real thing, somatic disturbances must be understood as secondary symptoms; and (c) insofar as one practices psychology, the object of inquiry is the psyche, not the soma, i.e., the connections with the soma are secondary; (d) because of (a), it does not follow from the Jungian point of view that the psychosomatic fashion is a reaction against medical materialism.

At the back of the second utterance lies the conviction that we physicians know nothing of consequence about the subject and that laymen can speak equally well about it, inasmuch as the psycho-physical connection is commonplace and can be looked up by everyone in a thousand and one reported cases.

To revert to my historical point, we know that Jung's clinical psychiatric career began with the discovery of the *complex*. The twelve or more complex indicators are all based on emotional reactions. Emotions, which certainly belong to the psyche, play a leading role in complex formation and complex effects. This was established experimentally by C. G. Jung, and it was precisely the clinical confirmation of his findings that brought Freud and Jung together.[1] It is one of the most important criteria of the emotions that they produce effects on and irradiate the bodily sphere. The connection between complexes and somatic changes, on the basis of the phenomena described by C. Féré[2] and O. Veraguth,[3] was first investigated and confirmed experimentally by

---

1. C. G. Jung, "Association, Dream and Hysterical Symptom," in *Experimental Researches* (Coll. Wks. 2, 1973), 353-407 [original German version 1906]. Also C. G. Jung and F. Peterson, "Psycho-Physical Investigations with the Galvanometer and Pneumograph in Normal and Insane Individuals," in *Experimental Researches* (Coll. Wks. 2, 1973) 492-553 [original English version 1907].

2. The Paris school made most important contributions to the psychosomatic problem as early as 1888. Cf. C. Féré, *The Pathology of Emotions* (London, 1899) [original French version, 1892], which contains many case-studies.

3. O. Veraguth, "Das psycho-galvanische Reflex-Phänomen," *Monatschr. Psychol. Neurol. Berlin*, 21 (1906, 1907; enlarged 1909).

C.G. Jung,[4] taking into account the analytical point of view; subsequently it was dealt with in detail by L. Binswanger.[5] The galvanometer was used for these purposes. Then followed the work by C. G. Jung and C. Rickscher, who applied the pneumograph in addition to the galvanometer;[6] Nunberg introduced a third recording instrument by Sommer (tremograph).[7] C. G. Jung and F. Peterson continued their investigations with galvanometer and pneumograph.[8] In 1908 the American authors B. Sidis and H. T. Kalmus occupied themselves with the galvanometer graph in great detail.[9] B. Sidis and L. Nelson subsequently dealt with the same problem more exhaustively.[10]

Thus by the application of different methods of measurement the responses of several physiological functions to psychical stimuli were investigated as follows:

1. Electrical skin resistance — Galvanometer and Wheatstone's Bridge, respectively

2. Involuntary tremors — Sommer's recording instrument: frequency and amplitude

3. Breathing — Pneumograph: frequency and amplitude

4. Pulse — Sphygmograph: frequency and amplitude

5. Blood supply — Plethysmograph

---

4. C. G. Jung, "On Psychophysical Relations of the Associative Experiment," in *Experimental Researches (Coll. Wks.* 2, 1973), 483-491 [original English version 1907].

5. L. Binswanger, "Über das Verhalten des psychogalvanischen Phänomens beim Assoziations Experiment – Diagnostische Assoziationsstudien," Beitrag XI. *J. Psychol. Neurol.*, 10 (1907).

6. C. G. Jung and C. Rickscher, "Further Investigations of the Galvanic Phenomenon and Respiration in Normal and Insane Individuals," in *Experimental Researches (Coll. Wks.* 2, 1973), 554-580 [original German version, 1907/8].

7. Nunberg, "Über Körperliche Begleiterscheinungen assoziativer Vorgänge," *J. Psychol. Neurol.*, 16 (1910).

8. Jung and Peterson, "Psycho-Physical Investigations."

9. B. Sidis and H. T. Kalmus, "A Study of Galvanometric Deflections Due to Psycho-Physiological Processes," pts. I and II, *Psychol. Rev. Balt.* 15, 16 (1908/1909).

10. B. Sidis and L. Nelson, "The Nature and Causation of the Galvanic Phenomenon," *Psychol. Rev. Balt.* 17 (1910).

Some of these instruments have been combined in a single device, now known as the polygraph or "lie detector." All the above investigations were overlooked until medical men began to apply chemical and physical methods to a more systematic investigation of changes in the functioning of organs and organic systems. As a result, it has been established that there is no organ (with the exception, perhaps, of bones and teeth) whose functioning is not influenced by affects.

I remind readers that as early as the eighteenth century, Boerhaave, as cited by Wittkower,[11] wrote as follows: "Affectus animi violenti aut diu permanentes iidem cerebrum, nervos, spiritus, musculos mirabiliter efficacissime mutant, figunt, depravant, unde quoscumque fere morbos valent producere et fovere pro sua diversitate et duratione." [Violent or long-persisting affects of the soul change, attach themselves to, and corrupt the brain, nerves, spirits and muscles in an extraordinary, most effective manner, and consequently in accordance with their diversity and duration are capable of producing and fostering practically every kind of disease.] A detailed discussion of the problem with clinical material may be found in Boerhaave.[12]

These facts were even known to the Greek physicians, as can be gathered from Herodotus and other sources. In any case, already Erasistratus (304-240 B.C.) must be already regarded as a physician with an exemplary psychosomatic approach. As an instance of his deep insight, I quote his case history of Antiochus, son of Seleucus, and his stepmother Stratonice, which has been handed down to us by Plutarch and Appian. I quote the version of Plutarch in Bernadotte Perrin's translation:

Antiochus fell in love with Stratonice, who was young and was already mother of a little boy by Seleucus. Antiochus was distressed and resorted to many means of fighting down his passion, but at last, condemning himself for his inordinate desires, for his incurable malady and for the subjugation of his reason, he determined to seek a way of escape from life and to destroy himself gradually by neglecting his

---

11. E. Wittkower, *Einfluss der Gemütsbewegungen auf den Körper* (Vienna and Leipzig, 1930).

12. Hermannus Boerhaave, ed. Jacobus Van Eems. *Praelectiones Academicae de Morbis Nervorum.* 2 vols. (Frankfurt and Leipzig, 1762).

person and abstaining from food, under pretense of having some disease. But Erasistratus, his physician, perceived quite easily that he was in love, and wishing to discover who was the object of his passion (a matter not so easy to decide), he would spend day after day in the young man's chamber, and if any of the beauties of the court came in, male or female, he would study the countenance of Antiochus and watch those parts and movements of his person that nature has made to sympathize most with the inclinations of the soul. Accordingly, when any one else came in, Antiochus showed no change, but whenever Stratonice came to see him, as she often did, either alone, or with Seleucus, lo, those telltale signs of which Sappho sings were all there in him—stammering speech, fiery flushes, darkened vision, sudden sweats, irregular palpitations of the heart and finally, as his soul was taken by storm, helplessness, stupor and pallor. Besides all this, Erasistratus reasoned further that in all probability the king's son, had he loved any other woman, would not have persisted to the death in refusing to speak about it.[13] He thought it a difficult matter to explain the case fully to Seleucus, but nevertheless, relying on the father's kindly feelings toward his son, took the risk one day and told him that love was the young man's trouble, a love that could neither be satisfied nor cured. The king was amazed and asked why his son's love could not be satisfied. "Because, indeed," said Erasistratus, "he is in love with my wife." "Then canst thou not, O Erasistratus," said Seleucus, "since thou art my son's friend, give him thy wife in addition to thy friendship, especially when thou seest that he is the only anchor of our storm-tossed house?" "Thou art his father," said Erasistratus, "and yet thou wouldst not have done so if Antiochus had set his affections on Stratonice." "My friend," said Seleucus, "would that someone in heaven or on earth might speedily convert and turn his passion in this direction, since I would gladly let my kingdom also go if I might keep Antiochus." So spake Seleucus with deep emotion and many tears, whereupon Erasistratus clasped him by the hand and told him he had no need of Erasistratus, for as father, husband, and king he was also the best physician for his own household. Consequently, Seleucus called an assembly of the entire people and declared it his wish and purpose to make Antiochus king of all Upper Asia, and Stratonice his queen, the two being husband and wife; he also declared it to be his opinion that his son, accustomed as he was to be submissive and obe-

---

13. This "moment of truth" has been portrayed by Ingres in an impressive painting with the title *Antiochus and Stratonice*, which is in the Musée Condé at the Chateau de Chantilly (exhibit No. 432).

dient in all things, would not oppose his father in this marriage, and that if his wife were reluctant to take this extraordinary step, he called upon his friends to teach and persuade her to regard as just and honorable whatever seemed good to the king and conducive to the general welfare. On this wish, we are told, Antiochus and Stratonice became husband and wife.

This influence of the affects on the bodily organs raises, among other things, the question of symmetry: that which causes the illness also heals. This reminds us of shock treatment and of κάθαρσις (*katharsis*) [ritual cleansing] in the ancient sense; the latter in turn leads to εὐκρασία (*eukrasia*) [good temperament], the equilibrium of the humors of the body or temperaments ἀταραξία (*ataraxia*) [impassiveness]. Also relevant here is the James-Lange theory of the affects, where the inquiry after the cause has resulted in a 180-degree turn: "We do not cry because we are sorry, but we feel sorry because we cry," or "My theory is that the bodily changes follow directly the perception of the existing fact, and that our feeling of the same changes *is* the emotion." Viewed historically, this one-sided approach leads from Darwin and William James, by way of Watson and Pavlov, to a purely materialistic behaviorism, and thus away from psychology, or rather to a psychology of the Russian brand, i.e., without soul.

In the course of time, however, a large amount of clinical material was collected and elaborated upon by various investigators (A. Adler, Oswald Schwarz, Wittkower, Heyer and others). These authors were able to show that the persistence of complexes could produce not only symptomatic actions and accident proneness but also symptoms that manifested themselves somatically and might result in genuine organic damages. The inference is drawn that it is a task of psychosomatic medicine to remove these pathogenetically significant complexes. My impression from the literature is that it is the symptoms rather than the complexes that are removed in psychosomatic medicine. A psychosomatic case *par excellence*,[14] of which I had been informed by Professor Bruno Klopfer of Los Angeles, was indeed cured of his bronchial asthma. A few years after the publication of this

14. Leon Saul, a paper in *Psychosom. Med. Monogr.* II, 2 (New York, 1941).

success, however, he developed an ulcus ventriculi.

Finally, there is another point of view that belongs to the historical part of this paper, raised by Jung just as early: the hypothesis of a *toxic factor* in the pathogeny of schizophrenia, an idea first put forward in 1907 in his study on dementia praecox already mentioned. According to this view, the postulated toxin would be responsible for the perseverance of the complex effects, or, as Jung also put it, for their fixation. One may recognize the analogy with the origination of organic changes from psychogenetic bodily symptoms.

This statement of Jung's fell on no more fertile soil than did his complex theory and, just like the latter, was not taken up until decades later, at approximately the same time as the psychotherapy of schizophrenia (Rosen et al.). In clinical psychiatry, however, intense work on the problem is being undertaken today with the resources of modern biochemistry, and as a result it has now become probable that Jung's toxic factor has a close chemical affinity with adrenalin. The *psychotomimetic* substances, too, such as mescaline, LSD, psilocybin, and the like, with which we can produce model psychoses, show a chemical affinity with adrenalin. Adrenochrome and adrenolutine (colored derivates of the colorless adrenalin) have intense psychotomimetic properties of a remarkably long, persistent effect. It is precisely this fact, however, that makes their experimental investigation exceedingly unpleasant.[15] Still, the protracted effects may enable us to gain a better understanding of the notorious fixation of the complex effects in schizophrenia. Robert G. Heath and colleagues,[16] on the other hand, have traced a protein in the serum

---

15. Cf. H. Osmond, "Inspiration and Method in Schizophrenia Research," *Dis. Nerv. Syst.* 16, 4 (Galveston, 1955) and "A Review of the Clinical Effects of Psychotomimetic Agents," *Annals N.Y. Acad. Sci.*, 66 (1957); H. Osmond and J. Smythies, "Schizophrenia: A New Approach." *J. ment. Sci.*, 98 (1952) and "The Significance of Psychotic Experience," *Hibbert J.* (1958); A. Hoffer and H. Osmond, "Schizophrenia – An Automatic Disease." *J. nerv. ment. Dis.*, 122, 5 (1955) and "The Adrenochrome Model and Schizophrenia," *J. nerv. ment. Dis.*, 128, 1 (1959) and "A Small Research in Schizophrenia," *Canad. med. Ass. J.*, 80, 91-4 (1959); and the most recent summary account of the findings: A. Hoffer and H. Osmond, *The Chemical Basis of Clinical Psychiatry* (Springfield, Oxford, Ontario: C. C. Thomas, 1960).

16. Robert G. Heath et al. *Amer. J. Psychiat.* (1956).

of schizophrenic patients that exhibits psychotomimetic properties, which they call taraxein (from the Greek ταρακτικός (tarak-
tikos) [confusing]). Another American author, Nicholas A. Bercel,[17] by administering the serum of schizophrenic patients to
the spider Zilla-x-notata, produces behavioral changes that
impress one as psychotoid: the spider spins schizophrenic webs.
His work is based on Peters, Witt and Wolff;[18] Wolff and Hempel;[19] Witt;[20] H. Fischer's work is also of great importance to
our theme.[21]

Already in 1907, Jung was of the opinion that the exaggerated
effect of complexes in schizophrenia was due to a peculiar ego
weakness (for which quite a number of factors, mainly family
factors, were held responsible) and that the fixation of the symptoms was due to the presence of the toxic factor. Inasmuch as the
toxin was considered only as an adjuvant of the fixation and not
as a cause of the exaggerated complex effect, the psychogenetic
approach was maintained. In his 1958 lecture to the Second
International Congress of Psychiatry at Zürich, Jung once more
repeated his fifty-year-old suggestion, this time, however, on a
more concrete basis. Jung was circumspect enough to leave open
the question whether the connection might not be the other way
around.

Let us examine, however, whether in the realm of psycho-physical relations the question of cause and effect may not become
altogether meaningless. We assume naïvely that once we know a
physical cause, the physical effect will necessarily follow. This
approach begins with the stimulus-response model and goes
right up to modern psycho-pharmacology. Such (psychic) effects,
to be sure, are repeatable and can be recorded experimentally

---

17. Nicholas A. Bercel, *AMA Arch. Gen. Psychiat.* 2 (Chicago, 1960).

18. H. M. Peters, P. N. Witt and D. Wolff, "Die Beeinflussung des Netzbaues
der Spinnen durch neurotrope Substanzen," *Z. vergl. Physiol.*, 32 (1950).

19. D. Wolff and V. Hempel, "Versuch über die Beeinflussung des Netzbaues
von Zilla-x-notata durch Pervitin, Scopolamin und Strychnin," *Z. vergl.
Physiol.*, 33.

20. P. N. Witt, *Die Wirkung von Substanzen auf den Netzbau der Spinne als
biologischer Test* (Berlin-Göttingen-Heidelberg, 1956).

21. H. Fischer, "Die Tierwelt im Lichte der Pharmakologie," *Neujahrsbl.
Naturf. Ges Zürich*, 164 Stck. (1962).

and statistically, but *how* the *physis* acts upon the psyche remains as great an enigma as the reverse process of psychic action on the *physis*. For instance, I recall the embarrassment that is always felt in connection with the James-Lange theory because, though in accord with the naïve idea of physical action on the psyche, it amounts to an unsatisfactory epiphenomenalism. Dealing with questions of psychosomatic medicine, we find ourselves more or less unwittingly, though inevitably, in the midst of the problems of psycho-physics. For good reasons these problems begin for us with the doctrine of the affects, which in turn has been basically enriched by Jung's theory of complexes. Emotion and complex are inseparable Siamese twins. The former must of necessity be accompanied by bodily changes, and for this reason both have become factors of the first order in psychosomatic medicine.

In view of these connections, we can easily see why the physicians and philosophers of antiquity regarded the affects as noxious and despicable. *Ataraxia* [freedom from passion] was rated as the highest desirable good; similarly μετριοπάθεια (*metriopatheia*) [moderation] and even ἀπάθεια (*apatheia*) [apathy]. The last was ascribed by the Fathers of the Church to God the Father, who was incapable of suffering and therefore, by way of compensation, had to produce the Son of Man who was capable of suffering. Apart from that, it seems really necessary to remain sufficiently human to be capable of succumbing to a *pathos*; the fact that we can be affected emotionally is of importance to us if only for the reason that in the state of *e-motio* the psyche as such may be experienced in its sheer dynamic immediacy, i.e., as libido. P. Janet's view that the emotions are excessive excitations due to an inability to react adequately probably goes back to the ancient contempt of the affects. An unbiased assessment of the emotions might very well make us conscious of a weakness in ourselves — note here the functional analogy with projection. Instead, what as a rule occurs is an *abaissement du niveau mental* accompanied by a regression to more primitive mechanisms (cf. complex symptoms), and thus the reaction after all remains undesirable.

We may here recall the discussion Περὶ παθῶν (*Peri pathon*) [Concerning affects] in Poseidonius. According to him, the cause of the affects is an excess of, or increase in, the *hormē*, i.e., the normal rational impulse. This, in turn, may occur either through the exaggerated size of the imagined object or through a peculiar weakness of the imagining subject (cf. trauma, shock or ego weakness). This view again reminds us of Jung's opinions about the psychogenesis of schizophrenia (see above).

For the purposes of this paper, I must give a brief sketch of the doctrines that today pass for psychosomatic medicine:

It is frequently forgotten that in 1907 Alfred Adler published his studies on organ inferiority and, on the basis of his clinical observations, worked out the theory that a person's ability or inability to cope with his organ inferiority would determine whether or not he was to become a neurotic. Subsequently this doctrine was decried as "organ mythology," yet it is a highly intelligent theory inasmuch as it ascribes a definite role to the somatic factor without bringing in causal explanations. It is occasionalistic. What the psyche makes of the somatic disturbance is the decisive factor. As an antiparallel, we find Freud's concept of conversion (put forward at the same time), according to which the psyche produces somatic symptoms, and which really amounts to a first definition of psychogenesis. The Freudian notion became considerably more popular than the Adlerian. There followed quite a number of summary accounts, e.g., by Oswald Schwarz,[22] who belongs to von Bergmann's and von Krehl's school of internal medicine, also by V. von Weizsäcker and A. Mitscherlich. Wittkower was the first to make a survey of the findings.[23] Now the Anglo-Saxon world seizes upon the idea with full force: we see the astounding achievements of Flanders Dunbar taking shape and roughly at the same time, Weiss and English, and Grinker and Robbins join the discussion.

The American literature was mainly based on psychoanalysis and, consequently, interpreted somatic disturbances almost exclusively as conversion symptoms until Alexander made the important distinction between conversion hysteria and vegetative neurosis, assigning a significant pathogenetic role to oral

---

22. Oswald Schwarz, *Psychogenese und Psychotherapie körperlicher Symptome* (1925).
23. E. Wittkower, *Einfluss der Gemütsbewegungen auf den Körper* (Vienna and Leipzig, 1930).

inhibition. F. Dunbar, on the other hand, is not concerned to the same extent with the psychogenesis in the causal sense, but attempts to reduce the sixteen hundred available cases to more or less specific illness syndromes as common denominators. She attempts to establish a significant correlation between certain somatic symptoms and specific psychological characteristics of the patients. In this way we get corresponding pictures of illnesses and personalities. No doubt all the literature mentioned has, as a matter of principle, adopted the Freudian point of view, treating bodily symptoms as causally dependent upon psychic factors. Somatic phenomena are thus reduced to physical phenomena. To what lengths these authors go becomes more obvious in reading the symposium *The Psychological Variables in Human Cancer*, where the psychodynamics of the personality are found relevant to the rate of growth of malignant tumors;[24] cf. also Klopfer[25] and the formation of an International Psychosomatic Cancer Research Association, which held its first congress in Amsterdam in the summer of 1960.

After this attitude had been predominant for approximately forty years, a new phase began. Under the influence of the remarkable progress achieved in psychopharmacology, psychosurgery, neurophysiology, and biochemistry, the younger generation of psychiatrists is again inclined to acknowledge the precedence of the soma over the psyche. These variations in the course of the history of research have their good reasons. For instance, M. Bleuler as cited by von Wyss says: "One must not be oblivious of the old rule that the possibility of understanding a certain development psychologically does not by a long way prove its psychological genesis."[26] Indeed, it is perfectly clear that the psychosomatic problem must be investigated from both sides. Whether the tunnels driven from either side will ever lead to a

---

24. J. A. Gengerelli and F. J. Kirkner, eds., *The Psychological Variables in Human Cancer* (Berkeley and Los Angeles: University of California Press, 1954 and London: Cambridge University Press, 1955).

25. Bruno Klopfer, "Psychological Variables in Human Cancer," *J. Projective Techniques* 21 (1957): 4

26. Walter H. von Wyss, *Aufgaben und Grenzen der Psychosomatischen Medizin* (Berlin-Göttingen-Heidelberg, 1955).

breakthrough remains an open question. Jung, to judge from his address to the Congress, seemed to take an optimistic view.[27] Those alterations of viewpoint are perhaps due to a deeper problem as H. G. Wolff surmised when he said in 1952 that "the affects that are evoked by the threatening situation are not the cause of the bodily changes. Both occur simultaneously and belong together, but the 'how' remains open."[28] Similarly von Weizsäcker: "The introduction of the psyche into pathogenesis means a transformation in which the causal point of view takes second place."[29]

It must be emphasized that the concept of psychogenesis is mechanistic and causal, which would be unobjectionable if, for fundamental philosophical reasons, we did not know that the connection between physis and psyche cannot be resolved in terms of cause and effect. Whether we adopt the standpoint of interactionism or that of parallelism is of no consequence. The "how," as Wolff rightly says, remains open, and according to one's temperament one may stop either at Dubois-Reymond's *ignoramus* [we are ignorant] or project into the future as an *ignorabimus* [we will be ignorant].

I now come to the second question raised at the beginning, the question of the acausal correlation between psyche and soma [physis].

$$\phi \underset{2}{\overset{1}{\rightleftarrows}} \psi$$

We will take our departure from the general question of psychophysical correlation. While we usually understand sense "1" as commonplace (I have already mentioned that this is not the case), the same certainly does not apply to sense "2", notwithstanding the fact that it normally functions similarly to "1". It seems unintelligible to us how the psyche can produce an arrangement in the physis, no matter whether the physis is *intra corpus* (cf. psychosomatic symptom) or *extra corpus*, that is,

27. C. G. Jung, "Schizophrenia," in the *Psychogenesis of Mental Disease* (*Coll. Wks.* 3, 1960), 256-271 [original German version 1958].

28. Wyss, *Psychosomatische Medizin.*

29. Wyss, *Psychosomatische Medizin.*

whether it is part of the subject or not. We still gladly agree with Kant when he says, "That my will moves my arm is not any more intelligible to me than when someone asserts that he can arrest the cycle of the moon; the only difference is that I experience the former, while the latter has never been presented to my senses." This difficulty was always known to philosophers, and has in no way been resolved by the neologism *psychosomatic medicine*. *Tertium non datur* [a middle term is not given], and if medicine wanted to be the *tertium* [third one], then it would at best consist of nothing but miraculous cures. Soma and psyche form a pair of opposites whose reconciliation in the case of a disturbance appears to depend upon the emergence of a symbol. For this reason the attempt was made very early on to replace the dichotomy by a trichotomy, which has its advantages. If we wish to adhere to the simple model of psychical complexes and emotional somatic effects, then we may follow Poseidonius who concluded that the imagination must be the mediating *tertium quid*.[30]

Plotinus says that the πάθη (*pathē*) [experience] belongs neither to the soul nor to the inanimate body, but to a συναμ-φότερον (*synamphoteron*) [combination][31] of soul and body.[32] Proclus speaks of the same entity as a body that does not consist of the four elements but of a fifth. This body is spherical, viz, its εἶδος (*eidos*) [form or image] is spherical. What Plotinus says of a circular course applies also to anything spherical: circular movement is the most perfect (cf. stars).[33] Something of that is also present in our bodies, and this is connected with the σῶμα πνευματικόν (*soma pneumatikon*) [breathing body] as *tertium quid*. We may here remember the *opus circulare*, the *rota* of the alchemists or the circular course of light in Taoism. This *soma*

[30. Ed. Note: *Tertium quid* translated literally means "third something." It refers to something that escapes a division into two groups supposed to be exhaustive, a third part of ambiguous status.]

31. συναμφότερον (*synamphoteron*) [both together] is the term for a *complex magnitude*, following Schwyzer (1960). The expression occurs already in Plato (*Alcib.* 130a) and Euclid (*Elem.* VII, 5) according to information received from H. R. Schwyzer and A. Szabó.

32. Plotinus, *Enneads* IV, 4. [28], 18, 19.

33. Plotinus, *Enneads* IV, 3, 9, 15.

pneumatikon has many names: it is also called πνεῦμα σωματι κόν (*pneuma somatikon*), ἀστροειδὲς σῶμα (*astroeides soma*) [starlike body], αὐγοειδὲς σῶμα (*augoeides soma*) [ray-like body], or in Proclus[34] αὐγοειδὲς ὄχημα (*augoeides ochema*) [radiant vehicle], or ἀστροειδὲς ὄχημα (*astroeides ochema*). Synesius has the synonym φανταστικὸν πνεῦμα (*phantastikon pneuma*) [visible breath], which, in accordance with what was said above, may go back to Poseidonius.

Generally the *astroeides soma* (or its synonyms) after death is transformed into the εἴδολον (*eidōlon*) [image], the *imago*, the *simulacrum* or the shade (Greek σκία *skia*, Latin *umbra*).

In Paracelsus we meet the same notion again, for he speaks of a "second, invisible body that forges the bodily symptoms."[35] Here we have to consider what a *symptom* really is by recalling its etymological history: σύμπτωμα (*symptoma*) is the coincidence into one, or the convergence of at least two distinct magnitudes, also the point of intersection of two curves. If Paracelsus is right, then it is this second body, the *tertium* between soma and psyche, that is responsible for symptom formation. Thus he would be very close to Plato's interpretation of σῶμα (*soma*) = σῆμα (*sema*);[36] whereas the Alexandrians seemed to think that consciousness of the *soma astroeides* would terminate bodily suffering, similar to the *Samkhya* teaching that the contamination of soma and psyche must be ended in order to recover health.

All these ideas lead up and belong to the theory of the "subtle body," the notion of a subtle vehicle of the soul as *tertium quid*, standing midway between the animal soul and the body. The work of G.R.S. Mead informs us of the development of these ideas in late antiquity and in Christianity.[37] Whatever homeopathic medicine may achieve will be affected through that third part of our system. The speculations concerning the subtle body

---

34. Proclus, "Commentaries on Plato's *Timaeus*," 384B.

35. Wyss, *Psychosomatische Medizin.*

36. This is a famous pun in Greek literature: σῶμα (*soma*) = body and σῆμα (*sema*) = tomb; but the original meaning is "sign," "mark," "token." Cf. Plato, *Phaedrus* 250C.

37. G. R. S. Mead, *The Doctrine of the Subtle Body* (London: Watkins, 1919).

and their magnificent amplification in the Iranian Shiite religion are now available for study, thanks to Henry Corbin's work. Compare in particular the parallels with Proclus.[38]

With the theory of the subtle body, we have apparently found the symbol that avoids the difficulties of the psycho-physical relation, but for the time being it has landed us beyond the reach of experiment and verification. This is not quite true, for in this connection I am able to draw on the result of an experiment that, to begin with, can only be understood by introducing something like the subtle body. In order to record volume variations, S. Figar, a Czech physiologist, made simultaneous plethysmographic investigations on the forearms of two persons who did not know of each other's presence.[39] One of them was subjected to certain psychical stimuli, which could be recognized in characteristic volume oscillations; but the volume graph of the second person, who took absolutely no part, showed a significant congruence with that of the first person. This surprising result reminds me of a passage by the anonymous author in the *Musaeum Hermeticum*: "Anima autem, quo homo a caeteris animalibus differt, illa operatur in corpore, sed majorem operationem habet extra corpus; quoniam absolute extra corpus dominatur." [But the soul by which man differs from other animals operates inside his body, although it has greater efficacy outside the body, for outside it rules with absolute power.][40] Figar's findings have been checked in the United States on a great number of subjects and with improved methods, and have been confirmed by Douglas Dean, New York.

At this point, we will once again revert to our physis-psyche schema, and, concentrating on sense "2", ask whether similar effects are known from elsewhere, in particular when φ lies *extra corpus*. This is the case in all methods of divination. For instance, when throwing the *I Ching* oracle it must be assumed that the psyche arranges forty-nine yarrow stalks in such a way that afterwards a definite hexagram comes into being by means of defined

---

38. Henry Corbin, *Terre Céleste et Corps de Résurrection* (Paris, 1960), esp. 148ff.

39. S. Figar, "The Application of Plethysmography to the Objective Study of So-Called Extrasensory Perception," *J. Soc. Psych. Res.* 40, 702 (1959).

40. *Musaeum Hermeticum* (Francofurti, 1677), 617.

grouping. In principle this applies to all mantic methods, and all of them give rise to an image. Inasmuch as images are orderly arrangements, they have a formal character, in most cases straightforwardly geometrical. This would fit the definition of the archetype quite well. Jung thinks that archetypes are more likely to appear in critical situations, and on the whole it may be assumed that we consult oracles when we find ourselves in a crisis. If our assumption of an actual correspondence between

$$\begin{array}{ccc} \text{Inner} & & \text{Outer} \\ \text{Subject} & \text{and} & \text{Object} \\ \psi & & \phi \end{array}$$

is correct, then that correspondence is as little causal in character as that between psyche and φύσις (*physis*) (= soma). The *I Ching* oracle was considered by Jung also under the aspect of synchronicity.[41] The mantic procedure, however, gives us a method which, if followed, promises that we shall unfailingly obtain a correspondence between psyche and physis. This looks thoroughly causal and does not satisfy the principle of *acausal connection.*

Here we are up against a difficulty that I am unable to resolve; however, this difficulty is in no way unique. The psycho-physical problem, too, presents us with such a situation: here also a causal correlation is unthinkable, and yet the system — the συναμφότερον (*synamphoteron*) of Plotinus — functions smoothly inasmuch as the physis continually produces arrangements in the psyche, and similarly the psyche in the physis; moreover these arrangements are always meaningful. At the worst, we do not readily understand them; for instance, when it is a question of symptoms (σύμπτωμα [*symptoma*] = Greek synonym of Latin *coincidentia*), but whoever possesses the art of the physician and knows how to read them will on every occasion come to something very useful, namely a *diagnosis* (= discernment). Therefore, I suggested as early as 1950 that, in view

41. C. G. Jung, "Foreword to *The I Ching* or Book of Changes," in *Psychology and Religion: West and East (Coll. Wks.* 11, 1958), 589-608.

of the failure of causal explanations, the psycho-physical functioning should be interpreted synchronistically. Jung at first attacked me violently on this account, but after lengthy discussions accepted my suggestion;[42] although in subsequent oral communication he was again inclined to reserve synchronicity for rarer and more striking coincidences. I cannot see how this restriction to a special theory of synchronicity can be maintained if causality and synchronicity, in the well-known quarternary schema,[43]

$$E \text{ or } p$$
$$\text{causality} + \text{synchronicity}$$
$$t \text{ or } q$$

(E = energy; t = time; p = impulse and q = coordinates, in physics.)

are to be treated as opposites of equal value. As a matter of principle, it may be advisable to take more serious account of synchronicity in this case. In the field of synchronicity, analogous to Einstein's work in the field of relativity, it will become necessary one day to develop a *general theory* besides the special theory. The psycho-physical functioning would then be regarded as only one special case of the general theory and, for example, the mantic methods as another.

Theoretically it makes no difference whether the *physis* arranges something acausally in the psyche, or vice versa: the cases are symmetrical, and probably always come into play together. What is common is the arrangement that seems to take place by virtue of the archetypal structure of the one that arranges. The phenomenon of imprinting (Lorenz) as described by students of ethnology appears to be a relevant example. Probably the synchronistic model applies also to the cognitive and learning processes. In any case, I believe there is a close correspondence between this schema and the Platonic ἀνάμνησις (*anamnesis*) [recollection].

---

42. C. G. Jung, "Synchronocity: An Acausal Connecting Principle," in *The Structure and Dynamics of the Psyche (Coll. Wks. 8, 1960), 500, 505ff. [original German version, 1952].

43. Jung, "Synchronicity," 514.

We may say, then, that effectiveness and archetypal evocation run parallel, and this surely applies also to psychosomatic medicine. Here, as elsewhere in medicine, therapeutic success may be obtained—other things being equal—in identical cases by different physicians who use different methods and maintain different theories. These are sometimes often downright absurd, which does not seem to impair healing. What one does is therefore relatively irrelevant, and to this irrelevance of the *what* corresponds the inconceivability of the *how* in the psycho-physical process. It seems that the decisive factor is only this: that an arrangement of wholeness = soundness comes into play. *How* this is brought about is irrelevant *qua* effect, as long as the archetype of wholeness and therefore—*post hoc aut propter hoc*—healing appears.[44] But here, too, as in methods of divination, it seems that certain steps can be taken which may make the appearance of the "wholesome" archetype more probable. For this reason, I occupied myself intensely at one time with the cult of Asklepios.[45] I will only emphasize seven of my findings:

1. The ancient health divinities originally were all possessors of oracles.

2. The patient was cured suddenly whenever he had dreamt the right dream.

3. The healing symbolism is a *creatio*, often sexual in character.

4. Dream and cure were obviously constellated by the cult, and perhaps by a personal relation with the priest.

5. A pure rational attitude on the part of the patient often caused a relapse.

6. His permanent cure meant at the same time that the ex-patient had become a *religiosus*.

7. The climate at the shrines of Asklepios, and of their festivals (the *Asklepieia*) and the whole cult, was apt to engender a harmony between macro- and microcosm.

In this connection I wish to report a case that represents the perfect counterpart of the Greek temple cures. For the treatment

---

44. Probably neither *post* nor *propter*, but acausal synchronistically.

45. C. A. Meier, *Ancient Incubation and Modern Psychotherapy* (Evanston, Ill.: Northwestern University Press, 1967) [original German edition, 1949].

of a Navajo woman in Arizona a sand painting was made. I was interested in the diagnosis of her illness, but neither diagnosis nor illness existed. The healing ceremony was enacted exclusively because the woman had had a bad dream. One may, therefore, conclude that an archetype was disturbed, and that it was the purpose of the ritual to put it right again, i.e., to restore its order, and to this end the patterns of sand paintings, which manifestly resemble mandalas, are preeminently suited.

In comparison, our psychosomatic "rituals" appear rather scientific and rational, but perhaps this makes them all the more primitive. Indeed, we assign a paramount role to the transference, of which the Greeks and Navajos—if it occurred at all—remained completely unconscious. Now I have a suspicion that may sound like heresy to psychoanalysts: perhaps the transference is the more "wholesome" the less conscious it is, at least in the psychosomatic realm. As we can see from a case already mentioned[46]—and here I have a suspicion that may seem heretical to the psychosomatic specialist—what ultimately matters in psychosomatic medicine is a symptomatic cure. It does not seem at all incredible to me that quaternity, for instance, may by itself produce a whole-making, i.e., a healing, effect. The position is of course different in the case of the few people of whom greater consciousness is demanded in the interest of the individuation process; presumably, in their case neither homeopathy nor allopathy can by themselves promise healing. On the other hand, probably every analyst regularly comes across cases where the analytic process is complicated by intercurrent somatic disturbances or even illnesses. Accidents, too, may be part of the picture, and then a physician must inevitably be called in. Psychology alone will not always do. In this context it appears doubtful whether in such cases one is right in reproaching oneself with having overlooked or misinterpreted something or in believing that, with greater knowledge, the complication might have been avoided. Life and man form a whole, which even medicine has to accept, so that it can dispense neither with *cura corporis* [care of the body], nor with *cura animae* [care of the soul]. This truth means a *crux* to the layman as well as to the physician and the

---

46. Saul, 1941.

psychosomatic practioner. I should not be surprised if the answer were to be found in that enigmatic synchronicity, the Jungian *transgressiveness of psychoid archetypes*, for phenomena of this kind seem to me indispensable for the attainment of right psycho-physical functioning, that is to say, for physical as well as for mental health, including individuation. No doubt the self must also comprise all the physical exponents of the body. That this is so we know not only from the Tantric Chakras and similar systems, but it has been strikingly brought home to us by the work of S. Bach at the Neurosurgical University Clinic in Zürich.[47]

These loose ends should suffice to protect us from the danger of understanding psychosomatic correlations without further thought, as explanations in the causal sense. Plutarch's tormenting question, *utrum animae an corporis sit libido* — whether the libido belongs to the soul or to the body — is still open.

SUMMARY

A Jungian approach to psychosomatic medicine emerged very early in Jung's career when he perfected his association experiments during the years 1907 to 1909. His discovery of complexes enabled him to demonstrate concurrent effects in psyche and soma. These could be measured by the use of the electrical skin reaction, the pneumograph, sphygmograph, plethysmograph, etc., ultimately resulting in the combination known today as the lie detector.

At first the theory was dominated by the fact that emotions and affects irradiate and produce effects on the body. Very soon Jung proposed the theory that, in schizophrenia, a third element may enter in the form of a toxin responsible for the fixation of the complexes; in addition, he left open the question whether the cause-effect movement might not run the opposite way — soma to psyche. A great body of subsequent additional

$$\phi \underset{2}{\overset{1}{\rightleftharpoons}} \psi$$

_____

47. S. Bach, "Spontanes Malen und Zeichnen im neurochirurgischen Bereich. Ein Beitrag zur Früh-und Differentialdiagnose," *Schweiz. Arch. Neurol. Psychiat.* 87, 1 (1961).

work, mainly in the Anglo-Saxon world, centered on this very question, yet remained safely within the sphere of cause-effect relationships.

It is proposed to approach the entire problem of psychosomatic phenomena as an acausal relationship, in accordance with the views held by the physicians of ancient Greece, expressed in the word *symptoma*, the acausal but meaningful coincidence of at least two distinct magnitudes. This concept is identical with that expressed in the modern term *synchronicity*; it presupposes a *tertium*, higher than soma or psyche, and is responsible for symptom formation in both – approximating to the theory of the *subtle body*.

Such concepts were set forth in ancient times by the Greek physician Erasistratus and by Poseidonius and Plotinus, and later by such medical authorities as Paracelsus and Boerhaave.

It appears that healing can take place only through the constellation of a *tertium* of a higher order – a symbol or the archetype of totality – but as a synchronistic event and not as a cause-effect chain. As with mantic methods or with the healings of the Asklepieia, it is the healer's task to create a climate and to take measures – their type being immaterial – which are favorable to the appearance of this third or higher order, the symbol or the archetype of totality.

Further References

Alfred Adler, *Studien über die Minderwertigkeit von Organen* (Berlin & Vienna, 1907).

Appian, *Roman History*, x, 59ff.

Nicholas A. Bercel, *AMA Arch. Gen. Psychiat.* 2 (Chicago, 1960).

C. G. Jung, "The Psychology of Dementia Praecox" (*Coll. Wks.* 3, 1960) [original German version, 1907].

C. A. Meier, *Zeitgemässe Probleme der Traumforschung* (Zürich, Kulturstaatswiss. Schriften E.T.H., no. 75, 1950).

H. R. Schwyzer, "Bewusst und Unbewusst bei Plotin," in *Sources de Plotin* (Genève, Entretiens V, Vandoeuvres, 1960).

Bibliographical Appendix

A further selection of papers on the psycho-galvanic phenomenon, not referred to in the text yet all instigated by Jung's interest (in order of publication):

Hugo Muller, "Experimentelle Beitrage zur physikalischen Erklärung der Entstehung es psycho-galvanischen Phänomens," Diss. (Zürich, 1909).

Jacob Abeli, "Zur Analye der physikalischen Vorbedingungen des psychogalvanischen Reflexes mit exosomatischer Stromquelle," Diss. (Zürich, 1910).

Esther Aptekmann, "Experimentelle Beitrage zur Psychologie des psychogalvanischen Phänomens," *Jb. psychoanal. psychopathol. Forsch.* III (1927).

Jacob Klasi, "Über das psychogalvanische Phänomen," *J. Psychol. Neurol.* xix.

Victor Kuhne, "Résumé des récherches psycho galvanométriques sur l'émotivité de M. Edouard Abramowski," *Bull. Inst. gén. psychol.* 3 (1913).

Victor J. Muller, "Zur Kenntnis der Leiungsbahnen des psycho-galvanischen Reflexphänomens," *Monatsschr. Psychol. Neurol.* xxxiii (1913).

Hans C. Syz, "Psycho-galvanic Studies in Schizophrenia," *Arch. Neurol. Psychiat. Chicago*, 16.

Carney Landis and Wm. H. Hunt, "The Conscious Correlates of the Galvanic Skin Response," *J. Exp. Psychol.* 5 (1926).

Chapter 8

The Dream in Ancient Greece
and its Use in Temple Cures (Incubation)

How the dream was viewed in ancient Greece has a long history:
at the beginning, the attitude was purely religious, whereas in
the end the dream had become prey to cheap imposters found by
the dozens in every marketplace, at every festival or country fair.
Incidentally, the wide diversity of esteem accorded the dream is
manifested in many other cultures so that it might almost appear
to be either a cultural pattern or the result of something inherent
in the phenomenon itself. However, the wide variety of meanings
attributed to dreams has not only been a function of the
dreamer's lifetime but also demonstrably of his social standing,
education or philosophy. Here the correlation may have been
direct or inverse, just as it is in our day. If we try to find a *constant*, it probably consists in the dreamer's attitude toward the
irrational.

One phenomenon connected with dreams has survived the
tides of changing opinion for several thousand years; incubation
was practiced in the most archaic *spelaea* of Amphiaraus at
Oropus or Trophonius at Lebadea, and is still flourishing at
many Christian shrines today, and not only in Greece.[1] I will
later point out some of the reasons for this striking fact. Following, in chronological order, are some of the more important
things that Greek poets, philosophers, and medical men had to
say about the dream.

─────────

Paper read to the "International Colloquium on 'Le rêve et les societés
humaines' " in Royaumont, France in 1962. First published in: *The Dream and
Human Societies* (Berkeley and Los Angeles, 1966), 303 ff.

1. Mary Hamilton, *Incubation* (London, 1906).

In Homer, ὄνειρος (*oneiros*) [dream] is always a personified, and at the same time divine (θεῖος, *theios*) and winged being that appears to the dreamer ὑπὲρ κεφαλῆς (*hyper kephalēs*) [at the head of his bed] and disappears again, being independent of time and space. Nestor, for instance, visiting Agamemnon in a dream, says: "Διός δέ τοι ἄγγελος εἰμί" ("Dios de toi angelos eimi") ["I am a messenger of Zeus"], and his task is to tell Agamemnon the will of God.[2] This example may be taken as a model for almost all Homeric dreams, and they all come from Zeus. In the so-called Homeric hymn of Hermes this god is called the ἡγητήρ ὀνείρων (*hēgētēr oneirōn*), the guide or mediator of dreams. It certainly strikes us as significant that the gods, as a rule, appear in person and speak directly to the dreamer: "quod ipsi di cum dormientibus colloquantur" ["the gods themselves speak to men when they sleep"].[3] From innumerable dreams related in ancient literature it is apparent that dreams were commonly considered messages from gods. More theoretically, and theologically or philosophically, this may be explained by the Orphic idea of σῶμα-σῆμα (*sōma-sēma*) (which we find again in Plato's *Phaedrus* 250 c), since in sleep the soul is freed from its tomb (the body) whereby it is sensitized and so is able to perceive and converse with the higher beings, a thought that was also held by the Pythagoreans. This idea can be found in Aeschylus and Euripides still, as well as in Pindar[4] and Xenophon.[5] It goes without saying that dreams of such dignity must be carefully observed and interpreted, an attitude that is reflected in Aeschylus' *Prometheus Bound*, where it is said that dream interpretation is one of the most important inventions of Prometheus.[6] The high dignity of dreams also made it imperative to go to any length in order to avert the evil that, according to the dream, was impending. Either such a dream had to be told to Helios whose bright daylight would frighten away its dangerous implications,[7] or sacrifices had to be made to the apotropaic

2. Homer, *Iliad* II.26.

3. Cicero, *De Divinatione* I.64; Homer, *Iliad* X.496; *Odyssey* XVI.21-24; XX.32.

4. Pindar, *Fragment* 131S.

5. Xenophon, *Cyropaedia* VIII.7, 21.

6. Aeschylus, *Prometheus Bound* 486.

7. Sophocles, *Electra* 424 and scholia; Euripides, *Iphigenia in Tauris* 42.

gods.[8] In minor cases lustration with water seems to have been sufficient.[9] In Euripides we find another interesting aspect of dreams when he calls Lady Earth "Ὤ πότνια Χθῶν μελανοπτέρυγος μῆτηρ ὀνείρων" ("ō potnia Chthōn, melanopterygōn mēter oneirōn") ["Mother of black-winged Dreams"].[10] This chthonic origin of dreams has survived to our time in the practice of incubation. More about this presently.

Plato did not create a theory of dreams except that in his psychology it becomes clear that the content of a dream is determined by the particular part of the psyche that is active, namely the λογιστικόν (logistikon) [reasonable element], the θηριοδές (thēriōdés) [savage element] or the θυμοειδές (thymoeides) [passionate element]. If the logistikon prevails, we may have a dream that reveals to us the all-important truth.[11] In regard to such dreams, Xenophon, in his Commentary, clearly advocates interpretation, as ordinary knowledge may not suffice for their understanding. In the Symposium, moreover, Plato calls a man who knows how to judge dreams a δαιμόνιος ἀνήρ (daimonios anēr) as opposed to the βάναυσος (banausos) [artisan].[12] But these are the words of Diotima, his specialist on Eros, and according to her, demons are the originators of dreams and oracles, and one of these demons is Eros. It should be noted that Plato attributes this view to a woman.

We deal briefly now with Aristotle, the most powerful authority on dreams. Two opuscula contained in the Parva Naturalia are in relatively good condition: (1) Περὶ ἐνυπνίων (Peri Enypniōn) [About Dreams] and (2) Περὶ τῆς καθ' ὕπνον μαντικῆς (Peri tēs kath' hypnon mantikēs) [About Prophecy in Sleep] (especially 464b). According to these, the dream is the result of the affection of the κοινὸν αἰσθητήριον (koinon aisthētērion) [common organ of sensation], that is, the heart as the central seat of representations, by those minimal movements during

---

8. Xenophon, Symposium IV.33; Hippocrates Peri Enypnion II.10, ed. D.C.G. Kuhn (Lipsiae, 1826).

9. Aeschylus, Persians 200; Aristophanes, Frogs 1339; Apollonius Rhodius, Argonautica IV.662; for further examples, see B. Buchsenschutz, Traum und Traumdeutung im Alterthume (Berlin, 1868).

10. Euripides, Hecuba 70.

11. Plato, Republic IX.571 C ff.

12. Plato, Symposium 203 A.

sleep left over from the waking activities of the senses. These residual movements are of course present in the waking state also, but remain unperceived – unheard, as it were, because of the violent movements of the senses, that is, because of the far greater noise they make. This is how veridical dreams are possible because during sleep the dreamer is much more sensitive to small disturbances of an organic nature. A skilled doctor can therefore predict illness, cure or death from such dreams.

Dreams about people we know well can, according to Aristotle, also be veridical or precognitive, because we know these people's motivations well and are consciously deeply involved with them, so that from such knowledge we can reach certain conclusions concerning their future actions.

Also, according to Aristotle, the dream is an incentive to future actions of the dreamer. Concerning the diagnostic and prognostic use of dreams, Aristotle closes his treatise "On Prophecy in Sleep" with an interesting simile by which he shows how dreams can and should be understood and interpreted:

The most skillful judge of dreams is the man who possesses the ability to detect likenesses, for anyone can judge the vivid dream. By likenesses I mean that the mental pictures are like reflections in water.... In the latter case, if there is such movement, the reflection is not like the original, nor the images like the real object. Thus *he* would indeed be a clever interpreter of reflections who could quickly discriminate and envisage these scattered and distorted fragments of the images as representing a man, say, or a horse or any other object.... Now in the other case, too, the dream has a similar result, for the movement destroys the clarity of the dream.[13]

Generally speaking, Aristotle paradoxically sides with Diotima when he attributes *demonic* origin to dreams. Were they sent by God, he argues, they would only be bestowed on the best and wisest men, which is most obviously not so. This sweeping devaluation of the dream has had a lasting effect. For example, the Epicureans, as well as the New Academy philosophers such as Carneades, naturally had as little use for dreams as did the Cynics. In the Stoa, however, dreams again play a prominent

---

13. Aristotle, "On Prophecy in Sleep," *Parva Naturalis*, trans. by W. S. Hett, *On the Soul; Parva Naturalia, On Breath* (Cambridge: Harvard University Press, 1936), 385.

part. The ancient Stoics seem to have been the first to classify dreams by their sources: they come either from God or from demons or from the activity of the soul itself.[14] Apart from this, the Stoics allow for prognostication through dreams by virtue of the interrelation of the human soul with the soul of the universe. Because of these correspondences, man is aware of the coherence of all things when his senses are at rest—that is, in his sleep—and thus he is able to know the future.[15] Poseidonius claims that the *divine* has three ways of acting upon man in dreams:[16] (1) the soul may see the future by virtue of its own godlike nature; (2) the air is full of immortal souls carrying obvious signs of truth, who penetrate the sleeper's system through the πόροι (*poroi*) [channels] of the senses;[17] and (3) the gods themselves talk to the sleepers.[18]

These thoughts, together with the idea of the macrocosm-microcosm relation, give a causal explanation for all mantic belief: the order of the universe consists of the concatenation of causes and effects. Certain signs let us perceive certain causes that will lead to certain effects. In turn, these signs are perceived in certain dreams: "Poseidonius esse censet in natura signa quadam rerum futurarum" ["Poseidonius held that nature gives certain signs of future events"].[19]

This theory certainly allows for precognitive or veridical dreams or, rather, dreams to be so interpreted, whereas for the possibility of the so-called telepathic dreams one must resort to a theory that had already been proposed by Democritus, astonishingly enough. His εἴδολα (*eidōla*) [atoms] have all the qualities of an *individuum*, the Latin word created by Cicero in translating the Greek ὁ ἄτομος (*hō atomos*) [the indivisible] of Democritus. The air is full of atoms—individuals that offer themselves as carriers of messages from one person to another, which

---

14. *Stoicorum Veterum Fragmenta* III.605.
15. *Stoicorum Veterum Fragmenta* II.1198.
16. Cicero, *De Divinatione* 1.30.
17. Plutarch, *De placitis philosophorum* V.2; *Quaestiones conviviales* VIII.10.2.
18. Karl Reinhardt, *Poseidonios über Ursprung und Entartung* (Heidelberg: Carl Winters Universitätsbuchhandlung, 1928), 457-459.
19. Cicero, *De Divinatione*, 1.52-57.

should indeed make it easy to transmit telepathic effects.[20] As I have already committed an anachronism by going back to Democritus, let me do so again by calling your attention to the well-known *Fragment* 89 D of Heraclitus "τοῖς ἐγρηγόροσιν ἕνα καὶ κοινὸν κόσμον εἶναι, τῶν δὲ κοιμωμένων ἕκαστον εἰσ ἴδιον ἀποστρέφεσθαι" ("tois egrēgorosin hena kai koinon kosmon einai, tōn de koimōmenōn hekaston eis idion apostrephesthai") ["the waking have one world and a common one, but when asleep everyone turns away from it into his own one"]. His *own one*, therefore, must be his dream world, where he is all by himself, in a primordial condition; in other words, the dreamer finds himself in a mythological realm and what happens there is actually cosmogony. In this sense, Heraclitus' saying corresponds exactly with Jung's concept of the meaning of dreams "on the subjective level."

To outline the medical approach to dreams in Greece, we go back to the fifth century B.C. where we find a Hippocratic writer dealing with the problem in Περὶ Ἐνυπνίων (*Peri Enypniōn*) [About Dreams].[21] According to this treatise, the soul is preoccupied with bodily functions during the waking state, whereas in sleep she is the unrestricted ruler of the house, since the sleeping body has no perception. While the body sleeps, the soul, always awake, has all the psychological and physiological functions at her disposal, so that he who is able to judge this relationship correctly possesses a good deal of wisdom. Hippocrates also admits that there can be divine influences in dreams through which we can know things otherwise unknowable. Regarding the diagnostic value of dreams, he thinks the soul can perceive the causes of illness in *images* during sleep. Here we see for the first time that a symbolic quality of the psyche is assumed. When Hippocrates is particularly interested in the medical aspect, he shows very clearly that the health of the dreamer is reflected in his dream. There are, of course, *divinely* inspired dreams, interpretation of which he leaves entirely to the dream specialist. There are the *natural* influences whereby the soul perceives the bodily condition and thus becomes a hygienic system. As long as the dreams simply repeat what has happened during the day, the

---

20. Cicero, *De Divinatione*, I.43; II.67.
21. Hippocrates, *Peri Enypniōn*, II.1-16.

body is obviously in order. When the dream pictures strife, war and the like, however, this means disorder in the body. For instance, when we dream of the sun and the moon as they appear in nature, this is a sign of good health, but when something is wrong with these planets in our dream, then there must be something the matter with those systems in us that correspond to sun and moon according to the macrocosm-microcosm relation. Springs and wells correspond to the uropoietic system, rivers to the circulatory system where flood or drought would be the same, for example, as hypertonia or anemia.[22] Galen had little more to say about this problem. The diagnosis, as the examples have shown, was reached exclusively from the dream text by what we might call "thinking in analogies." And this technique has been called by several authors the only significant point in the art of dream interpretation.[23]

It is evident that there is hardly anything new in the dream theories of Hippocrates and Galen as compared with those of Plato, Aristotle and Democritus. Plato already had the conception that dreams were the perception of residual movements in sleep — τὰς ἐντὸς κινήσεις (*tas entos kinēsis*) [literally "movements inside"] — and Aristotle the κινήσεις φανταστικαὶ ἐν τοῖς αἰσθητηρίοις (*kinēseis phantastikai en tois aisthētēriois*) [movements perceived in the sense organs], meaning that those inner movements are the dream images that are exclusively based on an inner faculty of perception — *phantasia*. Aristotle's psychology could be called a differential computation of the mutal inhibitions, stimulations and superpositions of those inner movements. Medical men, however, could apply this dream theory to therapy only by cutting out all extraneous sources for dreams. The *somnia a deo missa* [dreams sent by God] had to be excluded. And here we touch upon a decisive distinction regarding the immanence or transcendence of the source. Medical and rationalistic influence became very strong and almost replaced the purely religious attitude of the earlier days. It is clear that the transcendent source had been the only one that interested the

22. Hippocrates, Περὶ διαίτης (*Peri Diaitēs*) [About Diet] IV.88ff., trans. H. S. Jones (London and New York, 1931), IV, 421-447.

23. Aristotle, "On Prophecy in Sleep" 464-5; Artemidorus, *Oneirocritica* II.25.

Greek peoples earlier. Dreams were considered to be objective facts, things that happened to you. The Greek was visited by a dream, ἐπισκοπεῖν (*episkopein*), at best he "saw" a dream, ἐνύπνιον ἰδεῖν (*enypnion idein*). They would never have dreamed of saying, as the French do nowadays, *J'ai fait un rêve*, or the Italians, *Ho fatto un sogno*. We could therefore predict that after this rationalistic period the pendulum would swing again in the other direction. We have but to look at the Hellenistic period of which I take Philo as an example. To him the most important organ is the πνεῦμα (*pneuma*) [breath, spirit]. It is the ψυχὴ ψυχῆς (*psychē psychēs*) [the soul of the soul], that has the cleanest and best οὐσία (*ousia*) [substance], namely a divine one. The dream is to him a phenomenon in which the pneuma is the protagonist; therefore all dreams are interesting mainly for their prophetic quality. He has three categories of dreams: (1) dreams prophetic by direct divine influence, (2) dreams prophetic by virtue of the movement of the *ratio* (reason) inasmuch as it is in symphony with the general divine movement, and (3) dreams that spring from purely psychic emotion because of the powers of enthusiasm. Only dreams in the last category need interpretation, although here too the enthusiastic powers point to divine origin, and generally speaking, all is irrational again. This trend prevailed to Roman times.

This lopsided, enthusiastic view is of course as unsavory as the purely rationalistic one. The early Homeric distinction should never be forgotten.[24] There will always be confused, relatively unimportant dreams that penetrate the Gate of Ivory, and clear and very significant dreams that come through the Gate of Horn (Penelope's dream of the geese and the eagle, by the way, is interpreted purely allegorically and not symbolically in Jung's terminology). It is rather on the strength of such a dichotomy that dreams can be taken seriously at all, as is shown very impressively by Greek dreamers who had temples built, sacrifices performed, and so on, because of dreams.[25]

I am strongly disposed to believe that almost all the observations of the Greeks on dreams still hold good. There are a few obvious exceptions owing to changes in condition: for instance,

---

24. Homer, *Odyssey* XIX.560ff.
25. Aelius Aristides (A.D. 117 or 129-189).

with everything so utterly secularized with us, there are rarely any divine epiphanies in our dreams. For the same reason it is no longer true nowadays that only kings, priests or medical men have dreams of great import.

So far the scanty sources about dreams in ancient literature have had to be carefully and painstakingly collected, a task carried out mainly by B. Büchsenschütz,[26] and to some extent by E. R. Dodds.[27] Unfortunately, all the important books on dreams written in antiquity have been lost, and for synopses of them we must look to authors of the second and fourth centuries A.D., namely Artemidorus (who calls himself of Daldis, although he was born in Ephesus) and Macrobius and Synesius of Cyrene. Artemidorus had the advantage of having known all the antique literature on dreams as well as having been in practice for a lifetime. He not only collected more than three thousand dreams but also took a good look at the dreamers themselves, their history, and the outcome of their dreams. Compared to him, Macrobius and Synesius were highly educated men, much less influenced by the earlier dream literature, and much more scholarly. Macrobius was an initiate into the Neoplatonic mysteries, and Synesius became a Christian bishop (with wife and children!), though he had never been baptized, a fact that testifies to his scholarly merits and prestige. Contrary to Artemidorus, who is an eclectic, Macrobius and Synesius are both true to their Neoplatonic convictions. Briefly, Synesius' book Περὶ Ἐνυπνίων (*Peri Enypniōn*) [On Dreams] was written in one night at God's command.[28] With him, dreams are prophetic inasmuch as through and in them we practice what will eventually, according to cosmic harmony, happen to us later. They are the preludes to the events and they may tune us into them. They are the best kind of prophecy because they come to all men, poor and rich. Dreams arise from the soul, which contains the images of things to come. These images are reflected in "phantasy," which is a kind of life on a deeper level. Its sense organs are finer, more divine, hence more reliable than ours, but its perceptions are blurred, which is a wise limitation and accounts for the need for

---

26. Büchsenschütz, *Traum und Traumdeutung im Altertum* (Berlin, 1868).

27. E. R. Dodds, *The Greeks and the Irrational* (Berkeley and Los Angeles, 1956).

28. Synesii Episcopil, *Opera omnia*, ed. Petavius Dionys (Lutetiae, 1612).

interpretation. Synesius gives no general rule for interpretation but strongly recommends that we keep "nightbooks" instead of silly diaries. Macrobius' *Commentariorum ex Cicernone in Somnium Scipionis libri duo* first gives a classification of dreams closely resembling that of Artemidorus.[29] Then he gives a long and exhaustive context to Scipio's dream text and goes to great lengths to give exactly what we would today call an amplification of the material according to C. G. Jung. In this way we learn that the dreamer by means of his dream was not only given a thorough lecture on contemporary psychology but was truly initiated into the mysteries of his soul, an initiation that winds up with the mystagogue's assertion *deum te esse scito* [know that you are a god!]. Toward the end of the book Macrobius also presents a very useful and reliable synopsis of most of the Greek philosophers' ideas about the nature of the psyche. (Macrobius' interesting classification has been available since 1952 in a good annotated English translation.[30])

What follows are some of the more unusual qualities of Artemidorus' five books of Ὀνειροκρίτικα (*Oneirocritica*), or dream interpretation.[31] His views give us a chance to compare ancient ideas with modern ones. We must keep in mind, however, that he scrutinized three thousand dreams and carefully investigated the dreamers' personal circumstances as well as the outcome (anamnesis, catamnesis and epicrisis).

What stands out as important is (1) the fact that in contradistinction to modern dream material a large proportion of his dreams contain divine epiphanies. Here he knows of one and only one absolutely reliable criterion, that is: (2) as long as the god appears true to his attributes and to his cult image, the dream is favorably interpreted. The slightest flaw in this respect, however, renders its meaning ominous. This conviction clearly reveals a totemistic element. With aborigines of northwestern Australia, odd behavior of the totem animal in dreams is always

---

29. Macrobii, *Opera* (Societas Bipontina, Biponti, 1788). His commentary refers to Cicero's *De Republica* VI.

30. W. H. Stahl, *Macrobius' Commentary on the Dream of Scipio* (New York: Columbia University Press, 1952).

31. Artemidorus, *Oneirocritica*, ed. Rigaltius (Lutetiae, 1603). Also available in a critical edition: Artemidori Daldiani, *Oneirocriticon Libri* V, ed., Roger A. Pack (Leipzig, 1963).

interpreted unfavorably.[32] Gods appearing in a wrong costume may easily lie. It seems that such deviations had the quality of blasphemy, which psychologically meant that the dreamer was in conflict with whatever deeper psychological truth or quality the particular god represented. This would of necessity call down the god's wrath upon the dreamer. Generally speaking, we notice here the common features of ancient ὀνειρομάντεια (*oneiromanteia*) [dream interpretation], namely, that all dreams are mainly judged (3) in terms of future actual events and (4) as to whether they will turn out favorably or unfavorably. (5) The particular dreamer's god also has to obey the rule of *suum cuique* [to each his own], so that goddesses, for instance, are considered more appropriate for women than for men. (6) Gods may appear only as their attributes (*pars pro toto* [the part stands for the whole]), which is another reason why the interpreter (as well as for [2]) had to be very well informed in mythology. (7) Gods may make prescriptions, even in the medical sense, in the event of physical illness. These prescriptions are very simple and need no interpretation. A god speaks in riddles only in order to make us ponder the dream (IV. 22). (8) There are two kinds of dreams: (a) θεωρημάτικοι (*theorēmatikoi*) [visionary] and (b) ἀλλεγόρικοι (*allēgorikoi*) [story-telling]. The dreams in group (a) correspond exactly to reality, and very soon after being dreamed are *tale quale* lived out by the dreamer. The dreams in group (b) have a deeper meaning, showing *di' ainigmata* [through enigmas], and take a long time to come true, sometimes years. (9) There are dreams that come from within and dreams that come from without. All dreams containing unexpected elements belong to the latter category since they are regarded as θεόπεμπτον (*theopempton*) [being sent by the gods].

   Concerning the principles of interpretation, I point out a few pecularities that compare favorably with modern principles: (1) There are relatively few standard equations for typical dream elements, as for instance:

business   = mother, because it is nurturing
business   = wife, because of the close connection between a
                 man and his business
head   = father

---

32. Personal communication with Rix Weaver, Perth, W. Australia.

```
foot        = slave
right hand  = father, son, friend, brother
left hand   = wife, mother, mistress, daughter, sister
pudendum    = parents, wife, children
```

(2) There are six στοιχεῖα (*stoicheia*) [elements] to be found in all dreams: nature, law, custom, professional skill, art, and name. Everything in the dream that takes its course in harmony with its nature, law, and the rest, is of good omen; what deviates in one way or another is of bad omen. (3) You must know all about the dreamer's life – ἀνάμνησις (*anamnesis*) [literally "recollection"] – and situation; if necessary you must seek information from others (objective anamnesis). (4) You must know the dreamer's character. (5) You must consider the dreamer's actual mood. (6) You must be given the whole dream; fragments must not be interpreted (IV. 3). (7) You must be familiar with the customs of the place and of the people in order to judge the dream correctly according to (2). (8) Etymology should always be used, particularly in the case of proper names. (A Greek dreaming of a Εὐτύχης (*Eytuchēs*), or a Roman of a Felix, should take this as a good sign because both names mean literally "happy" or "lucky.") (9) We now dwell a bit on the most prominent feature of Artemidorus' approach, the *polarity* and *ambivalence* of dream motives, of which I give some examples:

  a. To have asses' ears is a good omen only for a philosopher because the ass will not listen and give in easily. To all other people it means servitude and misery (1.24).

  b. Taking a bath: formerly this was performed after tedious work and would consequently have indicated sweat and tears. Nowadays it is a sign of wealth and luxury and consequently a good omen (1.64).

  c. To sleep in the temple indicates a cure to the sick, illness to the healthy (1.79).

  d. Gold as such is of good omen, but should a man, for instance, wear a gold necklace it would be the opposite (II.5).

  e. Being struck by a flash of lightning takes from you what you possess. As the poor possess poverty and the rich wealth, the portent of such a dream is accordingly good or bad (II.9).

  f. A dolphin *in* water is of good omen, *out of* water of bad omen (II.9).

  g. Something bad happening to your enemies is of good omen to you (1.2).

h. If you are happy and are promised happiness in the dream, this means bad luck; if you are unhappy, good luck. Conversely, should you be unhappy and dream that you will be unhappy it means good luck.

i. Simple people dream directly, whereas people who know a lot about dreaming in their dreams translate the crude facts into symbols (iv. Introduction). This is in the genuine Sophoclean tradition: "For wise men author of dark edicts aye,/For dull men a poor teacher, if concise."[33] Generally speaking people have pleasant dreams when they live under unpleasant conditions. Explaining this ambivalence or multivalence of dream "symbols," Artemidorus simply points out that the facts in life *are* ambivalent.

j. In iv.67 he gives a striking paradigm for seven different meanings of an identical dream dreamed by seven different pregnant women: all dreamed that they had given birth to a dragon. The interpretation had to be adapted to the particular circumstances of the dreamer's life, her anamnesis, for in each case the ἀπόβασις (*apobasis*) [literally "what turned out"] was actually different.

k. Artemidorus makes allowance for wish fulfillment in dreams by saying that we want the god to help us to see more clearly what is going on in us. In this sense we are αἰτηματικοι (*aitēmatikoi*) [disposed to ask], and so are our dreams. But, he adds, we should never ask the gods undue questions either! If the answer has been granted, we must not forget to sacrifice and give thanks (iv.2).

l. In the art of dream interpretation you must skillfully synthesize all these and many more principles and never forget *respicere finem* to adapt your verdict to the personality of the dreamer before you (iii.66). Many a dream may be ἄκριτος (*akritos*) [uninterpretable] before its *apobasis* (iv.24).

m. In iv.20 we find advice for the scribes among analysts. He says in so many words that the analyst should, after due consideration of all the circumstances mentioned above, present his interpretation purely and simply, and not try to justify it by reasoning and quoting authorities, as in doing so he would simply be trying to impress the client with his scholarliness and

---

33. Sophocles, *Fragment* 704, ed., A. Nauck (Leipzig, 1889).

intelligence. (This and other remarks about decorum are often delightful.)

There is no end of sound advice, as modern as can be, in Artemidorus' *Oneirocritica* [Dream Criticism], but it requires close philological scrutiny. Artemidorus makes difficult reading and there are no reliable translations. This may account for the fact that most modern psychologists turn up their noses at him, in spite of the fact that Freud has taken quite some trouble to discuss him—but even with Freud, strangely enough, Artemidorus did not stick. He apparently had to hurry on to develop his own *new* ideas, which were shattering enough, so that we can well understand that he got completely wrapped up in them.

We have seen that in ancient Greece dreams were thought of as real oracles. But where the many existing techniques for receiving answers to problems (*auguries, haruspicy* and the like)[34] had fixed systems of reference and only a relatively limited number of possible answers, the dream lacks these points of reference altogether. It is so polymorphous that its proper interpretation either takes a great deal more skill and knowledge or leads to quackery, as in fact it mostly did.

Probably because of this difficulty, the Greeks very early limited the scope of dreams to one particular purpose by accepting them exclusively as oracles regarding sickness and cure. It seems that this specialization required two main adaptations: (1) one had to have recourse to a god who specialized as a healer and the appropriate cult had to be established, and (2) one had to resort to the chthonic deities, as *body* and *Mother Earth* are practically synonymous. Moreover, the age-old belief that πότ-νια Χθῶν (*potnia Chthōn*) [Mother Earth] is the mother of dreams was helpful. Chthonic gods have their definite abodes to which they are confined, so one must make a pilgrimage to the shrine. In the course of time the shrine will accumulate an enormous amount of prestige and mana. There were archaic models for worship of primitive chthonic gods or heroes who had the

---

[34. Ed. Note: Auguries were divinations made from interpretation of omens or portents (such as configurations of the flight of birds) or chance phenomena (such as the fall of lots). Haruspicy refers to an art of divination which relied on inspection of the entrails of sacrificial animals for its predictions.]

reputation for answering questions about illness and for working miraculous cures, such as Amphiaraus and Trophonius,
already mentioned. Moreover, there was an old mythical doctor
who had later been granted apotheosis, Asklepios. There had
been many in other cultures who also shared the same specialty,
but Asklepios' fame knew no boundaries, and his cult was certainly the most elaborate. The following is an extremely con-
densed description of the practice of incubation as it was performed at the shrines of Asklepios. A study of the older and contemporary parallels, including the cults of Trophonius,
Amphiaraus, Calchas, Faunus, Isis, and more particularly
Serapis, as well as others, would put Asklepios in the right perspective, but we treat him as a representative sample.[35]

I take Epidaurus to illustrate what went on at an Asklepieion.
The place is beautifully situated far out in the country with a *via
sacra* five miles long connecting it with the port. Its buildings are
world famous for their beauty, particularly the theater and the
rotunda called θόλος (*tholos*). The place swarms with harmless
snakes. Lots of trees, predominantly Oriental plane trees, and a
plentiful supply of water are found in the sanctuary. Near the
entrance are six stone stelae with inscriptions telling the case
histories of more than a hundred cures that had become famous.
(Seventy of them are still extant and are accessible in a fine edition by Rudolf Herzog.[36])

As a patient you would readily be admitted to the sacred precinct, unless you were moribund or a pregnant woman near con-
finement, as the sanctuary had to be kept ritually pure from
death and birth. After having performed certain purificatory
rites, ablutions, and preliminary sacrifices, you would go to sleep
on your κλίνη (*klinē*) [couch — whence clinic] in the ἄβατον
(*abaton*) or ἄδυτον (*adyton*), [the place not to be entered by the
unbidden]. To have to be bidden by the god into his temple is a
locus communis [common characteristic] in many mystery cults
(e.g., Isis, cf. Apuleius) and most probably depended on the out-

35. See C. A. Meier, *Ancient Incubation and Modern Psychotherapy*
(Evanston: Northwestern University Press, 1967) for a full account of the
sources. [Original German, 1949.]

36. Rudolf Herzog, *Die Wunderheilungen von Epidauros* (Leipzig, 1931).

come of your preliminary sacrifice. Once admitted, all will depend upon your having the *right* dream while sleeping in the *abaton*. This was the actual process of incubation. *Incubare* means "sleeping in the sanctuary," the Greek word being ἐγ-κοίμησις (*enkoimēsis*). Whether the dream was the right one was decided by its result, for if it was the right one, the patient awoke cured. Apparently he was always cured if in his dream he experienced an epiphany of Asklepios. The god then appeared to him ὄναρ (*onar*) [in the dream], to use the technical expression, or else ὕπαρ (*hypar*) [in the waking state or, as one should say, in a vision] in case he was too excited to sleep. The god came either alone as the bearded man of his cult image, or as a boy, or he might be accompanied by his virgin wife or daughter Hygeia and sometimes by Panacea or Iaso. Instead of appearing personally, he might delegate one of them or prefer to show himself in his theriomorphic aspect, as a dog or snake. In one or another of his aspects he would then touch the stricken part of the patient's body and disappear. In early times the patient was apparently regarded as incurable if he did not experience a dream epiphany on the very first night. He then was probably regarded as *unbidden*. Later this decision seems already to have been made as the result of the preliminary sacrifices. Because of this ritual it became customary to stay at the Asklepieion until the sacrifice turned favorable, thus indicating the καιρὸς ὀξύς (*kairos oxys*) [the decisive moment]. The place eventually turned into a thriving hotel.

This development had another, genuinely religious aspect. The normal situation seems to have been that the former patient became a strong believer in the god's power and kindness, an experience that turned him into what was technically called a *religiosus*. This must have been of considerable importance, psychologically speaking, in determining whether the cure was lasting. The patient did not have to become a *fanatic* who could not tear himself away from the *fanum*, the sacred precinct. In other words, he did not have to develop an unsavory transference, but only a healthy one. There are cases on record of patients who spent very long periods in the precinct and who remind us, therfore, of the institution of κατοχή (*katochē*) [confinement] recognized especially at shrines of the most prominent of Asklepios' colleagues, Serapis. The κάτοχοι (*katochoi*) [temple prisoners], voluntary prisoners of course, must have spent a good deal of time in the ancient theurgic clinics. One of the most famous habitués of many an Asklepieion was the rhetor Aristides of Smyrna. Another famous man, Apuleius, called himself a *desmios* of the goddess Isis.

As can be seen there was no need for dream interpreters in these places. Nor were there any physicians in the sacred precinct and no medical therapy of any kind was practiced.

The applicants were obliged to write down their dreams or have them written down. Aristides tells us that the "prisoners" carefully noted down their dreams until a *symptōma*, a coincidence with the dream of the priest, occurred. Referring to the Asklepieion, he says that the priest with whom he lodged outside the Hieron, or else the priest's slave, sometimes dreamed for him. This certainly indicates that the spirit of healing pervaded the whole atmosphere of the place, and if we sought a theoretical concept for such a possibility we certainly would find an answer in the ideas of Democritus, Aristotle and Hippocrates mentioned above. Apuleius sums up the imprisonment during the Isis mysteries in the apt saying, "Neque vocatus morari nec non jussus festinare" ["do not hesitate when called, nor hasten when not commanded"], and the day on which he was bidden to initiation was "divino vadimonio destinatus" ["destined for him by divine guarantee"]. Sometimes a definite vision was required as a sign that the applicant was ready for initiation. This corresponded to what was known in the Asklepian cult as the ἐνύπνιον ἐναργές (*enypnion enargēs*) [dream made manifest] the effective dream or healing dream that immediately brought about the cure.

After the cure the former patient was expected to pay certain fees and make thank offerings. We have on record instances in which the god administered a sharp lesson to tardy debtors or people who regressed after the cure into their earlier rationalistic skepticism—by promptly ordaining a relapse.

You will be able to appreciate the absolute authority these dream decisions possessed from Plato's *Republic*, where it is said that Asklepios refused to treat those who had not lived according to the established order as they were of no use to the community.[37] On the other hand, some patients seem to have established a jovial sort of relationship with the divine doctor,

---

37. Plato, *Republic*, III.14, 15.

reminiscent of the modern dialectical concept in psychotherapy. We hear, for example, the amusing anecdote of a certain Polemon who, being forbidden by Asklepios to drink water, replied, "What would you have prescribed for a cow?"[38] or of a certain Plutarchus who asks, when Asklepios ordered him to eat pork, "What would you have prescribed for a Jew?"[39] Asklepios reacted amiably to these waggish objections and varied the treatment accordingly. In other cases, when it was necessary to heal by means of paradoxes and the forbidden thing was at the same time the remedy, the god remained firm—ὁ τρώσας ἰάσεται (*ho trosas iasetai*) [he who wounded will cure]—even if a Syrian should have to partake of a roast pig or a Greek Adonis-worshipper eat wild boar's meat—*contraria contrariis* [the way to one principle is through its opposites], a principle that you find as frequently as *similia similibus curantur* [like cures like]. As you can see from these examples, there are cases where the god made actual medical prescriptions. This is an exception, though, and can be found only in relatively late periods. But it had already given rise in antiquity to much conjecture about the origins of the art of medicine. They even went so far as to say that Hippocrates learned his therapy from the temple cures in Kos, although archaeology proves that the famous Asklepieion of Kos was founded after Hippocrates' death. Nevertheless, it was founded by members of his *medical* school, so that we may justifiably say that, sooner or later, even the famous rational Hippocratic medicine had to take account of theurgic competition.

The symbolism of healing accruing at these shrines certainly shows striking similarities to that developed at the equally famous centers of the mystery cults. The cure, in effect, was given all the dignity of a rebirth, but it was brought about by contact with the Earth element in its divine aspect. Demeter and Zeus καταχθόνιος (*katachthonios*) [of the earth], therefore, were always worshiped in the Asklepieia along with Asklepios and his divine father, Apollo. Many opposites were united in the cult as well as in the mythology of Asklepios. Thus Apollo and his arts, music and theater, held a prominent place in the Epidaurian cult, so that it can be said that what actually was provided for in

---

38. Philostratus, *Lives of the Sophists*, 1.25.
39. Damaskos, *Suidas, s. v. Domninos.*

these clinics of antiquity was the *cura animae* [cure of the soul], and it was really a *cult of the psyche,* which in itself should be the object of true therapy. The ensemble of water, snakes, trees, art, music, theater, and a chthonic cult whose acme came about at night in a dream, seems to explain much of the miraculous effects. It is certainly more inclusive than what is offered at healing places these days, whether at a university clinic or at Lourdes. The most famous of the approximately four hundred and twenty Asklepieia in the whole of the ancient world, such as Epidaurus, Kos and Pergamon, are all situated in a natural environment of exquisite beauty; this fact should not be overlooked because it is most conducive to establishing harmony between the inner and outer worlds (macrocosm and microcosm). Nor must it be forgotten that in antiquity illness was equivalent to the lack of something, or πενία (*penia*) [poverty] which could, under such circumstances of plenitude, be converted into health, which in turn, according to ancient thinking, is equivalent to πλοῦτος (*ploutos*) [wealth], which again is equivalent to wholeness, holiness, or health. All these words are etymologically connected. This is actually how illness became the remedy. And this remedy was provided by a god who had himself been a patient and, being a god, had been able to overcome the disease and consequently to know the cure and, by divine intervention, to bestow it on the patient as well.

With all this in mind it becomes understandable that Epidaurus jealously guarded the tradition of the cult and saw to it that new foundations of Asklepieia elsewhere had to be closely affiliated with the one at Epidaurus. The mode of *translatio* of the cult from Epidaurus to any other place had to be the strictly ritualistic transportation of one of the holy snakes to the new center. Thus, the possession of the true tradition could never give rise to such unpleasant discussions as we now witness when doctors, analysts, or schools of thought, bogged down by their personal prestige, vainly claim to be the only possessors of the true spirit of the master.

Incubation seems to me to be only one example of something you will notice at once when you go to Greece: the whole country is imbued with myth even today. All the old gods are still alive. And if you take a map of the country in one hand and Pausanias' *Baedeker* (if possible in Frazer's edition with commentary)[40] in the other, you will soon realize that what you are actually looking at is the geography of the human soul. Not the Greek, not the "Western," but the human soul, *tout court*. Spread over the peninsula and its islands are hundreds of places, each of which has its special myth, its cult and cult legends, and sanctuaries, each of which would take care of one or another of the most basic problems of human life in the most varied, complete, beautiful, and healing way. If you had been in need of help in those days, you would have known exactly where to go to find enacted for you the appropriate archetype. Let me close with a pun: *Nomina mutantur, permanent numina* [the names change, but the numinous effects remain the same].

Further References

Ludwig Deubner, *De Incubatione* (Leipzig, 1900).
Emma J. and Ludwig Edelstein, *Asclepius* (Baltimore, 1945).
Erwin Preuschen, *Mönchtum und Sarapiskult* (Giessen, 1903).

---

40. Pausanias, *Description of Greece*, trans. and with commentary by J. G. Frazer (London, 1913).

Chapter 9

A Jungian View
of Modern Dream Research

First of all, by now those interested in dreams ought to join forces and make a serious attempt at producing a number of working hypotheses for the application of this new experimental technique in dream research related to the deeper *psychological* function and meaning of dreaming. Secondly, in this endeavor, the many schools of thought ought to stop forming pious denominations adhering to one orthodoxy or another and stop religiously repeating the gospel truth they so faithfully believe in. They should, at long last, be open enough to the fact that dreams are far from being satisfactorily understood, and that so far every one of the schools has succeeded only in making it more or less probable that the convictions of each have contributed to the understanding of one or the other of the untold aspects of this inexhaustible phenomenon. In view of past history, each school should humbly admit that we are far from having heard the last word about a phenomenon that has been such a vital riddle to men for thousands of years. In such discussions all participants should, therefore, have a completely open mind; no "religious" or "political" climate should be allowed to prevail.

Just in the last thirteen years, we have had to learn from Kleitman and Dement something totally new about dreams which is

---

Paper read to the "Symposium on Dream Psychology and the New Biology of Dreaming," October 1967, in Cincinnati, Ohio. First published in a book of the same title (Springfield, Illinois, 1969), 101ff.

absolutely fundamental (i.e., *periodicity*). Whenever in biology we come across a periodicity, we can be sure that we have discovered a basic law that needs the most thoroughgoing and careful investigation. Since no one had been aware of this law before it was shown to us by these two pioneers, we should all admit that we have been sadly unaware of a basic fact concerning dreams. Consequently we must be prepared to make an entirely new start and, if necessary, to review at least some of our treasured convictions.

I should like now to present the Jungian point of view regarding those findings. In 1967 my friend Dr. Thomas B. Kirsch of Menlo Park, California, presented a paper on just this subject before the annual convention of the American Psychological Association.[1] This paper was entitled "The Relationship of the Rapid Eye Movement State to Analytical Psychology." I would like here to add my own ideas to those of Dr. Kirsch. In his paper, readers will find a discussion of the relevance of the few general convictions about the function and structure of dreams held by Jung. It is difficult to say anything more precise because there *is* virtually no Jungian theory of dreams.

Immediately after its publication in 1900, Freud's book *Die Traumdeutung* had a very deep effect on Jung and was, after long and intense consideration, wholeheartedly accepted by him.[2] Only years later did Jung begin to take exception to the monotony of the sexual interpretation in which he thought the concept of the *censor* often was nothing but a *petitio principii* [begging the question]. If, for one reason or another, most items in dreams had to have sexual significance without overtly saying so, then of course lack of veracity on the part of the manifest content has to be introduced. Jung thought that the censor was introduced by Freud only in order to make his preconceived idea tenable.

As we now have the chance to bypass the censor by waking our subjects after every REM phase and thus making them aware of almost all of their dreams, however successfully they

---

1. Thomas B. Kirsch, "The Relationship of the Rapid Eye Movement State to Analytical Psychology," *Amer. J. Psychiat.* 124 (1968): 1459-63.

2. S. Freud, *Die Traumdeutung* (Leipzig, 1900) [The Interpretation of Dreams, London, 1913].

might have been suppressed under normal conditions, we now may have the chance to check the old theory. Supposing the censor theory was correct, such procedure ought to have a terrifying effect on the subject, as he thus would become conscious of so many "facts of life" from all this dream material that he could hardly stomach them. Such an effect, however, has not been shown in the laboratory; thus we have to say that, from this point of view, the censor theory has not been proven. Perhaps my tacit identification of censorship with the usual forgetting of most dreams is wrong and one simply would have to introduce an additional helpful hypothesis in order to make the censor idea tenable. However, I prefer Occam's razor (*Entia explicandi non sunt multiplicanda praeter necessitatem* [explanations ought not to be multiplied except out of necessity]) and therefore would rather reduce the *principia explicandi*. While we have not succeeded in finding any experimental proof of the censorship, how about the counterargument?

Admittedly the *dreamwork* may already have succeeded in "explaining away" the true nature of our desire when the experimenter artificially interrupts our sleep. Why, then, should we still lose so many of our dreams when they have already been rendered innocent or innocuous enough by the dreamwork put in action by the censor? With regard to this question, REM-deprivation experiments seem to help, since dream inhibition does produce some bad effects. These facts suggest that dreams by themselves serve a biological purpose or, more precisely, have a homeostatic function, as is also generally accepted nowadays. And here I should like to repeat that their periodicity alone almost asks for such an interpretation.

I think that here we are facing the most tantalizing problem modern dream research has so far produced: if dreams have a homeostatic function in themselves, even when they are not remembered, we can safely leave them alone. They are doing their nightly job anyhow and may do it even better unobserved. The folkloristic theory of the goblins safely putting the house in order at night, washing up the dishes and so forth — as long as they are left unobserved — seems to be the answer. On the other hand, as analysts we are convinced that catching these specters (i.e., making them conscious and, if possible, analyzing them) has the most beneficial effect on our mental health. That would appear to be an obvious contradiction.

I have to admit that the work at our own laboratory, from its very origin, followed the working hypothesis that by the Kleitman-Dement technique the analytic work could be speeded up considerably as the analysand could in this way be made conscious of many more of his problems in a much shorter period of time. One of our subjects who spent well over fifty nights in the laboratory, for example, produced seventeen times more dreams during this period than during a period of preexperimental analysis of equal length. However, he became rather uneasy, a symptom we cannot fully account for as an effect of sleep loss only. Even then he could not be analyzed to rock bottom, so we had to admit that this time-saving device did not work. How are we going to account for this negative effect? Let me offer a tentative explanation which, by the way, will lead us to a more Jungian consideration.

The unconscious part of our system is of course not really interrupted by our waking. It is only the conscious part that begins to make more noise so that we can no longer hear the continuous background music of the unconscious, which, according to Aristotle, consists of much finer vibrations than those prevailing in the waking state. Only during sleep does this music become perceivable in order to achieve a state of κοινὸν αισθητήριον (*koinon aistheterion*) [perception by the common organ of sensation], as dreams, the theory of which seems to be a venerable old version of what is nowadays called *internal sensory input*. Aristotle believed that the diagnostic value of dreams lay in their capacity to indicate the condition of the body. Making use of the new technique, we now are able to switch onto this background music much more frequently in the laboratory than under normal conditions. In this way we are getting a lot of information that normally would be lost, at least for the time being—I say "for the time being" because I think that exactly here lies the answer to our problem. To Jung, the unconscious is a continuum in space-time. Superimposed on it there is the periodic phenomenon of consciousness (i.e., waking). This waking state then is mainly open to bodily condition and external stimuli, but also to some extent to the inner world of the psyche, from which it not only receives all kinds of stimuli, but also, as we now know, periodically and unavoidably receives dreams.

Consciousness is steadily augmented in life by assimilation of more and more knowledge about the outer as well as the inner world, the latter mainly by dream material. Just as learning can only be achieved step by step, none of which can be skipped, so can the unconscious material *only* be assimilated step by step. There must, in this sense, be a kind of hierarchical structure of the unconscious just as there is one in consciousness. (One cannot learn higher mathematics before having understood arithmetic and algebra first.) It may, therefore, happen sometimes that, through a remembered dream, material from the unconscious is exposed to the conscious mind, which is still far from being capable of mentation. The material may still be too strange, too alien or too "advanced," and consequently will make either a very strange but strong impression or be immediately forgotten, not necessarily because of repression, but simply because the conscious system still lacks the necessary concepts to assimilate it properly. Should this hypothesis be confirmed, it would in most cases be superfluous to revert to the theory of the censor.[3]

Now the question is how this Jungian view is to be reconciled with the well-known fact that dreams with high emotional tone are more readily and spontaneously remembered than those with little emotionality – a fact which has been statistically proven in our laboratory. In special cases, this may be so because highly emotional events in dreams simply overwhelm the censor, so that the dreamer emerges higher than *emerging stage I*, that is, he wakes up and thereby already makes the connection of dream with consciousness. However, these may be exceptional cases only. It will be difficult to validate the theory since we awaken our subjects after every single REM period so that all dreams are brought to immediate consciousness independent of their emotionality; this practice will automatically have its effects on their being remembered.

I should like to remind you here of the Jungian concept of *archetypes* and *archetypal images* and so suggest how highly probable it is that, whenever a dream proves to be highly emotional, this is so because it has some archetypal content. It is well

---

3. C. A. Meier et al., "Forgetting of Dreams in the Laboratory," *Percept. Mot. Skills* 26 (1968): 551-557.

known from clinical experience that archetypal images are always accompanied by strong emotions.

Here I have touched upon another of our original working hypotheses which may or may not be verifiable and about which, so far, we have only met with difficulties. Archetypal dreams are considered most important in Jungian analysis. That they seem to occur more frequently at crucial points of the patient's development or process thus far is an empirical statement only. Much work is needed to verify this methodically, which, in my view, can be possible only by using Calvin Hall's method of *content analysis*. Clinically, however, the statement can be confirmed. For a striking example, I refer to my monograph *Ancient Incubation and Modern Psychotherapy*.[4]

Psychologically speaking, emotions seem to serve the purpose of driving home some truth to which there are resistances. Emotions also release a certain additional amount of energy. This energy manifests itself, for example, in a kind of motion (e-motion) that alters our state of mind and which can be almost measured, for example, in the degree of deflection of the galvanometer needle.[5] These facts are far from being properly understood, physiologically no less than psychologically. As is well known, emotions also occur in dreams – more specifically in archetypal dreams of a decisive nature. They sometimes seem to have a direct healing quality as can be seen in the case histories of the Asklepieion in Epidaurus.[6]

Such a dream was called ἐνύπνιον ἐναργές (*enypnion enargēs*) [the effective dream, the dream made manifest]. These effects remind us of their reverse, that is, the unpleasant effects of Dement's dream-deprivation experiments. Suppose we observe a highly emotional dream in the laboratory, what are the corresponding phenomena on the somatic level, the periphery? And would they help us understand the homeostatic function of dreams, let alone their healing function? As you know, it is easy

---

4. C. A. Meier, *Ancient Incubation and Modern Psychotherapy* (Evanston: Northwestern University Press, 1967) [Original German edition 1949].

5. C.f. H. Flanders Dunbar, *Emotions and Bodily Changes* (New York 1949), 3rd ed.

6. C. A. Meier, in *The Dream and Human Societies* (Berkeley: University of California, 1966).

to show a number of the physical concomitants of emotions in the waking state. You have only to think, for example, of the pneumogram or the Galvanic Skin Response effects, which have been known ever since the beginning of our century, or rather, since classical antiquity.[7] Now it becomes apparent that some of these effects seem not to work in the sleeping stage, and, what is more, there are puzzling differences between these autonomous reactions during REM and NREM periods.

The neurophysiologists will have to look for an answer to this problem, but for us it remains a fact that certain autonomous responses do not occur during sleep. From here I allow myself to make a bold conjecture: does it not look as if a censor were at work seeing to it that these emotional reactions will not reach the periphery? Maybe it is they who would wake me up if they were perceived at the periphery, so that there is good reason enough to suppress them. By this suggestion, I do not mean to support the rather unlikely theory of Freud that the dream is the guardian of sleep. We should here rather think of the effect of a neurophysiological inhibition. It may, however, be very difficult to measure the immediate effects of dreams on bodily functions. Our instruments still seem to be too blunt or crude, or we may have to look for new transducers allowing us to measure parameters not yet considered. So far, I have the impression that the plethysmograph is particularly sensitive to such changes, to the extent that it has even been used to monitor ESP effects.[8]

It is of particular interest that in the waking state we all show Galvanic Skin Responses to almost any kind of sensory stimulus, whereas there is no response during sleep. We had originally hoped to get such responses during emotional dreams, but so far we have not seen a single such response. I know of no explanation for this phenomenon but cannot help thinking of the big question already mentioned earlier: how do the dreams go about putting the house-body in order (homeostasis)? If these emo-

---

7. C. A. Meier, "Pychosomatic Medicine from the Jungian Point of View," *J. Analyt. Psychol.* 8(1963): 103ff.

8. Douglas E. Dean, "Non-conventional Communication," *Proceedings of the First Space Congress*. Sponsored by the Canaveral Council of Technical Societies, April 20-23, 1964.

tions experienced in certain dreams do not reach the periphery, how else are they taken care of? Do they remain on an inner level as purely mental experiences? If so, is the "emerging stage I," the means by which psyche and soma are linked directly, where, so to speak, translations of their different "languages" are given to each other, or where both speak a common language? I admit that this is a lot of speculation, but I also have to confess that I cannot see much progress in this kind of work unless we have the courage to indulge in all kinds of fantasies.

As I mentioned earlier, there can be no escape from the fundamental problem of the psychophysical relation, or, if you prefer, the psychosomatic riddle. Epistemologically, it will never help to declare it, in a grandiose manner, a pseudoproblem or to try to evade it by using such neologisms as *oneness*, *wholeness* or whatnot. These terms are only trivia or truisms and are sadly lacking in their capacity to make these transitions from psyche into soma and vice versa better understood. Has anybody ever explained *how* body chemistry turns into a thought, concept or dream; or *how* the mind, in psychosomatic medicine, merely using mental operations, results in the cure of a bodily symptom or disease?

The inescapability of the psychophysical problem on the one hand, and the relevance of modern experimental dream research for the Jungian point of view on the other, urge me here to say something about one of Jung's most treasured concepts, though it is practically impossible to make this clear in a limited amount of space to those who do not know much about it. I mean the concept of *synchronicity*.[9]

We sometimes observe events that show a most striking coincidence of outer and inner conditions while there is absolutely no causal explanation. For example, when one thinks of a friend it may happen that the next telephone call will be from that person, even though there has been no contact of any kind for a number of years. One may dream of something that actually happens the next day, without the slightest possibility of its having been foreseen, inferred, or caused. Causality collapses and

---

9. C. G. Jung and W. Pauli, *The Interpretation of Nature and the Psyche* (New York: Pantheon, 1955).

still (or maybe therefore) the event strikes us as meaningful. Jung called such meaningful coincidences *synchronistic events*. You may call me superstitious or unscientific, but I am convinced that these things happen frequently, more frequently than we think or perceive them, and in rare cases we can determine almost irrefutably that these incidents cannot be just coinciden- tal, particularly when the likeness of the two coinciding phenom- ena is photographic to the minute details. Phenomenologically, it appears in these cases as if an inner fact (my fantasy or dream) has brought about an outer event, or vice versa – which is causalistically impossible. In other words it seems as if psyche and physis were interchangeable.

Could it be that the world of the dream state is the place where the two realities of psyche and soma coincide, in which case this stage would be the *tertium*, the strange elusive something that through the ages has been called the *subtle body*?

I am afraid that this is still more speculation, and I am sure that you want me to come back to harder facts – supposing there are any in this field. One of my collaborators, Dr. Rüf, thinks that the facts contradict the simple theory of the homeostatic function of dreaming as soon as this theory is thought of as a doing away with toxins accumulated during the waking state: the toxins would have reached their highest level at the maximum of tiredness, just before going to sleep. REM periods, however, instead of showing their strongest activity right then and there, reach their climax only during the later hours of sleep. The dreams are longer at the end of the night and show more of the characteristics of classical dreams, of the *drame intérieur*, and they contain fewer day residues.

Shall we conclude from these data that earlier REM periods and dreams deal more with the manifold disjointed remnants from diurnal mental activities, and that hence they are kaleido- scopic and closer to hypnogogic visions than to actual dreams? These dreams, then, would have an aspect of the "junk removal" of computers, as suggested by some engineers. Furthermore, would these images represent visual images of the toxins, the tantalizing problems of everyday life that account for tensions and resultant fatigue? Could it then be that in later REM periods the observer turns more to the background which I have been talking about, to truly psychological problems pertaining more strictly to the unconscious mind? Would not what I said earlier concerning the inner process of learning and the hierarchical structure of the unconscious also apply?

More and longer *deafferentation* (i.e., decrease of information and signals with growing length of sleep) will force the mind back on itself and, as it literally almost consists only of images, the information it receives or creates in this way about its own genuinely psychological problems or queries will simply be more images. On this level, they are the "stuff" myths are made on; myths show us the age-old archetypal way of handling basic psychological problems, so that one might be tempted to assume that this is the way in which dreams can have a beneficial, if not healing, effect by themselves.

You certainly know that according to Jung, the real purpose of analysis is the establishment of a dialectical relationship with exactly this very unconscious, a relationship which itself consists of a give-and-take, a feedback, whereby what Jung calls the *process of individuation* is created.

Chapter 10

The Psychological Parameters of the Examination Situation

I first thought of writing on the psychological background of the (scholastic) examination situation, but the word *background* seemed to me to be somewhat nebulous. I finally hit on the term *parameter*, which denotes a more scientific approach. What I am going to discuss are the unconscious determinants that necessarily enter into every situation involving an examination (or test). I have selected this topic because such factors, in the majority of cases, become extraordinarily disturbing, and furthermore, very little on this particular subject can be found in the literature.

Fairly recently, psychologists have come to realize that an understanding of psychological phenomena depends on some acquaintance with their genesis or history. This is similar to medical procedure, which traditionally begins with the patient's history. I will first outline the phylogenetic antecedents, so to speak, of the practice of giving academic examinations.

It is certain that the Chinese – along with many other intellectual achievements – invented the technique of the examination. In imperial China candidates for higher offices had to undergo a rigorous examination, and those who passed were promoted to the rank of mandarins, approximately corresponding to our higher academic degrees.

The Bible does not explicitly mention examinations; however,

First published in German: *Neue Zürcher Zeitung*, March 1, 1970, and later in: *ETH-Bulletin*, 111/21 (Zürich, 1970). English translation by Fred Engreen.

the concept of trial *is* frequently mentioned. It is Jahweh who tries men and, more specifically, their *kidneys and heart*—a recurrent phrase. It becomes relevant to us if *heart* is understood as feeling, while *kidney* is taken to represent moral discrimination.

In ancient Greece we find nothing relating to examinations. The closest parallel would be selection on the basis of athletic achievement, probably derived from the idea that a healthy mind could exist only in a healthy body (*mens sana in corpore sano*).

During the Middle Ages, students were obliged to memorize the scholastic texts built on the philosophic systems of Aristotle and Thomas Aquinas. Centuries later, the Jesuits still employed a similar method in their colleges. During the Renaissance, the emphasis was on familiarity with the works of the pre-Christian philosophers. In order to guide the candidate through the rigorous examination required for attaining a doctor's degree, teachers took a very personal interest in the student, and thereby the entire university training assumed almost the character of an apprenticeship.

The history of a term often discloses important information about its psychological background. The Latin word *examinare* means to weigh precisely on the scales; *examinator* is consequently the person who carefully weighs or tests. *Examen*, on the other hand, connotes a swarm of bees leaving the hive. This meaning is directly applicable to our investigation because this exodus is equivalent to *establishing a new status*, which, in turn, represents the main object of every examination.

Leaving the *old status*, however, amounts to separation. Each such separation is dangerous and, according to C. G. Jung, is an archetypal experience. It represents a critical phase. In this context I am always reminded of the hermit crab, whose abdomen lacks the protection of armor and who therefore occupies the empty shell of a snail; when the crab grows, a shell of larger size is needed. Since this means that the crab must look for a new home and must give up the security of the old shell, he indeed is confronted with a critical phase.

Each human being passes through several critical phases of this kind. From earliest times, we may observe an instinctive tendency to give support to the person who finds himself in such difficulties. This is achieved by the institution of appropriate rites. As such ceremonies are intended to assist in the transition from one state to another, van Gennep has described them as *rites de passage.* The puberty rites constitute a particular form of these.

Even today we celebrate with special solemnity the most important phases in the life of a person — marriage, birth and death — although it may seem to us that the ceremony has become extenuated. Generally speaking, these are always occasions of initiation, the meaning and purpose of which are to give the subject undergoing such rites the license and power henceforth to perform acts that are denied to others.

Frequently the initiated does not know how to utilize his new state. For example, he may fall into the so-called *Examensloch*, a "letdown," which is known to occur after outstanding intellectual achievements (e.g., Champollion following his success in deciphering the Egyptian hieroglyphs). He has received the doctor's cap bestowed by *society*, that is, the collective whole, for an explicit and extremely personal accomplishment. It is important to celebrate this step with certain ceremonies — in the United States, for example, by the graduation ceremony. In Switzerland we are rightly beginning to give more dignity to the presentation of diplomas and the celebration of achieving a doctorate.

Moreover, these ceremonies are important because after the candidate's attainment of rank and title, society must change its attitude toward him. The title is, of course, also a reward for the fortitude required to overcome the cruel trial that proves the candidates's ability to perform even under conditions of stress. According to Freud, the examination is truly a judgment, a *dies irae* [day of wrath].

In view of these facts it cannot be overemphasized that in this situation anxiety is absolutely normal and even necessary. Any maximal accomplishment depends on anxiety as a precondition. We have only to think of the stage-fright of performing artists. Anxiety, thus, becomes a stimulus and prompts accomplishment. Altogether, anxiety represents the *dira necessitas* [dire necessity] of life and will continue to be needed. Without anxiety man is inhuman. On all counts, anxiety is a basic factor in the development of consciousness. I mention only the fairytale of the man who set out to learn what fear was and won the princess only after he had learned to be afraid. Hubris, as the Greeks said, is the greatest threat to man — or, according to our proverb, pride goeth before a fall. It follows that the examination is a highly mythological, archetypal situation on the life of man.

The *new status* amounts to an ascent in a given hierarchy and therefore has a *social* aspect. All of nature is arranged in a hierarchical order. In man, naturally, the question is how the impulse originated that compels him to ascend from state A to state B and then to state C, and so on. This constantly creates, in a wellnigh perverse manner, new sources of anxiety until we reach the upper limits of our specific capacity. The question remains as to what impels us to such behavior.

Let us assume that we are faced with a particular aptitude which is being artificially overcultivated. The inevitable consequence is specialization, resulting in knowing more and more about less and less. Thus, we tend increasingly to move along the fringes of life. If this tendency is followed too far, failure can easily be understood as due to compensation – more and more must be repressed, and it is the very material that is being repressed, the things we never knew or no longer know, that creates anxiety of different degrees, even neurotic anxiety.

Anxiety is especially prone to become neurotic when one no longer wants to see this psychological background as something normal. Then the examiner – through the mechanism of projection – becomes a devil. One sees him as a sadist, forgetting that he, too, is beset by anxiety since it is his students and his teaching ability that are being tested, and the grades they earn apply equally to him.

At this point, we must resort to so-called depth psychology. The student-teacher relationship of natural trust is disturbed to the degree congruent with the quality of the projection. Depending on whether the projected father image is of a positive or a negative nature, the examiner is assimilated as a benevolent, paternal friend or as a representative of the repressive "Establishment," to use a current expression. In the psychoanalytic view, students are constantly in search of parent figures. The Alma Mater would personify the mother, the professor (or father) would represent intellectuality. Accordingly, the student's quest of knowledge would be legitimized. The only remaining question would be the degree of objectivity.

All these aspects appear to be irrational and often create disturbing factors in the normal college routine, which aims exclusively at cultivating and rewarding rational-critical thinking.

Aesthetic considerations are neglected, and in this connection one might recall that σχολή (scholē), the Greek word from which our term school is derived, means leisure, repose, freedom from occupational labor. During college years, emotional stress is almost uninterrupted, culminating in final exams. Cannon demonstrated how such emergency situations affect normal physiologic functioning: pulse rate and blood pressure increase and the blood glucose level rises; the flow of saliva decreases markedly; there is sweating and pallor as well as other manifestations. In short, the vegetative nervous system is abnormally excited. This prevents any objective test of the candidate's potential, presumably the purpose of the examination. Small wonder, then, that many students who have learned the subject and may even have fully mastered it remember nothing during the exam.

The "laboratory conditions" of the examination situation are seen as far from ideal, because the irrational psychological components cannot be measured or objectified. Therefore, according to Dörner,[1] the most stupid candidates and those who qualify as geniuses come off best, while the large group in the middle (the "average" students) produce the most unreliable results. It is assumed that these "problem" students suffer from an unsatisfactory personality development. Since we don't know whether we are dealing with late adolescents or with young adults, it has been concluded that in some ways their personality development has been paradoxical. The average intelligence quotient is reported to be around 110, so that the level of intelligence cannot be said to be the determining factor.

These findings again confirm that personality traits are highly significant. Because the student must simulate more maturity than is warranted, the risk of failure is increased. According to Dörner, mathematicians and students of the natural sciences show more control in this respect; in other words, they behave more conventionally, with a favorable effect on the outcome of the examination. This proves only that the candidate has learned to think along prescribed lines, that he has actually been indoctrinated, which of course completely represses the spontaneous and imaginative elements.

---

1. Klaus Dörner, *Die Hochschulpsychiatrie* (Stuttgart: Ferd. Enke, 1967).

The personality as a whole embraces many important facets that are neglected or even suppressed by one-sided training. Some kind of backlash is inevitable, and the examination situation provides the perfect opportunity. The candidate is exposed, isolated, without support; subjectively, he is in agonizing suspense, and objectively he is bombarded with a host of questions that only bewilder him. At this moment, of course, previously repressed material has an ideal chance to trip us up. Such stressful situations hit us just where we are weakest.

This is also the juncture, unfortunately, where a mechanism which Edgar Allen Poe called the "imp of the perverse" comes into play. It is the tendency to self-destruction. The candidate, whose first failure does not awaken him to recognize the situation and accept his weakness with good grace, will certainly repeat the perverted pattern of behavior at the second examination. According to current rules, this could spell doom for the student's academic career, however unjust it might be, since the failure was not due to his stupidity. The only "stupidity" was that he did not utilize the time before the second examination to fill in the nonintellectual or noncognitive voids. He felt compelled to act as if these gaps did not exist; in other words, the catastrophe occurred because he presumed himself to be more mature than he really was.

Psychologists know that such neglect or repression must always bring repercussions. They may occur only much later in life, and even with the candidate who has finally passed all exams with good grades. Indeed, such repercussions may not involve his professional career but, for example, disturb his married life in which nonintellectual attributes are decisive. Thus, a double failure in the academic examination can, in spite of its immediate negative consequences, be a boon, at least if a personality development takes place under the *dira necessitas*. Failure, then, has its aspect of compensation and, if the subject learns his lesson, may become a blessing in disguise.

Even so, a degree of injustice remains, because, as mentioned, in many cases of failure that which was intended to be tested was not tested at all, namely, the knowledge and ability of the candidate. How could that come about? Psychologists have learned that the outcome of an experiment — no matter how cleverly and carefully set up — is not independent of the so-called experimental situation, which among other factors includes some irrational ones. On principle, it is not possible to exclude these completely. Yet the manner in which the subject of the experiment assimilates the investigator is of critical importance. The response depends partly on personal and partly on collective factors.

One of the personal factors, for instance, is whether the *imago* of a good or a bad father is present. The generation problem, of course, plays a vital part with every student. It is accentuated because of a phase shift: the student acts even younger than his chronological age in handling life situations. The inevitable problems inherent in the relationships between fathers and sons, a younger and an older generation, teachers and students, examiners and examinees, are thereby aggravated.

Among the collective factors, the trend to question the authority of the older generation is manifested by a gigantic projection of the younger generation, in which older people are seen as pillars of the Establishment. Every projection has a kernel of truth insofar as the time element heralds a cyclic change of consciousness. In this case it embodies the overcoming of the father. But only he who is himself prepared to be a father can overcome the father.

Psychologically, however, father signifies intellect and creative performance – two qualities demanded by the inner man. Historical changes are of course inevitable, but their successful accomplishment depends on some knowledge of history and on a correct perspective. Otherwise one simply creates a *bête noire* and puts the cart before the horse: dissatisfaction with oneself turns into dissatisfaction with the world – in the present case, dissatisfaction with the Establishment. This is a classical example of projection.

With a positive father image, projection is useful in motivating emulation. With a negative image, projection produces nothing but protest: one sees himself as mature and superior, that is, advanced beyond his actual stage of development – which, of course, being untrue, cannot fail to have repercussions.

Negative projection can certainly be provoked by the inappropriate behavior of the examiner. As so often happens, here it is *le ton qui fait la musique*. Undoubtedly, this situation could stand much improvement. For instance, written examinations are intended to eliminate subjective factors as far as possible.

But where "good music" is being played, its favorable effect is eliminated also. Emphasis put exclusively on mechanizing the testing techniques carries a great danger; it may further dehumanize the already inhuman examination. When all human factors have been conjured away, the irrational elements are freed, beyond control, isolated, and therefore unmanageable. Such education or instruction produces nothing more than "specialized idiots."

Between Scylla and Charybdis only a middle path is possible, always fraught with danger. This way out, however, would require the candidate to be completely aware that he is not yet a finished product and that the examiner's function is to help him. My proposal should not be misunderstood as an idealistic fancy; it is entirely practical, taking full account of the psychic imponderables, the irrational elements (emotions, etc.), and in line with Goethe's observation: "Human nature, divided by reason, still leaves a remainder." On principle we can see no way to resolve this remainder, since we are faced with a fundamental constant that is ubiquitous – as, for instance, the generation problem.

The psychoanalysts, not without cause, hold Oedipus responsible for everything. In the conventional psychoanalytic version, however, the problem has been oversimplified. According to this view, each candidate would want to murder the examiner in order to sleep with his wife. It is easy to understand that in such a state of mind any candidate's saliva would dry up. Taken literally, success in an examination would be restricted to the *reo nato* [born criminal]. What is missing in the psychoanalytic concept is a psychological interpretation. One must first be able to be a son and, after surmounting infantile inhibitions, become a father; only then can one fully enjoy the Mother-World.

In this context we should remember the meaning of the term *Maturität*.[2] However, even this interpretation is still too individualized. For, Oedipus – through unconscious guilt and conscious atonement – becomes deified by apotheosis (at Colonus)

---

2. In Switzerland, "Maturität" is the title of the examination given at the end of high school; if successful, the candidate is considered "mature" enough to start university.

and ends up as a fertility hero (creative man). In this myth, the span is stretched as far as possible and projects far beyond the secular dimension of a trivial college examination. Seen in this perspective, each examination represents *one* of the many hierarchical levels of life which must be attained as an absolute psychic requirement to make life fascinating and interesting.

I call it a psychic requirement because human nature is organized in such a way that a gradual realization of the potentialities bestowed on each individual is well-nigh enforced. As Seneca said, "Ducunt volentem Fata, nolentem trahunt" [Fate guides him who is willing, he who resists is compelled]. Therefore, we have to understand the institution of examinations and their hierarchical arrangement as a social development, which is psychologically predestined. Consequently, it would be perverse to interpret this invention as a repressive device intended to maintain the power of the Establishment.

However, anything can be abused and corrupted. Under such conditions the examination becomes the prototype of an asymmetrical power situation; an examination should never be permitted to degenerate to this because such abuse leads to a betrayal of its innermost essence, the productive outpouring of the fatherly intellect. Whenever such productive participation is absent, the examination situation might easily lapse into a power struggle. Therefore, it is necessary always to be on guard. If the Establishment itself is not alert, it automatically behooves the students to keep their eyes open, we hope for the benefit of the school and of society as a whole.

In summary, anxiety is inherent in any examination situation because it represents a transition phase and is, therefore, full of risk. Fear of the actual situation, however, is not a satisfactory explanation. More powerful are the archetypes that constellate the background of each ascent to a new level. The hierarchy of stages is immanent in the nature of things and also in personality development (maturation). In this sense, it is incorrect to ascribe the invention of examinations to the work of the devil or the heinous Establishment. On the contrary, they are necessary for deep-rooted reasons, and the ceremonies connected with them should support the candidate. On both sides, archetypal forces come into play; therefore, careful and continuous attention should be given to increasing human values in examinations.

For the same reason, emphasis on the technical structure of examinations is obviously questionable.

How the respect for human values can be fostered in examiner and candidate is quite another problem. I believe it would be necessary to give more consideration to immaterial issues rather than to specialized information, command of subject matter, and memorized data. It is here that the deeper significance of the father problem, so much distorted by the Freudians, comes into the picture. My remarks are based on the concept of an unconscious psyche which is primitive and archaic. Particularly under conditions of stress, it can break through and take over the situation autonomously. Depending on the degree of intensity, such an eruption is called stupor or panic. Because the unconscious psyche is unchanging and cannot be influenced, the best protection against its intrusion is to be aware of its threat. Fortified with this knowledge, one is able to accommodate himself gracefully to the traditional examination ceremonies. In doing this, however, care must be taken that balance is preserved.

Bibliographical Appendix

Klaus Dörner, *Die Hochschulpsychiatrie* (Stuttgart: Ferd. Enke, 1967).

Michael Lukas Möller, "Untersuchung zur Psychodynamik der neurotischen Prüfungsangst," Diss. (Berlin, 1967).

Th. Spoerri and W. Th. Winkler, eds., *Student und Neurose* (S. Karger, Basel-New York, 1969) also in *Proc. of the VII. Intl. Congress of Psychotherapy*, pt. VI, Wiesbaden, 1967).

Hans Biäsch, "Psychologische Hintergründe des Examensverhaltens," *Jb. für Psychol., Psychoth-u. mediz. Anthropol.* 16-1/2, 115 - 129 (Freiburg-München, 1968).

Aage Rosendal Nielsen, ed., *Lust for Learning* (New Experimental College Press, Denmark, 1968).

M. L. Möller, "Psychotherapeutische Beratung für Studierende an der Universität Giessen," *Nervenarzt* 40, 155 - 163 (Springer, Berlin, 1968).

———, *Zur Psychoanalyse der Prüfungsangst* II, "Aspekte der Prüfungsangst, betr. Erziehung," Nr. 1, 16 - 20 (1969).

Chapter 11

Dynamic Psychology and the Classical World

Because it would take a series of lectures to cover the realm of "Dynamic Psychology and the Classical World" appropriately, I offer here a limited presentation. I shall confine myself almost exclusively within the proverbially classical Greek time of the fifth to fourth century B.C.

When G. S. Blum, in the title of his study, draws the unmistakable equation, *Psychodynamics: The Science of Unconscious Mental Forces*, this could be misleading.[1] The real dynamism only comes into action in the interplay between conscious and unconscious parts of the system. It is clear that as long as dynamic psychology is understood as the psychology wherein the unconscious is included, our old authors have not read any Freud or Jung. Our research will be restricted to the manifestations of the irrational and emotional parts of the psyche, to passions and the like.

Let me explore the history of the word *dynamis* for this purpose: philosophically it always meant an ability or capability, a potential, a force or a power, be it physical or mental including magic power. With Plato, *dynamis* is the category of being that

Paper read to the "Conference on Methodology in the History of Psychiatry," April 1967, at Yale University. Published in: George Mora and Jeanne L. Brand, eds., *Psychiatry and Its History* (Springfield, Illinois, 1970), 159ff.

1. G. S. Blum, in E. L. Walker, ed., *Basic Concepts in Psychology Series* (Belmont, Calif.: Wadsworth, 1966).

enables us to do what we are *capable of doing* — γένος τι τῶν ὄντων (*genos ti ton onton*) [a generation of things that are]. It can be attained by sacrifices to the gods δύναμις ἐκ θεῶν (*dynamis ek theon*) [capability derived from the gods]. Plato's strongest *dynamis* is *episteme*, knowing. It also designates the healing power of plants, animals, stones — for example, the σωφρονίστηρ λίθος (*sophronister lithos*) [healing stone] which in Thebes restored reason to Heracles and the stars.[2] With Pythagoras the δεκάς is a *dynamis*, more particularly a *dynamis* ἰσχύουσα (*ischuousa*) [continuing, on-going], a power expressing itself in forceful actions. In the Stoa, it becomes a world power and a world deity and eventually is equated to *nous* and the world soul. With Poseidonius we then find the ζωτικὴ δύναμις (*zotike dynamis*) [living capability], which is a force vivifying the whole cosmos and has a decidedly biological aspect (over against the *dynamis* which is physical), or κινητικὴ (*kinetike*) [moving element]. In religion, *dynamis* is directly equated to God. Apollo, for example, has four *dynameis*: τοξική (*toxike*) [of the bow], μαντική (*mantike*) [of divination], ἰατρική (*iatrike*) [of medicine] and μουσική (*mousike*) [of artistic inspiration].[3]

In witchcraft and magic, *dynamis* is closely related to sympathy and antipathy. The sorcerer has ὑπερβάλλουσα δύναμις (*hyperballousa dynamis*), an extraordinary gift. In Neoplatonism all these qualities are included in the same word, so that Nilsson rightly calls it *dynamic pantheism*.[4] The Latin *virtus* also covers miracles. In later Judaism it becomes a hypostasis of God, similar to wisdom with the Greeks. The Torah, for example, becomes such a *dynamis*, exactly as the Gospels do in Christianity. Whereas the Old Testament remains theocentric, in the New Testament God becomes a will-power which imposes itself on the world, but in a Christocentric way, from which the apostles and martyrs derive their power.

The third limitation imposed herein concerns the term *psychology*. We should not forget that no such science really existed

---

2. Pausanias, *Description of Greece* IX, II.2.

3. Menander, *Rhet.* 440 Sp.

4. M. P. Nilsson, *A History of Greek Religion* (Oxford: Oxford University Press, 1925).

in antiquity; psychology was part of philosophy and ethics on the one hand, and religion on the other. Then as now, psychological phenomena were primarily the concern of physicians confronted by clinical manifestations. But even in ancient medicine, we observe the same dichotomy as today: there are psychiatrists and psychotherapists. Hippocrates would belong to the former class, whereas most of what happened in the cult of Asklepios belonged to the latter. I hope to have taken care of this aspect in my monograph, whereas the Hippocratic point of view is still not sufficiently dealt with in literature.[5]

In antiquity there was no concept of consciousness and the unconscious, nor of their alleged opposition. There is no correspondence between our author's terminology and modern medical or philosophical terminology. This basic opposition must be hidden behind such philosophical terms as the *rational* and the *irrational*, which have had many other names through the centuries. (Refer to the tentative table of synonyms included later in this chapter.) In comparing these "synonyms" we emphasize their similarities rather than their differences. The differences are most important for the history of philosophy and epistemology, however, although here we are interested primarily in a comparative or genealogical point of view.

As there was no dynamic psychology as such in those days, I shall ruthlessly mix whatever we know about it symptomatically, whether from philosophy, medicine, religion and cult, or even folklore, assuming that man functioned dynamically then just as he does today. There is, however, one definite difference: in Greek antiquity there were a number of institutions that took care of people's emotions, whereas today, with the constrictions of our Calvinistic and Victorian backgrounds, emotions are frequently dealt with negatively or ignored.

The Greek gods were temperamental; they must, therefore, have been understanding concerning human passions. They could be placated and they accepted offerings; in some cases, they could even be bribed, whereupon the patient's balance was restored. *Menadism* with its ὀρειβασία (*oreibasia*) [wandering on mountains] and ὠμοφαγία (*omophagia*) [eating raw flesh]

---

5. C. A. Meier, *Ancient Incubation and Modern Psychotherapy* (Evanston: Northwestern University Press, 1967) [original German edition 1949].

helped abreact dangerous emotions. Dionysus was, therefore, called Βὰκχος καὶ Λύσιος (*Bakchos kai Lusios*) [the inspired and curse-releasing one]. Madness was stimulated to the extreme, reaching its λύσις (*lysis*) [solution].[6] This is nothing other than the homeopathic principle of *similia similibus curantur* [like cures like; poison as remedy].

The Corybantes had a ritual for the cure of madness (phobias and anxiety feelings). Diagnostically and therapeutically it was essential to know which god or goddess you were possessed by, so you could placate him or her by the adequate ritual.[7] An additional remedy was music.[8] According to Theophrastus, hearing is the most emotive – παθητικωτάτη (*pathētikōtatē*) – of all the senses.[9]

Let us see how Plato philosophizes with regard to our question: in his early writings, ἀρετή (*arētē*) [excellence] is more or less equated with rational living. Later, after all the political upheaval, he had to take the *irrational* more realistically, so that he created a "metaphysical extension" of rationalism, a kind of "magico-religious view of the psyche." Whereas sins were, until then, only pollutions of the soul by the body, "the folly of the body" (*Phaedo*), the irrational factor becomes now part of mind itself. At this juncture the hitherto more or less *physiological* origin of conflicts is abandoned and is replaced by a *psychological* conflict proper, which is then called στάσις (*stasis*) – moral position.[10]

Still later, this development results in the *soul* becoming the source of all motions (e-motion), good and bad,[11] so that in the *Republic* (441 B.C.) we find the two parts of the soul in dialogue. The one and the only therapy advocated remains the critical control by reason. Socrates seems to have been the one who

---

6. E. Rohde, *Psyche: The Cult of Souls and Belief in Immortality among the Greeks* (London: Kegan Paul, 1925), chapter IX, 308, n. 21.

7. E. R. Dodds, *The Greeks and the Irrational* (Berkeley: University of California, 1951), 79.

8. I. M. Linforth, "The Corybantic Rites in Plato," *U. of Calif. Publ. Class. Philol.* 13 (1946): 121-161.

9. Theophrastus, fr. 91 W. παθητικωτάτη, Dodds, 78; cf. Plato, *Republic*, 398 C-401A.

10. Dodds, *The Greeks and the Irrational*, 209-213.

11. Plato, *Timaeus*, 89E.

urged Plato to take the *irrational* more and more seriously, since it was he who was prepared to take his dreams, his *daimonion*, and Pythias' utterances very realistically.

It is true that in later life Plato was moving toward a certain dualism, which has puzzled the historians, particularly with regard to the possibility of its being caused by Zoroastric influence.[12] To some extent in the course of this development, *Eros* becomes the mediator between these opposites as it has its roots in nature (sex), but at the same time reaches far beyond into the spiritual realm, thus constituting the dynamics of the whole human being.[13] Obviously, modern *libido* theory – more specifically in the Jungian sense – is faithfully Platonic. It may be that the parallel can be carried further in placing Freud side by side with Aristotle, who took the irrational far more realistically than Plato did. Should this be more than a bold conjecture, the differences between the two modern analytic schools would be but another example of the typological difference between introversion and extraversion. For a full-scale elaboration of the relationships that may be drawn among Freud's, Aristotle's, Jung's and Plato's concepts, I refer the reader to C. G. Jung's *Psychological Types*.[14]

I turn now to a brief outline of typological discussions in classical antiquity, simply because typological classification and differences are always based upon ἐναντίοται (*enantiotai*) [pairs of opposites] and because energy, *libido*, or psychological dynamics, presupposes tension between opposites. From here we may return to our table of "synonyms" and then consider classical pathology.

---

12. Cf. Plato, *Timaeus*, 69C.

13. Plato, *Symposium*, 186A.

14. C. G. Jung, *Psychological Types* (New York: Harcourt, 1924), *Collected Works* 6.

TABLE I

Author (Chronological Order)	Concepts (Enantioses)	Disease (Pathology)	Telos Health (Therapy)*	Typology
Anaximander				
Pythagoras	apeiron peras or peraion nous, episteme doxa, aisthesis	cakodaimon	harmonia, tetractys (songs)	
Alcmaion	4 dynameis (enantiotetes) even/odd, good/bad, cold/warm, sweet/bitter	Monarchia	isonomia (gymnastics)	
Empedocles	4 rhizomata (elements) + 4 dynameis thermon/psychron, xeron/hygron = 2 pairs of opposites	(blind) philia	symmetria, sphairos (Katharsis by madness)	
Heraclitus	logos, sophon + pyr (calor vitalis)	passions	enantiodromia of all opposites[1]	
Ionian philosophers	1 primal matter developing into 4 rhizomata			
Parmenides Anaxagoras Atomists + Democritus	neikos + philia (Philotes) spirit + matter rational + irrational parts of psyche. Orge and epithymia[2]	allophonein[3]	1 sphairos homoiomeria by nous euthymia, harmonia, symmetria, eudaimonia, ataraxia, to isom	
Herodicus of Selymbria	2 humors			
Hippocrates	kata physin/para physin stoicheia/archai. 2 blood vessels (hepatitis + splenitis)	dyskrasia, dysharmonia (mania + deimata[5]) hyperbole & ell psis[6]	eukrasia − isomoiria of humors harmonia + symmetria of elements xynesis[7] through which awareness of man's spiritual existence	2 types: 1. rich in phlegm 2. rich in gall

TABLE I (continued)

1 Author (Chronological Order)	2 Concepts (Enantioses)	3 Disease (Pathology)	4 Telos Health (Therapy)*	5 Typology
Anon. Londinensis			eurhoia of pneuma, rhythmic circulation	
Polybus	4 humors 4 blood vessels (phlebas haimatidas, sphagitides).			4 kraseis
Plato	4 stoicheia 4 dynameis, body/soul, rational/irrational	akrasis	eukrasia (balance) = sophrosyne Eros for idea (music) arete hygieinou episteme definite numerical proportions between stoicheia and dynameis	4 characters** (1) timocratic (2) oligarchic (3) democratic (4) tyrannic
Aristotle	1 horme (basic drive) brain/heart pairs of opposites cf. Metaph. 986 a 22 Ethic + dianoetic virtues	pathos	harmony under hegemonikon, eutonia, mesotes[9] (katharsis, music, tragedy)	
Philistion	4 elements.			4 characters
Peripatus	4 cardinal virtues eschaton orecton			4 characters
Epicurus	pleasure/displeasure	hedone, lype,[10] epithymia,[11] phobos[12], boulesis,[14] eulabeia[15]	symmetry, metriopatheia hegemonikon	
Stoa	pyr technicon/pyr psychicon	aegritudo, laetitia, metus, libido	eupatheia synectice dynamis,[16] apatheia	

Author				4 temperaments
Chrysippus	4 humors + 4 qualities. Many polarities (e.g., misogyny + philogyny).	symmetry		
Posidonius	*logisticon/patheticon* = rational/irrational.	harmony of macro/microcosm (*phantasia*[17])		
Pneumatics[18]	*Pneuma*			
Galen	body/soul; *physike orexis/psychike orexis*. 4 humors	*eukrasia* — health, strength, beauty, wholeness of body; prudence, temperance, fortitude, justice of mind	*dyskrasia*; *pathē dyskraton*: coma, morosis, phrenitis, paraphrosyne, melancholy	
Paracelsus			"cho era," melancholy, phlegm, gall	

KEY

1. Taoism, 2000 years its predecessor.
2. Anger and passionate desire.
3. Senseless mixup.
4. Teacher of Hippocrates.
5. Terrors.
6. Excess and defect.
7. Partnership?
8. State in which Love of Honor is the ruling principle.
9. Proper middle position.
10. Pain.
11. Desire, passion.
12. Fear.
13. Joy, delight.
14. Desire.
15. Timidity.
16. Fit for folding together.
17. In alchemy + *imaginatio*.
18. From Athenaios of Attalia.

*Words in brackets in column 4 indicate the prescribed alleged therapy.

**These four characters are arranged in decreasing order from 1 to 4.

Table I is based on the fact that dynamism only exists where there are tensions between opposites. In this way, I have tried to give a synopsis of philosophers' concepts constituting pairs of opposites or *quaternios* [four-fold divisions] of such ἐναντιώσεις (*enantioses*) [oppositions]. This must be understood as a comparison only, and in no way is it meant to give equations. From the fragments, however, it becomes clear that all philosophers were convinced that health depended upon a balance between these opposites, whereas a lack of balance was responsible for various mental and bodily diseases (column 3). From this theory the philosophers often developed the further concept of a goal to be attained by the "practice of philosophy," whereby a kind of therapy is hinted at (column 4). A few philosophers also developed a kind of typology based on the assumption that one can observe in people a kind of habitual preponderance of one or the other of the δυνάμεις (*dynameis*) [capabilities], ριζόματα (*rhizomata*) [root-mass elements], στοιχεῖα (*stoicheia*) [elements] or humors (column 5). This idea appears only relatively late, and with Paracelsus I have transgressed my chronological limitations.

1. Until Hippocrates, there was no discrimination among natural philosophy, religion and medicine. Medical treatment, therefore, included incubation, menadism and other rituals and devout actions. Diagnostics were more or less folkloristic; we hear of Musolepsia [under the spell of the muses], nympholepsia [under the spell of nymphs], boanthropy [bull-man madness], kynanthropy [dog-man madness], lycanthropy [wolf-man madness], daimonism [demonic possession] and the like, all due to gods or godlings of disease. It should not be forgotten that phenomenologically this is a most adequate description of psychotic intervals. There is a corresponding awe of madness, and therapy consists of ritual purification from the *miasma* of madness. With Empedocles a certain madness is even its own catharsis. There are purifying stones used, for example, by Heracles and Orestes. One god, Asklepios, specializes in medicine; he becomes extremely popular and refuses to die for several Christian centuries. Nor did he succumb to Hippocrates' "scientific medicine," as can be seen from the fact that after Hippocrates' death his disciples reactivated the old Asklepieion at Kos, where a purely theurgic treatment was practiced. Generally speaking, the therapy of this whole group obeys the law of homeopathy (*similia similibus*).

2. With the growth of Greek philosophy, the dynamic manifestations of the psyche became a concern of the philosophers, and much of the discussion of ethics was based upon psychiatric experience. Socratic θεραπεία ψυχῆς (*therapeia psyches*) [treatment of the soul] particularly became such an essential concern since the psyche really always comes first. But here we meet with several difficulties: either these philosophers were rather far removed from reality and did not care for the pragmatic test of their theories, or their philosophy must have been much more powerful than modern philosophy.

In any event, according to the testimony of Epictetus, the philosophers' lecture room was in fact a kind of dispensary for sick souls.[15] A third possibility seems more plausible: the Greek minds were more susceptible than ours to philosophic argument, just as they must have been to music and drama. Music, theater and art therapy remain in the philosophers' arsenal from Pythagoras down to Aristotle. It still is puzzling to us, however, that they should have cured patients by such argument as the following: passions are diseases of mind or body. Philosophy is the medicine of the soul since it helps you either to see that the objects of your passions are vain, or simply to suppress your excitement, as they are always only the result of a wrong opinion. This all can be read easily in Cicero's *Tusculan Disputations*, Book IV, which is a complete dissertation περὶ πάθων (*peri pathon*) [about affects] from a stoic point of view. Cicero clearly states, "Est profecto animi medicin philosophia" (III, 6) [philosophy indeed is the soul's medicine]. But he also makes clear that "magnum opus et difficile, quis negat?" [Who would deny that this is a great and difficult task?] (III.84). "Animorum salus inclusa in his ipsis est" (IV,58) [the souls contain their own health] certainly gives the most fundamental prerequisite of all psychotherapy. Passions lack reason and can, therefore, not be according to nature "an quicquam est secundum naturam 'quod fit repugnante ratione?" [is there anything according to nature that happens contrary to reason?] (IV,79). Keeping an even keel comes from knowledge, whereas passions come from mistakes (IV,80). We simply have to "sibi imperare" [dominate ourselves] (II,47-58) and care for the "cultura animi" (II,13b).

---

15. Epictetus, *Discourses*, 3, 23, 30.

3. It was Plato who was particularly interested in the μανία τελεστική (*mania telestike*) [madness of initiation], and who emphasized the etymological connection between μανία (*mania*) [madness] and μαντική (*mantike*) [divination] of the ἐκστατικός (*ekstatikos*) [literally "one outside himself"]. He, too, was the first to point out the moral causes of psychoses and thereby the patient's responsibility.

4. Aristotle made a heroic attempt to bring the Platonic ideas down to earth, whereupon the *stoicheia* [elements] and *dynameis* [capabilities] (cf. Table I) became located in certain bodily centers. It appears that the famous overestimation of the melancholic type, which played such an important part in Neo-platonic discussion during the Italian Renaissance, went back to his passages in probl. xxx, 1 and 14, where Aristotle equates the melancholic to genius, using Heracles, Aias, Bellerophon, Empedocles, Plato and Socrates as examples. He also almost reaches the level of modern analytic or psychosomatic medicine, or the level on which it should be, when he says that "affect" (i.e., πάθος [pathos]) is a movement of the body that leads to conscious knowledge of the soul.[16]

5. Hippocrates has not yet sufficiently been sifted regarding his views on dynamic psychology – but this would definitely be worth someone's hard work. When he pronounced (over against the "sacred disease") πάντα θεῖα καὶ πάντα ἀνθρώπινα (*panta theia kai panta anthropina*) [they all are divine and all human], this should never be misinterpreted either as the beginning of scientific medicine or as a pure statement of a rationalist. Hippocrates was, of course, mainly an empiricist, which Plato did not like, and his more or less unchallenged theoretical presupposition was τὰ ἐναντία τῶν ἐναντίων ἐστὶν ἰήματα (*ta enantia ton enantion estin iemata*) [opposites are cures for opposites]. Whenever an attempt was made at a θεωρία (*theoria*), it seems to have based itself almost automatically on the concept of one or, more commonly, two pairs of opposites, which in turn have apparently archetypal roots (*tetractys, quaternio*). It is well known that this theme has been one of the primary concerns of Aristotle, as is shown in the *Metaphysics* and *Prior Analytics*. Hippocrates does not seem to have had the four humors, but

---

16. Aristotle, *Problemata* xxx, 403, a. 16.

they appear with the writings of his son-in-law Polybus and have survived ever since. Empirically, he seems to have soundly relied on the fact that "Nature, however uneducated and uninstructed,—ἀπαίδευτος (*apaideutos*) [without culture] — always does the right thing" (*Epidemics*).

6. To see how the classical mind actually experienced dynamic psychology, one can do no better than to read ancient drama. (For this purpose I have listed some of the most impressive passages in the Bibliographic Appendix.) The role of catharsis was discussed from Aristotle to Goethe and down to our days. A pathetic example was the schizophrenic at Argos, who kept being socially adjusted by sitting daily in the empty theater, enjoying the hallucinated spectacles immensely: "in vacuo laetus sessor plausorque theatro" [happily he sat alone in the empty theater applauding].[17] Ponder on the well-attested fact that theatrical performances in ancient Greece were most effective therapeutic institutions, for which reason they played a predominant part in the Asklepieia. The Greeks always saw σῶμα καὶ ψυχή (*soma kai psyche*) [body and soul] as one.

Appendix: Ancient Drama

Aeschylus, *Prometheus Bound*, 554ff (Io); *The Libation-Bearers*, 1023 (Orestes); and *The Eumenides*, 40ff (Orestes).
Sophocles, *Ajax*, 51ff and 232ff (Ajax).
Euripides, *The Madness of Herakles*, 858 and 1089ff (Herakles); *Iphigeneia in Tauris*, 281-310 (Orestes); and *Orestes*, 34ff and 210-277 (Orestes).

---

17. Horace, *Epistles* II, 2.130.

Psychological Types and Individuation: A Plea for a More Scientific Approach in Jungian Psychology

Jung's most important contribution to psychology was the discovery and practice of the process of individuation. In spite of the supremacy of this concept, its origins in terms of chronology are far from being as clear as they should be, and in this respect not even Jung's memoirs yield the needed biographical information. That is just the trouble: we don't have a biography of our *heros eponymos* yet. And, since those who grew up with the development of, and were dyed in the wool with, Jungian thought are slowly but surely disappearing from this planet, I thought it might be useful if I tried to give some hints concerning the genesis of the idea of individuation, for there is no better way of understanding a living thing than by tracing its embryology.

But before I give you the prehistory, history and an account of the survival of the concept of individuation, I shall ask you to remember: *Individuation begins and ends with typology.* I shall now try to elucidate this statement.

Whereas Freud's chief interest was to find a common denominator for the varieties of human behavior, which he believed he found in the Oedipus complex, Jung was never quite happy with this simplification. *His* mind was open to, and rather struck by, the almost unlimited psychic complications the species produces all the time. In view of them, he too was eager to find a compass,

Paper read to the "Fourth International Congress for Analytical Psychology" in Zürich in September 1968. First published in German in: *Zeitschrift für Analytische Psychologie*, vol. 1 (Berlin, 1970), 6; in English in *The Analytical Process* (New York, 1971), 276ff.

as he put it, for his own orientation in his patients' and his own nightly sea journeys. As early as 1904 he thought he had struck upon a significant dichotomy in the attitude of his subjects to the Word Association Test. The classification of their answers or reactions showed that some consistently preferred to relate to the stimulus in an egocentric, subjectively evaluating way, whereas other subjects preferred to take the stimulus in an impersonal and abstract way. Jung's preoccupation with the diagnostic and psychiatric purpose of the test at the time made him believe that the first group – those who reacted egocentrically, subjectively and evaluatingly – constituted the hysterical group of patients, whereas the latter group would constitute the schizophrenic, or, as it then was called, dementia praecox group.[1] Jung soon realized that this discrimination was of a much more general validity, and it reminded him immediately of the dichotomy made by William James when he discussed the differences between tough- and tender-minded people, where the tough-minded would correspond to the extraverted and the tender-minded to the introverted attitude.

This amplification encouraged him to coin the concepts of extraverted and introverted attitude, and in 1913, exactly fifty-five years ago, he read a paper to the Munich Psychoanalytic Congress, wherein he asked for nothing less than a psychology that would do justice to the existence of those two basically different and almost completely opposite types of persons. This demand proved to be a first, almost innocently blown, attack against the absolute monarchy of Freudian principles, which made Freud faint and became subsequently a *cause célèbre*. Consequently, Jung's paper could never be published in German and only appeared in French in 1915 in the *Archives de Psychologie* under the auspices of Claparède.[2]

I quote this incident simply in order to call to your attention the fact that, from the beginning, typology created quite an out-

---

1. C. G. Jung and Franz Riklin, "The Associations of Normal Subjects" in *Experimental Researches* (Coll. Wks. 2, 1973), 3-196 [original German edition: Leipzig, 1904].

2. C. G. Jung, "Contribution à l'Etude des Types Psychologiques" in *Archives de Psychologie* XIII, 52 (Geneva, 1913): 289-99. Available in English in *Coll. Wks.* 6 (1971).

burst of psychodynamics. Freud must have been rather apprehensive at the time since this problem had its precursor in the first part of the "Wandlungen und Symbole der Libido," published in the *Jahrbuch* of 1911[3] where, in the introductory chapter, Jung had already made this discrimination of the two types of thinking, which can easily be related to the two attitudinal types.

In this connection it should not be overlooked that Freud made an attempt at giving the introvert, or the introverted attitude, a more specific meaning in his treatise on narcissism, which was published in 1914, but it is obvious that Freud quite misinterpreted this introverted attitude—shall we say—for the benefit of his own purposes.[4] These two types, by the way, have subsequently found their way into two most vivid monographs in literature, namely the typically extraverted American *Babbitt* (1922) and the typically introverted *Arrowsmith* (1925) by Sinclair Lewis. So it was a writer who, as an amplification, provided us with this very acute characterization of two types of American personalities.

From 1913 on, Jung devoted all his time to the amplification and further differentiation of the typological problem. The additional aspect of the four functions had also blossomed forth from some of the early observations with the Word Association Test, namely that the extravert tended to react to the stimulus word in the association experiment with a feeling tone (the subjectively evaluating, value predicative type). This feeling tone was subsequently demonstrated physically by the strong Galvanic Skin Response that went with those reactions, and the thinking function came in handy for the objective type of reaction in the Word Association Test.

In many papers read to the Psychological Club in Zürich and subsequent discussions with his friends, colleagues, and pupils, Jung's concept was clarified step by step. It was Dr. Hans Schmid-Guisan who made it clear to Jung that extraversion was not of necessity correlated to feeling as he had originally been

---

3. C. G. Jung, "Wandlungen und Symbole der Libido," *Jahrb. Psychoanal. u. Psychopathol. Forschungen* III/I (Leipzig and Vienna, 1911): 124-152. Available in English in *Coll. Wks.* 5 (1956).

4. S. Freud, "Zur Einführung des Narzissmus," in *Jahrb. Psychoanal. Psychopathol.* VI (Leipzig and Vienna, 1914): 1-24.

advocating, and Toni Wolff was highly instrumental in introducing sensation and intuition as two indispensable orienting functions of consciousness. In particular, intuition was dealt with more critically in those days by Dr. Emil Medtner.[5]

Discussions subsequently became extremely dynamic, particularly when Jung had to defend introversion against the accusation of its being nothing but a benign metonymy of narcissism or schizoid autism. To this discussion we owe the formulation of the *subjective factor* that at long last gave introversion a decent definition, whereas extraversion remains to this day more or less taken for granted.

At all events, Jung must have been working very hard on the typological problem during the eight long years between 1913 and 1921, when the monolithic tome *Psychological Types* appeared.[6] Wanting a relevant biography, this, the lengthiest of Jung's publications, must always look like a miraculous birth to the understanding reader, or must seem wholly incomprehensible to those who would not have it as a product of long experience and would therefore interpret it as a bone-dry abstraction. (The very same year, in 1921, Kretschmer's book *Körperbau und Charakter* appeared, and it is rather a shame that this most genial contribution to psychiatry has never been decently evaluated in respect to its relation to Jungian typology.)[7]

At this point you must allow me to become a bit more personal. When I read the book on the types in 1922 it simply hit me between the eyes. It had such an impact upon me that I could not help telling Jung immediately. He could hardly understand my reaction, for so far all the reviews of the book had been more than cool and totally lacking in deeper understanding. When he asked me what it was that had moved me so deeply, I said I thought that he had given nothing less than the clearest pattern for simply all the *dynamics* of the human soul. He said that this was exactly what he had intended to do, but so far nobody seemed to have noticed.

From here you can see why I believe the types are the begin-

---

5. Emil Medtner, *Über die sog.* "Intuition," *die ihr angrenzenden Begriffe und die an sie anknüpfenden Probleme. Vorgetragen im Psychologischen Club Zürich, 1919* (Moscow and Zürich, 1923) 8, 179ff.

6. C. G. Jung, *Psychologische Typen* (Zürich, 1921).

7. Ernst Kretschmer, *Körperbau und Charakter* (Berlin, 1921).

ning of the individuation process. I was, however, astonished to find much later that Baynes' translation of the types book was given a subtitle; it was now called *Psychological Types or The Psychology of Individuation.*[8] In a preface, Baynes laconically remarks that Jung himself had suggested this addition. In the book, the term *individuation* is hardly used and is only discussed rather timidly in the last chapter, where it is given a tentative definition.

Jung must have suffered a great deal from the lack of enthusiasm with which his theory of types was greeted, and he only made two more attempts at advertising it: one in 1923 at an international conference on education in Territet—this was later published in English[9]—and the other in a paper read to the Medical Society in Zürich in 1928, later published in *Seelenprobleme der Gegenwart.*[10] On both occasions he seemed not to have been interested in elaborating the aspect of individuation at all and confessed that typology served him as the only reliable compass for what he called a *critical psychology*, which, as he says, he should indeed hate to miss.

Later he occasionally made remarks about the differences between Freud and Adler in terms of their belonging to the two different attitudinal types, and this of course has to be borne in mind throughout our discussion. To judge from his scientific work published since 1928, one might be tempted to think that he abandoned typology altogether, but this would be a mistake. What he really did was to devote the rest of his life to the amplification of the dynamics of the individuation process, the blueprint of which is already neatly given with typology.

Let me now try to make it clear how this typological pattern connects with the individuation process. For that purpose we shall have to go into the laboratory—as the alchemists would call it—to the workshop or consulting room of the analyst, where traditionally attempts at individuation are made.

---

8. C. G. Jung, *Psychological Types*, H. G. Baynes, trans. (London: Kegan Paul; New York: Harcourt Brace, 1923); *Coll. Wks. 6*, 1971.

9. C. G. Jung, "Psychological Types," in *Contributions to Analytical Psychology* (London, 1928): 295-312.

10. C. G. Jung, "Psychologische Typologie," in *Seelenprobleme der Gegenwart* (Zürich, 1931), 115-143.

I will use a schema for the situation we meet with in the consulting room (Fig. 1). We have the two persons of analysand and analyst, i.e., we have the two systems; and these two systems in themselves are again polarized, as you might call it, into the two realms of the conscious and the unconscious psyche. Thus you

Fig. 1

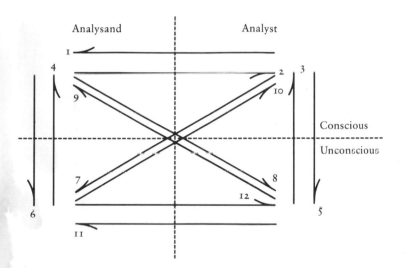

automatically have two pairs of factors or entities, which you always have to bear in mind. In the case of this encounter between the two systems, we can discriminate between the analysand's consciousness and the analyst's consciousness, and the interaction between those two systems can more or less be taken for granted. We give this interaction, which can and should work both ways, the numbers (1) and (2). Then we have the two *un*conscious systems, and we assume that in the case of the analyst there is a living connection to his unconscious and also some influence from his unconscious into the conscious system. These relations would be represented by the arrows (3) and (5). The same is supposed to exist in the case of the analysand (4) and (6), with whom there naturally is always a question of those relations really functioning, and functioning properly. We still have another possibility, namely that the analyst's conscious system has an effect on the patient's unconscious (7); and, as there is a demand for symmetry, we must also assume that there is a possibility of its working both ways (10). And still more, the same would apply in another direction, showing the influence of the patient's or the analysand's consciousness on the analyst's unconscious, or vice versa, i.e., the well-known constellating effects. These symmetric effects would be shown by the arrows (8) and (9). Now there remains a gap at the bottom of our schema. Here an interaction between the unconscious of the analysand and the unconscious of the analyst and vice versa would then make the pattern complete (11) and (12).

Whereas (1) and (2) are more or less trivial, and while, in view of the compensatory relation between conscious and unconscious, (3) to (6) can be taken for granted, (7) to (10) can hardly be rationally understood. In order to admit their existence and functioning we have to make the supposition that the two systems of analysand and analyst have (at least partly) merged, so that a clear-cut discrimination (dotted vertical line) is no longer quite so easy.[11] With (11) and (12) epistemological difficulties reach their culmination, and yet I think they are far from being merely theoretically posited. At all events they will have to be considered effective wherever parapsychological phenomena occur during analysis, whether inside or outside the consulting room. In this connection I should like to remark that the various brave psychoanalytic attempts at an understanding of such phenomena are hardly sufficient.[12] The Jungian view of the *omniscience* of the unconscious, however, which is indispensable in this connection, may be too hard to swallow as long as we think purely causalistically. At all events it is obvious that on the level of (11) and (12) we are moving in the matrix of synchronicity.

In praxi, we will always meet with difficulty in that most of these relations cannot really be taken apart, as they are probably

---

11. Cf. C. A. Meier, "Projection, Transference and the Subject/Object Relation in Psychology," *Journ. Anal. Psychol.* IV/I (London, 1959).

12. Cf. Jan Ehrenwald, *New Dimensions of Deep Analysis* (London, 1954) and Emilio Servadio, "Psychoanalysis and Parapsychology," in *Science and ESP*, ed. J. R. Smythies (London, 1967).

all working and functioning simultaneously, if only in a more or less infinitesimal degree. What I want to say, though, is that the constellating influences and everything we can talk about – the difference, the interaction, the polarity, the tension of opposites and all these famous compensatory constellations, etc., in short, all the dynamics playing between the two systems – are all to be regarded as being contained in this pattern.

Fig. 2

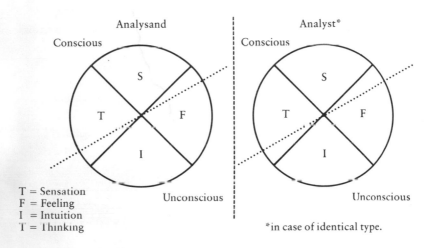

T = Sensation
F = Feeling
I = Intuition
T = Thinking

*in case of identical type.

Another way of describing these facts, which Jung advocated as early as 1925, takes the role of the four functions more particularly into account.[13] Again we have the situation of the analyst in the consulting room. Figure 2 would again represent the two systems of analysand and analyst. We have the four functions – thinking, feeling, sensation and intuition – in a particular setting or distribution, whereby we would have an interesting kind of measuring rod as to the nature of the interaction of those two systems. Let us assume that we have to deal with two identi-

---

13. C. G. Jung, "Notes on the Seminar in Analytical Psychology, 1925," Diagrams 8, 178 (Zürich, 1926) [privately multigraphed].

cal types which, incidentally, would be a disastrous proposition because in such a case most probably nothing would ever happen. No interaction could possibly take place because the two systems are so identical that no potentials can result—I am sure you all know that such things happen. Identities between analyst and analysand not only exist, but also can be produced artificially, *per nefas*, of course. In any case the situation would be stale and the analyst would have to refer the analysand to a colleague differing in pattern. For his own benefit he certainly should start developing more than one auxiliary function, to bend the dotted line toward F, for example, or as I shall call it later, to "rotate" his system. From this way of describing a respective situation you can easily see the nature of the limitations in the situation. We know where the limitations of the analyst are according to the given case, and we know where the limitations of the analysand are, and—supposing that we know the exact structure of our two systems—we can give a prognosis of the development of the process that is to take place. Naturally enough this instrument (Fig. 2) is no Laplacean intelligence that would allow you to predict the exact course of events from this very moment, where you have a complete and thorough diagnosis of the present situation, for the fulfillment of such a prognosis is already impossible if only because of the existence of the *uncertainty principle*. The situation has to be understood as a dynamic one, and let us hope that there is no such *a priori* identity. I would like to emphasize only this, that in view of the fact that the two systems have to be understood as constantly interfering, we must assume that whatever the analyst's system looks like to begin with, he should always be able to change altogether every single moment of the process, so as to produce a tension of opposites with regard to the system of the analysand. If he can do this, then something really can happen and things can really be constellated, and problems can really come to a head. For that purpose, of course the analyst has to be capable of rotating and revolutionizing his own system, time and time again. If not, you get stuck in shadow projections and complete blockages of development which, as we know all too well, happen in both the case of incompatibility and the case of too good a compatibility between characters.

It is important to notice at this juncture that we have to attempt a synthesis of those opposites that are in play all the time, and we must come to a point where the well-known *exclusion principle* between the opposite functions gets less and less exclusive, so that a synthesis is at long last possible. Whenever the exclusion principle is no longer dominating the situation, or also when it is absolutely valid, then one can expect the formation of a *uniting symbol*, and in such a way a constructive or a healing effect can take place. The healing always is the begetting of a new microcosm. If you like, you can call all these schemata or mandalas an attempt to describe what can be called microcosmogony.

The conclusion of all this would be that the indispensable prerequisite for any success in analysis would be the training analysis, which in itself is absolutely identical with analysis *tout court* and in no way different, so that the trained analyst is really capable of undergoing this continuous "revolution," as I have been calling it.

I have always wondered why Jung never took the trouble to support his typological concept with its earliest predecessors. You only have to think of the four elements of Empedocles (fifth century B.C.) and his two powers of νεῖκος (*neikos*) [contention] and φιλότης (*philotes*) [amiability] (the separative principle in the cosmos and its opposite). Or you have the four cardinal humours of Sextus Empiricus (second century A.D.) and, concerning my last remark, the goal of *eukrasia* (harmonious mixture of them), which would exactly correspond to individuation, as can be seen for example from Honorius of Autun (twelfth century) and William of Conches (1080-1154 A.D.), who called it a *paradisiacal condition*. Incidentally, he also says that whenever one of the four elements (functions) too strongly prevails, this means a depravation to the brute level, and he uses animal symbolism to describe such conditions.

What I would like to mention now, specifically in favor of a more scientific approach in Jungian psychology, is simply that according to my conviction, the four functions are the most basic, the most elementary, the most neatly defined concepts in Jungian psychology. For this reason, they lend themselves to simple testing, providing that the subjects for the tests do not reflect on answers too long, since all the obvious interactions between the conscious opposites have to be avoided. This of course is a great danger. But may I emphasize that we have a possibility to test our analysand by the Gray-Wheelwright test,[14] which has enormous advantages; it is simple enough so that we can always change and improve it, and it makes no difference whether you have a patient of high intellectual development or not. Any patient would be capable of answering these simple questions. You would have an enormous number of subjects very quickly, and the result could be easily evaluated statistically, even computerized. May I also emphasize here that it is imperative that we support our own convictions by statistical evaluations, as statistics are the closest we can come to the truth in psychology. We should remind ourselves of the fact that Jung himself started his scientific work in the Word Association Test by using statistics, and he made use of them again in his later work. I need only remind you of his Eranos lecture of 1935, and the study on synchronicity.[15]

Academic psychologists are right in wanting things shown to them statistically; and it is we Jungians who have the *onus* of showing them that our ideas stand their tests. Only in this way can the unconscious be reintroduced into a scientific discussion. We should have the chairs of the psychology departments of the universities held by Jungians, and they could have their real institutes, their assistants, their student population, their funds, their statisticians, and their computers; then we could have high dynamic discussion and a living thing instead of the scientific stagnation in Jungianism during the last several years.

Jung was a pioneer who gave us such an enormously great number of fascinating ideas, all of which eagerly await to be proven, and we still have to collect the necessary clinical data for this evaluation. We have a *responsabilité de l'esprit*, because if this is not done by Jungians, it will be done by others. They will,

---

14. Joseph B. Wheelwright and John A. Buehler, "Jungian Type Survey" (The Gray-Wheelwright Test], *Manual* (1st ed. 1944, 15th revision 1964. Society of Jungian Analysts of Northern California, San Francisco, 1964).

15. Cf. Jung's Eranos Lectures (1935): C. G. Jung, "Traumsymbole des Individuationsprozesses," in *Eranos Jahrbuch* 1935 (Zürich, 1936) n.1, 131; and "Synchronicity: An Acausal Connecting Principle," in *The Structure and Dynamics of the Psyche* (*Coll. Wks.* 8), 417-519 [original German edition: Zürich, 1952].

of course, all mistake Jungian terms from the word *go* and then show that it is all a lot of nonsense and completely wrong. With that, Jungianism will disappear from the discussion, and in the next couple of generations nobody will ever care to come near our field. The unconscious has lately become a *numerus clausus* [closed subject], beginning with Freud himself who not only discovered it but very quickly created the most successful system of reducing it to "nothing but" a big illusion.

He was bound to fail in this titanic fight of "moving his *Acheronta*." He only did so in order to become afraid of it and consequently had to mark it as nothing but an illusion. *His* concept of the unconscious, therefore, had to be replaced by more scepticism on the one hand or by still more cloudy concepts on the other, such as *Dasein* or *Existence* or whatever other more fashionable ones there may be.

I repeat: younger psychologists want statistical proof. They could have it. We could procure it. We should even go so far as to make membership to this society dependent on an oath that our members will give all their patients the Gray-Wheelwright test to start with and again during the process, in order to find out how the pattern changes. Why have we not done anything about this? Obviously the answer is that we are all much too much fascinated by the unconscious instead of giving the typological mandala the due scope and application it so urgently is asking for.

When I said that the typological tests are already taken out of our hands by non-Jungians and that they get adopted without Jung's name ever being mentioned, this is a fact that can easily be proved. You all know that extraverted and introverted attitudes, for example, are not only adopted by many academic psychologists, but also, it has to be admitted, these people have tried to make something of it. We need only think of McDougall[16] who in 1929 already talked about those two types in terms of the differences in their chemistry — a very interesting, probably a rather fantastic idea. Still, it was obviously a very intuitive hit.

---

16. William McDougall, "A Chemical Theory of Temperament Applied to Introversion and Extraversion," in *J. Abnorm. Soc. Psychol.* 24 (1929): 393-409.

What follows is a tentative chronological enumeration of important contributors to Jungian typology since McDougall, as far as they are not included in the references at the end of the Gray-Wheelwright *Manual*. We first have A. R. Root[17] and J. P. Guilford, (from 1930-1959),[18] as well as R. B. Cattell (since 1946),[19] and H. J. Eysenck.[20] P. M. Garrigan (1960)[21] is of considerable value as well as, of course, the Myers-Briggs type indicator (1962).[22] The most interesting contributions come from 1962 to 1964 by L. J. Strickler and J. Ross,[23] wherein apart from the attitude, the functions are discussed more carefully. Since 1966 we have a fine German study by E. Wolpert and L. Michel.[24]

Some of these authors are far ahead of us, which of course implies that some of them know even better than Jung. And it is we Jungians who are responsible for this trouble. Some of these scientists reach interesting results, which should only encourage

17. A. R. Root, "A Short Test of Introversion-Extraversion," *Pers. J.* 10 (1931): 250-253.

18. J. P. Guilford and K. M. Braly, "Extra- and Introversion," in *Psychol. Bull.* 27 (1930): 96-107; J. P. Guilford and R. B. Guilford, "An Analysis of Factors in a Typical Test of Intro- Extraversion," in *J. Abnorm. Soc. Psychol.* 28 (1933/34): 377-99; J. P. Guilford, "Intro- Extraversion," in *Psychol. Bull.* 31 (1934): 331-354; *Personality* (New York: McGraw Hill, 1959).

19. R. B. Cattell, *Description and Measurement of Personality* (New York: World Books, 1946); *Personality and Motivation Structure and Measurement* (New York: World Books, 1957).

20. H. J. Eysenck, *Dimensions of Personality* (London: McMillan, 1947); *Dynamics of Anxiety and Hysteria* (London: Praeger, 1957); *The Structure of Human Personality* (London: Methuen, 1960); *The Biological Basis of Personality* (Springfield, Illinois: Charles C. Thomas, 1967). Also: H. J. Eysenck, ed., *Extraversion-Introversion*, 3 vols. (London: McGibbon & Kee, 1969).

21. P. M. Garrigan, "Extraversion-Introversion as Dimensions of Personality," in *Psychol. Bull.* 57 (1960): 326-360.

22. I. B. Myers, *Manual*, "The Myers-Briggs Type Indicator" (Princeton, New Jersey, 1962).

23. L. J. Strickler and J. Ross, "An Assessment of Some Structural Properties of the Jungian Personality Typology," in *J. Abnorm. Soc. Psychol.* 68 (1964): 62-71; "Some Correlations of a Jungian Personality Inventory," in *Psychol. Rep.* 14 (1964): 623-643.

24. Wolpert and L. Michel, "Die Typologie C. G. Jung als Gegenstand empirischer Persönlichkeitsforschung," in *Psychol. Forschg.* 29 (1966): 112-131.

us to do something more in our own field. Astonishingly enough, even in the Psychological Institute of Zürich University something concerning the attitudes has recently been undertaken.[25]

Since 1944, some Jungians themselves have realized that Jungian typology offers many questions and answers, and it is with pleasure that we have seen the articles by M. J. Dicks-Mireaux,[26] K. Bradway,[27] F. B. Brawer and J. M. Spiegelman,[28] I. N. Marshall,[29] H. G. Richek and O. H. Brown,[30] and H. Mann, M. Siegler and H. Osmond[31] in our *Journal*.

A small number of German-speaking Jungians have also made attempts to elaborate the typological idea, among whom Toni Wolff[32] came first, whereas J. H. van der Hoop[33] took it upon himself to teach Jung a lesson. K. W. Bash[34] has been the first one to make use of Jungian typology for general psychopathology, and H. K. Fierz[35] has tried to show the clinical relevance of the difference in attitude, whereas Markus Fierz[36] neatly demon-

---

25. Ilka S. von Zeppelin, *Die Variablen der Holtzman Inkblot Technik in iher Beziehung zur Introversion und Extraversion* (Bern and Stuttgart, 1966).

26. M. J. Dicks-Mireaux, "Extraversion-Introversion in Experimental Psychology," in *J. Anal. Psychol.* 9 (1964): 117-128.

27. K. Bradway, "Jung's Psychological Types," in *J. Anal. Psychol.* 9 (1964): 129-135.

28. F. B. Brawer and J. M. Spiegelman, "Rorschach and Jung," in *J. Anal. Psychol.* 9 (1964): 137-149.

29. I. N. Marshall, "Extraversion and Libido in Jung and Cattell," in *J. Anal. Pschol.* 12 (1967): 115-136; "The Four Functions: A Conceptual Analysis," in *J. Anal. Psychol.* 13 (1968): 1-32.

30. H. G. Richek and O. H. Brown, "Phenomenological Correlates of Jung's Typology," in *J. Anal. Psychol.* 13 (1968): 57-65.

31. H. Mann, M. Siegler and H. Osmond, "The Many Worlds of Time," in *J. Anal. Psychol.* 13 (1968): 33-56.

32. Toni Wolff, "Einführung in die Grundlagen der Komplexen Psychologie," in *Die Kulturelle Bedeutung der Komplexen Psychologie* (Berlin, 1935): 51-122 and *Studien zu C. G. Jung's Psychologie*, ed. C. A. Meier (Zürich, 1959): 77-171.

33. J. H. van der Hoop, *Bewusstseinstypen* (Bern, 1937).

34. K. W. Bash, *Lehrbuch der allgemeinen Psychopathologie* (Stuttgart, 1955).

35. H. K. Fierz, *Klinik und Analytische Psychologie, Studien aus dem C. G. Jung Institut Zürich*, xv (Zürich, 1963).

36. M. Fierz, "Die vier Elemente," in *Traum und Symbol*, ed. C. A. Meier (Zürich, 1963).

strates the age-old activity of the Pythagorean *tetractys* in science.[37]

Bruno Klopfer and Marvin Spiegelman[38] gave an interesting study of types of analyses and analysts that has something to do with our kind of mandala, and they use interesting parameters; unfortunately not only are the statistics completely lacking, which is natural enough, but also the parallel to the process or to the development (rotation) that takes place is amiss. So it seems that even in Jungian circles the interest in our topic is starting again.

You may all say that this whole business is an old dream of mine, and that the typological mandala simply struck me almost in childhood and that now in old age I regress to it again. This is true, but it does not invalidate the argument that, of all the basic concepts of Jung, the four functions are the most basic. The attitudes are already widely accepted, as I said, even though only a few of the authors seem to give Jung credit for them; but the functions should be even more easily acceptable. That they have not been accepted is in part due to the fact that the Jungians themselves have never really made much of them. The rest of the Jungian psychology is really what Jung sometimes calls *Komplexe Psychologie*, i.e., a description of highly complicated phenomenological data and their metamorphoses. The

---

[37. Ed. Note: The concept of the *tetractys* typifies the focus the Pythagoreans placed on the mystical significance of numbers, conceiving of them as representing the harmonious order of the universe. Literally, it refers to the numbers 1 to 4, which or all add up to the sacred number 10, and constitute the ratios underlying the intervals of the musical scale. "The core of the Pythagorean belief in universal harmony is the music – heard or inaudible – of the celestial elements. But the sublunary world also partook of this harmony: the elements of fire, air, water and earth; the seasons; the days of the week; the flow of rivers and the tides of the sea; the direction of winds; the growth of plants. These and many other earthly phenomena were viewed as directly related to the heavens, and so governed by the same principles of harmonics or musical mathematics .... Man, the microcosm, shares in this harmony: everything from the gestation period of the human embryo and bodily proportions to the smallest details of human behavior is governed by analogy with, or dependence upon, celestial harmony." – *Dictionary of the History of Ideas*, ed. Philip P. Wiener (New York: Charles Scribner's Sons, 1973) IV: 40.]

38. Bruno Klopfer and J. M. Spiegelman, "Some Dimensions of Psychotherapy," in *Spectrum Psychologiae* (Zürich, 1965): 177-183).

dynamics, however, are far from being adequately, clinically described in terms of attitudes and functions, for which reason, in the United States, the term *dynamic psychology* has become almost synonymous with Freudian psychoanalysis, which, however, lacks the complex images, and more particularly misses completely the effects of the transcendent function of the true symbol. That Freudians freely avail themselves even of the most Jungian terms and misuse them is made apparent in the title of the book by Margaret Mahler: *On Human Symbiosis and the Vicissitudes of Individuation.*[39]

The one symbol Jung brought up as early as 1902 in his doctoral dissertation was the mandala.[40] It may well be that the *Types* are really a later upshot of it, as can be seen from the fact that ever since the 1925 seminar he used to represent the types in this sort of diagram (Fig. 2).

Later in his life, whenever he wrote about the mandala in the individuation process, he always omitted hinting at the connection with the typological pattern, which, however, constitutes the dynamics of the process itself. But it should never be forgotten that almost all Eastern mandalas, in their graphic representations, make it very clear that they are ever vividly rotating, thus indicating the dynamics, the process, the character of the ever-repeated night-sea-journey during the "dark night of the soul." He who is not prepared to get literally revolutionized in this way, time and again, cannot very well be a Jungian analyst.

To conclude, I will try to do justice to the origin of my argument that individuation is of necessity already dynamically anticipated in the concept of typology. We have seen what its origins were in Jung's own development, but here as always big discoveries have their *archetypus*, as the philologists would call it. In our case, it is the archetype of the *tetractys*, which was first formulated by Empedocles. This idea comes at the beginning of dynamic psychology in classical antiquity, and it proved to be so

---

39. Margaret Mahler, *On Human Symbiosis and the Vicissitudes of Individuation*, vol. 1: *Infantile Psychosis* (International Psycho-Analytical Library, no. 83) (London: The Hogarth Press, 1969).

40. C. G. Jung, "On the Psychology and Pathology of So-Called Occult Phenomena," in *Psychiatric Studies* (*Coll. Wks.* 1, 1957), 3-88. [original German edition: Leipzig, 1902, p. 53.]

useful that Greek philosophy and medicine literally lived on it for centuries, and it actually dominated the field right down to the Renaissance. The dynamics of the tension of the pairs of opposites was not only made responsible for disease and health, but also for all creativity. It is a shame that Jung never made much use of those sources, conspicuous as they are.

When I prepared a paper to be read at Yale University Medical School entitled "Dynamic Psychology in Classical Antiquity," I researched a great number of ancient texts and fragments.[41] I should like here to quote one that greatly impressed me when I reread that paper. It is Fragment 119 of Heraclitus which reads as follows: Ἦθος ἀνθρώπῳ δαίμων (*ethos anthropo daimon*) [character is man's daimon]. Ἦθος is the *character* as in Theophrastus' Ἠθικοὶ Χαρακτῆρες (*Ethikoi Charakteres*), i.e., the particular pattern or type; ἀνθρώπῳ (*anthropō*) means "to man," δαίμων literally means *daemon*, which in this context means nothing more or less than "dynamism," the force that is in him and makes him tick, and, as we would now say in this respect, also makes him rotate. In these three words you have the gist of everything I tried to show and I think also of everything Jung tried to show with his typology. But of course in order to make this whole thing clear, to show how it works, and how it both can and should be done, Jung had to live it out for us.

---

41. C. A. Meier, "Dynamic Psychology in Classical Antiquity," *Psychiatry and Its History*, eds., G. Mora and J. Brand (Springfield, Illinois: Thomas, 1969).

Chapter 13

Cultural Education as Symbol*

Comparative research into the history of the term *Bildung*, from antiquity to Pestalozzi, comes up with findings which are of interest in many respects from a psychological point of view.

Bildung (the noun) and *bilden* (the verb) have disappeared from the psychological dictionary and have become the exclusive prerogative of pedagogics, but even here their meanings have undergone a secularization and are confined to the imparting of knowledge (information) and its methodology, with the emphasis almost solely on the discussion of the increasingly technical aspect of teaching methods and aids. This sector has become barren ground with regard to a general psychological method of observation and it remains to be seen whether or not psychology, without wishing to pretend to a *Bildung* psychology, is in a position to create fertile ground for the concept.

Although the term no longer offers a basis for psychological discussion and is rarely understood in its original meaning, it has nevertheless stood its ground in the life of the individual. Like it or not, in our everyday lives we are all judged by these criteria even if the judgment is not based on any clear definition

First published in German as "Bildung als Symbol" in: *Buch der Freunde für J. R. von Salis* (Zurich, 1971), 331. English translation by David N. Roscoe.

*[Translator's Note: I have opted for the term *cultural education* as a translation of the German *Bildung* because the author's use of the term goes beyond the purely pedagogic aspect to include cultivation of the mind. An interesting comparison may be made here with the French *éducation*.]

or if it is made unconsciously; whether he realizes it or not, the average person is consciously striving to improve himself in this respect.

Nevertheless, there is no denying that nowadays *Bildung* is a vague term, more precisely an empty one, with its meaning lost. Since C. G. Jung, we in the field of psychology have grown accustomed to dealing with such vague concepts by the method of amplification. In other words, we collect as much (historical) material as possible that has accumulated around the concept with the passage of time. If we work on the assumption that this material has piled up concentrically around the original concept, the focal point emerges with greater clarity when this approach is adopted.

Within the scope of an essay of this nature it is impossible, of course, even to list the variations on the subject of *Bildung* that have built up over the past two thousand years. Nor is it a good thing that, in our amplificatory approach, we psychologists are forced to make uninvited forays into other specialized fields where our discretion cannot be guaranteed. For the sake of brevity I shall confine myself to those amplifications that I feel substantiate the psychologically most interesting result of my investigation, namely, that the traditional concept of *Bildung* and the modern Jungian concept of *individuation* clearly converge.

Let our first foray be a look at what light etymology throws on this expression. What do the etymologists have to say about *Bildung* and *bilden*?

The untranslatable, subtle German word *bilden* is said to be a word borrowed from the Latin *formare* [to form]. We recall that the scholastic term *forma* means the Aristotelian μορφή (*morphē*), in other words the spiritual form. As a consequence, whenever Shaftesbury speaks of *formation*, the German translators have always translated it with *Bildung*.

On the other hand, the following etymological link exists for the German word *Bild: bi-lipi* (Goth.), *bilidi* (AS), *lipu* (G) = limb, *bilipu* = artificial limb. This last term is an indication of the magical use of such structures, be it for casting evil spells or for healing purposes.

Keeping these two aspects of etymology in mind, let us now turn to an outline of the cultural history of the ideal form of *Bildung*.

Werner Jaeger has shown us clearly that the major concern of the Greek policy of *Bildung* was to *form* real people, just like the potter with clay and the sculptor with stone.[1] The living human being is seen as the highest work of art. The formative principle is the idea, the *typos*, the form that is seen from the *Theoria*—from θεωρεῖν (*theorein*) [to look at]—and interpreted from the *Bild* (image). Anything else is merely training for specific purposes (instruction, indoctrination, information), in the face of which the human being as microcosm has a totally different dimension. What it is actually is an anthropoplastic whose πλάστης (*plastes*) is the human being himself as molder of the soul, πλάστειν τὰς ψυχάς (*plastein tas psychas*). This is the real meaning of humanism, the *mentes formare* [to form with the mind], the *studia humanitatis* [humanistic studies] of Cicero, the becoming aware of the actual laws of being of Man. The becoming manifest of the "spiritual form," μορφή (*morphē*) that lies behind such a process, or is at its very essence, is introduced by the παιδεία (*paideia*) [education]. Learning and practicing belong to the προπαιδεύματα (*propaideumata*) [pre-studies], the *pueriles artes* or *disciplinae*, but must be pursued with a sense of instructional creativity. Already with Plato, the aim of the *Paideia* is the *Trias*: ποιητής (*poietes*) πολιτικός (*politikos*) and σοφός (*sophos*) [poet, citizen, wise man]. In the sense that it also comprises the preparation for death, it even has eschatological significance[2] and makes possible a knowledge of God (*Epinomis*). Apart from the sciences of numbers, special emphasis is laid by Plato on the Muses, in particular the chorus dance.[3]

In Alexandria the Platonic-Aristotelian *Paideia* becomes the ἐνκύκλιος παιδεία (*enkyklios paideia*, whence encyclopaedia), first in Dionysios of Halikarnassos, the secularizing misunderstanding of which only comes to its sad conclusion with Diderot and D'Alembert. In actual fact it is always a system of liberal arts as a prerequisite for each special field of study and once again is connected with dance ἐνκύκλιος (*enkyklios*) [in a circle]. Only once again does this idea arouse genuine interest and appreciation with the Renaissance Platonists. Special mention must be made here of Gianfrancesco Pico, nephew of

---

1. Werner Jaeger, *Paideia*, 3 vols. (New York: Oxford University Press, 1943-1945).
2. Plato, *Phaedo*, 107d.
3. Plato, *Laws*, 2.654A.

Giovanni Pico della Mirandola, who recognized the decisive importance of the *Bild* (picture, in the sense of example) in the process of *Bildung*, seeing that it had an effect – in other words, was formative. Later more importance was attached to facts, i.e., natural sciences, a.id what was originally meant by *Bildung* was to a large extent lost.

Although the term acquired more materialistic connotations, we can see in the Age of Enlightenment a genuine German deepening of the old ideal in mysticism and pietism, and this provides us with the most impressive use of the verb *bilden*. It depicts once again a forming *process*, whereby the forming is based on a *Vorbild* (example) and an *Urbild* (ideal), comprising both a spiritual and physical form. The aim is to *înbilden* = the imprinting of God on the mind. According to Jakob Boehme, all life is the wish for *Bildung* in the *Bild* (image) of God (Genesis 1, 27); the Holy Ghost "appears in everything and shapes everything" or "he forms everything, shapes everything and loves everything." Johann Georg Gichtel has a markedly alchemistic-Paracelsic natural philosophy language, so that for him *Bildung* is production, and he makes use of erotic pictures. With him the *word* (rhetoric) has productive characteristics (which reminds one of the *logos spermatikos*) and leads to God's birth in Man, i.e., re-birth. Valentin Weigel achieves *Bildung* through a kind of *studium universale* "for which no other book is needed than the Bible, and even he who cannot read has the words in his inner self." Gottfried Arnold believes more in education than his predecessors and he prays: "Oh form me in your image," his wish being to lead (shape) Man from an ἄνθρωπος ψυχικός (*anthropos psychikos*) [ensouled man] to an ἄνθρωπος πνευματικός (*anthropos pneumatikos*) [breathing man] which reveals Gnostic influences. Friedrich Christoph Oetinger (1702-1782), as a genuine pietist, speaks of "forming the heart, forming the feelings and formative love." "Love is a fire and has in its roots the power of *Bildung*," so that one becomes uniform with the object of one's love. Love shapes Man into the form of the one who has created it (made himself the image) and given him Christ as the ideal and example. This brings us to the roots of the new humanistic *Bildung* movement of the early eighteenth century (Herder, Goethe, Schiller, W. von Humboldt), the humanistic gymnasium, and the Humboldt-style university.

I recall one aspect of *Bildung* that may all too easily be forgotten in the present discussion: *Paideia* originally meant child education and was only extended by the Sophists to mean human education and culture. The Latin equivalent is *disciplina*, from the verb *dis-cipio*, meaning intellectual understanding. But it also means teachings, law, and breeding, which is particularly important to the Romans. So alongside the intellectual, there was also a strong ethical and moral factor. *Disciplina* stands for order in the world, venerable tradition, and transmission. In the religious context it has the same meaning as *fides* and in the Vulgate is even related to wisdom and epistemology. Varro wrote, "IX disciplinarum libri," where, in acknowledgment of the importance of Muses in *Bildung*, two further Muses are added to the *septem artes liberales* to make the number complete.

Given the considerable ethical factor which was attached to the Trivium and Quadrivium by the Romans, it is understandable that the Church Fathers began to concern themselves seriously with the canon of *Bildung*. We first find this with the Areopagus speech of Paul (Apg. 17) and then in I. Thessal. 5.21: "Examine everything and keep the best." In the second letter to the Corinthians (3.18) the symbol of the *Bild* (image) emerges in all its central significance, as it has done previously in this essay with the German mystics and Gianfrancesco Pico, namely, in its power to transform: "But reflected in all of us is the clearness of the Lord with bared countenance and we shall be transfigured in the same image," etc., *in eandem imaginem transformamur*, μεταμορφούμεται (*metamorphoumetai*) [we shall be transformed]. Here the Aristotelian μορφή (*morphē*), the *forma*, the *Bild*, leads to the μετάμορφή (*metamorphē*), *transformatio*, which means transforming, in other words, changing. What this is is the "putting-on of the new man."[4]

Here we recall once again the *inbilden* of the mystics and the effectiveness (reality) of the *Bild* with Gianfrancesco Pico, as well as the magic powers of the *Bild* in Germanic etymology (see above), which sheds light on C. G. Jung's so-called "transcendental function of the symbol." It is common knowledge that the

---

4. Ephesians 4.24.

alchemists pursued lengthy discussions on the *imaginatio* [active imagination], which is not the same as imagination or fantasy but an *imaginatio vera non phantastica* [true imagination and not just fantasy] (Rosarium), namely an active evocation of internal images which have informative powers. The alchemist attempted to change material with these powers, to transmute by creating images, which amounts to a creation of reality.[5]

As we have stated, the Church Fathers held heated discussion on the pros and cons of the old ideal of *Bildung* of the *Enkyklios Paideia,* with the Eastern church very much in favor of the concept of *Bildung* and the Western church viewing genuine faith as largely independent of scholarly philosophy (*Enkyklios Paideia*). A dramatic swing in this direction is seen in the young Augustine (*De Ordine, De Quantitate Animae*) and the old St. Augustine (*De Civitate Dei*). Despite these discussions, the attitude toward *Bildung* in the Middle Ages was transferred to the monastic orders in the largely unchanged style of the old heathen Trivium and Quadrivium, albeit edified by theology. A cultural education still included a command of the *artes liberales* stamped with late ancient Christianity, as seen in Hugh of St. Victor's *Didascalion* and John of Salisbury's *Metalogicon.* From this point on, the instruction of *Bildung* became the preserve of the humanistic gymnasium and the ancient universities.

From the few examples given above of the meaning attached to the concept of *Bildung* over the centuries, the following facts emerge:

1. The verb *bilden* should only be used in the reflexive form, for it indicates a *process* for which the individual is left to his own devices. In this respect we fully agree with Herder when he says, "*Bildung* must grow out of necessity." As a representation of such process, we think here of the type of novel known as the *Bildungsroman* in which traditionally a young man receives his education in life. Novalis' *Heinrich von Ofterdingen* also comes to mind, where wandering and the "path" are so strongly emphasized.

2. *Bildung* must come out of self-determination; a person

---

5. Cf. C. G. Jung, *Psychology and Alchemy (Coll. Wks.* 12, 1953) [original German edition, 1944].

must be open and ready to educate himself in this sense of the term, on a life-long basis and willing to work constantly at it.

3. Although *Bildung* is imbued with the historical figures of our spiritual past, it must continually come to terms with the spirit of the age and its duties and amalgamate them; thus it is traditional as far as objective spirit is concerned but also protestant in its criticism of tradition. This makes it a paradox, as witness the fact that —

a. it "forms" both mental powers and heart, thus uniting the classical opposites, and
b. in this way it creates the prerequisites for ethical and social culture, for really learning to deal with the world and understand it, for human confirmation, and for creative achievement.

4. In the words of Pestalozzi, *Bildung* is the "essence and objective of Man." Like a genuine *telos*, it has been given countless "names," i.e., definitions over the centuries; it has been devalued, then revalued, declared dead and has always risen again. It has shifted from the "most profane" and "most practical" to the "most sacred" and has lost none of its fascination, not even with our modern "educational policy" (*horribile dictu!*).

5. *Bildung* features prominently in any discussion on spirit, culture and conscience.

This has been the case within living memory. It represents such a challenge, the fulfillment of which remains so much with the individual and gives him such a feeling of being involved in a process with its contradictory aspects. It contains both rational and irrational elements, represents an asymptote, and fits in closely with the *cultura animae* [cultivation of the soul] of Cicero. When the Jungian psychologist comes across this term he recognizes it as the model of the genuine symbol, which, according to C. G. Jung, is the best possible expression for a relatively unknown but necessary and "fixed" set of circumstances. Seen this way, the symbol has a transcendental function, i.e., it enables the person who seeks to do so to bring about changes that would not be possible without the effect of the genuine symbol. *Bilden* as a path or process thus acquires the dimension of the individuation process. Thus the person with *Bildung* remains a *Desideratum*, maybe even a paradox, as was said of St. Benedict, "scienter nescius, sapienter indoctus" [wisely uninformed].

Chapter 14

Localizations of Consciousness

Mankind has always been concerned with the location of consciousness, although as often as not it was the soul or the psyche that was being referred to and not consciousness itself. Definitive assumptions have been made about their localization in different centuries or millennia and in various cultures. As we shall see, the Greeks debated for centuries about the location of the ruling principle. These century-long discussions about the seat of the Aristotelian ἡγημονικόν (*hegemonikon*) are an especially striking example for us of this insecurity regarding the location of the psychic in general. Fortunately, M.-L. Putscher has gone to the trouble to research these transformations in accordance with this concept, so that we can refer here to her valuable book.[1] With reference to Jung's four "orientation functions of consciousness," we should like to point out that Thomas Aquinas already sticks to a *quaternio* [fourfold division], as opposed to Avicenna, who postulated five psychic powers. With regard to the cerebral localization, we now have a lucid compilation recently published by Clarke and Dewhurst.[2]

From the standpoint of the so-called Complex Psychology of C. G. Jung, the available variants represent comparative material, which makes possible an evaluation of the level of consciousness of each of the respective cultures and peoples. However, we do not suffer from hubris, which would lead us to

---

Published in *The Shaman from Elko* (San Francisco, 1978), 102ff.

1. M.-L. Putscher, *Pneuma, Spiritus, Geist* (Wiesbaden, 1973).
2. E. Clark and K. Dewhurst, *An Illustrated History of Brain Function* (Oxford, 1972).

assume that our contemporary level of consciousness, with its apparent localization of consciousness in the brain, is the highest step in this sequence. On the contrary, we are disposed to regard the entire organism as the locus of the psyche and accordingly to accept specific organ locations as coordinates for special aspects of the psyche.

Certainly our scientific approach and methodology have shown us that by experimentally eliminating the cortex, consciousness is also extinguished. The same empirical research shows, however, that the continuity of the psyche then ceases as well. In addition, observations have been made in cases of accidents involving brain trauma, such as those which occur in war when the brain is pierced by a bullet: psychic processes continue that are no different from those in a normal state of consciousness but in an apparently unconscious state.[3] Along the same line are the well-documented cases of out-of-the-body experience such as those collected by Celia Green.[4] To be sure, they lie almost on a parapsychological plane, but that must not disturb us. (We will return to this later in another connection.) The clinical observations of Jantz and Beringer throw an interesting light on Dunne's observance of the observer.[5] Also, the trivial fact that we have the most lively experiences every night in a state of almost total unconsciousness belongs to this problem. Thus it can be said that the matter of unconsciousness and indirectly of consciousness is not easily explained. Certain experiences at the bedside of the ill have shown every doctor that even with the most severely comatose patients, not all consciousness and perception are extinguished with certainty. Nevertheless, it has been established that the cortex has priority for processes of consciousness and that the subcortical processes have only a conditional influence on consciousness.

Inasmuch as the brain, like the skin, is of ectodermal origin, it is an organ of the senses and perceptions; its perceptions are for the most part of an optical and acoustic nature. This can be seen

---

3. I. Jantz and K. Beringer, "Das Syndrom des Schwebeerlebnisses unmittelbar nach Kopfverletzungen," *Der Nervenarzt* 17 (1944), 202, cited in C. G. Jung, *Coll. Wks.* 8, par. 949, n.1.

4. C. Green, *Out-of-Body Experiences* (London, 1968).

5. J. W. Dunne, *The Serial Universe* (London, 1934).

in sleep activity, that is, in the dream, where it is to a large degree shielded from external sensory stimulation. Thus, the brain is, for the most part, our psychic orientation system; it is by no means the psyche itself.

We will examine several of the older localization theories using the comparative approach referred to earlier.

We know of the *bush soul* that is embraced by many "primitives." They believe that their soul and thus their most intimate identity — we would be inclined to say their conscious ego — can be found in a certain place in the bush, in a particular animal for instance, or a tree, or a stone. Its location would, therefore, be *extra corpus*. This is dangerous because the soul can easily get lost, and then the owner becomes physically or psychically ill and can even die, as the soul has a "participation" with him or he with it.[6] The medicine man must get it back to him. This can be done, for example, as follows: the medicine man goes into the bush with his bird cage and captures several escaped "soul birds." When he returns, the patient lies on the ground and the cage is opened. The medicine man is situated some distance from the head of the patient, to which a row of seeds leads, the last one lying on the forehead of the patient. The birds, having been released, eat their way along the row of seeds, and the bird that picks the last seed from the forehead of the patient proves itself to be the escaped soul bird. In this manner it reintegrates itself with the sufferer. The "loss of soul," the illness, is cured. Examples of a similar kind are numerous. The location of the soul outside the body, typical of primitives, and the resulting *participation* greatly affect the relationship of the human being to external objects and vice versa. In primitive culture this relationship is regarded as a matter of course, but it must be understood as purely parapsychological from our point of view, that is, as psychokinesis (PK). It also recalls the old doctrine of sympathy, which nonetheless does not relieve us of the unsolved problem of the subject/object relationship. Especially difficult problems arise when both are separated spatially, and no known channels for the transmission of the effects are conceivable. During certain "mystical" moods, such sympathy conceptions of significant poetic valency also easily befall us.

---

6. L. Lévy-Bruhl, *How Natives Think*, trans. I. A. Clare (London, 1926).

If we now want to pursue a comparative localization theory, only anatomy – that is, the body – remains as a frame of reference. We shall have to proceed, then, from the lower to the higher segments.

Localization in bladder and rectum would be the most primitive. There are life phases (early childhood) in which these regions are of dominant importance or in which (later in life) they assume more or less pathological significance. Here one is inclined to think of the "mentality" of the dog.

For the next step, the stomach is the characteristic organ. I do not mean that class for whom the satisfaction of the stomach becomes the high point of existence, and even less those peoples for whom almost everything else in life has fallen away in the face of satisfying hunger. Yet there were cultures in which there was not sufficient motivation, for example, to go hunting until the stomach growled so persistently that any further attempt to tighten the belt became futile.

It can also happen to us that we do not become conscious of certain facts until they begin to make us sick (to our stomach). The *plexus coeliacus* (also popularly called the solar plexus), which lies at this level on the aorta, appears to be a kind of organ of expression for the various contents of the psyche. Especially impressive in this regard, as Sir Laurens van der Post told me, are the Bushmen. They become aware of approaching strangers at enormous distances and thus can make predictions on the basis of an urgent, monitory tapping that, in all probability, comes from the *plexus coeliacus*.

The diaphragm, from the Greek φρήν (*phren*), shows itself to be a psychic localization in the passage in the *Iliad* where Achilles kills Hector: "And Hector knew the truth inside his heart ἐνὶ φρενί (*eni phreni*) and spoke aloud."[7] Today in psychiatry we speak of schizo*phrenia*, the illness that most severely impairs consciousness, although with this expression nothing is said about the location. For the Romans the diaphragm was the seat of thought and sensation. Another name for it is *praecordia*, from which the expression *intima praecordia movit* [his own heart (diaphragm) moved him] comes if something especially moving happens.

---

7. Homer, *Iliad* XXII, 296.

Even for us today, the heart is the actual seat of the soul and not just a poetic metaphor, at least to the extent that it makes itself felt by strong feelings and passions. The corresponding Greek expression is θυμός (*thymos*) and actually means the breath of life, the Latin *passio, affectus* or *perturbatio*, that is, all emotions that belong in particular to our humanity. On the heart as the seat of the κοινὸν αἰσθητήριον (*koinon aistheterion*) [the central organ of sensation], see Aristotle's *De Insomniis* (On Dreams).

As the highest level in this hierarchy, the brain is reserved to us moderns. This localization can hardly be contested, but it by no means eliminates the lower levels from also having their representation in the brain. There is even less possibility that the brain will ever manage completely to control or make ineffective the lower localizations. In that event we would have lost the direct contact with our biological and psychic prerequisites and have become a formidable super- or, more accurately, a non-human being. It can be said without compunction that the robot, run with a pure brain computer, is an absurd extrapolation. The whole person is the one who functions satisfactorily and in proportion on all these six levels: brain, heart, diaphragm, stomach, bowels and bladder and, finally, even *extra corpus*.

In a private seminar in 1930, C. G. Jung presented the case of a female patient who engaged in active imagination and produced drawings and pictures during the course of analysis. These created the most extraordinary impression and were not understandable until Jung made the acquaintance of a book that had appeared for the first time in Madras in 1918; this was *The Serpent Power* by Sir John Woodroffe, alias Arthur Avalon. This book presents the Sanskrit text, with an English translation, of the *Shat-Chakra-Nirupana* ("Seven Circles Description") and is essentially a yoga meditation text. It is concerned with the special (for the most part Bengali-South Indian) Tantra yoga, also called Kundalini yoga. Tantra simply means "book," and this Tantrism comprises yoga sects that have their holy books just as we have the Bible. Kundalini—related to the Greek χύλινδος (*chylindos*) [round, cylinder]—is conceived as a serpent and symbolizes, as is clearly evident from the text and the practice of meditation, psychic energy, that is the libido as understood by Jung. It is set in motion in the yoga process and circulates throughout the entire body, which in turn shows a striking similarity to the "circulation of light" in Chinese Taoism, as so cogently described by Erwin Rousselle.[8] The Kundalini (serpent) proceeds in this process ascending and descending through seven *chakras* (Sanskrit for "circles"), which are imagined to be hierarchically located in different body segments. These localizations exhibit amazing analogies with those we described above, although we arrived at them independently on the basis of clinical observation, comparative religion, and ethnological reflections.

That this Western approach should find such a widespread analogy in the East is not only sufficient confirmation, but should also lead us to see that the psychobiological basis of the human being is to a large extent the same everywhere. To use Jung's language, we see how much the realities of the collective unconscious are ubiquitous and identical, i.e., archetypal, and to what degree they are identified in the East with physical structures. At the same time we should not forget that these representations have become much more differentiated by cultures in the East than they are by us, owing to thousands of years of tradition, observation, and experience, so that there is a good deal we can learn from them.

Nevertheless, we are not interested in making propaganda for yoga with the following presentation, because the difference between the essence of our spiritual makeup and that of Eastern man is too great for us to be able to adopt Indian philosophy. If the *Shakta* (member of the Bengali Tantra sects) says, "whoever makes *chakra-puja* [*puja* = "veneration"] without having fought the powers of the world and tradition will not succeed but come to harm," it is clear from the text that this attitude is identical with that which Jung always required for analysis. But yoga is also the specifically Indian road to master experience by means of introspection.

I shall attempt to make a table of the seven centers, using Avalon's version, although I must omit many details. Not until I finish will I be able to elaborate on several of those *chakras* that are suitable for making a number of things clear to us in the West. I shall give only the basic details of the *chakra* description

---

8. E. Rousselle, "Spiritual Guidance in Contemporary Taoism" (Orig. 1933), in *Spiritual Disciplines* (Papers from the Eranos Yearbooks, 4, B.S. XXX, 1960).

1	2	3	4	5	6	7
1. *Muladhara*	root-support	perineum	plexus pelvicus	earth	4	elephant
2. *Svadhisthana*	own place	bladder	plexus hypogastricus	water	6	*makara*
3. *Manipura*	jewel-abundance	navel	plexus coeliacus seu solaris	fire	10	ram
4. *Anahata*	unassailable	heart	plexus cardiacus	air	12	gazelle
5. *Vishuddha*	purification	larynx	plexus pharyngeus	ether	16	white elephant
6. *Ajna*	episteme	between the eyes	pineal gland		2	0
7. *Sahasrara*	pure consciousness	on the scalp = *extra corpus*	0	empty space	1000	0

in the following sequence: (1) Sanskrit name of the center, (2) English translation, (3) location in the body, and (4) where this is probable, the corresponding localization of the ganglia of the vegetative nervous system, because it would be easier to assign them psychic representations, should such a coordination be possible, at least to a certain degree, (5) the assignment to the "elements," (6) the number of petals of the corresponding lotus — that is *chakra* — without reference to the very differentiated number and letter symbolism which is connected with them in India,[9] and (7) the corresponding animal symbols.

The yogi should now meditate, from bottom to top, on one center after another; that is, not only imagine in all detail, but construct them from the elements and physically call them forth, and in *dhyana* (submersion), in a manner not readily understandable to us, realize them. (That which I think becomes here that which thinks me. I am thought.) The energy-libido necessary for this process is supplied by Kundalini, which has been slumbering in the lowest center and now awakens and is gradually sent upward through the other centers, where at any given time it leads to the realization, that is, to the almost physical sensation of the *chakra* in question. Each of the previous steps is maintained, and then the next highest one is attempted. Having reached the top, the order is reversed and the way is retraced, step by step, until the Kundalini in the *Muladhara* is again in a position of rest. Then the yogi returns to his daily routine.

Given this hierarchy, we are reminded of the "progressive cerebration" of Hughlings Jackson, which, although the points of departure are very different, bears a similarity to these conceptions.

In the hope of better understanding the Tantric-like drawings of the patient referred to at the beginning, Jung invited the Indologist and Sanskrit scholar J. W. Hauer (Tübingen) to a private seminar in 1932. At its conclusion, Jung gave an appropriate psychological commentary, so that I am in the fortunate position of often being able to draw on those very talks.

1. In *Muladhara*, on the lowest rung, the level of consciousness

---

9. Cf. Avalon, *The Garland of Letters* (Madras, 3rd edition, 1955), where further information can also be found about the mystic aspect of sound.

is that of our daily existence, psychologically speaking, of our family, profession, and the like. The four petals of the lotus are symbolic of the material reality in its entirety, which is why the element of earth has been assigned to it. Because we are to a large degree bound up with this reality, this is a quasi-latent state where everything divine is still asleep, just like the Kundalini, and where it only softly hums to itself "like a swarm of love-struck bees" entwined as it is three and one-half times around the lingam (phallus), represented here at the base, and covering the mouth with its head. The major animal symbol for the whole is the elephant, which represents the domesticated libido in India. Beginning with this state, it is now time to ascend to higher consciousness, that is, to awaken and mobilize Kundalini — to ascend.

2. In *Svadhisthana*, we are somewhat surprised to find two symbols, which, like water, unmistakably point to the unconscious: the half moon and a water monster, the *makara*. In the latter we can recognize a type of leviathan, the reverse side of the elephant of *Muladhara*. Here we are reminded of the shadow as the first step toward confrontation with the unconscious on the way to consciousness. That which is applicable for us in the West is expressed in the East as a necessity, namely to realize rather negative tendencies as a prerequisite for more consciousness.

3. With *Manipura*, the picture is of a crucible on the fire and the symbolic animal is the ram, which corresponds to Agni, the fire god. (In our astrology the ram is also the house of Mars, and Mars is a close relative of Agni.) The *chakra* is relegated to the element of fire. And also in the *bindu*, the point which is on top of the inscribed Sanskrit letter, is *Rudra*, the destroyer of creation, because the animation of passion threatens to destroy everything again. Here we are reminded of Heraclitus who said, "It is difficult to fight with lust and what it wants it buys with the soul." Here we are concerned with the θυμός (*thymos*) [breath of life], with the affects, with a purely emotional psychology where I become aware only of that which makes me uncomfortable or affects my stomach (hunger) or the gall bladder; that is, with an unfree state of being and nevertheless with the beginning of a real psychology. But here we are still below the diaphragm; the conscious psychology begins above the aforementioned.

4. *Anahata* means "the unassailable," and refers to the symbol

of the "Self," of the Indian *Atman* that appears here for the first time. The term "Self," as it was coined by Jung, represents a more highly ordered center of the personality, which is exhaustively described in the phenomenology of the *Atman* in Indian philosophy. The element associated with it is the air, because from earth comes water, and from this, through fire, air is derived. The element of air is represented by the lungs, in which the heart is embedded. Further, the fleeting animal symbol of the gazelle indicates air. Neurophysiologically we are also at the level of the already partly conscious control of the functions, to which the breath is subordinate. It is at this point that the human being begins to contemplate, to judge, to differentiate. He becomes capable of setting himself apart from pure emotion. At the same time he here becomes aware for the first time of his impersonal side (Self equals *Atman*). This is the actual beginning of our conscious psychology. At this level the Christian "mystique of the heart" could be understood. The Self is something extraordinarily impersonal, and to the extent to which I regard it as something objective, I myself become impersonal. The unpleasant phenomenon we know in English as "personality" is thus eliminated. For those of us in the West, however, there is a danger in this connection — namely identification with the Self, which is tantamount to inflation, to a type of delusion of grandeur. We cannot warn often enough against this danger. I remember an impressive experience that Jung had with the Pueblo Indians in Taos, New Mexico. His Pueblo friend there complained about the Americans, saying they were all crazy because they maintained that they thought here (referring to his forehead) when everybody knows that we think here (referring to his heart).

5. With *Vishuddha*, it becomes increasingly difficult for us with our Western way of thinking to imagine clearly which psychic characteristics are being referred to in the higher centers. Thus, *Vishuddha* is associated with the element of ether. We would say that ether is matter and at the same time no longer so; it is a purely abstract concept, whereupon this *chakra* becomes one of the pure concepts, that is, something purely psychic. Thus it is also the *chakra* of the *reality of the psychic* in general where, unfortunately for us, it assumes an insubstantial position about which little can be said. Western man seems to be at approximately this level of *Anahata*. Against this background, the world

and its game here become an image of our psyche, that is our own *drame intérieur*. For the Indian, sound, language, and singing belong here. In *bindu* Ardhanarishvara is in the form of a half-male half-female, that is, an androgynous god who unites in one, the sun and moon, gold and silver—that is, the elementary opposites.

6. *Ajna* is the place of union, of the *unio mystica*. There are no more animal symbols because here the psychic experience requires no support in outer reality. Not even a god is found here because the yogi himself has become the psychic content of god through the *unio mystica*, which means he himself is the content of the psychic. The lingam once again appears, this time, however, as *itara shiva*, as another lingam, which has only the form in common with the one at the first level. All of this is hardly imaginable for us in the West.

7. For *Sahasrara*, the qualities of *Ajna* apply to an even greater degree. But here we find an interesting paradox: in it is the emptiness, *shunyata*, of which is said: "That is the place where all being is no longer being. Not until now has the real been reached. Whoever has gone completely into this emptiness has achieved complete fullness. Not until this emptiness has been achieved does this knowledge which has been gathered during the course of this process become real." Here there is only *brahman*. And the *brahman* cannot itself experience, as it is *advaita*, that is, "not two." It is being-not being, which is the same as the idea of the *nirvana*, which is *nir-dvandva*, that is, free of contradictions. As a result of the completed union of the Kundalini (*shakti*) with Shiva, which equals a ἱερός γάμος (*hieros gamos*), in *Sahasrara*, a nectar (*amrita*) flows from here which means complete release (solution = *mucti*), so that the yogi comes to enjoy *advaya* (no second), that is, is identical with Kundalini.

Our difficulties with the beloved Indian metaphysical speculation on the pure subject of cognition, which is not opposed by any object, make it impossible for us to judge here any longer. We must, as Wolfgang Pauli aptly said, reject it as an indefensible extrapolation inasmuch as our consciousness presupposes the duality of subject and object or the division of the two. Pauli correctly goes on to reason that our Western idea of the unconscious begins at just this point, that is, instead of at the idea of an all-encompassing consciousness without an object as here in

Tantra. We don't want to overlook the fact that with *Sahasrara* we again find ourselves outside the body, whereby an unusual similarity with the primitive's bush soul (located *extra corpus*) originates. If we audaciously wish to describe this curve as the Tantrists do, we go from the bush soul of the primitive, which is completely outside the body, to the caudal end through different, always higher levels, to the top on the cranial end—so to say, again outside the body.

Only the libido and its circulation remain as the connection that makes itself felt, in this case by *affecting* the body or the different organs. Not to be forgotten is the fact that the expression "affect" originates from this experience. But it is also known here in the West that this is not the whole activity of the psyche. In this connection, I should like to repeat an important passage from an alchemist: [10]

Corpus enim nihil scit, quicquid in corpore fortitudinis sive motus est, mens facit ista; corpus tantum est menti sicut instrumenta alcujus artificis. Anima autem, qua homo a caeteris animalibus differt, illa operatur in corpore, sed majorem operationem habet extra corpus; quoniam absolute extra corpus dominatur, et his differt ab animalibus quae tantum mentem et non animam deitatis habent. [The body knows nothing of what is in it as power or movement; this the spirit knows; the body is to the spirit only what the instrument is to an artist. Nevertheless, the soul, which differentiates the human being from other organisms, has those functions in the body. But its more significant effect is outside the body, because outside the body it governs in itself.]

Gerardus Dorneus also says, "Mentis a corpore distractio necessaria est" [The spirit must be separated from the body]. [11] Recently we learned from a Gnostic-early Christian source of the same spirit: "Jesus said, 'woe betide the flesh [σάρξ, *sarx*] that is dependent on the soul [ψυχή, *psyche*]; woe betide the soul that is dependent on the flesh.' " [12]

---

10. Sendivogius, "De Sulphure," *Musaeum Hermeticum* (Frankfurt, 1677), 617.

11. G. Dorneus, "Philosophia Meditativa," in *Theatrum Chemicum* I (Ursellis, 1602).

12. *Evangelium nach Thomas*, ed. A. Guillaumont (Leiden, 1959), 55 (*Logion* 112). Now available in *The Nag Hammadi Library*, ed. James M. Robinson (San Francisco, 1977).

Of late the West appears to be greatly impressed by Tantrism, which accounts for the fact that Tantric texts are also now available in English. We believe that everything that is said and written in the West about levels of consciousness has afforded interesting illustrations and empirical foundations as a result of these experiences and our Jungian approach.

Chapter 15

Altered States of Consciousness and Psi*

Since I have no new staggering experimental data to produce concerning psi and altered states of consciousness (ASC), I thought I might seize the opportunity to make a few unconfidential confessions to you about the way I see this question, hoping that they might be of some use in future research.

Off and on, as analysts, we observe the occurrence of cases of indisputable telepathy, clairvoyance or precognition with one or another of our analysands. Trained in parapsychology, our observation is supposed to be both sensitive and accurate. Furthermore, we routinely take precautions to have everything carefully documented. In this way a good many convincing cases have been gathered, and some of them have been published by Servadio[1] and Ehrenwald.[2] Telepathic or precognitive phenomena, however, occur all the time in everyday life, but in most cases

---

First published in: *Psi and States of Awareness*, (New York, 1978), 238ff.
[*Ed. Note: Psi (process): "An intra-individual process that cannot be described in terms of presently accepted natural laws. The term is somewhat narrower than *parapsychological*, since the latter may refer to the extra-individual outcome. The psi process consists in whatever it is that enables the individual to "send" or receive telepathic messages (provided, i.e., the process turns out to be not conformable to accepted scientific descriptions)." – Horace B. English and Ava Chempney English, eds., *The Comprehensive Dictionary of Psychological and Psychoanalytical Terms* (New York: David McKay Co., 1965).]

1. Refer to the bibliography.
2. J. Ehrenwald, *New Dimensions of Deep Analysis: A Study of Telepathy in Interpersonal Relationships* (London, 1954).

they escape our attention. What I want to say is that they are much more frequent than we notice. But when we find ourselves in such a close personal relationship with the subject, as we usually do with our analysands, such events do not escape our attention so easily. To draw the inference, however, that under analytical conditions psi phenomena occur more frequently than under so-called normal conditions would be unwarranted. We have in these cases only a better understanding of the subjects' motivation for illegitimately penetrating into our own as yet unlived lives (in the case of precognition) or in the case of telepathy into our own conscious preoccupations that are unknown to them. In either case, we usually take refuge in our beloved hypothesis of the unconscious, knowledge of which we grant the subject to be sufficiently motivated to want to have (e.g., of our more or less secret hopes or wishes to cure them). This, however, is far from explaining the mechanism of *how* they get access to such knowledge, knowledge of facts neither we nor they could possibly possess, as in the case of true precognition.

Whenever such a case occurs, and it is dramatic enough and seemingly beyond any doubt, I am not only duly impressed, but I feel confronted with a real *tremendum*. I begin to be fully superstitious. One such case – and I have witnessed a number of them – suffices to convince me of the reality of psi, as long as it is beyond any legitimate doubt of being merely coincidental, statistically speaking. But that is beside the point. What I want to stress more vigorously is this: when we come to consider such occurrences seriously, we are immediately at a complete loss, scientifically speaking, since time and space parameters are here totally "out of joint," as we have to admit in old-fashioned physical terminology. Causal connections in such cases are unthinkable, and purely psychological investigation of all the possible conditions could only give a person an inkling of conditioning circumstances without telling a thing as to *how* it was at all possible.

Experimental research of all sorts has tried to isolate one or another possibly relevant factor facilitating (or inhibiting) the occurrence of psi, or as it is now called *psi-conducive conditions* or *states*. I once had a discussion with Eileen Garrett, complaining to her about our having only insignificant results in thousands of card-guessing experiments with hundreds of subjects. Her answer was, "But you must get your subjects excited, highly excited!" This sounded familiar to me, and I will try to explain why. As you know, Jung was always deeply impressed by ESP phenomena.[3] His impression was that they occurred more frequently under conditions of what might today be called stress, i.e., suffering from an acute problem. This is simply another way of saying when finding oneself in an *archetypal* situation. Jung's experience was that at such times a patient would produce particularly significant dreams, so-called archetypal dreams. The content of such dreams seemed to sum up symbolically the problem in question and possibly to include a suggestion as to its solution. He thought that at such moments particularly, he had observed the occurrence of parapsychological phenomena more frequently, and he also observed that they then were connected with the problem in question in a peculiarly "meaningful" way. This is why he speaks of *meaningful coincidence* or *synchronicity*. (Recently the usefulness of this Jungian concept was emphasized by Lila L. Gatlin.)[4] The concept of synchronicity means nothing less than that. For such phenomena we should simply relinquish or do away with our scientific prejudice of causality, even if only for the fact that in such cases the time-space parameters no longer seem to work. Such phenomena have to be considered as acausal coincidences or connections. This would simply amount to the fact that, in parapsychology, we are totally outside of the range of causality or natural science *tout court*. The original choice of the term *parapsychology*, probably quite unconsciously, hints at something of this kind, since the Greek preposition *para* has as one of its connotations the meaning of something *more than* or *beyond*. Schopenhauer has stated: "Dem Zufall eine Absicht unterzulegen ist ein Gedanke der, je nach dem man ihn versteht, der absurdeste oder der tiefsinnigste sein kann" [To attribute to chance an intention is an idea which,

---

3. C. G. Jung, "Synchronicity: An Acausal Connecting Principle," in *The Structure and Dynamics of the Psyche* (*Coll. Wks.* 8, 1969), 417-519 [original German edition: Zürich, 1952; C. A. Meier, ed.]; and also *The Interpretation of Nature and the Psyche* (New York, 1955).

4. Lila L. Gatlin, "Meaningful Information-Creation: An Alternative Interpretation of the Psi-Phenomena, New York: *Journal of the American Society for Psychical Research* 71/1 (1977): 1-18.

depending only on how it is understood, can be either most absurd or very deep].[5] We are too timid to admit openly that in our field we are hopelessly outside science as it is understood today and continue to be greatly concerned about finally becoming acceptable to the scientific community. Moreover, we are so conditioned by our Western tradition and education that it is healthier to forget it altogether.

In the Graeco-Roman tradition, however, of which our self-same science is a legitimate offspring, miracles of this and all other kinds did not seem to contradict the otherwise strictly scientific approach that had so convincingly and successfully become part of its spirit. Oracles played a decisive part in the politics of the ancient world, which otherwise was undoubtedly extremely rationalistic and realistic. With the Greeks the rational and irrational were still happily married, as has been masterfully described by E. R. Dodds.[6] The temple cures of Asklepios or Serapis and others, which were always performed with the help of healing dreams, were extremely popular, so much so that the pupils of Hippocrates, the father of scientific medicine, after their master's death reestablished the cult of Asklepios at Kos. In other words, they reverted as fast as possible to theurgy and faith healing. They seem to have been able to produce *meaningful coincidences* between dreams and bodily processes. Those medical men *cum* priests seem still to have known how to bring about such phenomena. We, on the other hand, seem to have lost that *tertium quid*, and our laboratories are of course far from being temples (not even "temples of science" unless we use computers!). Fortunately, there seem to have been places of "grace" at certain periods of time, such as Duke University, or special persons being gifted with a charisma conducive to psi.

What I really mean to say is simply that we have almost completely lost access to psi-conducive conditions. In antiquity they played a prominent part in the culture and were firmly estab-

---

5. A. Schopenhauer, "Transzendente Spekulation über die anscheinende Absichtlichkeit im Schicksal des Einzelnen" [Transcendent Speculation on the Apparent Premeditation in Personal Fate] in *Parerga und Paralipomena*, 1851 [available in English as *Essays from the Parerga and Paralipomena*, 1951].

6. E. R. Dodds, *The Greeks and the Irrational* (Berkeley, Calif., 1956); "Supernormal Phenomena in Classical Antiquity," in *Proceedings of the Society for Psychical Research* 55 (London, 1971) 189-237, and in *The Ancient Concept of Progress* (Oxford, 1973) 3-25.

lished and rooted in religion and philosophy. At the present time, however, there seems to be little or no interest or concern on the part of philosophy or religion in what we are discussing here. We start from one end, but lose sight of the other. There always are two ends to a spectrum, and I propose that we should never lose sight of the opposite end while we work on the other. Our scientific approach in the laboratory should always be compensated by our parascientific point of view. We should have the courage to harbor unadulteratedly fantastic theories and still not take refuge in such pseudoscientific alternatives as psychedelic drugs or trance. It is highly questionable whether any of the possible lines in the spectrum of consciousness is particularly conducive to psi. Dreams are only one of those lines, as they seem to happen at only one of the five possible stages of sleep. I am, however, personally convinced that this is a *non liquet*. All that can be said without bias is that the REM state is the one sleep- or dream-state out of which we can *remember* dreams more easily. The unconscious activity is certainly not interrupted by sleep stages one to four. The unconscious activity is rather a continuum of images, and represents a spontaneous and gratuitous imagery that coexists with our process of living, accompanying it as another primary or secondary continuum. So far, only general anesthesia seems to interrupt this parallelism (which is a *true* parallelism as opposed to the psycho-physical one still lingering). For the rest of our lives we seem to be constantly dreaming, wherefore the question of whether we are only dreaming, or that we are conscious of who we are, has to be taken seriously. The continuum from total to near-total unconsciousness (deep sleep, coma, general anesthesia) to such other altered states of consciousness as REM sleep, hypnosis, tiredness and utter distraction, and finally to the allegedly highest state of attention, awareness, vigilance—*Samadhi* or *Satori*—or whatever you may call it, are all one and the same thing, i.e., various degrees of consciousness or unconsciousness.

It is highly questionable to naïvely accept the Eastern contention that *Samadhi* or *Satori* or any kind of *dhyāna* [meditation in the strict sense] equals a higher state of consciousness in our Western sense. For us, it is rather close to auto-hypnosis, since the ego is supposed to disappear in union with *Ātman* [Self]. In this sense, it is hardly distinguishable from the experiences of our Western mystics. Whether any of these states is more conducive to psi, we simply don't know. Deep meditation may serve to lead to deep levels of the unconscious, or rather into the collective unconscious, where we all are equal if not identical. Participating in that realm may indeed be conducive to psi phenomena, which is explicitly stated in Yoga texts and would be in full agreement with Jung's theory of synchronicity. Should you empty your mind (your consciousness) completely, as demanded by most Yoga texts, you might arrive at pure physiology on the one hand or then at manifestations of the pure spirit on the other. Here, to us, metaphysics becomes psychology of the unconscious. In Hindu philosophy there exists a "state of consciousness," during which all sorts of ESP phenomena may occur, so that you would be able to produce them intentionally (rope trick!), but you are always strongly discouraged against bringing them about. They are regarded as unfortunate side effects, having the tendency of luring you back into *sangsara*, i.e., into further illusion, instead of experiencing the reality of the Self.

While our consciousness has its periodic ups and downs (circadian rhythms), the unconscious seems to be relentless, as are most of the physiological oscillators (heartbeat, breathing, etc.). Whenever the level of consciousness goes down (physiologically or pathologically), the unconscious has automatically a higher potential and gets a chance of showing its imagery (e.g., dreams) and of being clearly perceived. These messages may, to an extent, consist of day residues, elements from previous waking experiences or of actual facts of the present and perhaps also of future elements, occurring in the next day or two. The latter elements may still be purely coincidental. A few of them, however, may be quite specific, and quite different from all inference or altogether contrary to hopes, wishes or fantasies, and yet may appear in outer reality before too long. They already confront us with a veridical or precognitive element, and time and space are violated. It is always rather precarious to isolate certain specific items out of the more embracing content of a dream. In my own laboratory we have had little luck with Hall and Van der Castle's method[7] when we wanted to isolate specific data.

In the early thirties, when I was still in analysis with C. G.

---

7. Calvin S. Hall and R. L. Van de Castle, *The Content Analysis of Dreams* (New York, 1966).

Jung, I kept a very careful record of my dreams. In two instances, they definitely contained precognitive motives. From then on, I used to go through the whole record regularly one and two and three days later, a week later, and a month later. From the elements identifiable in them, I computed that about fifty percent stemmed from the past and the other fifty percent from the future. The latter fifty percent may have been trivia or inferences, but certainly not all of them. The method, of course, was very crude, although I don't see how we can improve on it today, for methodologically, we seem to be confronted here with an *aporia*. The result, however, seems to point to the fact that the unconscious seems not to pay attention to space/time limits, that in fact, it is ubiquitous and omniscient. This is, of course, blasphemous. The fact that we are invariably tied to time and space in our conscious mind is responsible for the fact that the temporal and spatial location of such paranormally or rather unconsciously received messages is impossible. But there are always rare exceptions that offer such minutiae that we feel obliged to try to interfere with facts. In the few cases I happened to witness, such intentions were deleterious in that the whole system broke down, so that it looked as if the unconscious had only been kidding.

I said earlier that genuinely paranormal experiences were always numinous, in short, a *tremendum*. It is worth noting that throughout the history of humanity they were always carefully kept either strictly secret (mysteries) or within a carefully observed (religious) ritual in the Asklepieia or at the oracle of Delphi. We now know for certain that the Pythia in Delphi was always a very carefully selected medium. We even know the method for her selection. We also know that she was always in a trance-like condition whenever she acted. We know equally well that drugs were never used for that purpose. As psychologists, we then simply draw the inference that in order to make "the lot spring," as they say, she got into a trance whereby she was capable of producing PK (psychokinetic) phenomena, and that she must have been a woman permeable to the unconscious or more specifically to the collective unconscious. Those were the psi-conducive conditions, when men still knew about their reality, and such conditions will very probably remain as mysterious as they always were.

Are we thus operating or trying to operate in a secularized

religious realm? If so, how are we going to reconstruct those conditions the ancients had such apparently foolproof methods for producing? Or does parapsychology have to become a substitute for religiousness? *horribile dictu!* I am afraid that survivalism and spiritualism definitely smack of such an unappetizing mixture, but *we* must make every effort to keep on the safe side and leave it to them to abide by Goethe's statement in *Faust* that "das Wunder ist des Glaubens liebstes Kind" [the miracle is faith's most beloved child]. For the medical man, to keep on the safe side means to stick to clinical experience. Neurosis and psychosis are undoubtedly altered states of consciousness. Do they produce more psi? According to my experience, they don't. On the other hand, clinical experience has taught us to look at normal psychological phenomena in the light of their pathological equivalent (e.g., dreams compared to hallucinations, and vice versa). In this way we have also learned something about normal madness, namely moments when we are *possessed* by a complex. Complexes are normal elements of our system, but they tend to produce an *abaissement du niveau mental*.[8] In sleep, our level of consciousness is naturally lowered and our complexes are, therefore, acted out quite freely, which accounts for an analogy between emotional waking states and dreaming. In view of Jung's concept of synchronicity and its more regular occurrence with highly emotional states (stress, problems, impressive dreams) it might be expected that the vicinity of such conditions may be psi-conducive. I must, however, leave it to the younger generation of researchers to devise methods and find means to tackle this question experimentally, and to verify or disprove it.

---

8. Pierre Janet, "Les Oscillations du Niveau Mental," *Nouveau Traites de Psychologie*, IV/3 (Paris, 1937).

Chapter 16

Science and Conscience
as Seen by Analytical Psychology

"Science sans conscience n'est que ruine de l'ame."
                                    —François Rabelais

By way of introduction, let me tell you what happened to me
when I first heard the general theme of our colloquium: I
immediately assimilated "Science + Conscience" as a stimulus-
word to my own conscience. "Conscience" was apparently functioning with me as a critical stimulus word and hit my own complex, my conscience. Consider what I say as an attempt at a kind
of analysis of my complex concerning this passion-evoking
theme of science and conscience.

We are all scientists and we tacitly assume to know what science is, but are we all so sure of having a conscience, and if so,
one that is functioning well? What is this conscience really, and
what can psychology as a science say about it?

In order to talk to you about this subject, I must give you an
idea about what part conscience plays in analytical psychology.
Knowing the approximate answers to these preliminary questions, it may be easier to say something relevant about our
kephalaion, our central theme.

I should like to begin this discussion with a statement that
has, so far as I know, never been made before: analytical psychology (Jungian psychology) begins and ends with conscience. I am
using the word *conscience* in the classical French sense of *conscience morale*, for it took an untold amount of moral courage

---

Paper read to the "International Colloquium on Science and Conscience,"
organized by 'France-Culture' of Radio France in Cordoba, Spain in October
1979. Published in French in: *Science et Conscience, les deux lectures de
l'Univers* (Paris, 1980), 221ff.

in the early years of this century to take seriously, along with Freud, all those manifestations of the unconscious, and it still is a crucial demand throughout analysis to this day.

We make use of the word *conscience* in another way here: Latin *scire* means to know; *con-scire* to know one thing and the other as well. In our technical language this means to fully know what can be said from the point of view of conscious mind (consciousness) as well as (*con, cum*) what the *unconscious* has to add to it, which in most cases will amount to a painful *conscientia*. Analysis invariably starts with the encounter of what Jung calls the shadow, which personifies mostly unsavory aspects of our personality, hitherto not cognized. The *conscientia* of both aspects constitutes by itself conscience, whether good or bad, and consequently demands discrimination and decision. Conscience constitutes a fundamental requirement of analysis, and it has a highly moral quality. Moral, from the Latin *mores*, cannot be reduced to more elementary qualities but is one of the most specifically human achievements, without which we would be amoral beasts or suffer from "moral insanity" and be locked up in asylums, for to be insane is to be capable of all sorts of crimes without the least twinge of conscience. At least here the law and psychiatry are certainly reasonable.

For the reasons previously given, we can understand why Jung devoted one of the very last papers he published (1958) to the discussion of conscience.[1] By summing it up I can answer the question: what does analytical psychology as a science have to say about conscience? Jung first of all makes it clear that conscience, as we observe it clinically, as well as in everyday life, cannot be reduced to the Freudian superego, which is a product of human authority exerted upon us from early childhood.[2] Conscience is not the product of the moral code, but rather precedes it in origin. It is a rational product of those collective representations as they were already described in 1909 by L. Lévy-Bruhl.[3]

---

1. C. G. Jung, "A Psychological View of Consciousness," *Civilization in Transition* (*Coll. Wks.* 10, 1964), 437-55 [original German version, 1958].

2. See also Ernst Spengler (diss.): *Das Gewissen bei Freud und Jung* (Zurich, 1964).

3. L. Lévy-Bruhl, *La mentalité primitive* (Paris, 1909).

Conscience is closely connected to primitive fear, which always crops up when we deviate from the moral code and thus do the unusual, the immoral, that without *mores*. The primitive man already has a bad conscience, not only whenever he does the unusual, but even when he simply experiences or observes it, from which can be seen that the unusual as such creates conscience, albeit only on the primitive level of its emotional component. In this way it reveals itself as highly autonomous, which brings it formally into close vicinity with the complex. These primitive roots, according to Jung, have further consequences: they change in the course of cultural development and they begin to be given symbolic expression. So conscience manifests itself as the *daimonion* with Socrates, and then it begins also to be called one's genius, one's guardian angel, one's better self, one's inner, higher man or "inner voice." Then it begins to be called *vox Dei*. Once conscience is received in that way, we have to draw the conclusion that it has become a purely psychological fact. Here the popular dichotomy of "good" or "bad" or "false" conscience becomes handy for Jungian thinking in terms of pairs of opposites. The polarity of conscience shows itself clearly when it comes to the symbolic expressions for a false conscience over against the ones mentioned previously for the good conscience, i.e., devil, seducer, tempter or evil spirit. This polarity constitutes tension, emotion and hence becomes a *fascinosum*. Here Jung reminds us of the numinosity of the *vox Dei*, but also of its ambivalence. After all, the old Jahweh, besides being terribly moralistic, can also be quite amoral: "God made everything in pairs (twins), of which one is the opposite of the other," and: "I am the Lord and there is none else, I form the light, I create darkness, I make peace and create evil. I am the Lord that does these things."[4] This dual quality of the Godhead has served early Christianity very well, for had not the thousands of martyrs been burnt, the Church would lack a good deal of its foundations, so that evil eventually served good. Recall the line Goethe gave to Mephistopheles in *Faust*: "I am part of the power that always wants the evil and always creates the good."

This ambivalence of the inner voice is a tremendous mystery against which we can only take refuge in the Johannine *trying of*

---

4. Isaiah 45: 6-7.

the Spirits: "Beloved, believe not every spirit, but try the spirits whether they are of God . . . . Hereby know ye the Spirit of God: every spirit that confesseth that Jesus Christ is come in flesh is of God; And every spirit that confesseth not that Jesus Christ is come in flesh, is not of God; and this is that spirit of Antichrist, whereof ye have heard that it should come; and even now already is it in the world."[5]

We should indeed be happy to still have such clear-cut criteria of discrimination when it comes to the ambivalence of our conscience. In such a dilemma we will most naturally simply take refuge first of all in the moral code of our particular culture, assuming that it represents the "true spirit," which it might indeed do in a majority of cases.

This would be what Jung calls the *moral conscience*, which only to some extent would correspond to Freud's superego. As we have seen, however, there is usually a good deal more involved when we find ourselves in such a quandary. The irrational emotional effects of such a conflict point at something transcending our ego to such an extent that we cannot but attribute it to what Jung calls the *collective unconscious*, housing the archetypes. Those among you conversant with Jungian psychology must long have guessed that Jung winds up with an archetypal root of conscience. Ending his paper, he consequently made the statement that a genuine conscience only comes into action when we have to cope with conflicts of duty. It is only then that the problem begins to be a genuinely psychological one insofar as we then have to consider the conflict between the conscious and the unconscious view of a situation. For example, do we or do we not have to reveal all we consciously know for the sake of truth and thereby possibly vitally endanger our neighbor? "The truth, the whole truth, and nothing but the truth" – doctors, psychiatrists and priests in the confessional can tell you something concerning this problem. It is therefore a highly accurate name the Catholic Church gives to those priests, calling them *directeurs de conscience*, conscience in its most appropriate psychological meaning. It is right there, in the midst of this conflict of duty, that the *ethical conscience*, as Jung calls it, originates. Here it becomes obvious that the archetype with its transcendence of

---

5. I John 4: 1-3.

the ego comes into play. Should you have the courage to fight this battle, to really undertake a thoroughgoing scrutiny of both positions, the conscious as well as the unconscious, you may, with some luck, arrive at a creative solution to this problem of opposites. This possibility exists because of the *transcendent function*, as Jung named it, inherent in a discursive cooperation of conscious and unconscious factors, or, as Jung says, "of reason and grace, in the theological language." This is, as you will understand, what we call *ethos*: exactly the point at which I began this paper. Or, we are back to the old Heraclitus Fragment 119: Ἦθος ἀνθρώπωι δαίμων (*ethos anthropoi daimon*) [*ethos* is man's daimon or fate], where *ethos* simply means the person's character, whereby we are back some 2500 years.

The authenticity of Jung's statement can also be elucidated by another of the typically Jungian methods: whenever a Jungian analyst is confronted with a psychological item hard to understand, as is often the case with particular dream figures or dream motives, he takes refuge in the method of *amplification*. This means that we scrutinize the history of the particular item and try to see what intelligent people of all times and cultures (preferably our dreamer's own) have thought about it. Now, through lifelong experience, I am aware of the fact that people who are not familiar with Jungian thought, or who have little awareness of the unconscious imagery, find it particularly hard to see what we are talking about when we introduce the term *archetype*. It is to be hoped that the archetypal root of conscience becomes more clearly visible when we go into the many definitions given for conscience in philosophical and theological literature. For that reason, I have consulted various encyclopedias and I feel compelled to give you, amplifying *conscience*, a summary of the relevant articles, however tedious this may become.[6]

The Greek synonym for our conscience is συνείδησις (*syneidesis*), which most appropriately has been translated into Latin *conscientia* by Cicero from whom we still have *conscience* as it is written in English and in French. In Homeric times, nothing of the kind existed; when θυμός (*thymos*) [heart, pas-

---

6. Henry Chadwick, "Gewissen," *Reallexikon für Antike und Christentum* 10(Stuttgart, 1976); and H. Reiner, "Gewissen," *Historisches Wörterbuch der Philosophie* 3 (Basel, 1974).

sion] or φρένες (*phrenes*) [when you are frantic] overcame you, this was due to the fact that God had sent it, so that you were exonerated. Achilles and Agamemnon both finally understood their terrifying conflict in this sense and did not feel guilty in our modern sense.[7] We can see that their ego was not yet split or, as Jung would say, the ethical conscience was not yet born, and as their deeds were sanctioned by the gods, they remained purely a question of *moral* conscience in the Jungian sense. The beginning of a *truly* moral consciousness comes with the tragedians in the fifth century B.C. They began to ask why a man should suffer from, and be punished for, a deed he never intended to do or was not even aware of having done—as was the case with Oedipus. Conscience, however, is still represented by the chorus (in Aeschylus, for example) or by the Erinyes, in other words, it is still projected. I think that the very first case of a conflict of duty and consequently of truly ethical conscience is described in *Philoctetes* by Sophocles, where Neoptolemos is its victim.[8] Another classic example is Euripides' *Orestes* (396). When the hero is asked by Menelaos what disease it is that eats him away, Orestes says: "My synesis, because I am *conscious* of having done a terrible deed." One can see that here the furies are already introjected.

I think that thereafter the existence of what Jung would call an *ethical conscience* is always present. The *daimonion* of Socrates is to him a divine warning and definitely more than pure reason.[9] It is only on account of the *daimonion's* intervention that Socrates becomes the model of a protestant and that he is perfectly willing to die for his beliefs, knowing full well that his conscience or *daimonion* is the highest authority, hence a true ethical conscience in Jung's sense. With Socrates' *daimonion* we can already clearly see that it owes its existence to the possibility of the splitting of the ego and thus of facing the conflict between the two. Therefore the Cynics rightly identified the Socratic *daimonion* with conscience.

Aristotle in the *Nicomachian Ethics* repeatedly states that reason gives commands but that we may obey them or not[10]

---

7. Homer, *Iliad* IX: 109f, 119f.
8. Sophocles, *Philoctetes*, 88, 902f.
9. Plato, *Phaedrus*, 242c; and *Apology*, 29b; 31c, d; 40b.
10. Aristotle, *Nicomachian Ethics*, 3, 7; 1115b, 12; 3, 8; 1117a, 8.

since we have free choice, whereby ethical values alone decide.[11]

Then comes the Stoa with its bitter discussion with the Epicureans about the objectivity or subjectivity of ethical judgment. It seems that this time the Epicureans won the battle with their argument for its subjectivity. I believe they not only conquered the Stoa, as we shall presently see with Seneca, but that eventually Christianity as well subjectivized moral judgment. Let us not forget, however, that even the Comedian Menandros (an Epicurean) said: ἅπασιν ἡμῖν ἡ συνείδησις θεός (*Hapasin hemin he syneidesis theos*) [for us all, conscience is a God].

For Cicero conscience plainly is a piece of God within us.[12] When he cites Poseidonius, he says that our difficulties really begin whenever we do not obey the inner demon which, to him, corresponds to the "protecting demon" of Chrysippus. "Morderi est melius conscientia" [It is better to be bitten by conscience].[13] Cicero also wrote "recta conscientia, non scripta, sed nata lex ... quae a nobis divelli non potest" [Real conscience is not a law written, but one we are born with and it cannot be torn from us].[14] There is a gnome of allegedly Pythagorean origin which says that "in our youth it is the *paidagogoi*, in our grown age conscience, that teaches us right behavior."

It can easily be shown that the Stoics as well as the Epicureans knew what we would call the scrutiny of conscience, but they also issued a *cave* (warning) against morbid self-indictment. Seneca calls conscience a great *numen*, "majus quam cogitari potest" [bigger than we can think].[15] They also knew how unpleasant a task scrutiny of conscience is and how hard it is therefore to arrive at *metanoia*, which in fact means *to reach insight*. Conscience with Seneca then remains a *scintilla* [spark] from the stars and thus becomes something pretty close to the *pneuma*.[16] *Conscientia* for him is a divine spirit in us.

Conscience is a topic of primary importance to Philo of Alexandria since it is a witness (martyr) of our most secret inten-

11. Aristotle, *Magna Moralia*, 1, 12; 1187b, 33.

12. Cicero, *De Legibus* 1, 24f, 59; *De Finibus* 2, 1114; *Tusculanae Disputationes* 5, 38.

13. Cicero, *Tusculanae* 4, 45.

14. Cicero, *Cluentio* 159h.

15. Seneca, fragment 17.

16. Seneca, *De Otio* 5, 5.

tions. Quintilian calls it a *mille testes* [thousand witnesses].[17] When Marcus Aurelius describes the good man, he calls him simply εὐσυνείδητος (*eusyneidetos*) [a man with a good interior].

When it comes to the Old Testament, I am no expert and therefore only remind you of the fact that Adam hides from God, which clearly shows his guilty conscience.[18] Philo calls conscience the true man within our soul, because it cannot be bribed.

In the New Testament, the concept of conscience does not play much of a part in the Gospels, whereas in the Epistles and the Acts it becomes very decisive. For Paul, all moral values depend on the judgment of conscience. For him, conscience is obligatory, even while erring, and only liberation from the law (Torah) creates true freedom (cf. the martyrs). He also knows the problem of conflicts of duty. He gives the example of the wife committing adultery in order to save her husband's life, and says, when Scripture is silent, conscience helps you on. The autonomy of conscience becomes obvious in 1 Cor. 10:29 and Rom. 14:23 because it is a con-science of God and is in this way connected to *pistis* = faith.[19]

We will now briefly go through some of the Patristic literature: for John Chrysostom, the highest judge's seat on earth is conscience. When you are accused by everybody, but your conscience is clean, then you are blessed (*makarios*). He highly recommends scrutiny of conscience, particularly during Lent. Origen dwells particularly on the conflicts of duties wherein reason and conscience are equal participants, which view corresponds closely to that of John Cassian, who asks you to use *diakrisis* (discrimination) in such cases.[20] For Origen, *Gehenna* is already here with us on earth in terms of conscience. With this statement, it becomes clear that conscience is subjectivized. Fortunately, conscience is then also equated with man's guardian angel,[21] i.e., to divine grace. We can even find a direct equation of God with conscience in Zeno of Verona, who says: "Qui suam con-

17. Quintilian, *Institutiones Oratoriae* 11.41.
18. Josephus, *Jewish Antiquities* I, 47.
19. 2. Corinthians 1:12; Acts 23:1.
20. Johannes Cassianus, *Conferences* 6, 8f: 214.
21. Origen, *Commentaries on Romans* 2, 9.

scientiam non timet, id est qui Deum non timet" [He who does not fear his conscience, does not fear God].[22]

Personally, I think that Saint Augustine has the last word in this discussion. He speaks of conscience, in his usual simplicity and clarity, as the *intus hominis* [the interior man],[23] for we find ourselves with conscience directly *coram Deo* or *in conspectu Dei* [face to face with God], where, consequently, God speaks directly to us.[24] Conscience, according to him, because it has understood the universal laws of God, can judge the authority of the earthly, local laws, and then permit us to act accordingly.[25] In Saint Augustine's precept "dilige et quod vis, fac" [find out and do what you will], *dilige* equates the scrutiny of conscience with *diakrisis*.[26] From this, he also reaches the "golden rule" not to inflict anything on anyone which you would not be prepared to endure yourself.

I will now rush through the Middle Ages, Reformation, humanism, and Enlightenment by quoting only a very subjective and small selection of authors: Abelard, for example, states that "non est peccatum nisi contra conscientiam" [there is no sin except the one against conscience]. Calvin calls conscience *sensus divini iudicii* [sense of divine judgment]. It becomes at all events increasingly clear that conscience coincides with the acceptance of one's responsibility, when we are responsible to God for our actions and conscience remains a purely subjective principle. This is literally expressed by Kant who is convinced that everyone of us has this inner judge within him or her *ab origine*, so that it becomes quite feasible to equate this inner authority with Kant's 'transcendental subject.'

From the many examples I have given you, it would be easy to extract a long list of attributes which have been associated with conscience through the ages. This fact alone testifies to the archetypal nature of our concept. Archetypes always have "a thousand names." The considerable variety of the qualities attributed to conscience also allows us to better understand what the otherwise ill-defined term of *conscience* amounts to in the last

---

22. Zeno of Verona, *Tractatus* [Sermones] 2, 3, (CCL, 22, 154).
23. Saint Augustine, *Enarrationes in Psalmos* 45, 3.
24. Saint Augustine, *De Sermones Dom* 2, 19, 32.
25. Saint Augustine, *De Doctrina Christiana* 3, 22.
26. Saint Augustine, *In Jonam.* 7, 8.

analysis, and this is what is called amplification. This list shows us that conscience was always regarded as something transcending our ego, being of near-divine nature, i.e., numinous, but fallible at the same time. It embraces inherent polarity and can be extremely powerful or even too weak. I could go on much longer, but my enumeration would only contribute more evidence to the statement already made, that conscience is of archetypal origin.

When I studied the history of the concept of conscience (*Gewissen*) in order to give you an idea of what we in Jungian psychology are talking about when we use this term, I could not help being deeply impressed by having found out in this way that Jung himself had come to formulations which are almost literally identical with those to be found in literature of all ages. Although he was entirely ignorant of those testimonies, he reached these formulations purely as an upshot of his clinical experience. This fact, together with the equally striking one of the astonishing *consensus gentium* when conscience has been discussed throughout the centuries, again testifies to the ubiquitous archetypal nature of conscience.

I hope that I have shown that conscience has indeed been attributed great importance throughout the ages, although or perhaps because it escapes a clear-cut definition in the rational sense. This is exactly what proves that we are dealing with an archetypal representation in Jung's sense. I hope it is also clear that in the course of time, conscience became more and more of a subjective factor and thereby came closer to Jung's ethical conscience. Regarding my first question as to whether we all have a conscience and a well-functioning one, we may say that we would certainly be monsters were we lacking that function, whether you call it archetypal or not.

Let us now turn to the second point, which concerns the relation of conscience to science, and vice versa. To tackle this most difficult problem, I think I had best take refuge in some "casuistry." First there will be two examples showing the effects of a badly functioning or nonfunctioning conscience in scientific research and then a few cases testifying to its well-functioning counterpart.

Concerning my first case, you have to know that, for professional reasons, I am deeply interested in parapsychology and that I have been working in this area as one of science. That such an approach to parapsychology was at all justified remained questionable until J. B. Rhine at Duke University, Durham N. C. gave it its first and so far only sound foundation.[27] This was in the early 1930s. However, in science we never feel quite satisfied with our findings until other researchers, preferably at a totally different place and possibly of a different persuasion, have been able to produce the same results.

It therefore was a great comfort to me and to all specialists in parapsychology when, in 1954, S. G. Soal and F. Bateman of London published a book entitled *Modern Experiments in Telepathy*, in which they replicated Rhine's experiments, producing results much more stunning than Rhine's had been.[28] The publication was, in other words, most spectacular and has since been quoted as a pillar of parapsychology. This was particularly so because the two authors were highly respected professors of mathematics in Great Britain and their methods were impeccable. (My friend W. Pauli, a mathematician of the highest caliber, stated after having studied the book most carefully that the publication convinced him completely of the reality of the alleged phenomena.)

In 1978, twenty-five years later, Betty Markwick of London took an enormous amount of trouble to go again through the many hundred protocols of those experiments, since, as a crucial piece of parapsychological research, she felt they had to be foolproof.[29] What she found in fact was that Soal had manipulated his data! After this revelation I felt as if the rug had been pulled from under my feet. For many reasons, I am still fully convinced of the reality of certain parapsychological phenomena, but their scientific proof, under those conditions, is again still lacking. It is now open to question as to whether Soal was deliberately cheating or whether it was his unconscious playing him a bad trick in terms of unconscious wishful thinking. At all events, I wrote letters to some people concerned with parapsychology, to the

---

27. J. B. Rhine, *Extra-Sensory Perception* (Boston, 1934).

28. S. G. Soal and F. Bateman, *Modern Experiments in Telepathy* (London, 1954).

29. Betty Markwick, *Proceedings of the Society for Psychical Research 56*, part 211 (May, 1978): 250-281.

effect that I had always been convinced of the fact that in research you can never trust the results of so-called scientists without knowing their character very well. I am afraid to say that I regard this element of subjectivity on my part as gospel truth, whether this be in parapsychology or whatever branch of orthodox science. Such disappointments and discussions, I am afraid to say, have happened more times than one would like in the history of science and I therefore hope you can understand my own deep-rooted skepticism when it comes to the question of scientists' conscience.

Just recently, another courageous man has unmasked another scientific fraud performed by the eminent grand old man of British psychology, Sir Cyril Burt.[30] Burt quite consciously manipulated the results of his I.Q. experiments with certain populations and published lies about this work. He did so intentionally, not only to support his own theory or subjective conviction, but maybe even to block promotion of a colleague who was of an opposite persuasion to his.

Soal and Burt both were first-class scientists on the one hand, and fakes on the other. Their consciences malfunctioned when it came to certain personal prejudices. Psychologically speaking, they were swallowed up by their respective complexes, their egos were assimilated by the overestimated giant idea (alias complexes), so that their moral standard was annihilated together with some of their clear thinking.

It is a clinically well-known fact that in order to compensate or substitute for a defective conscience, people unconsciously develop compulsions and obsessions of all kinds, so that they begin to lack the formerly well-functioning *diakrisis* and thus may become scientific criminals. Psychologically it becomes clear from these facts, that we had better scrutinize our consciences most carefully when it comes to our personal prestige and to publishing our discoveries. If you do not question your motivation most seriously and thereby discover your own wishful thinking, however unconscious it may so far have been, you are doomed to injure your very prestige and also to mislead research. But I shall not wind up on this sad note and prefer to remind you of better positive paradigms of the problem of sci-

30. L. S. Hearnshaw, *Cyril Burt, Psychologist* (London, 1979).

ence versus conscience, where the latter was victorious.

Albert Einstein, by means of his equation $E = mc^2$, long ago provided us with the theoretical means for exploitation of nuclear energy. When the time came to manufacture the atomic bomb, however, he refused to have anything to do with it and very firmly declared that his personal conscience would not allow him. This decision was certainly anything but easy in those critical years for a Jewish guest in the United States.

Although it has been of such decisive influence in world history, Einstein's connection with the construction of the A-bomb is already forgotten. This, however, is what always happens to facts of a moral nature: they are inconvenient and therefore are rapidly repressed. Einstein was a highly moral man and as such was a confirmed pacifist and antimilitarist; so, when he reached the decision to sign the two letters to President Roosevelt, strongly petitioning him to urge the construction of an A-bomb against the evil power of Hitler, he had to fight a bitter battle with his *conscience morale*.[31] The decision was strictly against his former convictions and was at cross purposes with the popular image of Einstein as a pure scientist, idealist and wise old man, and compelled him to sacrifice this image and his conviction. Moreover, by convincing the U.S. government to go ahead with the plans for such a devilish contraption in order to win the battle against the devil Hitler, he had to pay with his own soul's contamination with darkness. This is the inevitable price we pay and constitutes another reason why we tend to forget such problems of conscience quickly and dislike talking about them. Einstein's conscience would not let him get away with it, and so he signed the papers.

When Switzerland was under heavy threat by Nazi Germany, my Jewish friend W. Pauli moved to Princeton, New Jersey. He made it clear the very first day that he would not have anything to do with the problem of the atomic bomb. Had he not been in such high repute, this would have been the end of his safety in the American harbor, but his inner voice left him no choice. It was certainly not just a eulogy when Victor F. Weiskopf, his former assistant, now at M.I.T., pronounced at Pauli's funeral that with Pauli's death physics had lost its conscience.

---

31. B. Hoffman and H. Dukas, *Albert Einstein* (New York, 1972).

I am sure you all remember the famous case of Robert J. Oppenheimer, then president of the Institute for Advanced Study, who went through hell in his lifetime because he would not let them manufacture the H-bomb. Had it not been for the courageous intervention of the brothers Alsop, Oppenheimer would without any doubt have been totally annihilated.[32] His conscience would have utterly ruined if not killed him. His stamina was unprecedented, and the "stamina" of American justice could not break his back.

The scientist's curiosity knows no limitations, be it in the macrocosm or the microcosm. The two unite in our own soul, anyhow, but in the individual case they frequently constitute a problem because they encounter conscience in exactly that place. However, once the scientist's creation becomes common property, is seized by technology, and is adopted in the name of so-called "progress," it easily gets out of hand because there is no longer a single man who is taking responsibility to save his soul. Technological "progress" often becomes a compulsion and thus a crime against humanness. A sad and impressive example of this may be witnessed in the scene between Philemon and Baucis at the end of Goethe's *Faust*.

It is one of the saddest aspects of mankind that conscience disappears with the masses. It only takes one madman to declare that he takes the responsibility for a whole people for the people's morale or conscience to get divided up by the number of citizens participating in the so-called movement, which then has already the power of compulsion or obsession and is consequently incurable. Its "leader" has then already become the "sorcerer's apprentice."

It seems we are getting into politics, and I should hate to generalize. As there is naturally much more to conscience than can be touched upon in a single lecture, I can only hope there is some grace permitting me to have a modicum of a good conscience concerning my effort. If I consider this lecture as a sin, there is a chance I may be granted a pardon.

It is always very moving to read Saint Augustine, who so openly confesses all his sins in his *Confessions*, and then winds

---

32. Joseph and Stewart Alsop, "The Case of J. Robert Oppenheimer," *Harper's Magazine*, vol. 209, no. 1253 (October 1954).

up with a clean conscience because, due to his belief, he knows that divine grace does not hold him fully responsible for his contemptuous deeds and thoughts and so forgives him. How many of us, though, in our far-progressed age, are blessed Saint Augustines? I pose this question seriously, for there is no shortcut or easy method to acquire an ethical conscience. It remains a lifelong, lonely, individual effort, requiring patience, love and humility – and a quest that needs some grace as well.

Chapter 17

Wilderness and the Search for the Soul of Modern Man

First of all I should like to give a definition of *wilderness*. Wilderness is Nature in her original condition, undisturbed, unadulterated by man. Does that mean Paradise? As we know, Paradise has been forbidden to us ever since the original sin, but there is a Jewish legend that says that it had been removed by God and relocated at the end of time. Then it becomes eschatological, Utopia, a goal, or ἀποκατάστασις τῶν πάντων (*apokatastasis tōn pantōn*) [reestablishment of everything]; indicating that it was originally in order, which brings us to the question of how human interference created disorder. Here we are confronted with the age-old problem of opposites:

> nature vs. culture
> matter vs. spirit
> evil vs. good

with mankind in the middle having to cope with the tension between them.

In *Genesis*, we are encouraged (or ordered) to make use of everything present and to multiply. We certainly did so, right down to the atom bomb and the population explosion. We have abominably exaggerated this liberty to a point where we are about to extinguish ourselves by behaving as if we ourselves were the *creators*. In other words, we are suffering hubris to an extent that cannot go unpunished. We have made use of the laws of Nature in humble obedience to the original commandment, e.g., inventing physics, chemistry and biology as best we could and only up to our own limitations. Where, then, is the mistake

---

Inaugural speech given to the "Third World Wilderness Congress" in Inverness, Scotland on October 8, 1983.

or the sin? My humble answer, coming from some fifty years of experience with disordered human beings, is that, with all this frantic "progress" in the outer world, all this terribly lopsided extraversion, we became intoxicated and forgot about our soul.

Then we paid for it: neurosis became the plague of our days, the penalty of modern man for his hubris (and here I am more in my own professional field). Man is estranged from his soul, therefore from his own inner nature, by being lost in the outer world. Excessive interference with *outer* nature creates of necessity disorder of the *inner* nature, for the two are intimately connected.

Here I must request your patience for a somewhat lengthy detour into history. Since we cannot understand ourselves and our motivation without knowing something about our spiritual ancestors, I would like to give you some fragmentary information concerning the spiritual history of these predecessory ideas about wilderness conservation.

According to the pre-Socratics, the universe, man included, was one big organism with many organs, of which mankind was only one. The organs functioned in perfect harmony. This was the belief of Heraclitus and also of Parmenides. For the latter, it had consisted of two components, νεῖκος (*neikos*) and φιλότης (*philotēs*), hatred and love, repulsion and attraction. The result was a cyclic change from one to the other in time, in due course. We were, of course, included in this process (and aren't we now?). This view already tacitly presupposed the existence of what was later called συμπάθεια τῶν ὅλων (*sympatheia tōn holōn*) [sympathy of all], an interrelatedness of all things in the cosmos, an idea which found its fundamental place in the philosophy of Poseidonius (135-50 B.C.).[1] We must admit that as long as this idea prevails, we are peacefully contained in something ever so much bigger than ourselves.

To understand better the deeper meaning of sympathy of all things in macrocosm and microcosm, we would have to go into alchemy, Jung's idea of synchronicity, and his speculations on *unus mundus* (Dorneus), as well as the "psychoid" factor of matter, which space here does not permit. Something of the alchemistic idea of *unus mundus* must have been functioning as the unconscious root of Wendell Wilkie's prophetic message,

---

1. Cf. Karl Reinhardt, *Kosmos und Sympathie* (Munich, 1926).

"One World or No World" (*One World*, 1943), however much it was projected onto the macrocosm by him.

Poseidonius' idea did prevail for many centuries, and was widely discussed, mainly in terms of the relationship between macrocosm and microcosm. Man was conceived of as a small cosmos, containing everything in the world, right up to the stars. We could argue that if this were not so, how could we ever understand anything out there? Epistemologically, for example, in the case of sympathy, Plotinus says that our perception is only possible through sympathy between subject and object. Or, according to Sextus Empiricus: perception, cognition, understanding are only possible by an outpouring of the macrocosm into the microcosm (us). Porphyrius said that the soul, when it encounters the visible, recognizes itself there as it carries everything within itself and the *all of things* is nothing else than the soul.

I could add many more quotations attesting to this conviction, but will now move to a discussion of another, adjoining aspect of the macrocosm-microcosm relation, which will bring us closer to a more current problem in psychology, i.e., the thorny problem of the relation between the psyche and the soma, physis and psyche — body and soul. (Here we border on the problem of psychosomatic medicine, psychophysical dualism or parallelism, and the like, of which we still understand next to nothing. I can say with full conviction, and with regard to the teachings of philosophers and theologians, that this problem inevitably culminates in a religious question.)

It must be understood that, from the times of Poseidonius, the concept of macrocosm-microcosm was never conceived of as a pair of opposites, but rather as *complements* which are related by the aforementioned sympathy of all things. Kepler, in his usual prudent way, spoke of a certain proportionality of the two worlds, and with Poseidonius this relationship includes the macrocosm within man, as we know from Cicero (to whom we owe most of what we know of Poseidonius). With Iamblichus it is exactly this relation that, for example, justifies the function of the priest: [2]

---

2. Iamblichus (Syrian, d. 330 A.D.), Sec. IV, chapter 2, "On the Mysteries of the Egyptians, Chaldeans and Assyrians," ed. Thomas Taylor (London, 1895), 207.

For these things, also, another reason may be assigned, and which is as follows: in all theurgical operations the priest sustains a twofold character: one, indeed, as man, and which preserves the order possessed by our nature in the universe; but the other, which is corroborated by divine signs, and through these is conjoined to more excellent natures, and is elevated to their order by an elegant circumduction – this is deservedly capable of being surrounded with the external form of the gods. Conformably, therefore, to a difference of this kind, the priest very properly invokes, as more excellent natures, the powers derived from the universe, so far as he who invokes is a man; and again, he commands these powers, because through arcane symbols, he, in a certain respect, is invested with the sacred form of the Gods.

You can see that hereby Iamblichus brings down into us, into our microcosm, the macrocosmic – divine actions. However, since we are not the mediators between God and ourselves, we have to be careful not to suffer inflation and, in order to prevent this dangerous sickness, to maintain our awe and respect of macrocosm, i.e., *Nature*. The discussion of the macrocosm-microcosm problem went on to become a fundamental notion of Renaissance philosophy. In it, microcosm became the mirror of the macrocosm, to the extent that the perspective was inverted. The world became a μακράνθρωπος (*makranthropos*) or μέγας ἄνθρωπος (*megas anthropos*) and man was, therefore, a concentration of everything of importance in the cosmos, thereby indeed bordering on inflation. Cf. Pico's *Heptaplus* 56 q.v.: "Nam si homo est parvus mundus, utique mundus est magnus homo" [For if man is a small world, then the world is a great man]. In our time psychology would step in and warn: "Watch out, lest you become like God!" In John Scotus Eriugena (c. 820 A.D.) something similar is to be found: "Homo veluti omnium conclusio quod omnia in ipso universaliter comprehenduntur" [Man is the inclusion (or end) of all, since everything is enclosed in him].[3] And our Swiss, Philippus Aureolus Paracelsus: "Omnia una creata sunt, macrocosmos et homo unum sunt." [Everything was created in One, macrocosm and Man are one]. This was his basic conviction and it most probably accounts for his world-wide success as a man of medicine, for he always tried to bring

---

3. John Scotus Eriugena, *De Divisione Naturae* IV, 10.

about this macrocosm-microcosm harmony, loss of which, according to him, accounted for his patients' sicknesses.

When we speak of man as microcosm, we cannot, of course, help but think of the monads of Leibnitz. He mentions the term by saying "Le microcosme est un monde en raccourci" [The microcosm is a world in miniature], or "un miroir vivant perpetuel de l'univers" [a perpetual living mirror of the universe]. Nikolaus Cusanus had already remarked that the *parvus homo* mirror reflects things (including those of the macrocosm). This, of course, presupposes consciousness (as later with Leibnitz's "monads"). Consciousness means reflection of things perceived, discrimination over against indiscrimination. We try to learn more and more about those objects and begin to analyze and dissect them, thereby eventually killing them, if they are in fact living beings. In other words, as the natural sciences developed, respect for Nature as a whole disappeared. We no longer bring sacrifices to her, we think of having dominated her, and to a large extent we *have* dominated her to a point where the original fear of Nature has disappeared. What does inner nature (microcosm) say to that loss of fear? At this point, we find that we have lost something equilibrating, equalizing, healthy, sane, and valuable, a loss for which we have to pay. Thus, anxiety neurosis has become very widespread, and this has its concrete reasons. With our knowledge of the laws of Nature, we brought about its domination to the point of constructing A-bombs, and we became destructive to Nature in many ways. The dangerous aspects of Nature that kept our forebears watchful and humble have now almost disappeared outside; but they have turned inward (wilderness without—wilderness within!) so that the whole of Western society rapidly approaches the physical and mental cracking point from the inner dangers alone. This is no joking matter, for should the outer wilderness disappear altogether, it would inevitably resurrect powerfully from within, whereupon it would immediately be projected. Enemies would be created, and its terrifying aspects would take revenge for our neglect, our lack of reverence, our ruthless interference with that beautiful order of things. The wilderness is by no means chaos, it is most admirably ordered and organized, quietly and beautifully obeying the laws of Nature. In modern terminology, this is called *cybernetics*, meaning self-regulating. The father of cybernetics, Norbert

Wiener,[4] has already written a book entitled *The Human Use of Human Beings*, meaning that, in spite of all the machines, we must behave according to our level – the human level. What, then, of the self-regulation of Nature, when she is no longer left to herself, when she is excessively interfered with, and too badly wounded to be able to recover? The repercussions of this sacrilege in the psyche of the single human being are unpredictable, but one thing is certain: we are in great danger of losing our humanity as a result of this unrelenting process of destruction. If, therefore, you equally relentlessly make attempts at preserving the wilderness, you are not only doing something idealistic or ideological, but rather something substantial for the health of human beings globally.

I shall now return to more fundamental considerations concerning your endeavor. It is one of the basic laws of physics that action equals reaction. When you interfere in some way or another with the wilderness, something will inevitably happen to *you* as a reaction, i.e., to the wilderness within, and vice versa. How can we conceive of this? There is a dichotomy in man: on the one hand, we are just a part of Nature, but, on the other, we are different, and that different part of our system tries very hard to understand about the One (cf. Plato, Parmenides: ταὐτόν (*tauton*) [identical], and θάτερον (*thateron*) [in the other way]). This natural curiosity of the human would be perfectly innocent in itself if it were not insatiable. For centuries, Christianity has emphasized that a mature man should be completely freed of his natural carnal being. But such a man turns sour! We must learn to live with both natures and with their opposites, and we must also learn to cope with the suffering of this tension. Our inner "nature" does not tolerate too much interference such as repression, askesis, and the like. As there is now this correspondence between the two worlds alluded to earlier, we must respect this subtle balance. The wilderness within would really go "wild" if we should badly damage the outer wilderness. So let us keep the balance as best we can, in order to maintain sanity.

How can this be practiced? As a psychologist, I am not going

---

4. Norbert Wiener, *The Human Use of Human Beings: Cybernetics and Society* (London, 1950).

to give you technical advice, but I shall try to intimate to you how psychology may help. First of all, we must frankly admit that, in spite of our culture, we are still mammals, *natural* beings. This aspect of our being, last but not least, is forgotten by that selfsame culture; we are, as we say, unconscious of its archeological, prehistoric existence and reality in the unconscious part of our psyche. Now everything in us of which we are unconscious is automatically projected. You only have to think of the primitive fear of animals, whether it be of spiders, mice, snakes or tigers, almost all of them perfectly harmless if left unmolested. But those powers in the unconscious are overwhelming, so that we are tempted to project them as far away as possible, onto the stars, for example, more particularly when we have to deal with fate. And this in spite of the fact that already in 1798 Schiller let Illo say to Wallenstein's astrologer Seni: "In your bosom are the stars of your fate."[5] And, I do not have to tell you how, with the increasing insecurity on this planet, people tend more than ever to believe in this projection of secular astrology. Scientifically those allegedly extremely personal effects of specific stars on Tom, Dick, or Harriet are inconceivable.

How does the case look when this astrological illusion is analyzed psychologically? To begin with, we have populated the starry sky with a vast collection of gods and myths. Planets are named for the gods. Concerning myths, you have only to think of Andromeda, Orion, and so forth. First of all, we created constellations out of purely statistically distributed single stars; and secondly, we endowed them with mythological names. It has become a psychological truism that such images have an archetypal origin, which means that they correspond to certain pre-existing images and processes in our collective unconscious, and therefore get projected. But, however unconscious, they are having their effects upon our behavior, and thus constitute our fate. This projection onto the stars is not altogether harmless, since projection is a psychological reality, an *action*, which consequently has its *reaction* upon us. So this is the way in which these benevolent or malevolent stars or constellations in turn

---

5. Friedrich Schiller, *The Piccolomini* II.6,2069. Compare also what, more than a hundred years earlier, Shakespeare had already said in *Julius Caesar* 1.2, 139-141: "Men at some time are masters of their fates: / The fault, dear Brutus, is not in our stars / But in ourselves, that we are underlings."

have their effects upon us. We need only remain unconscious of them, and the archetypes go to work, and the boomerang of projection hits back.

The reality of psychological factors is a hard fact, and should no longer be denied in the name of exact science. Archetypes are frighteningly contagious, as evidenced by the many mass movements in history. The Huns, Vandals, Turks, French and Russian Revolutions, Napoleonism and Hitler are classic examples of the phenomenon of mass projection. "Plus ça change, plus ça reste la même chose" [The more things change, the more they remain the same]. It is only the names that change. Suffice it to say, no matter how civilized one may be, identification with an archetype can lead to the megalomania of a ruler of the world, something close to God Almighty.

Concerning the efficacy of projections and the relation of macrocosm and microcosm, I will relate a true story, which to my mind illustrates all this most beautifully. It is the story of the rainmaker of Kiao Chow, which I owe to Richard Wilhelm. At the Psychological Club in Zürich he told us this true story, which he had witnessed himself.

He lived in a district of China that happened to be threatened with famine and a terrific drought. The inhabitants tried to produce rain with the help of their own local rainmakers, processions, etc., but to no avail. So they sent for China's most famous rainmaker, who lived far away in Kiao Chow. They asked him what they could do to assist him, but he only wanted a secluded place in the wilderness, where he was to be left alone, except for the delivery of his daily meals.

After a couple of days without rain the people became impatient and sent a delegation to ask him why there was no success, but he simply sent them back. On the next day it began to snow (in mid-summer!) and then the snow turned into pouring rain. On his return to the village, they asked why it had taken him so long. He explained: "When I came to this district, I immediately realized that it was frighteningly out of Tao, whereby being here myself, I naturally was also out of Tao. All I could do therefore, was to retire into the wilderness (Nature) and meditate, so as to get myself back into Tao." (Recall here that Jesus also had to retire into the wilderness whenever he was confronted with a problem that needed meditation.) With that, the rainmaker returned to Kiao Chow, happy as a lark.

You may dismiss this whole event as sheer coincidence, as such things may happen in full accord with the laws of Nature once in a blue moon. Snow in mid-summer, however, is still less likely. What is its probability from a purely meteorological point of view? Recalling the story, we can say the following: the magician comes to a place which is physically out of order and notices this immediately, thereby falls out of order himself (being contaminated, taking macrocosm into microcosm, introjecting), so that he becomes a part of unbalanced, sick Nature. He then attempts to put himself back in Tao again, which is hard work, but he succeeds. With that, Nature herself is healed, and it rains; in other words, the boomerang hit the target.

Here we have not only a beautiful example of the reestablished harmony of macrocosm and microcosm, but also of the way in which we, the microcosm, are capable of contributing to this harmony, i.e., *corriger la fortune* [directing our destiny]. The archetypes are *in us*, and some of them represent the chthonic part of our soul, by which we are linked to Earth and to Nature. That can certainly be linked to the wilderness.

We are fascinated by, as well as afraid of, these archetypal components of Nature, and so we want to know more about them. Historically speaking, this is a very new attitude which only began to dawn with the Renaissance, as when Petrarch climbed Mont Ventou, thereby becoming the father of mountaineering. Mountains are obviously one kind of wilderness, which asks for many human sacrifices every year. There are other dangerous wildernesses that are just as hostile as mountains: the Arctics and Antarctics with their icy coldness and darkness; the desert with its heat and dryness; the impenetrable jungle; the sea with its frightening storms and unfathomable dark depths. I assure you, they can all be found in our own depths, in our own unconscious. The tragedy is that with more and more knowledge of this outer wilderness we cannot tranquilize the inner wilderness. Nature cannot be placated by artifacts. She stands in her own right and will never surrender her position. Why is it that we cannot make peace with her? We have explored the macrocosm too extensively, ill-advisedly, and with too much success, and thereby lost sight of the microcosm. The more I think of this quandary, the more I begin to understand humankind's endeavor. It is a much healthier attitude to try to preserve the outer wilderness than to negate the inner wilderness and thereby let it go rampant, whereupon it inevitably becomes projected onto your fellow beings, whether friend or foe. In order to keep in harmony with the concept of Wilderness equaling Nature unspoiled, apart from analysis I know of nothing better than to keep the outer wilderness alive and to not let it be ruined. Thus, you will find Nature an idyllic landscape where the law of the jungle still holds. For as long as you don't interfere with it too badly, Nature functions beautifully. I should like to quote here a famous Persian-Egyptian alchemistic authority (thought to have lived in the fourth century B.C.) by the name of Ostanes.

1. ἡ φύσις τῇ φύσει τέρπεται (*he physis te physei terpetai*) [Nature enjoys Nature];

2. ἡ φύσις τῆν φύσιν νικᾱ (*he physis ten physin nika*) [Nature vanquishes Nature];

3. ἡ φύσις τῆν φύσιν κρατεῖ (*he physis ten physin kratei*) [Nature rules Nature].

These three lines may sound trivial, but at the same time they are very deep.

1. Let her be as she is, and she will enjoy herself like a virgin.
2. She will always be victorious, self-regulated.
3. She will religiously obey her own rules.

Psychology gives us many good reasons for keeping in touch with the "Wilderness equals Nature" concept. We live on the upper floor (consciousness). It is supported by the lower one (the unconscious), and eventually by its foundation, the cellar (let's not forget that we also keep wine in the cellar, which equals spirit). It represents the unconscious, the earth, our mother, Mother Nature and, in its original condition, virgin Nature, with which we live in a sort of *participation mystique* (Lévy-Bruhl); it is there that the archetypes live. The archetypes correspond to our instincts, which are the *psychological* aspects of the *biological* facts, the patterns of behavior by which we live. Inasmuch as we are unconscious of the archetypes, they are projected, i.e., they are experienced as if they were in the macrocosm. Usually they are personified (bush soul, animals, brother animal—think of Kipling's *Jungle Book*) and this is how we originally become "related" to animals.

This part of our psyche is thus experienced in the form of outside objects, although it belongs strictly to us, the subject, the microcosm. You need only think of phenomena such as *lycan-thropy* (werewolves), which is simply a symbolic identification with the animal. On this level of semi-consciousness, there can exist uncanny places outside in which demons dwell, wells popu-lated with nymphs or djinns; in short, the soul is divided up into many partial souls. So the wilderness is really the original biotope of the Soul.

With the development of consciousness in our Western civili-zation, these fragments slowly begin to be integrated, but how-ever strongly we believe in "progress" (of consciousness), a total integration remains a hopeless desideratum. The ideal outcome of this process was called *individuation* by Jung. Alas, the uncon-scious is as inexhaustible as Nature, and as deep as "the deep blue sea." This is our inner wilderness.

I will now return to my favorite idea of the correlation of mac-rocosm-microcosm, which seems to me to justify beautifully the enthusiasm for conservation of wilderness.

One of the protagonists of this whole idea was Robert Fludd, a humanist who wrote in Latin, and therefore called himself Robertus de Fluctibus (1574-1637). A medical man, Fludd was a Rosicrucian, an alchemist, and an admirer of Paracelsus. He is best known for his battle with Kepler, whom he accused of not paying enough attention to the "yeast" (*faex*) in matter. He pub-lished many beautifully illustrated books, and most of the excel-lent etchings by Johann Theodor de Bry therein are concerned with the connection of macrocosm and microcosm. His ideas, as we can see now, go back to Poseidonius, who said that man was a microcosm, having his being in common with stones, his life with plants, his perception with animals, and his reason with the angels. From here, Fludd claimed that we get in touch with the Supreme Being by means of the mediation of Nature (woman), who on the one hand sums up minerals, plants, animals (the ape being their summit), and on the other hand, *via aurea catena Homeri* [through the golden chain of Homer], is linked to the ineffable God (cf. fig. 1 and 2). There could not be a better exam-ple of the harmony of macrocosm-microcosm, mediated by Nature in her virginal aspect. Fludd had worked it out in endless detail in most of his many books, as for example his *Clavis Philosophiae et Alchymiae* (1633) and *Philosophia Moysaica* (1635). He was by no means alone, but found himself in full accordance with such people as Pico della Mirandola, Girolamo

Fig. 1 Robert Fludd, *Utriusque Cosmi,*
maioris scilicet minoris metaphysica,
physica atque technica historia.
Frontispice Tom. II. Oppenheim 1619

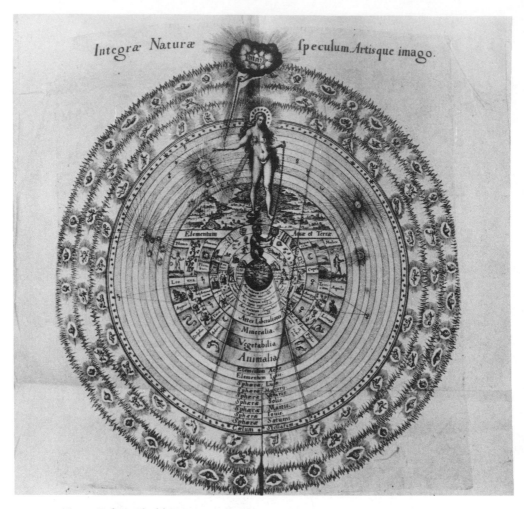

Fig. 2 Robert Fludd, Tom, ii Oppenheim 1619,
p.4, by Johann Theodor de Bry

Cardano, Tommaso Campanella, Giordano Bruno and most of the other prominent figures of Renaissance philosophy. These men were influenced by early Platonic ideas such as the *world soul* (the soul of the universe), the *anima mundi* (*Timaeus* 41 D). However, it looks as if Fludd's efforts did not have much of an echo in the world, or if so it is hard to locate. But Schopenhauer repeatedly refers to this concept, mainly in his magnum opus *The World as Will and Representation* (II, para. 29), where he wholly agrees with the macrocosm-microcosm idea, without, however, referring to Fludd.

According to Anthony Shaftesbury (1671-1713), the goal of man is to achieve harmony. Shaftesbury has a long prehistory, since a great number of the Fathers of the Church have dealt with the problem of macrocosm-microcosm by discussing Plato's *Anima Mundi*, the *pneuma* of the Stoa and Plotinus.

I was always shocked by the Jewish way of dealing with evil (Leviticus 16.2): loading the scapegoat (Azazel) with the people's sins and then driving him out into the wilderness to the "Lord of the Flies." I am sure you won't find *him* there, but rather you will find some of the many healing spirits of Nature! In any case, let us not forget the vandalism against Nature that is presently afoot. Let us also not forget that only recently even purely scientific ethologists came to believe that one can observe altruistic actions with certain higher animals, so that the origins or phylogeny of ethics are to be found already in unspoiled Nature.[6]

I should like to remind you of the way in which Voltaire concludes a long philosophical discussion by letting Candide say: "Cela est bien dit, mais il faut cultiver notre jardin" [All that is well said but we must cultivate our own garden]. I only hope not to have destroyed your enthusiasm but rather to have helped you to find something of this harmony and beauty during our outings, and to live it, which is the only way of properly relating to it and loving it. So, as Rudyard Kipling wrote:

> "Good hunting to all
> That keep the Jungle Law!"

---

6. Gunter Stent, ed., "Morality as a Biological Phenomenon," *Live Sciences Report* 9, Dahlem Konferenzen (Abakon Verlagsgesellschaft: Berlin, 1978).

Bibliography

[Ed. Note: Publication information for C. G. Jung's *Collected Works* used throughout *Soul and Body* is as follows:
Collected Works (Bollingen Series 20). 13 Vols. In Britain, London: Routledge & Kegan Paul, 1953-1978. In the United States, New York: Pantheon Books, 1953-1960; New York: Bollingen Foundation, distribution by Pantheon, a division of Random House, 1961-1967; Princeton, N.J.: Princeton University Press, 1967-1978.]

Chapter 1

Bardo Thödol (*The Tibetan Book of the Dead or the After-Death Experiences on the Bardo Plane*). According to Lama Kazi Dawa-Samdup's English rendering by W. Y. Evans-Wentz. London: Oxford University Press, 1927.

Carbonelli, G. *Sulle fonti storiche dell' Chimia e dell' Alchimia in Italia, tratte dallo spoglio dei manuscritti delle Biblioteche con speciale riguardo ai Codici 74 di Pavia e 1166 Laurenziano*. Roma: Instituto Nazionale Medico Farmacologico, 1925.

Colonna, Francesco. *Le Tableau des riches inventions...representées dans le songe de Poliphile...exposées par Beroalde [de Verville]* [The Dream of Poliphilo]. Paris: 1600. Original edition: Venice, 1499. Cf. also, *The Dream of Poliphilo* related and interpreted by Linda Fierz-David. Princeton: Bollingen Series 25, 1950.

Deecke, W. *Annali dell' Instituto di Correspondenza Archeologica*. Rome: 1881.

Deedes, C. N. "The Labyrinth." In *The Labyrinth: Further Studies in the Relation Between Myth and Ritual in the Ancient World*. Edited by S. H. Hooke. London: 1935.

Evans, Arthur. *The Palace of Minos I*. London: 1921.

Knight, F. W. J. "Maze Symbolism and The Trojan Game." *Antiquity* VI, 24 (1932).

Kircher, Athanasius. *Mundus Subterraneus*. Amstelodami: 1678.

Layard, John. "Maze Dances and The Ritual of the Labyrinth in

Malekula." *Folklore* XLVII (1936): 123-170; XLVIII (1937): 115-182.

Layard, John. "Der Mythos der Totenfahrt auf Malekula." *Eranos-Jahrbuch*. Zurich: Rhein Verlag, 1937.

Lucian, *De Saltatione* [On Dance]. LCL, Vol. V.

Maier, Michael. *Secretioris naturae secretorum scrutinium chymicum*. Francofurti: 1687. Emblema XXI.

Maspero, Gaston. *L'Archeologie Egyptienne*. Paris: Maison Quantin, 1887.

Matthews, W. H. *Mazes and Labyrinths*. 1922.

Morienus. "De Transmutatione Metallorum." *Artis auriferae quam chemiam vocant* XI. Basel: 1593.

Petrie, W. M. Flinders. *The Royal Tombs of the Earliest Dynasties*, II Egypt Exploration Fund, 21st memoir, 1901.

Philalethes, Eirenaeus [pseud]. *Erklärung der hermetisch poetischen Werke Herrn Georgi Riplaei* [An Exposition on Sir Ripley's Hermeto-Poetical Works]. Hamburg: 1741.

Pliny (the Elder). *Naturalis Historia*. XXXVI.

Schlesinger, Max. *Geschichte des Symbols*. Berlin: 1912.

Seabrook, W. B. *The Magic Island*. New York: Harcourt Brace, 1929. Published in German as: *Geheimnisvolles Haiti*. Berlin: 1931.

Suetonius. *Nero*.

Virgil. *Aeneid*.

Wheeler, R. E. M. *The Antiquaries Journal* XV, 3 (1935); XVI, 3 (1936).

Wilhelm, Richard, trans. *The Secret of the Golden Flower* [Chinese meditation text] with a commentary by C. G. Jung. New York: Harcourt, Brace & World, 1962. Original German edition: 1929.

Zimmer, Heinrich Robert. *Kunstform und Yoga*. Berlin: 1926.

Chapter 2

Bier, August. *Die Seele*. Munich: 1939.

Caton, R. *The Temple and Ritual of Asclepius*. London: 1900.

Deubner, L. *De Incubatione*. Leipzig: 1900.

Flournoy, Th. *Des Indes à la planète Mars*. Paris: 1900.

———. *Journal of the American Society for Psychical Research*. New York: 1907.

———. *Proceedings of the American Society for Psychical Research*. New York: 1907.

———. *Journal of the Society for Psychical Research*. London: 1907.

———. *Proceedings of the Society for Psychical Research*. London: 1907.

Hager. *Hdb. d. parmazeut Praxis*. Leipzig: 1913.

Hamilton, M. *Incubation*. London: 1906.

Herzog, R. *Die Wunderheilungen von Epidaurus*. Leipzig: 1931.

Jung, C. G. "On the Psychology and Pathology of So-Called Occult Phenomena." *Psychiatric Studies (Collected Works 1)*, 1957. Originally published as "Zur Psychologie und Pathologie sog. okkulter Phänomene." Leipzig: 1902.

———. "The Psychology of Dementia Praecox." *Psychogenesis of Mental Disease (Collected Works 3)*, 1960. Originally published as "Über die Psychologie der Dementia praecox," 1907.

———. "The Content of the Psychosis." *Psychogenesis of Mental Disease (Collected Works 3)*, 1960. Originally published as "Der Inhalt der Psychose," 1914.

———. *Archetypes of the Collective Unconscious (Collected Works 9, Part I)*, 1959. Originally published as "Über die Archetypen des Kollektiven Unbewussten." Eranos-Jahrbuch, 1934.

———. "Individual Dream Symbolism in Relation to Alchemy." *Psychology and Alchemy (Collected Works 12)*, 1953. Originally published as "Traumsymbole des Individuationsprozesses." *Eranos-Jahrbuch*, 1935.

———. "Concerning the Archetypes." *The Archetypes and the Collective Unconscious (Collected Works 9, Part I)*, 1959. Originally published as "Über den Archetypus." *Zbl. f. Psychotherapie* 9 (1936).

———. *Psychology and Religion: West and East (Collected Works 11)*, 1958. Originally published as *Psychologie und Religion*. Zurich: 1940.

———. "Psychotherapy and a Philosophy of Life." *The Practice of Psychotherapy (Collected Works 16)*, 1954. Originally published as "Psychotherapie und Weltanschauung." *Schweiz Z. Psychologie*, 1943.

Kehrer, F. "Wach-und Wahrträume bei Gesunden und Kranken." *Sammlg. Psychiatr. v. Neurol. Einzeldarst.* Bd, IX. Leipzig: 1935.

Liek, Erwin. *Der Arzt und seine Sendung*. Munich: 1934.

———. *Das Wunder in der Heilkunde*. Munich: 1936.

Schubert, G. H. von. *Die Geschichte der Seele*. Stuttgart: 1878.

Tappeiner, H. V. *Lehrb. d. Arzneimittellehre* 10. Leipzig: 1913.

Chapter 3

Dorneus, G. "Philosophia Meditativa." In *Theatrum Chemicum*. Vol. I. Ursellis: 1602.

Freud, Sigmund. *The Problem of Lay-Analysis*. New York: Brentano, 1927. Originally published as "Die Frage der Laienanalyse."

Vienna: 1926.

———. *Gesammelte Schriften* [*Collected Works*] XI. Vienna: 1928.

Meier, C. A. *Ancient Incubation and Modern Psychotherapy.*
Evanston, Ill.: Northwestern University Press, 1968. Originally published as *Antike Inkubation und Moderne Psychotherapie.* Zurich: Rascher Verlag, 1949.

Morienus. *Harmonia Imperscrutabilis.* J. Rhenanus, ed. Francofurti: 1625.

Musaeum Hermeticum. Francofurti: 1677.

Chapter 4

Jung, C. G. *Mysterium Coniunctionis. An Inquiry into the Separation and Synthesis of Psychic Opposites in Alchemy* (*Collected Works* 14), 1963. Originally published in German as *Mysterium Coniunctionis.* Zurich: Rascher, 1955.

———. *Psychological Types.* Trans. H. G. Baynes. London: Kegan Paul; New York: Harcourt Brace, 1923. Also in *Collected Works* 6, 1971. Originally published as *Psychologische Typen.* Zurich: Rascher, 1921.

———. *Psychology and Alchemy.* (*Collected Works* 12), 1953. Original German edition, Zurich: Rascher, 1944.

———. "Psychology of the Transference." In *The Practice of Psychotherapy. Essays on the Psychology of the Transference and Other Subjects* (*Collected Works* 16), 1954. Originally published in German as *Zur Psychologie der Übertragung.* Zurich: Rascher, 1946.

———. "The Spiritual Problem of Modern Man." In *Modern Man in Search of a Soul.* London: Kegan Paul, 1933; New York: Harcourt Brace. Also in *Collected Works* 10, 1964.

———. *The Structure and Dynamics of the Psyche* (*Collected Works* 8), 1960.

———. "Synchronicity: An Acausal Connecting Principle." In *The Interpretation of Nature and Psyche.* London: Routledge & Kegan Paul; New York: Pantheon, 1955. Originally published in German as "Synchronizität als ein Prinzip akausaler Zusammenhänge." *Naturerklärung und Psyche.* Zurich: Rascher, 1952.

Jonas, H. "Motility and Emotion." *Actes du XIe Congrès International de Philosophie,* 1953, 7. Amsterdam: Louvain, 1954.

Kemp, P. *Healing Ritual.* London: Faber, 1935.

Lindner, R. *The Fifty-Minute Hour.* New York: Rinehart, 1955.

Pauli, W. "The Influence of Archetypal Ideas on the Formation of Scientific Theories in Kepler." In *The Interpretation of Nature and the*

Psyche, Bollingen Series 48. London: Routledge & Kegan Paul; New York: Pantheon, 1955.

Plato, *Symposium*.

Rhine, J. B. *The Reach of the Mind*. Harmondsworth: Penguin Books, 1954.

Schopenhauer. "Animalischer Magnetismus und Magie." In *Über den Willen in der Natur*.

Soal, S. G. and Bateman, F. *Modern Experiments in Telepathy*. London: Faber, 1954.

Wickes, F. *The Inner World of Childhood*. New York: Appleton, 1927.

———. "Three Illustrations of the Power of the Projected Image." *Studien zur Analytischen Psychologie C. G. Jung's* 1. Zurich: Rascher, 1955.

Chapter 5

St. Augustine. *Retractationes*.

Frazer, Sir James George. *The Golden Bough; A Study in Magic and Religion*. New York: Macmillan, 1960 [Original version 1859].

Homer. *The Iliad* xv.

Jung, C. G. "Concerning the Archetypes," In *The Archetypes and the Collective Unconscious* (*Collected Works* 9, part 1), 1959: 54-72. Originally published in German as "Über den Archetypus, mit besonderer Berücksichtigung des Animabegriffes." *Zentralblatt für Psychotherapie*. IX (1936).

———. *Psychological Types* (*Collected Works* 6), 1971. Trans. H. G. Baynes. London: Kegan Paul; New York: Harcourt Brace, 1923. Also in *Contributions to Analytical Psychology*. London, 1928: 295-312. Originally published in German as *Psychologische Typen*. Zurich: 1921.

Maitland, Edward. *Anna Kingsford: Her Life, Letters, Diaries and Work*. London: 1896.

Plato. *Symposium*.

Wiener, Norbert. *The Human Use of Human Beings: Cybernetics and Society*. London: 1950.

Wilhelm, Richard, trans. *The Secret of the Golden Flower* [Chinese meditation text] with a commentary by C. G. Jung. New York: Harcourt, Brace & World, 1962. Original German edition, Munich: 1929.

Winthuis. "Das Zweigeschlechterwesen bei den Zentralaustraliern und anderen Völkern" [The Double-Gendered Being Among the Peoples of Central Australia and Elsewhere]. *Forschungen zur Völkerpsychologie und Soziologie* 5. Leipzig: 1928.

Chapter 6

Jung, C. G. "The Psychology of Dementia Praecox." In *The Psycho-genesis of Mental Disease* (*Collected Works* 3), 1960. Originally published in German as "Über die Psychologie der Dementia praecox," 1907.

Wiener, Norbert. *The Human Use of Human Beings: Cybernetics and Society.* London: 1950.

Chapter 7

Adler, A. *Studien über die Minderwertigkeit von Organen.* Berlin and Vienna: 1907.

Appian. *Roman History.*

Bach, S. "Spontanes Malen und Zeichnen im neurochirurgischen Bereich. Ein Beitrag zur Früh-und Differentialdiagnose." *Schweiz. Arch. Neurol. Psychiat.* 87, 1 (1961).

Bercel, Nicholas A. *AMA Arch. Gen. Psychiat.* 20. Chicago: 1960.

Binswanger, L. "Über das Verhalten des psychogalvanischen Phäno-mens beim Assoziationsexperiment-Diagnostische Assoziationsstu-dien," Beitrag xi *J. Psychol. Neurol.* x (1907).

Boerhaave, Hermannus. *Praelectiones Academicae de Morbis Ner-vorum,* 2 vols. Edited by Jocabus Van Eems. Frankfurt and Leipzig: 1762.

Corbin, Henry. *Terre céleste et corps de résurrection.* Paris: 1960.

Féré, C. "Notes sur les modifications de la résistance électrique sous l'influence des excitations sensorielles et des emotions." C. R. *Soc. Biol. Paris* 5, 8ème série (1888).

———. *The Pathology of Emotions.* London: University of London Press, 1899.

Figar, S. "The Application of Plethysmography to the Objective Study of So-Called Extrasensory Perception." *J. Soc. Psych. Res.* 40, 702 (1959).

Fischer, H. "Die Tierwelt im Lichte der Pharmakologie." *Neujahrsbl. Naturf. Ges Zurich* 164. Stück. (1962).

Gengerelli, J. A. and Kirkner, F. J. (Eds.). *The Psychological Variables in Human Cancer.* Berkeley and Los Angeles: University of California Press, 1954; London: Cambridge University Press, 1955.

Goldberg, Jane G. *Psychotherapeutic Treatment of Cancer Patients.* 1982.

Goldberg, Richard and Tull, Robert M. *The Psycho-Social Dimensions of Cancer.* 1984.

Heath, Robert G., et al. *Amer. J. Psychiat.*, 1956.

Hoffer, A. and Osmond, H. "The Adrenochrome Model and Schizophrenia." *J. Nerv. Ment. Dis.* 128, 1 (1959).

———. *The Chemical Basis of Clinical Psychiatry.* Springfield: C. C. Thomas, 1960.

———. "Schizophrenia – An Automatic Disease." *J. Nerv. Ment. Dis.* 122, 5 (1955).

Jung, C. G. "Association, Dream and Hysterical Symptom." In *Experimental Researches (Collected Works 2)*, 1973. Originally published in German as "Assoziation, Traum und hysterisches Symptom – Diagnostische Assoziationsstudien, Beitrag VIII." *J. Psychol. Neurol.* VIII (1906).

———. Foreword to *The I Ching or Book of Changes.* In *Psychology and Religion: West and East (Collected Works 11)*, 1958.

———. "On Psychophysical Relations of the Associative Experiment." In *Experimental Researches (Collected Works 2)*, 1973. Originally published in German in *J. Abnorm. Psychol.* 1 (1907).

———. "Schizophrenia." In *The Psychogenesis of Mental Disease (Collected Works 3)*, 1960. Originally published in German in *Schweiz. Arch. Neurol. Psychiat.* 81, 1-2 (1958).

———. "Synchronicity: An Acausal Connecting Principle." In *The Structure and Dynamics of the Psyche (Collected Works 8)*, 1960. Originally published in German as "Synchronizität als ein Prinzip akausaler Zusammenhänge," in *Naturerklärung und Psyche.* Zurich: Rascher, 1952.

———, and Petersen, F. "Psycho-Physical Investigations with the Galvanometer and Pneumograph in Normal and Insane Individuals." In *Experimental Researches (Collected Works 2)*, 1973. Originally published in *Brain* 30 (1907): 118.

———, and Ricksher, C. "Further Investigations of the Galvanic Phenomenon and Respiration in Normal and Insane Individuals." In *Experimental Researches (Collected Works 2)*, 1973. Originally published in *J. Abnorm. Psychol.* II, 1 (1907/8).

Kant, I. *Dreams of a Spirit Seer and Other Related Writings,* 1969. Originally published in German as *Träume eines Geistersehers* II, 3, 1766.

Klopfer, Bruno. "Psychological Variables in Human Cancer." *J. Projective Techniques* 21 (1957): 4.

Meier, C. A. *Ancient Incubation and Modern Psychotherapy.* Evanston, Ill.: Northwestern University Press, 1968. Originally published in German as *Antike Inkubation und Moderne Psychotherapie.* Zurich: Rascher Verlag, 1949.

———. "Zeitgemässe Probleme der Traumforschung." Zurich: Kultur und staatswiss. *Schriften E.T.H. no. 75,* 1950.

Musaeum Hermeticum. Francofurti: 1677.

Mead, G. R. S. *The Doctrine of the Subtle Body.* London: Watkins, 1919.

Nunberg. "Über körperliche Begleiterscheinungen assoziativer Vorgänge." *J. Psychol. Neurol.* XVI (1910).

Osmond, H. "Inspiration and Method in Schizophrenia Research." *Dis. Nerv. Syst.* XVI, 4 (1955).

———. "A Review of the Clinical Effects of Psychotomimetic Agents." *Annals N.Y. Acad. Sci.* 66 (1957).

———, and Smythies, J. "Schizophrenia: A New Approach." *J. Ment. Sci.* 98 (1952).

———, and Smythies, J. "The Significance of Psychotic Experience." *Hibbert J.* (1958).

Peters, H. M.; Witt, P. N. and Wolff, D. "Die Beeinflussung des Netzbaues der Spinnen durch neurotrope Substanzen." *Z. vergl. Physiol.* 32 (1950).

Saul, Leon. A paper in *Psychosom. Med. Monogr.* II (1941).

Schwarz, Oswald. *Psychogenese und Psychotherapie körperlicher Symptome.* 1925.

Schwyzer, H. R. "Bewusst und Unbewusst bei Plotin." *Sources de Plotin.* Geneva: Entretiens V. Vandoeuvres, 1960.

Sidis, B. and Kalmus, H. T. "A Study of Galvanometric Deflections due to Psycho-Physiological Processes." Pts. I and II, *Psychol. Rev. Balt.* XV, XVI (1908/1909).

———, and Nelson, L. "The Nature and Causation of the Galvanic Phenomenon." *Psychol. Rev. Balt.* XVII (1910).

Veraguth, O. "Das psycho-galvanische Reflex-Phänomen." *Monatschr. Psychol. Neurol. Berlin,* XXI (1906/1907) – revised and enlarged under identical title, 1909.

Witt, P. N. *Die Wirkung von Substanzen auf den Netzbau der Spinne als biologischer Test.* Berlin-Göttingen-Heidelberg: 1956.

Wittkower, E. *Einfluss der Gemütsbewegungen auf den Körper.* Vienna and Leipzig: 1930.

Wolff, D. and Hempel, O. "Versuch über die Beeinflussung des Netzbaues von Zilla-x notata durch Pervitin, Scopolamin und Strychnin." *Z. Vergl. Physiol.* 33.

Chapter 8

Aeschylus. *Persians.*
———. *Prometheus Bound.*
Apollonius Rhodius. *Argonautica.*
Aristophanes. *The Frogs.*

Aristotle. "On Prophecy in Sleep." In *On the Soul; Parva Naturalia, On Breath*. Trans. W. S. Hett. Cambridge: Harvard University Press, 1936.

Artemidorus Daldianus. *Oneirocritica*.

Büchsenschütz, B. *Traum und Traumdeutung im Alterthume*. Berlin: 1868.

Cicero. *De Divinatione*.

———. *De Republica*.

Damaskos. In *Suidas, s.v. Domninos*.

Deubner, Ludwig. *De Incubatione*. Leipzig: 1900

Dodds, E. R. *The Greeks and the Irrational*. Berkeley and Los Angeles: University of California Press, 1956.

Edelstein, Emma J. and Edelstein, Ludwig. *Asclepius*. Baltimore: 1945.

Euripides. *Hecuba*.

———. *Iphigenia in Tauris*.

Hamilton, Mary. *Incubation*. London: 1906.

Herzog, Rudolf. *Die Wunderheilungen von Epidauros*. Leipzig: 1931.

Hippocrates. *Peri Diaites* IV. Trans. W. H. S. Jones. London and New York: 1931.

———. *Peri Enypnion* II. Edited by D. C. G. Kuhn. Lipsiae: 1826.

Homer. *Iliad*.

———. *Odyssey*.

Macrobii. *Opera*. Edited by Societas Bipontina. Biponti: 1788.

Meier, C. A. *Ancient Incubation and Modern Psychotherapy*. Evanston, Ill.: Northwestern University Press, 1968. Original German edition, Zurich: Rascher, 1949.

Pausanias. *Description of Greece*. Trans. and with commentary by J. G. Frazer. London: 1913.

Philostratus. *Lives of the Sophists*.

Pindar. *Fragments*.

Plato. *Republic*.

———. *Symposium*.

Plutarch. *De Placitis Philosophorum*.

———. *Quaestiones conviviales*.

Preuschen, Erwin. *Mönchtum und Sarapiskult*. Giessen: 1903.

Reinhardt, Karl. *Poseidonios über Ursprung und Entartung*. Heidelberg: Carl Winters Universitätsbuchhandlung, 1928.

Sophocles. *Electra*.

Stahl, W. H. *Macrobius' Commentary on The Dream of Scipio*. New York: Columbia University Press, 1952.

Stoicorum Veterum Fragmenta.

Synesii Episcopi. *Opera omnia*.

Xenophon. *Cyropaedia*.

———. *Symposium*.

Chapter 9

Dean, E. Douglas. "Nonconventional Communication." In *Proceedings of the First Space Congress*. Sponsored by the Canaveral Council of Technical Societies, April 20-23 (1964).

Dunbar, Flanders. *Emotions and Bodily Changes*. 3rd. ed. New York: 1949.

Freud, S. *Die Traumdeutung*. Leipzig, Vienna: Deuticke, 1900. Published in English as *The Interpretation of Dreams*. London: George Allen & Co.; New York: Macmillan, 1913.

Jung, C. G. and Pauli, W. *The Interpretation of Nature and the Psyche*. New York: Pantheon, 1955.

Kirsch, Thomas B. "The Relationship of the Rapid Eye Movement State to Analytical Psychology." *Amer. J. Psychiat.* (1967).

Meier, C. A. *Ancient Incubation and Modern Psychotherapy*. Evanston, Ill: Northwestern University Press, 1968. Originally published in German as *Antike Inkubation und Moderne Psychotherapie*. Zurich: Rascher, 1949.

———. *The Dream and Human Societies*. Berkeley: University of California, 1966.

———. "Psychosomatic Medicine from the Jungian Point of View." *J. Analyt. Psychol.* 8 (1963).

———, et al. "Forgetting of Dreams in the Laboratory." *Percept. Mot. Skills* 26 (1968).

Chapter 10

Biäsch, Hans. "Psychologische Hintergründe des Examensverhaltens." *Jahrbuch für Psychologie, Psychotherapie und Medizinische Anthropolgie* $16^{1/2}$ (1968): 115-129.

Dorner, Klaus. *Die Hochschulpsychiatrie*. Stuttgart: Ferd. Enke, 1967.

Möller, Michael Lukas. "Aspekte der Prüfungsangst, betr. Erziehung." *Zur Psychoanalyse der Prüfungsangst* II, 1 (1969): 16-20.

———. "Psychotherapeutische Beratung für Studierende an der Universität Giessen," *Nervenarzt* 40 (1968): 155-63.

———. "Untersuchung zur Psychodynamik der neurotischen Prüfungsangst." Diss. Berlin: 1967.

Nielsen, Aage Rosendal (Ed.). *Lust for Learning*. Denmark: New Experimental College Press, 1968.

Spoerri, Tund and Winkler, W. T. (Eds.). *Student und Neurose*. Basel-New York: S. Karger, 1969. *Proceedings of the VIITH International Congress of Psychotherapy*. Wiesbaden: 1967. Part VI.

Clarke, E. and Dewhurst, K. *An Illustrated History of Brain Function*.

Oxford: 1972.

Dorneus, G. "Philosophia Meditativa." In *Theatrum Chemicum.* Ursellis: 1602.

Dunne, J. W. *The Serial Universe.* London: 1934.

Green, C. *Out-of-the-Body Experience.* London: 1968.

Jantz, H. and Beringer, K. "Das Syndrom des Schwebeerlebnisses nach Kopfverletzungen," *Der Nervenarzt* 17 (1944).

Levy-Bruhl, L. *How Natives Think.* Trans. L. A. Clare. London: 1926.

Putscher, M. *Pneuma, Spiritus, Geist.* Wiesbaden: 1973.

Robinson, James M. (Ed.). *Evangelium nach Thomas.* Leiden: 1959. Available in *The Nag Hammadi Library,* James M. Robinson, ed. San Francisco: 1977.

Rousselle, E. "Spiritual Guidance in Contemporary Taoism." In *Spiritual Disciplines.* Papers from the Eranos Yearbooks 4, B.S. XXX, 1960 [Original edition: 1933].

Sendivogius. "De Sulphure." *Musaeum Hermeticum.* Frankfurt am M.: 1678.

Chapter 11

Aeschylus. *Choephoroi.*
———. *Eumenides.*
———. *Prometheus Bound.*

Blum, G. S. In Walker, E. L. (Ed.) *Basic Concepts in Psychology Series.* Belmont: Wadsworth, 1966.

Chaignet, Anselme Edouard. *Histoire de la Psychologie des Grecs.* 5 Vols. Paris: Hachette, 1887-1893.

Euripides. *Heracleidae.*
———. *Orestes.*

Festugière, Andre-Jean. *Personal Religion Among the Greeks.* Berkeley: University of California Press, 1954.

Harkins, Paul W. and Riese, Walter. *Galen: On the Passions and Errors of the Soul.* Columbus: Ohio State University Press, 1963.

Klauser, Theodor (Ed.). *Reallexikon für Antike und Christentum.* Stuttgart: Anton Hiersemann, 1941.

Linforth, I. M. "The Corybantic Rites in Plato." *U. of Calif. Publ. Class. Philol.* 13 (1946).

Nilsson, M. P. *A History of Greek Religion.* Oxford: Oxford University Press, 1925.

Pauly-Wissowa (Eds.). *Realencyclopadie der klassischen Altertumswissenschaft.* Stuttgart: Alfred Druckenmüller, 1984.

Pohlenz, Max. *Hippokrates.* Berlin: W. de Gruyter, 1938.

Rather, Lelland J. *Mind and Body in Eighteenth Century Medicine*. London: Wellcome Hist. Med. Lib., 1965.

Rohde, E. *Psyche. The Cult of Souls and Belief in Immortality among the Greeks*. London: Kegan Paul, 1925.

Roscher, Wilhelm Heinrich. *Das von der "Kyanthropie" handelnde Fragment des Marcellus von Side. Abhandlungen der Königlich Sächsischen Gesellschaft der Wissenschaften*. Leipzig: S. Hirzel, 1897.

Schumacher, Joseph. *Antike Medizin*. Berlin: W. de Gruyter, 1940.

Siebeck, Hermann. *Geschichte der Psychologie*. Vols. 1 and 2. Gotha: Andreas Perthes, 1880-1884.

Stallmach, Josef. *Dynamis und energeia*. Meisenheim am Glan: Anton Hain, 1959.

Tambornino, Julius. *De Antiquorum Daemonismo*. Giessen: Töpelmann, 1909.

Vaughan, Agnes Carr. *Madness in Greek Thought and Custom*. Baltimore: Furst, 1919.

Zeller, Eduard. *Die Philosophie der Griechen*. 6 Vols. Leipzig: Reisland, 1920-1923.

Chapter 12

Bash, K. W. *Lehrbuch der allgemeinen Psychopathologie*. Stuttgart: 1955.

Bradway, K. "Jung's Psychological Types." In *J. Anal. Psychol.* 9 (1964): 129-35.

Brawer, F. B. and Spiegelman, J. M. "Rorschach and Jung." In *J. Anal. Psychol.* (1964): 137-49.

Cattell, R. B. *Description and Measurement of Personality*. New York: World Books, 1948.

———. *Personality and Motivation Structure and Measurement*. New York: World Books, 1957.

Dicks-Mireaux, M. J. "Extraversion-Introversion in Experimental Psychology." in *J. Anal. Psychol.* 9 (1964): 117-28.

Ehrenwald, Jan. "New Dimensions of Deep Analysis." London: 1954.

Eysenck, H. J. *The Biological Basis of Personality*. Springfield, Ill.: C. C. Thomas, 1967.

———. *Dimensions of Personality*. London: Macmillan, 1947.

———. *Dynamics of Anxiety and Hysteria*. London: Praeger, 1957.

———. *The Structure of Human Personality*. London: Methuen, 1960.

———. (Ed.). *Extraversion-Introversion*. London: McGibbon & Kee, 1969.

Fierz, H. K. *Klinik und Analytische Psychologie. Studien aus dem C. G. Jung-Institut Zurich* xv. Zurich: 1963.

Fierz, M. "Die vier Elemente." In *Traum und Symbol*. Edited by C. A. Meier. Zurich: 1963.

Freud, S. "Zur Einführung des Narzissmus." In *Jahrb. Psychoanal. Psychopathol. Forschungen* vi (Leipzig and Vienna: 1914): 1-34.

Garrigan, P. M. "Extraversion-Introversion as Dimensions of Personality." In *Psychol. Bull.* 57 (1960): 326-60.

Guilford, J. P. "Intro-Extraversion." In *Psychol. Bull.* 31 (1934): 331-54.

———. *Personality*. New York: McGraw Hill, 1959.

———, and Braly, K. M. "Extra- and Introverison." In *Psychol. Bull.* 27 (1930): 98-107.

———, and Guilford, R. B. "An Analysis of Factors in a Typical Test of Intro-Extraversion." In *J. Abnorm. Soc. Psychol.* 28 (1933/34): 377-99.

Van der Hoop, J. H. *Bewusstseinstypen*. Bern: 1937.

Jung, C. G. "A Contribution to the Study of Psychological Types." In *Psychological Types (Collected Works 6)*, 1971. Originally published in French as "Contribution à l'étude des types psychologiques." In *Arch. Psychol.* xiii. Geneva: 1913.

———. "Individual Dream Symbolism in Relation to Alchemy." In *Psychology and Alchemy (Collected Works 12)*, 1953. Originally published in German as "Traumsymbole des Individuations Prozesses." In *Eranos Jahrbuch* 1935. Zurich: 1936.

———. "Notes on the Seminar in Analytical Psychology 1925." In *Diagram 8*. Zurich: 1926 [privately multigraphed].

———. "Psychologische Typologie." In *Seelenprobleme der Gegenwart*. Zurich: 1931.

———. "On the Psychology and Pathology of So-Called Occult Phenomena." In *Psychiatric Studies (Collected Works 1)*, 1957. Originally published in German as *Zur Psychologie und Pathologie sogenannter okkulter Phänomene*. Leipzig: 1902.

———. *Psychological Types (Collected Works 6)*, 1971. Trans. H. G. Baynes. London: Kegan Paul; New York: Harcourt Brace, 1923. Also in *Contributions to Analytical Psychology*. London: 1928. Originally published in German as *Psychologische Typen*. Zurich: 1921.

———. "Synchronicity: An Acausal Connecting Principle." In *The Structure and Dynamics of the Psyche (Collected Works 8)*, 1960. Originally published in German as "Synchronizität als ein Prinzip akausaler Zusammenhänge." In *Naturerklärung und Psyche*. Studien aus dem C. G. Jung-Institut Zurich iv. Zurich: 1942.

———, and Rankin, F. "The Associations of Normal subjects." In

Experimental Researches (Collected Works 2), 1973. Originally published in German as "Diagnostische Assoziationsstudien," I. Beitrag. In *Journ. Psychol. Neurol.* III, IV. Leipzig: 1904.

Klopfer, B. and Spiegelman, J. M. "Some Dimensions of Psychotherapy." In *Spectrum Psychologiae.* (Zurich, 1965): 177-83.

Kretschmer, Ernst. *Körperbau und Charakter.* Berlin: 1921.

McDougall, W. "A Chemical Theory of Temperament Applied to Introversion and Extraversion." In *J. Abnorm. Soc. Psychol.* 24 (1929): 393-409.

Mahler, Margaret. "On Human Symbiosis and the Vicissitudes of Individuation." In *Infantile Psychosis* . International Psycho-Analytical Library, 83. London: The Hogarth Press, 1969.

Mann, H. Siegler, M. and Osmond, H. "The Many Worlds of Time." In *J. Anal. Psychol.* 13 (1968): 33-56.

Marshall, I. N., "Extraversion and Libido in Jung and Cattell." In *J. Anal. Psychol.* 12 (1967): 115-36.

Marshall, I. N. "The Four Functions: A Conceptual Analysis." In *J. Anal. Psychol.* 13 (1968): 1-32.

Medtner, Emil. Über die sog. "Intuition," die ihr angrenzenden Begriffe und die an sie anknüpfenden Probleme. Vorgetragen im Psychologischen Club Zurich, 1919. Moscow and Zurich: 1923.

Meier, C. A. "Projection, Transference and the Subject/Object Relation in Psychology." *J. Anal. Psychol.* IV/1 (London, 1959).

Myers, I. B. *Manual.* The Myers-Briggs Type Indicator. Princeton, N.J.: Princeton University Press, 1962.

Richek, H. G. and Bown, O. H. "Phenomenological Correlates of Jung's Typology." In *J. Anal. Psychol.* 13(1968): 57-65.

Root, A. R. "A Short Test of Introversion-Extraversion." *Pers. J.* 10 (1931): 250-253.

Servadio, Emilio. "Psychoanalysis and Parapsychology." In *Science and ESP.* Edited by J. R. Smythies. London: 1967.

Stricker, L. J. and Ross, J. "An Assessment of Some Structural Properties of the Jungian Personality Typology." In *J. Abnorm. Soc. Psychol.* 68 (1964): 62-71.

"Wandlungen und Symbole der Libido." *Jahrb. Psychoanal. u. Psychopath.* Forschungen II/1. (Leipzig and Vienna): 124-152.

Wheelwright, Joseph B. and Buehler, John A. "Jungian Type Survey" (The Gray-Wheelwright Test). *Manual* (1944). San Francisco: Soc. Jungian Analysts of No. Calif.: 1964. (15th revision).

Wolf, Toni. "Einführung in die Grundlagen der Komplexen Psychologie." *Die kulturelle Bedeutung der Komplexen Psychologie*, 51-122. Berlin, 1935.

――――. *Studien zu C. G. Jung's Psychologie.* Edited by C. A. Meier. Zurich, 1959.

Wolpert, E. and Michel, L. "Die Typologie C. G. Jung's als Gegenstand empirischer Persönlichkeitsforschung." *Psychol. Forschg.* 29 (1966): 112-31.

Von Zeppelin, Ilka S. *Die Variablen der Holtzman Inkblot Technique in ihrer Beziehung zur Introversion und Extraversion.* Bern and Stuttgart: 1966.

Chapter 13

Jaeger, Werner. *Paideia: The Ideals of Greek Culture.* 3 vols. Trans. Gilbert Highet. New York: Oxford University Press, 1943-1945.

Jung, C. G. *Psychology and Alchemy (Collected Works* 12), 1953. Original German edition, Zurich: Rascher Verlag, 1944.

Plato. *Phaedo.*

———. *Laws.*

Chapter 14

Clarke, E. and Dewhurst, K. *An Illustrated History of Brain Function.* Oxford: 1972.

Dorneus, G. "Philosophia Meditativa." in *Theatrum Chemicum.* Ursellis: 1602.

Dunne, J. W. *The Serial Universe.* London: 1934.

Green, C. *Out-of-the-Body Experiences.* London: 1968.

Jantz, H. and Beringer, K. "Das Syndrom des Schwebeerlebnisses nach Kopfverletzungen," *Der Nervenarzt* 17 (1944).

Lévy-Bruhl, L. *How Natives Think.* Trans. L. A. Clare. London: 1926.

Putscher, M. *Pneuma, Spiritus, Geist.* Wiesbaden: 1973.

Robinson, James M. (Ed.). *Evangelium nach Thomas.* Available in *The Nag Hammadi Library.* Edited by James M. Robinson. San Francisco: 1977.

Rouselle, E. "Spiritual Guidance in Contemporary Taoism." In *Spiritual Disciplines.* Papers from the Eranos Yearbooks, 4, B.S. XXX, 1960 [Original edition: 1933].

Sendivogius. "De Sulphure." In *Musaeum Hermetcum.* Frankfurt am M.: 1678.

Chapter 15

Dodds, E. R. "On Misunderstanding the Oedipus Rex." In *The Ancient*

Concept of Progress. Oxford: 1973.

——. "Supernormal Phenomena in Classical Antiquity." *Proceedings of the Society for Psychical Research* 55 (1971): 189-237.

Ehrenwald, J. *New Dimensions of Deep Analysis: A Study of Telepathy in Interpersonal Relationships.* London: 1954.

Gatlin, Lila. " 'Meaningful Information-Creation' an Alternative Interpretation of the Psi-Phenomena." *Journal of the American Society for Psychical Research* 71/1 (1977): 1-18.

Hall, Calvin S. and Van de Castle, R. L. *The Content Analysis of Dreams.* New York: 1966.

Janet, Pierre. "Les Oscillations du Niveau Mental." *Nouveau Traitès de Psychologie* IV/3 (Paris, 1937).

Jung, C. G. *The Interpretation of Nature and the Psyche.* New York: 1955. German edition: 1955.

——. "Synchronicity: An Acausal Connecting Principle." In *The Structure and Dynamics of the Psyche (Collected Works* 8), 1969. Original German edition, C. A. Meier, ed.: Zurich: 1952.

Schopenhauer, A. "Transzendente Spekulation über die anscheinende Absichtlichkeit im Schicksal des Einzelnen" [Transcendent Speculation on the Apparent Premeditation in Personal Fate]. In *Parerga und Paralipomena,* 1851. Available in English as *Essays from the Parerga and Paralipomena,* 1951.

Servadio, E. "Le Conditionnement transferentiel et contre-transferentiel des evenements pose au cours de l'analyse." *Acta Psychotherapeutica, Psychosomatica et Orthopaedagogica.* Suppl. to Vol. III (1955).

——. "The Dynamics of So-Called Paranormal Dreams." In *The Dream and Human Societies.* Berkeley: 1966.

——. "État present de la parapsychologie psychoanalytique." *La Tour St. Jacques.* n. 6-7, 1956.

——. "The Normal and the Paranormal Dream." *International Journal of Parapsychology.* IV (1962).

——. "A Presumptively Telepathic Precognitive Dream During Analysis." *Int. J. Psycho-Anal.* XXXVI (1955).

——. "Psicoanalisi e Parapsicologia." *Sperimentale di Freniatra.* Vol. XCVI. Suppl. al. fasc. II (1972).

——. "Psychoanalyse und Telepathie." *Imago* XXI (1935).

——. "The Psychodynamic Approach to Parapsychological Problems." *Psychotherapy and Psychosomatics* XV (1967).

——. "Telepathy and Psychoanalysis." *Journal of the American Society for Psychical Research.* 1.II (1958).

——. "Transference and Thought-Transference." *Int. J. Psycho-Anal.* XXVII (1956).

Chapter 16

Alsop, Joseph and Alsop, Stewart. "The Case of J. Robert Oppenheimer." *Harper's Magazine* 209, no. 1253 (October 1954).

Baylor, M. G. and Young, L. Action. "Conscience in Late Scholasticism and the Young Luther." *Stud. in Med. and Ref. Thought*, 209 (1977).

Chadwick, Henry. "Gewissen." In *Reallexikon für Antike und Christentum* 10. Stuttgart: 1976.

Hearnshaw, L. S. *Cyril Burt: Psychologist*. London: 1979.

Hoffman, B. and Dukas, H. *Albert Einstein*. New York: 1972.

Jung, C. G. "A Psychological View of Consciousness." In *Civilization in Transition (Collected Works* 10), 1964. Originally published in German as "Das Gewissen in psychologischer Sicht." *Das Gewissen*. Zurich: 1958.

Lévy-Bruhl, L. *La mentalité primitive*. Paris: 1909.

Markwick, Betty. *Proceedings of the Society for Psychical Research* 56, part 211 (May, 1978): 250-281.

Michaelis, A. R. and Harvey, H. (Eds.). *Scientists in Search of their Conscience*. Berlin: 1973.

Mokrosch, R. *Das religiöse Gewissen: historische und sozial-empirische Untersuchung zum Problem einer (nach) reformatorischen religiösen Gewissensbildung bei 15-bis 19-jährigen*. Urban Taschenb., 1979.

Petrilowitsch, N. (Ed.). *Das Gewissen als Problem*. Darmstadt: 1966.

Reiner, H. "Gewissen." *Historisches Wörterbuch der Philosophie* 3. Basel: 1974.

Rhine, J. B. *Extra-Sensory Perception*. Boston: 1934.

Soal, S. G. and Bateman, F. *Modern Experiments in Telepathy*. London: Faber, 1954.

Spengler, Ernst. *Das Gewissen bei Freud und Jung*. Diss. Zurich: 1964.

Chapter 17

Iamblichus. *On the Mysteries of the Egyptians, Chaldeans and Assyrians*. Edited by Thomas Taylor. London: 1895.

Reinhardt, Karl. *Kosmos und Sympathie*. Munich: 1926.

Schiller, Friedrich. *The Piccolomini*.

Stent, Gunter (Ed.). "Morality as a Biological Phenomenon." *Live Sciences Report* 9. Dahlem Konferenzen. Berlin: Abakon Verlagsgesellschaft, 1978.

Wiener, Norbert. "The Human Use of Human Beings." In *Cybernetics and Society*. London: 1950.

Index

abaissement de la tension
    psychologique, l', 108
abaissement du niveau mental, 108,
    113, 176, 286
Abelard, Pierre, 295
aborigines, Australian, 86, 130,
    199-200
About Dreams (Hippocrates), 195-96
accidents, 186
Achilles, 269, 292
active imagination, 264, 270
active projection, 47, 61
Acts of the Apostles, 101, 294
Adam, 294
Adler, Alfred, 68, 72, 173 on neurosis,
    135, 141-42, 156, 177; typology and,
    75, 246
adrenalin, 174
adrenochrome, 174
adrenolutine, 174
Aenid (Virgil), 19
Aeschylus, 191, 292
affect. See Emotion
affectus, 270
Agamemnon, 191, 292
Age of Enlightenment, 262
Agni, 274
Aias, 240
air, 272, 275
Ajna, 272, 276
Albertus Magnus, 62
alchemy, 87, 277; circularity in, 27,
    180; labyrinth in, 22, 26; projection
    and, 48-50, 264, 303
Alcmaion, 235
Alexander, 177-78
Alexandria, 261
Alexandrians, 181
aljiranga-mijina, 130
Alkadhir, 129-30
allēgorikoi, 200
all-round being, 85-86
Alma Mater, 223
Alsatian parsons, conference of, 64
Alsop, Joseph, 300
Alsop, Stewart, 300

alter ego, 69
ambivalence, in dreams, 201-202
Ambrosiana, 26
Amenemhet III, grave of, 21
American Psychological Association,
    211
amiability, 251
ammonite, 14, 24-25
Amphiaraus, 190, 204
amplification, 123-24, 125-28, 199,
    260, 291, 296
Amsterdam, 178
anagoge, Aristotelian, 124
Anahata, 272, 274-75
analogy, principle of, 139, 162, 196
analytic psychology, 215, 256, 271,
    279-80, 287-301; process of, 90-93,
    95-105, 157, 219, 247-52; religious
    factor in, 131, 150-51. See also
    Transference
anamnesis, 33, 184
Anaxogoras, 235
Anaximander, 235
Ancient Incubation and Modern
    Psychotherapy (Meier), 215
ancilla domini, 146
androgyny, 100, 276
anemia, 196
anesthesia, 283
anima, 50, 83, 104-105; in analysis, 56,
    92, 99-102; in dreams, 116, 144; as
    soul, 86, 88-89, 132
animals, 16, 23, 116, 251, 308, 311-12.
    See also specific animals.
anima mundi, 143, 315
Anima naturaliter christiana, 132
animism, 70
animus, 88, 92, 97, 103-105; in
    analysis, 50, 56, 99
Antaeus, 154
anthropō, 258
Anthropos, 166
Antichrist, 146, 290
Antiochus, 171-73
Antiochus and Stratonice (Ingres),
    172n

antipathy, 104, 231
anxiety, 222-23, 228, 306
apatheia, 176
apathy, 176
Apollo, 136, 138, 157, 162, 207, 231
Apollodorus, 138, 162
apperception, 73
Appian, 171
Apuleius, 206
Aquinas, Thomas, 221, 226
Arcanum, 153
archetypal dreams, 215, 281
archetypal image, 86-87, 88-90, 147,
    149, 214-15
archetypes, 47, 104, 240, 257;
    appearance of, 62, 148-49, 214-15,
    281, 295-96; collective unconscious
    and, 76-78, 83-90, 99, 290-91, 308-
    311; development and, 221, 228;
    healing and, 154, 183-88; projection
    and, 51, 55, 58-61, 62
archetypon eidos, to, 86-87
Archives de Psychologie, 243
Ardhanarishvara, 276
Areopagus 17 (Paul), 263
arētē, 233
Argos, schizophrenic at, 241
Ariadne, 22
Aristides of Smyrna, 206
Aristotle, 221, 234, 236, 292-93; on
    consciousness, 266, 270; on
    dreams, 192-93, 196, 213; healing
    and, 206, 239, 240, 241
Arizona, 186
Arnold, Gottfried, 262
Arrowsmith (Lewis), 244
Artemidorus, 110, 198-203
"artificial bloodlessness," 36
Artis Auriferae Quam Chemiam
    (Basel), 22
art therapy, 239
Ascension Day procession, 19
Asklepieia, 154, 215, 232, 241, 285;
    divine intercession and, 139, 153,
    162; treatment at, 185, 188, 204-
    208, 241, 282
Asklepios, 38, 146, 204, 238;
    Christianity and, 154, 166; dreams
    and, 146, 205, 206-207
"Association, Dream, and Hysterical
    Symptom" (Jung), 106
Assumption, myth of, 97
astroeides ochema, 181

astroeides soma, 181
astrology, 50, 308-309
ataraxia, 173, 176
Atlantide, L', (Benoit), 101
Atman, 275, 283
atomic bomb, 299, 306
Atomists, 235
atomos, hō, 194
atoms, 194
Atridae, curse of the, 110
augoeides ochema, 181
augoeides soma, 181
Augustine, Saint, 81, 86, 264, 295,
    300-301
Aurelius, Marcus, 294
Aurora consurgens, 44
Australia, 86, 199-200
automatic writing, 33
automatisme ambulatoire, 13
automatisme téléologique, 25
automobile, in dreams, 128
Avalon, Arthur, 270, 271
avataras, 25
Avicenna, 266
Aylward, Father James, 166

Babbit (Lewis), 244
Bach, S., 187
Bacon, Francis, 62
Baedeker (Pausanias), 208-209
Baer, K. E. von, 19
Bakchos kai Lusios, 233
baptism, 88
Bardo existence, 28-29
Bardo Thödol, 27-29
Basel University, 65-66
Bash, K. W., 255
Bastian, Adolf, 87
Bateman, F., 62, 297
Baubo, 100
Baucis, 300
Baynes, H. G., 246
behaviorism, materialistic, 173
Bellerophon, 240
Benedict, Saint, 265
Benoit, Pierre, 101
benzole molecule, 36
Bercel, Nicholas A., 175
Bergmann, Ernst von, 177
Beringer, K., 267
Beroalde de Verville, 25
Beromünster, 19
bête noire, 90, 118

Seni, 308
sensation, common organ of, 192-93, 213, 270
sensation function, 73, 74, 245, 249-51
sense organs, movements perceived in, 196
sensory input, internal, 213
sensus divini iudicii, 295
Serapis, 204, 205, 282
Serpent Power, The (Woodroffe), 270
Servadio, E., 279
"Seven Circles Description," 270
sewer lids, symbolism of, 18, 27
sexuality, 40, 185, 234; libido and, 72, 211; projection and, 53-54, 56
shadow, 102, 118, 223, 274; in analysis, 90-97, 98, 288
Shaftesbury, Anthony, 260, 315
Shakespeare, William, 97, 117, 308n
Shakta, 271
Shakti, 87, 276
Shat-Chakra-Nirupana, 270
She (Haggard), 101
shell-shock dreams, 121
Shiite religion, Iranian, 182
Shiva, 25, 87, 276
shock treatment, 173
shunyata, 276
sickness. See Illness
Sidis, B., 170
Sidpa Bardo, 28
Siegler, M., 255
sigillum confessionis, 43
Silberer, Herbert, 106-7, 113
similia similibus curantur, 139, 146, 162, 207, 233, 238
simulacrum, 181
sin, 233
sleep, 204-5; consciousness and, 108, 286; sensations and, 193, 194, 196, 213, 268; soul and, 191, 195; REM and, 211-14, 218, 283
slips of the tongue, 69, 160
smell, 14, 15, 18, 27
snake, symbolism of, 116, 146, 205, 208
Soal, S.G., 62, 297, 298
Socrates, 117, 233-34, 239, 240, 289, 292
sol, 87
solar plexus, 26, 269
soma, 120, 177-78, 183, 186, 241, 304; emotions and, 169, 176, 187;

tertium quid and, 180-81, 217-18. See also Emotion
soma kai psyche, 241
soma pneumatikon, 180-81
soma-sema, 191
somatic disturbances, 120, 169, 177-78, 180, 186
Sommer, Robert, 170
somnia a deo missa, 110, 120, 132, 147, 196. See also Dreams sent by God
Son of God, 166
Son of Man, 176
Sophia, 87, 101
Sophists, 263
Sophocles, 292
sophos, 261
sophronister lithos, 231
soul, 86, 209, 261, 304, 312; conscience and, 239, 294; dreams and, 132-33, 191, 194, 195, 198; emotions and, 233, 240, 270; loss of, 130, 173, 268, 303
spear, in dreams, 109, 125, 127-28, 139, 140, 149
sphairos, 85-86
sphygmograph, 170, 187
Spiegelman, J. Marvin, 255, 256
Spongia usta, 34-35
springs, 154, 196
stasis, 233
Steindans, 19
Stevenson, Robert Louis, 92
Stoa, 193-94, 231, 236, 293, 315
stoicheia, 238, 240
stomach, 269, 270
stone circles, 19
Stonehenge, 19
stones, healing, 231, 238
storms, god of, 127
story-telling dreams, 200
Stratonice, 171-73
Strickler, L. J., 254
strife, in dreams, 196
Studies in Word Association (Jung), 106
stupas, in Sanchi, 26-27
subcortical processes, 267
subjective factor, 73, 92-93, 245
subject-object relation, 57-62
subtle body, 181-82, 188, 218
Suetonius, 19
sulcus primigenius, 26
sun, in dreams, 196

Xenophon, 191, 192

Yale University, 131, 132, 143, 159, 238
yantra, 18
Yin-Yang, 87

Zener cards, 62
Zeno of Verona, 294-95
Zeus, 126, 127, 191, 207

Zilla-x-notata, 175
Zimmer, Heinrich Robert, 26-27
Zoser, grave of King, 20-21
zotike dynamis, 166, 231
"Zur Einführung des Narzissmus"
  (Freud), 244
Zürich, 77, 175, 187, 244, 246, 309
Zürich University, 46, 66, 77, 78, 137,
  255

Index of Greek Words and Phrases

*Entries in this index are listed in the
form they appear in the text.*

ἄλιος γέρων, 129
ἀλλεγόρικοι, 200
ἀνάμνησις, 33, 184
ἀπάωθεια, 176
ἀνθρώπῳ, 258
ἀρετή, 233
ἀρχέτυπον εἶδος, 86-87
ἀστροειδὲς ὄχημα, 181
ἀστροειδὲς σῶμα, 181
ἀταραξία, 173, 176
ἄτομος, ὁ, 194-95
αὐγοειδὲς ὄχημα, 181
αὐγοειδὲς σῶμα, 181

Βάκχος καὶ Λύσιος, 233

γενέθλιος, 127

δαιμόνιος ἀνήρ, 192
δαίμων, 258

δεκάς, 231
δυνάμεις, 238, 240
δύναμις ἐκ θεῶν, 231

ἐγκοίμησις, 205
εἴδολον, 181, 194
ἐναντίοται, 234
ἐναντιώσεις, 238
ἐνκύκλιος παιδεία, 261, 264
ἐνύπνιον ἐναργές, 206, 215
ἐνύπνιον ἰδεῖν, 197
ἐπισκοπεῖν, 197
εὐκρασία, 173

ζωτικὴ δύναμις, 166, 231

ἡγημονικόν, 266
ἡγητὴρ ονείρων, 191
'Ηθικοὶ Χαρακτῆρες (Theophrastus),
  258

θεόπεμπτον, 200
θεραπεία ψυχῆς, 239
θεραπευτής, 132, 154